Business Essentials

Supporting Pearson BTEC Higher Nationals and Foundation degrees

Management: Communications and Achieving Results

Course Book

In this July 2013 edition:

- Full and comprehensive coverage of the key topics within the subject

- Activities, examples and quizzes

- Practical, up-to-date illustrations and case studies

- Index

- Fully up-to-date as at July 2013

- Coverage mapped to the Pearson Edexcel Guidelines for the Pearson BTEC Higher Nationals in Business

Harrow College
Harrow Weald Campus, Learning Centre
Brookshill, Harrow Weald, Middx.
HA3 6RR   0208 909 6248

BPP
LEARNING MEDIA

Third edition July 2013
First edition 2007

Published ISBN 9781 4453 6833 7
(previous edition 9780 7517 9042 9)
e-ISBN 9781 4453 6853 5

British Library Cataloguing-in-Publication Data
A catalogue record for this book is available from the
British Library

Published by
BPP Learning Media Ltd
BPP House, Aldine Place
London W12 8AA

www.bpp.com/learningmedia

Printed in the United Kingdom by Ricoh

Ricoh House
Ulswater Crescent
Coulsdon
CR5 2HR

Your learning materials, published by BPP
Learning Media Ltd, are printed on paper
obtained from traceable sustainable sources.

We are grateful to Pearson Edexcel for permission to
reproduce the Guidelines for the Pearson BTEC Higher
Nationals in Business.

Contents

Introduction

BPP Learning Media's **Business Essentials** range is the ideal learning solution for all students studying for business-related qualifications and degrees. The range provides concise and comprehensive coverage of the key areas that are essential to the business student.

Qualifications in business are traditionally very demanding. Students therefore need learning resources which go straight to the core of the topics involved, and which build upon students' pre-existing knowledge and experience. The BPP Learning Media Business Essentials range has been designed to meet exactly that need.

Features include:

- In-depth coverage of essential topics within business-related subjects

- Plenty of activities, quizzes and topics for discussion to help retain the interest of students and ensure progress

- Up-to-date practical illustrations and case studies that really bring the material to life

- User-friendly uncomplicated style, of particular benefit to those for whom English is not their first language

- A glossary of terms and full index

In addition, the contents of the chapters are comprehensively mapped to the **Pearson Edexcel Guidelines**, providing full coverage of all topics specified in the Pearson BTEC Higher National qualifications in Business.

Each chapter contains:

- An introduction and a list of specific study objectives

- Summary diagrams and signposts to guide you through the chapter

- A chapter roundup, quick quiz with answers and answers to activities

BPP Learning Media's Business Essentials range is used by colleges and individual students throughout the world. Tried and tested on numerous different courses and for a variety of qualifications, the course books are ideal generic manuals for students and lecturers everywhere.

BPP Learning Media values your opinion. If you have any comments about this book, or suggestions as to how we could improve it, please email the Publishing Manager, Pippa Riley, at pippariley@bpp.com.

Other titles in this series:

Mandatory core units for the Pearson BTEC Higher Nationals in Business

Unit 1	Business Environment
Unit 2	Managing Finance
Unit 3	Organisations and Behaviour
Unit 4	Marketing Principles
Unit 5	Business Law
Unit 6	Business Decision Making
Unit 7	Business Strategy
Unit 8	Research Project

Pathways for the Pearson BTEC Higher Nationals in Business (specialist units)

Units 9 and 10	Finance: Management Accounting and Financial Reporting
Units 11 and 12	Finance: Auditing and Financial Systems and Taxation
Units 13 and 14	Management: Leading People and Professional Development
Units 15 and 16	Management: Communications and Achieving Results
Units 17 and 18	Marketing Intelligence and Planning
Units 19 and 20	Marketing and Sales Strategy
Units 21 and 22	Human Resource Management
Units 23 and 24	Human Resource Development and Employee Relations
Units 25 – 28	Company and Commercial Law

Generic titles

Economics

Accounts

Business Maths

Interactive CD ROMs are also available for separate sale in support of the three generic titles.

For more information, or to place an order, please call 0845 0751 100 (for orders within the UK) or +44(0)20 8740 2211 (from overseas), e-mail learningmedia@bpp.com, or visit our website at www.bpp.com/learningmedia.

Study guide

This Course Book includes features designed specifically to make learning effective and efficient.

- Each chapter begins with a summary diagram which maps out the areas covered by the chapter. There are detailed summary diagrams at the start of each main section of the chapter. You can use the diagrams during revision as a basis for your notes.

- After the main summary diagram there is an introduction, which sets the chapter in context. This is followed by learning objectives, which show you what you will learn as you work through the chapter.

- Throughout the Course Book, there are special aids to learning. These are indicated by symbols in the margin:

 Signposts guide you through the book, showing how each section connects with the next.

 Definitions give the meanings of key terms. The *glossary* at the end of the book summarises these.

 Activities help you to test how much you have learned. An indication of the time you should take on each is given. Answers are given at the end of each chapter.

 Topics for discussion are for use in seminars. They give you a chance to share your views with your fellow students. They allow you to highlight gaps in your knowledge and to see how others understand concepts. If you have time, try 'teaching' someone the concepts you have learned in a session. This helps you to remember key points and answering their questions will consolidate your own knowledge.

 Examples relate what you have learned to the outside world. Try to think up your own examples as you work through the Course Book.

 Chapter roundups present the key information from the chapter in a concise summary. Useful for revision and to consolidate knowledge.

 Quick quizzes are designed to help you revise and consolidate your knowledge. They test what you have learned (the answers often refer you back to the chapter so you can look over subjects again).

- The wide **margin** on each page is for your notes. You will get the best out of this book if you interact with it. Write down your thoughts and ideas. Record examples, question theories, add references to other pages in the Course Book and rephrase key points in your own words.

- At the end of the book, there is a glossary of definitions, a bibliography where appropriate and an index.

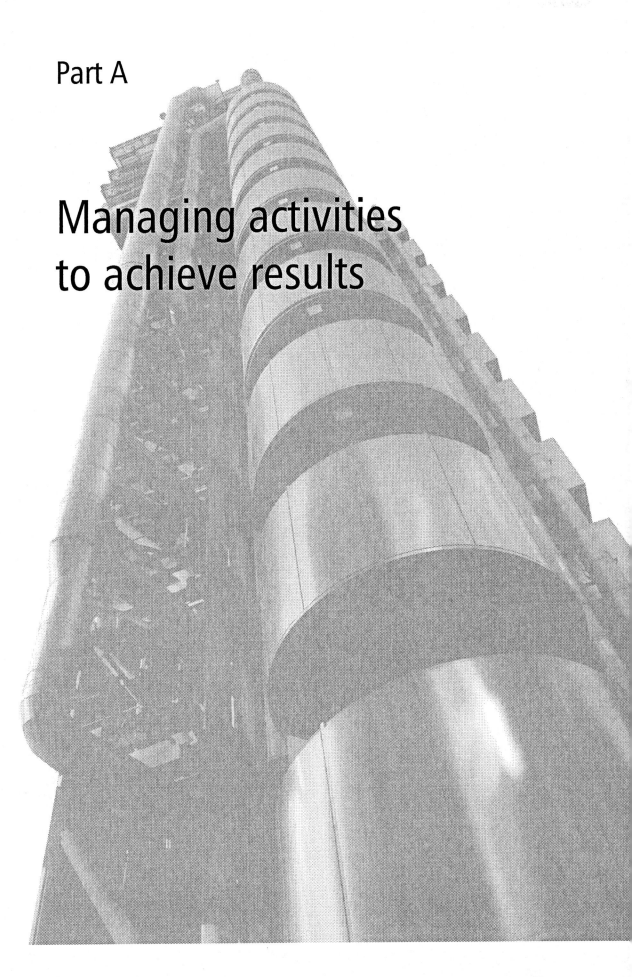

Part A

Managing activities
to achieve results

Chapter 01

Business processes and functions

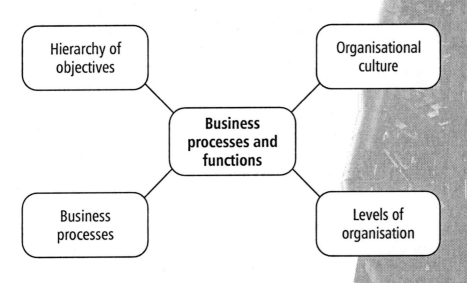

Introduction

Each business or organisation has **objectives**. The objectives of the organisation and what it does determine the type of structure that it has. An efficient structure for a government department might not be effective for an advertising agency. Changes in technology, such as the development of personal computers over the last decade or so, can radically change both the organisation's ways for working and their structures.

Your objectives

After completing this chapter you should be able to:

- Evaluate the interrelationship between the different processes and functions of the organisation

- Justify the methodology to be used to map processes to the organisation's goals and objectives

- Evaluate the output of the process and the quality gateways

SIGNPOST
First we look at the influences that shape organisations.

1 HIERARCHY OF OBJECTIVES

Today you want to drive to college. You know that you can call at a BP petrol station and fill the tank, pay with your visa credit card and go on your way along the district council's well surfaced road. If you break down you can call out the very, very nice man from the AA.

Suppose that none of the organisations involved with your journey to college outlined above had a formal structure. What would happen? For a start, you could not take it for granted that you could buy petrol at a petrol station. Without having people to take the decisions to drill for oil, extract it, refine it and ship the petrol to the pumps, there is no guarantee at all that it would all happen.

All organisations have some function to perform, some contribution to make. The function of the business organisation may be seen as the creation and/or supply of goods and services. This involves bringing together the factors of production and their successful mix and direction, to provide products or services in order to create value added.

It is the interaction of people, in order to achieve the aims and objectives, which form the basis of an organisation. Some form of structure is needed by which people's interactions are channelled and coordinated.

Organisations need:

- objectives
- people
- structure

Most writers agree with the idea that there is a hierarchy of objectives. *Mintzberg* uses the following:

(a) Mission – 'overriding premise' of the business
(b) Goal – 'general statement of aim or purpose'
(c) Objective – quantification or more precise statement of a goal
(d) Strategies – broad kind of action to achieve objective

Some writers ignore purpose and mission or use aims, goals, objectives and targets interchangeably. However, it is important to be able to clarify the ways in which you are using them.

1.1 MISSION

DEFINITION

Mission 'describes the organisation's basic function in society, in terms of the products and services it produces for its clients'.

(Mintzberg)

One view of the mission is that it is a broad statement of the purpose of an organisation. It is the primary raison d'être, set in advance of strategy. It can define why the company exists or why its managers and employees feel it exists. It outlines who the organisation exists for (eg shareholders, and possibly other stakeholders such as employees and customers). Possible purposes include those below.

- To create wealth for shareholders, who take priority over all other stakeholders.
- To satisfy the needs of all stakeholders (eg including employees and society at large).
- To reach some higher goals ('the advancement of society' and so forth).

1.2 MISSION STATEMENTS

DEFINITION

Mission statements are formal declarations of underlying purpose. They say what an organisation exists to do.

Mission statements might be reproduced in a number of places (eg at the front of an organisation's annual report, on publicity material, in the chairman's office, in communal work areas etc). There is no standard format, but they should have certain qualities

- **Brevity** will make them easier to understand and remember.
- **Flexibility** will enable them to accommodate change.
- They should be **distinctive**, to make the firm stand out.

Scott Adams, creator of Dilbert, defines a mission statement as 'a long awkward sentence that demonstrates management's inability to think clearly'. This illustrates the main problem with mission statements, which is getting people to take them seriously.

FOR DISCUSSION

The following statements were taken from annual reports of the organisations concerned. Are they 'mission statements'? If so, are they any good?

(a) **Glaxo** 'is an integrated research-based group of companies whose corporate purpose is to create, discover, develop, manufacture and market throughout the world, safe, effective medicines of the highest quality which will bring benefit to patients through improved longevity and quality of life, and to society through economic value.'

(b) **IBM (UK)**: 'We shall increase the pace of change. Market-driven quality is our aim. It means listening and responding more sensitively to our customers. It means eliminating defects and errors, speeding up all our processes, measuring everything we do against a common standard, and it means involving employees totally in our aims'.

(c) **Matsushita**: 'the duty of the manufacturer is to serve the foundation of man's happiness by making man's life affluent with an inexpensive and inexhaustible supply of life's necessities.'

(d) **Guinness Group**: 'Guinness plc is one of the world's leading drinks companies, producing and marketing an unrivalled portfolio of international best-selling brands, such as Johnnie Walker, Bell's and Dewar's Scotch whiskies, Gordon's and Tanqueray gins, and Guinness stout itself – the world's most distinctive beer. The strategy is to focus resources on the development of the Group's alcoholic drinks businesses. The objectives are to provide superior long-term financial returns for shareholders, to create a working environment in which people can perform to their fullest potential and to be recognised as one of the world's leading consumer brand development companies'.

(e) **British Film Institute**. The BFI is the UK national agency with responsibility for encouraging and conserving the arts of film and television. Our aim is to ensure that the many audiences in the UK are offered access to the widest possible choice of cinema and television, so that their enjoyment is enhanced through a deeper understanding of the history and potential of these vital and popular art forms.'

1.3 AIMS OR GOALS

Aims or goals are the secondary objectives derived from the mission and also set in advance of strategy.

Organisations have definite aims (or goals); by this we mean they try to make particular things happen. An aim or goal is a future expectation – a desired future state. It is something the organisation is striving to accomplish.

DEFINITION

Goals or **aims** give a sense of direction for the activities of an organisation and are sufficient for the satisfaction of the organisation's mission.

They can be used in a very broad sense to refer to the overall purpose of the organisation, eg to produce washing machines. They may also be used to refer to more specific desired outcomes, eg to produce and sell a given number of washing machines within a given period of time.

The aims of an organisation will determine the nature of its inputs and outputs, the series of activities through which the outputs are achieved and interactions with its environment.

The extent to which an organisation is successful in achieving its aims is a basis for the evaluation of organisational performance and effectiveness.

Aims serve a number of important functions.

- Aims provide a **standard of performance**. They focus attention on the activities of the organisation and the direction of the efforts of its members.

- Aims provide the **basis for planning** and management control of the activities of the organisation.

- Aims provide guidelines for decision-making and justification for actions taken.

- Aims influence the **structure** of the organisation and determine the nature of the technology employed.

- Aims or goals are the **basis for objectives and policies** of the organisation.

1.4 OBJECTIVES

In accordance with its ideology, the aims of the organisation are translated into objectives, which are expressed in a form that can be measured. All the organisation's objectives should be directed towards achieving the organisation's mission. In business organisations, a paramount consideration is profitability. The mission of a business, whether it is stated or not, must be to carry on its activities at a profit.

They should relate to the critical success factors of the organisation, which are typically:

(a) Profitability
(b) Market share
(c) Growth
(d) Cash-flow
(e) Customer satisfaction
(f) Quality of the organisation's products
(g) Industrial relations
(h) Added value

Objectives are normally quantified statements of what the organisation actually intends to achieve and should fulfil the SMART criteria outlined below.

Specific

Measurable

Achievable

Results-oriented

Time-bounded

Whereas mission statements describe a value system for the organisation and some indication of the business it is in, objectives are well defined. For example:

(a) mission: deliver a quality service

(b) aim or goal: enhance manufacturing quality

(c) objectives: over the next twelve months, reduce the number of defects to one part per million

Other examples of objectives include:

(a)   increasing the number of customers by x% (sales department objective)
(b)   reducing the number of rejects by 50% (production department objective)
(c)   responding to calls within ten minutes (hospital ambulance service)

Some objectives are more important than others. When there are several key objectives, some might be achieved only at the expense of others. For example, a company's objective of achieving good profits and profit growth might have adverse consequences for the cash flow or good product quality, or to improve market share, might call for some sacrifice of profits. There will be a trade-off between objectives when strategies are formulated, and a choice will have to be made.

1.5 STRATEGIES

A strategy provides the commercial logic for the company and so defines the nature of the firm's business, the markets it competes in and the competencies and competitive advantages by which it hopes to prosper.

DEFINITION

A **strategy** is a course of action, including the specification of resources required to achieve a specific objective.

Strategy is the organised development of resources (financial manufacturing, marketing, technological, manpower etc) to achieve specific objectives against competition from rival organisations. These perform a series of activities and they are all part of the inter-related sub-system of the organisation.

Resource planning will require answers to the following questions.

- What are the key tasks that have to be completed?
- What control systems exist?
- What changes should be made to resources?

As a result of this planning, organisations may decide to change their structure to meet the strategic requirements more closely.

1.6 POLICIES AND STANDARDS OF BEHAVIOUR

Policies provide the basis for decision-making and the course of action to follow to achieve objectives. For example, where the objective is to increase the number of customers by x%, the policy might be to sell to every retail outlet that is credit worthy. Some policy decisions are directly influenced by external factors, eg government legislation on equal opportunities.

Objectives and policy together provide corporate guidelines for the operation and management of the organisation. For example, specific decisions relating to personnel policy could include:

- giving priority to promotion from within the organisation

- enforcing retirement at government pensionable age

- permitting line managers, in consultation with the personnel manager, to appoint staff up to a given salary/wage level

Policies and strategies need to be converted into everyday performance. They are translated into rules, plans and procedures and relate to all activities of the organisation. For example, a service industry that wishes to be the best in its market must aim for standards of service, in all its operations, which are at least as good as those found in its competitors. In service businesses, this includes simple matters such as politeness to customers, speed at which phone calls are answered, and so forth.

ACTIVITY 1   (10 MINS)

Set out one of your new year's resolutions in terms of:

- mission
- goal (aim)
- objectives
- strategy

1.7 ORGANISATION STRUCTURE

Clearly defined and agreed aims and objectives are the first stage in the design of organisation structure and they help facilitate systems of communication between different parts of the organisation. As we have already noted, the aims are related to the input-conversion-output cycle. To achieve its objectives and satisfy its mission and aims the organisation takes inputs from the environment, through a series of activities transforms or converts them into outputs and returns them to the environment as inputs to other systems.

Figure 1.1: Input-output conversion

All organisations need lines of direction through the establishment of objectives and the determination of policy.

Other factors also influence the design of the structure. In total, the structure of a business organisation is determined by:

- its mission
- what it does
- its size
- where it operates
- who it deals with
- its culture
- technology
- the complexity of its operations
- its history and future expectations

For example, a hairdresser who provides haircuts to men and women within a two-mile radius is clearly going to have a very different market structure to a company providing air travel globally to a global market.

1.8 THE PUBLIC AND NOT-FOR-PROFIT SECTORS

Organisations in the public and not-for-profit sectors also have structures determined by the factors listed above. The public services and local government have some additional factors which influence them:

(a) the extent and type of duties and obligations imposed by Parliament, which they must perform;

(b) the changing expectations of society;

(c) changes in government policies and priorities.

Because they are closely associated with government and depend on it for funding, quangos, much of the voluntary sector, many arts and environmental bodies and local clubs and societies that use the facilities of the local authority are all affected by these factors.

FOR DISCUSSION

Consider your college's or university's structure of faculties and departments. Which of the factors listed above have been important in shaping its structure? How do you think that they compare with those that are important for:

(a) a news agent and sub-post office;

(b) the Royal Air Force?

BPP
LEARNING MEDIA

2 ORGANISATIONAL CULTURE

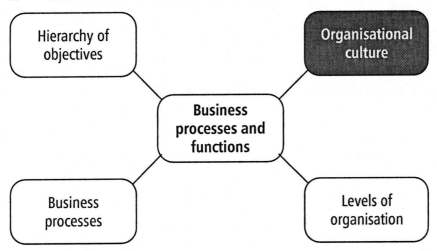

2.1 WHAT IS CULTURE?

There are many factors that influence the expectations that people are likely to have of an organisation, as shown in the diagram below:

Figure 1.2: Influences on organisational culture

The aims of the organisation will have an ideology based on beliefs, values and attitudes. This ideology is a means of control through shared beliefs and determines the culture of the organisation, providing a set of principles that govern the overall conduct of the organisation's operations, code of behaviour, the management of people and its dealings with other organisations. For example, a firm's moral principles might mean refusing an assignment if it believes the client will not benefit, even though this refusal means lost revenue. A sense of mission, or emotional bond, is where employees' personal values coincide with organisational values.

Culture may be identified as ways of behaving and ways of understanding that are shared by a group of people. Handy referred to it as 'the way we do things round here'.

DEFINITION

Culture is the commonly held and relatively stable beliefs, attitudes and values that exist within the organisation.

Culture in an organisation is the sum total of the beliefs, knowledge, attitudes of mind and customs to which people are exposed. Mintzberg refers to organisations as having an ideology. Ideology is a stronger word than culture: it means a set of beliefs, which are used to justify the position and activities of a ruling group.

Culture is both internal to an organisation and external to it. There are certain patterns of behaviour, assumptions and beliefs which members of the organisation have in common, because of their:

(a)   citizenship of the same society or country;

(b)   status or class position within that society;

(c)   profession (eg as accountants, marketers);

(d)   membership of the organisation.

All organisations will generate their own cultures, whether spontaneously or under the guidance of positive managerial strategy. Here are some aspects of culture.

(a)   **Customs and rituals**: there may be ceremonies, whether formal or informal, such as a Christmas party and awards to high achievers.

(b)   **Relationship between superiors and subordinates**: are bosses approachable?

(c)   **Symbols**: status may be reflected in things like size of office, or a democratic approach may be symbolised by an open plan office.

(d)   **Physical artefacts**: office layout and décor can influence communication.

(e)   **Common language**: the slang of the Royal Navy has grown up over centuries.

(f)   **Values** may be clearly stated or left unspoken and rather vague.

Trompenaars suggested that in fact there are different levels at which culture can be understood.

(a)   The **observable**, expressed or 'explicit' elements of culture include:

(i)   **Behaviour**: norms of personal and interpersonal behaviour; customs and rules about behaviours that are 'acceptable' or unacceptable.

(ii)   **Artefacts**: concrete expressions such as art and literature, architecture and interior design (eg of office premises), dress codes, symbols and 'heroes' or role models.

(iii)   **Rituals**: patterns of collective behaviour which have traditional or symbolic value, such as business formalities, social courtesies and ceremonies.

(b)   Beneath values and beliefs lie **assumptions**: foundational ideas that are no longer consciously recognised or questioned by the culture, but which 'programme' its ways of thinking and behaving. Examples include the importance of the individual in many Western cultures: this is taken for granted in designing HR (human resources) policies, for example.

(c)   Beneath values and beliefs lie **assumptions**: ideas that are no longer consciously recognised or questioned by the culture, but which 'programme' its ways of thinking and behaving. Examples include the importance of the individual in many Western cultures: this is taken for granted in designing human resources policies, for example.

Layers of culture, following Trompenaars' elements, include the following.

Item	Example
Beliefs and values, which are often unquestioned	The customer is always right'
Behaviour	In the City of London, standard business dress is still generally taken for granted and even 'dress down Fridays' have their rules.
Artefacts	Microsoft encourages communication between employees by setting aside spaces for the purpose.
Rituals	In some firms, sales people compete with each other, and there is a reward, given at a ceremony, for the salesperson who does best in any period.
Symbols	Corporate logos are an example of symbols, but they are directed outwards. Within the organisation, symbols can represent power: dress, make and model of car, office size and equipment and access to facilities can all be important symbols.

ACTIVITY 2 (10 MINS)

What do you think would differentiate the culture of:

(a)   A regiment in the army
(b)   An advertising agency?

2.2 CATEGORISING CULTURES

Deal and Kennedy (*Corporate Cultures: The Rites and Rituals of Corporate Life*) went beyond outlining the cultural elements within an organisation. They believe that the culture of a company affects its policies, decisions, activities and hence its success. Successful companies have strong and cohesive cultures where employees identify with the company goals and band together to achieve them. Alternatively, less well-performing companies have weak and disconnected cultures with minimal employee loyalty. Money is the prime motivator at work.

They suggest that an organisation is capable of being managed from a weak one to a strong one by the process of creating and implementing supporting rites, rituals and ceremonials. These act to communicate and reinforce the beliefs and values that senior management wants all employees to share.

Deal and Kennedy argue that two crucial factors shape an organisation's culture. The first is the degree of risk associated with the organisation's activities and the second is the speed of feedback provided to employees concerning the success of their decision strategy. They placed these factors on different axis to produce four distinctive types of organisational culture as follows.

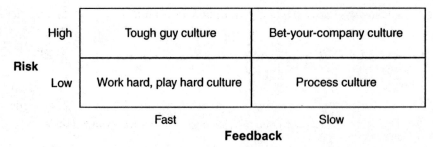

	Fast	Slow
Risk High	Tough guy culture	Bet-your-company culture
Low	Work hard, play hard culture	Process culture

Figure 1.3: Deal & Kennedy's cultural grid

- **Tough guy culture** – is made up of individualists who thrive on high risks and fast feedback on their performance. Unfortunately, the short-term need for feedback may divert attention from longer-term efforts. This type of culture is often found in construction, advertising and entertainment organisations.

- **Bet-your-company culture** – is characterised by high stake decisions with a delayed feedback. It is prevalent in oil and aircraft companies where the decisions that risk the company's future are made by technically competent people and necessitate attention to detail.

- **Work hard, play hard culture** – is characterised by low risk taking combined with quick feedback. High activity is the key to survival. This type of culture suits organisations with high volume sales of mass produced goods.

- **Process culture** – has little risk and little feedback. Typical process cultures include government agencies, banks and heavily regulated industries.

2.3 ANALYSING AND COMPARING CULTURES

Developing the ideas of Roger Harrison (*Understanding your Organisation's character*), Charles Handy created a typology which provides a useful basis for discussing and investigating variations in organisational culture. According to *Harrison*, the four basic classifications of the types of culture one might expect to find in an organisation are: power; role; task; and people cultures. *Handy* gave each of these types a Greek God's name:

- **Zeus** is the god representing the **power culture** or club culture. Zeus is a dynamic entrepreneur who rules with snap decisions. Power and influence stem from a central source, perhaps the owner-directors or the founder of the business. The degree of formalisation is limited and there are few rules and procedures. Such a firm is likely to be organised on a functional basis.

    – The organisation is capable of adapting quickly to meet change.

    – Personal influence decreases as the size of an organisation gets bigger. The power culture is therefore best suited to smaller entrepreneurial organisations, where the leaders have direct communication with all employees.

    – Personnel have to get on well with each other for this culture to work. These organisations are clubs of 'like-minded people introduced by the like-minded people, working on empathetic initiative with personal contact rather than formal liaison.'

- **Apollo** is the god of the **role culture** or bureaucracy. There is a presumption of logic and rationality.

    - These organisations have a formal structure, and operate by well-established rules and procedures. Individuals should perform their job to the full, but not overstep the boundaries of their authority. Individuals who work for such organisations tend to learn an expertise without experiencing risk; many do their job adequately, but are not over-ambitious.

    - The bureaucratic style can be very efficient in a stable environment, when the organisation is large and when the work is predictable.

- **Athena** is the goddess of the **task culture.** Management is seen as completing a succession of projects or solving problems.

    - The task culture is reflected in project teams and task forces. In such organisations, there is no dominant or clear leader. The principal concern in a task culture is to get the job done. Therefore the individuals who are important are the experts with the ability to accomplish a particular aspect of the task.

    - Performance is judged by **results.**

    - Task cultures are expensive, as experts demand a market price.

    - Task cultures also depend on variety, and to tap creativity requires a tolerance of perhaps costly mistakes.

- **Dionysus** is the god of the **existential** or **person culture.** In the three other cultures, the individual is subordinate to the organisation or task. An existential culture is found in an organisation whose purpose is to serve the interests of the individuals within it. These organisations are rare, although an example might be a partnership of a few individuals who do all the work of the organisation themselves (with perhaps a little secretarial or clerical assistance).

    - Barristers (in the UK) work through chambers. The clerk coordinates their work and hands out briefs, but does not control them.

    - Management in these organisations are often lower in status than the professionals and are labelled secretaries, administrators, bursars, registrars and chief clerk.

    - The organisation depends on the talent of the individuals; management is derived from the consent of the managed, rather than the delegated authority of the owners

---

ACTIVITY 3 (10 MINS)

Review the following statements. Ascribe each of them to one of Handy's four corporate cultures.

People are controlled and influenced by:

(a)   the owner's personally administered rewards, punishments and plans;

(b)   the impersonal exercise of economic and political power to enforce procedures and standards of performance;

(c)   communication and discussion of task requirements leading to appropriate action, motivated by personal commitment, to achieve the goal;

(d)   intrinsic interest and enjoyment in the activities to be done, and/or concern and caring for the needs of the other people involved.

2.4 MILES AND SNOW

Miles and Snow analyse three strategic cultures, and a fourth 'non-strategic' culture.

(a)   **Defenders**. Firms with this culture like low risks, secure markets, and tried and trusted solutions. These companies have cultures whose stories and rituals reflect historical continuity and consensus. Decision-taking is relatively formalised. There is a stress on 'doing things right' ie efficiency. Personnel are drawn from within the industry.

(b)   **Prospectors** are organisations where the dominant beliefs are more to do with results doing the right things ie effectiveness.

(c)   **Analysers** try to balance risk and profits. They use a core of stable products and markets as a source of earnings to move into innovative prospector areas. Analysers follow change, but do not initiate it.

(d)   **Reactors**, unlike the three above, do not have viable strategies. Arguably, they do not have a strategy, either deliberate or emergent, at all, unless it is simply to carry on living from hand to mouth, muddling through.

3 LEVELS OF ORGANISATION

BPP
LEARNING MEDIA

Organisation structure is the grouping of people into departments or sections and the allocation of responsibility and authority.

Organisation structure implies a framework intended to:

(a)   Link individuals in an established network of relationships so that authority, responsibility and communication can be controlled

(b)   Allocate the tasks required to fulfil the objectives of the organisation to suitable individuals or groups

(c)   Give each individual or group the authority required to perform the allocated tasks, while controlling their behaviour and use of resources in the interests of the organisation as a whole

(d)   Coordinate the objectives and activities of separate units, so that overall aims are achieved without gaps or overlaps in the flow of work

(e)   Facilitate the flow of work, information and other resources through the organisation

3.1   HIERARCHY AND SPECIALISATION

An organisation is a collection of groups joined in a common mission. Each group has its own specific objectives and functions. A group is unlikely to operate successfully without a leader who can take responsibility in seeing that the group performs its tasks. Current changes in management practice are leading to collective responsibility for work being given to groups themselves; however, there must still be an individual who interacts with other groups and with managers of wider groupings.

Many decisions need to be made within an organisation and someone must have the authority to make them at each of the different levels within it. This authority should be given to people who have the appropriate knowledge and experience. Along with the authority goes responsibility, and the need to ensure that decisions are carried out.

Organisations develop layers of authority to ensure that correct decisions are made and implemented. This results in the **organisation pyramid** as shown below. The more important a decision is to an organisation, the fewer are the people entrusted with the authority to make it.

Figure 1.4: Organisational pyramid

As organisations grow, specialist individuals or groups appear. These have to be coordinated, so further layers of management are required. Each department develops its own pyramid of authority. There can be specialism within a department, requiring more coordination. Thus increasing specialisation often leads to more layers of management.

EXAMPLE   BUILDING SOCIETIES

Building societies were originally formed to take deposits and lend funds as mortgages. They only required a few specialist departments; deposits, lending, administration, and legal. When they started to offer banking facilities, such as personal loans and savings and investments, they had to develop many more specialist departments.

ACTIVITY 4   (20 MINS)

Think about your local department store (or visit it if you do not know it well).

1   List the departments on all the sales floors.
2   Also list the support departments such as accounts.
3   Now suggest what advantages there are in having this degree of specialisation.

3.2   CENTRALISATION AND DECENTRALISATION

A centralised organisation is one in which authority is concentrated in one place. For example, if you meet a sales person who always says 'sorry, I'll have to refer that to head office', this implies that the organisation is centralised. We can look at centralisation in two ways.

(a)   *Geography.* Although councils can make decisions that affect their locality, they may be required to refer some decisions to central government in London.

(b)   *Authority.* Centralisation also refers to the extent to which people have to refer decisions upwards to their superiors.

The table below summarises some of the key issues.

Arguments in favour of centralisation and decentralisation	
Pro centralisation	Pro decentralisation/delegation
Decisions are made at one point and so easier to coordinate.	Avoids overburdening top managers, in terms of workload and stress.
Senior managers in an organisation can take a wider view of problems and consequences.	Improves motivation of more junior managers who are given responsibility-since job challenge and entrepreneurial skills are highly valued in today's work environment.
Senior management can keep a proper balance between different departments or functions — eg by deciding on the resources to allocate to each.	Greater awareness of local problems by decision makers. Geographically dispersed organisations should often be decentralised on a regional/area basis.
Quality of decisions is (theoretically) higher due to senior managers' skills and experience.	Greater speed of decision-making, and response to changing events, since no need to refer decisions upwards. This is particularly important in rapidly changing markets.

Arguments in favour of centralisation and decentralisation	
Pro centralisation	**Pro decentralisation/delegation**
Possibly cheaper, by reducing number of managers needed and so lower costs of overheads.	Helps junior managers to develop and helps the process of transition from functional to general management.
Crisis decisions are taken more quickly at the centre, without need to refer back or, get authority	Separate spheres of responsibility can be identified: controls, performance measurement and accountability are better.
Policies, procedures and documentation can be standardised organisation-wide.	Communication technology allows decisions to be made locally, with information and input from head office if required.

There is a good argument in favour of *centralising certain specialist functions* at head office to coordinate the strategy of the group as a whole. Central functions might include the public relations department, and a strategic planning department. Perhaps the most important example, however, is a research and development function, which might be centralised into a single unit, or broken up into separate R & D units for each product group/major subsidiary. A drawback, though, is that R&D can become too distant from the marketing function.

3.3 DEPARTMENTATION AND DIVISIONALISATION

Division of labour is one of the key principles of organisation. once an organisation grows beyond a certain size, this typically involves the grouping together and allocation of specific aspects of the work to different departments. This can be done on the basis of various criteria, such as functional specialisation, geographical area or product/brand.

Basic approaches to departmentation and divisionalisation are outlined below.

Functional organisation. This is departmentation by type of work done (eg finance department, marketing department, production function).

(a) Expertise is concentrated, enabling effective division of labour.

(b) Problems include poor communication between functional specialists, who might know little about other areas of the business.

Figure 1.5: Functional organisation

Geographic/territorial organisation. Reporting relationships are organised by geography. In each area functional specialists report to an area boss, who ensures coordination.

(a) This enables greater flexibility at local level, and allows experimentation.

(b) Some managerial work is duplicated. There may be problems in ensuring consistent standards.

Figure 1.6: Geographic organisation

Product/brand organisation. A divisional manager for each product is responsible for marketing and production. Some divisions are effectively run as independent businesses, in which case the division's finance specialists will report to the division's head.

(a) Individual product profitability can be easily identified.

(b) There is increased managerial complexity, and problems of resource allocation.

Multinationals can also divide up their activities by product, with each product division taking responsibility for worldwide production and sales, often with a territorial structure that has, in turn, a functional structure.

International charities tend to have territorial structures. For example, the Save the Children Fund has divisions for the UK, Africa, Asia and the Americas and the Pacific.

Customer/market segment organisation. reporting relationships are structured by type of customer.

Hybrid designs. In practice, organisations may draw on a number of these approaches. Product/brand departmentation for marketing and production, say, might be combined with a centralised R&D function. This is because some activities are better organised on a functional basis (for reasons of economies of scale) whereas others are more suited, say, to product/brand departmentation (eg marketing).

A *strategic business unit* (SBU) is normally defined as a division of the organisation 'where the managers have control over their own resources, and discretion over the deployment of resources within specified boundaries' (Ward). SBUs have an external market for goods/services, distinct from those of other SBUs.

ACTIVITY 5 (10 MINS)

What type of departmentation has:

(a) Central government?

(b) Independent television?

(c) Your college?

FOR DISCUSSION

As you can see from these examples, an organisation can use different methods of departmentation at different levels. Why is this so? What advantages are there for a multinational firm in having a territorial structure with regional divisions each structured into product divisions that are organised into functional departments?

3.4 THE MATRIX STRUCTURE

Despite its advantages, specialisation by department leads to problems of coordination and control. The matrix structure was developed to ensure coordination between different functional departments. This structure essentially 'crosses' functional and product/project organisation, so that staff in different functional or regional departments are responsible:

- To their department managers, in regard to the activities of the department;
- To a product or project manager, in regard to the given product or project.

An example of the matrix structure is shown in the diagram below:

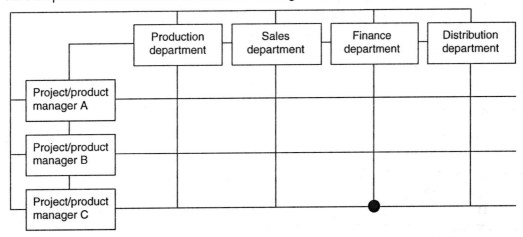

Figure 1.7: Matrix organisation

The employee represented by the dot in the above diagram, for example:

- is responsible to the finance manager for his/her work in accounting and finance;
- is responsible to the project manager for his/her work on the project team. This may be budgeting, management reporting, and payroll relevant to the project.

The purpose is to retain functional expertise while ensuring coordination. This is similar to *project organisation* where people from different functions are drawn together in a project team: however, matrix organisation is permanent.

- Advantages include better coordination and communication, and focus on the task.

- Disadvantages include the potential for conflict between, say, functional and area managers, and an increase in managerial overheads.

ACTIVITY 6 (15 MINS)

Jason, Mark, Gary and Robbie set up business together as repairers of musical instruments – specialising in guitars and drums. They are a bit uncertain as to how they should run the business, but when they discuss it in the pub, they decide that attention needs to be paid to three major areas: taking orders from customers, doing the repairs (of course) and checking the quality of the repairs before notifying the customers.

Suggest three ways in which they could structure their business.

4 BUSINESS PROCESSES

4.1 BUSINESS PROCESS ORIENTATION

DEFINITION

We define a **business process** as 'a set of related activities that collectively realise a business goal'.

The concept of business process-orientation is a recent development in organising. It can be described in terms of an organisation that is oriented towards processes, customers and outcomes as opposed to hierarchies.

The components of a business process oriented organisation include:

- a process view of the business – the cross-functional, horizontal picture of a business involving elements of structure, focus, measurement, ownership and customers;

- structures that match these processes – cross-functional process team structure, 'flat' hierarchy, process owners with leadership not control-oriented management;

- jobs that operate these processes – empowered, multi-dimensional, process team oriented – jobs that focus on processes not functions and are cross-functional in responsibility, e.g. 'product development process owner' rather than 'research manager'.

- management and measurement systems that direct and assess these processes – measures that include aspects of the process like output quality, cycle time, process cost and variability compared to the traditional accounting measures;

- customer focused, continuous improvement-oriented values and beliefs (culture) that are embodied in all components.

4.2 WHAT IS A PROCESS?

A business process:

- Has a goal
- Has specific inputs
- Has specific outputs
- Uses resources
- Has a number of activities that are performed in some order
- May affect more than one organisational unit.
- Creates value for the customer. The customer may be internal or external.

The environment

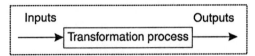

A process is a transformation; it converts its inputs into its outputs.

Inputs may include capital, raw materials, people, information, managerial and technical skills and knowledge.

The transformation process – Charles Handy considers these processes as sub-systems:

- **Production** – in a manufacturing organisation, the transformation of inputs into outputs would be the production department, in an insurance company it would be the underwriting department. The production sub-system is the heart of the organisation and all sub-systems are usually oriented towards it.

- **Maintenance** – keeps the organisation functioning. It may repair and service the building. Alternatively, the human resource department can be seen as a maintenance sub-system, recruiting, retiring and counselling employees.

- **Boundary spanning** – organisations must acquire inputs, raw materials data etc, and distribute output – the finished product or service. This sub-system can cover a variety of activities, such as purchasing and marketing.

- **Adaptation** – an organisation needs to adapt in order to survive. This sub-system can cover such activities as research, engineering, planning and development.

- **Management** – is the sub-system which coordinates all of the other sub-systems, by means of policies, plans, resolving conflict etc. It is the task of managers to transform the inputs, in an efficient and effective way, into outputs using the managerial functions of planning, organising, staffing, leading and controlling.

Outputs – the type of outputs will vary with the organisation. They generally include products, services, profits and rewards (the satisfaction of the goals of various claimants).

A process is not just about 'what people do', equal consideration should be given to 'what people produce'. Historically, there has been a lot of emphasis attached to the study of the way people perform their jobs, ie the activities they carry out. In process terms, the emphasis rests more heavily on the outputs a person produces – where a person does their job, the exact way they do it, what time of day they do it, or what they wear when they do it are largely irrelevant. A beach in Rio is a perfectly good office if the required output is produced on time and at the right level of quality.

Examples of processes are:

- Sales order processing
- Demand forecasting
- Sales operations planning
- Bought-ledger invoice processing
- New product development

Processes are identified from knowing an objective. If one of your objectives is to manage customer relationships effectively, you have a 'customer relationship management' process. If another objective is to bring innovative products to market ahead of the competition, you have an 'innovation' process or if the objective is to deliver product to customer on time, you have a 'delivery' process

Objectives are determined from the purpose of the organisation by establishing the factors upon which fulfilment of the purpose depends. These are the critical success factors (CSFs). The CSFs indicate the capabilities needed and therefore identify the objectives to deliver these capabilities.

4.3 THE COMPONENTS OF A PROCESS

A process is performed by using a procedure to combine basic assets with explicit and tacit knowledge.

- Basic assets consist of tangible and intangible assets. Examples of tangible assets are plant, machinery and cash. Intangible assets include reputation and brand strength

- Explicit knowledge is knowledge that is in the public domain. It is formal and standardised and can be easily shared and communicated. Examples would be the legal obligations of companies and the knowledge of how to undertake stock control.

- Tacit knowledge is personal and rooted in a specific context. Skill, the ability to do something well, especially because it has been learned and practised, is one form of tacit knowledge For example, once you learn how to drive a car and have been doing it for some time, you develop certain techniques (and bad habits) and driving becomes second nature. In contrast, much of the skill in an organisation such as Tesco is organisational skill eg, how to establish profitable relationships with suppliers.

- Procedures provide the ability to coordinate the basic assets, explicit and tacit knowledge to perform a process.

Processes link together to form a set that delivers a product or service to the customer. Two organisations competing for the same customers are differentiated on how well they manage to perform their processes. How well, for example, they transform market research into product design and development, or prospective customer interest into sales follow-up, and raw materials into building a product. An organisation with effective processes will meet or exceed customer expectation, whereas organisations with ineffective processes will fail to meet customer expectation and will therefore fail to retain those customers.

ACTIVITY 7 (15 MINS)

Give examples of the basic assets and the explicit knowledge likely to be found in a small local garage.

4.4 PROCESS MAPPING

Process maps are used to help analyse and understand a process and to aid its improvement or, ultimately, its replacement. The process map can show:

- what controls a process
- what it produces
- what areas it covers
- which elements make up the process.

It shows the sequence of activities, flow of information, decision points and the range of possible process outcomes The success of a process map rests in its ability to communicate a functional unit's core processes and key activities, how such processes and activities interrelate and the directional flow of the process. Maps are similar to flow charts, showing each step of the process in a way that is understood at every level of an organisation. An effective process map should provide a broad overview of a unit's activities – not an overly detailed description of individual tasks, responsibilities and the like. It should determine the unit's core purpose. It is vital that:

- all core processes are identified,
- all key activities are identified,
- process limits are defined.

Figure 1.8: Process map

The map will identify key stakeholders that will benefit from the outputs of the unit's processes and key activities. Stakeholders may be internal and/or external to the unit.

It will also identify the inputs to the process and the outputs eg, a service, process, a necessary outcome, process measures and/or process improvement.

The inclusion of performance measures that are related to client needs eg accuracy, timeliness, satisfaction, etc. should also be included.

Process maps should provide sufficient detail to allow an informed observer to understand the flow of work in the process/unit.

Figure 1.9: Content of a process map

Once the process mapping is done, there can be no uncertainty as to the requirements of every internal business process.

4.5 MANAGING THE PROCESSES

Business processes exist to realise business goals. By performing a business process, a necessary task is completed that contributes to the aims of the business. Thus, if a process does not make a contribution to a business goal, it should not exist.

The successful management of business processes requires the management of four different aspects of a process – process goals, performance, resources and interfaces. Process goals are derived from three sources – from business goals, from customer requirements and from benchmarking information.

There is a series of activities for managing processes effectively.

- Determine scope – identify processes, process ownership, boundaries and interfaces.

- Establish process objectives and express them in measurable terms.

- Document processes – develop process maps for all core and support processes.

- Define the key stages that convert the inputs into outputs.

- Define the resources, information and competences required to deliver the required outputs.

- Identify the risks and put in place measures that eliminate, reduce or control these risks.

- Establish measures of success – the factors that will indicate whether the objective has been achieved. Performance measures must relate to employee behaviour to tie in the strategic direction with employee action.

- Measure performance – identify customer requirements. Determine control points and specific process measures and targets. Collect data and develop statistical charts.

- Analyse performance – analyse results, determine process stability and the ability to meet customer requirements.

- Improve processes – plan and implement corrective action. Find better ways of achieving the process objectives and improve process efficiency.

- Establish whether the processes objectives remain relevant to the needs of the interested parties and if necessary change them.

Systems need to be established which will provide internal and external customer feedback on process outputs and track process performance against goals and sub-goals. Functions that play a role in the process must have feedback about their aspects of the process' performance and mechanisms must be established to solve process problems and continuously improve process performance. As new customer requirements are identified process goals must be adjusted to ensure the requirements are met.

4.6 QUALITY GATEWAYS IN THE REQUIREMENTS PROCESS

Requirements are the foundation for all that is to follow in the product or software development cycle. It therefore stands to reason that the requirements must be correct before they are given to the designers/developers.

The quality gateway is a quality control filter for all requirements. The basis of the gateway is simple: no matter how or where a requirement originates, it has to get through the gate to become an accepted requirement. It is a single point that every requirement must pass through before it can become a part of the specification document.

Figure 1.10: Quality gateway diagram 1

Quality gateways are normally set up so that one or two people, probably the lead requirements analyst and a tester, are the only people authorised to pass requirements through the gateway. If they are to be at all useful requirements must be measurable. That is, they must be given quantifiable characteristics so that testers can accurately determine whether the eventual solution satisfies a requirement, and so that the client can determine if the requirement's value is worth the cost of construction.

The steps to achieve good quality in requirements definition include:

- Elicitation – discovering the customer and user needs through consultation with stakeholders.

- Analysis – establishing an agreed set of requirements and discovering conflicts, missing, ambiguous, overlapping and unrealistic requirements.

- Representation – documenting individual requirements in a concise, understandable and unambiguous way.

- Validation – checking the requirements for omissions, conflicts and ambiguities and for ensuring that the requirements follow quality standards.

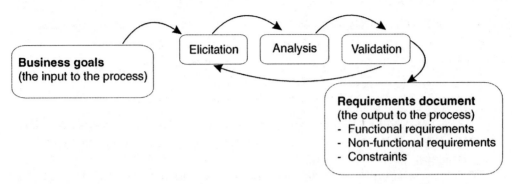

Figure 1.11: Quality gateway diagram 2

To make the requirements document easier to understand, it is a good idea to classify the requirements:

- Functional requirements define what the project/system will do

- Non-functional requirements describe project/system qualities. These include look and feel requirements, usability requirements, performance, operational, maintainability and portability requirements as well as security, cultural, political and legal requirements.

- Constraints are conditions that limit the choices available to designers and programmers , for example 'the system must run on Windows'

4.7 BUSINESS PROCESS MEASURES

The building blocks of business measures are goals (what is measured) and critical success factors (CSFs) – what has to be achieved for success. The measurement must quantify the advantage gained by the organisation. For example, if the goal is to give immediate and complete response to customers who order goods over the telephone, you have to ask what advantage that goal brings to the organisation. If immediate response will result in more satisfied customers, then the measurement must quantify that satisfaction.

Elements that could be measured include the increase in repeat business (on the basis that a happy customer comes back for more), the increase in customer approval ratings from surveys, the increase in revenue from returning customers, and so on.

The goal should be one of the following types:

- Service goal: this is measured by quantifying what it does for the customer

- Revenue goal: quantify how much revenue or revenue growth over what period of time. Alternatively, a revenue goal could be quantified by market share.

- Legal goal: this is not a quantification, but a way of knowing that the product or service conforms to a piece of legislation (this could be the law of the land or might be an industry or organisation standard).

The key to effective management of processes is the correct selection of the process outcome measures to provide data that can readily determine process health – for example:

- customer satisfaction

- cost of process outcome per unit measure

- quantity of output

- reliability of quality of output

- manner of delivery of output

- reliability of delivery of process outcome to defined programme

- delivery of process outcome within the defined timescale

- success or failure of process (eg tender process, win or lose)

- quantity of rejects, cost of rework

- quantity of waste

- extent of containment of risk (eg rise/fall in number of safety/environmental incidents or unexpected results)

The actual measuring of process performance can be done in a variety of ways and for different purposes. If the measurement is part of process performance management there will need to be a comparison made between how the process is operating now and 'something else'. This could be done by measuring the process over a period of time and making the comparison between 'then' and 'now' or by benchmarking – comparing it against a similar process performed elsewhere, often external to the business.

Process measurement performed as part of process performance management must be built in to the operational processes. Where possible the information required to measure the process should be captured by an automated recording system so that it can easily extracted and reported on.

Sometimes there is a requirement to measure all or specific parts of processes to determine the amount of actual time spent performing them, or to make a comparison between operating the process manually or using automated tools. In these cases a 'time and motion' study may be required which involves observation of the process being performed by other people using a stopwatch to record actual elapsed time.

CHAPTER ROUNDUP

- The first stage in the design of an organisation's structure is the definition of its mission, aims and objectives.

- The structure of an organisation is determined by influences such as its mission, operations, culture, technology and external factors like changes in government policy.

- Organisations develop the typical pyramid structure because of the need to establish lines of authority and responsibility.

- Culture is the commonly held and relatively stable beliefs, attitudes and values that exist within the organisation.

- Elements of culture include observable behaviour, artefacts, rituals and symbols: underlying values and beliefs; hidden assumptions

- Types of culture and related structures were identified by Harrison and Handy as follows:
    - Power culture (Zeus)
    - Role culture (Apollo)
    - Task culture (Athena)
    - Existential or person culture (Dionysus)

- Organisation structures can be classified into the following categories:

    - Specialisation – the typical line and staff organisation

    - Departmentation – functional, product or territorial

    - Matrix – authority is shared between the project manager and the line managers in departments

- Business process orientation can be described in terms of an organisation that is oriented towards processes, customers and outcomes as opposed to hierarchies.

- A process is performed by using a procedure to combine basic assets with explicit and tacit knowledge.

- Processes link together to form a set that delivers a product or service to the customer.

? QUICK QUIZ

1   Objectives should fulfil the SMART criteria. What do the letters stand for?

2   What are the elements of culture, according to Trompenaars?

3   Bureaucracy might be another name for a:

    A   Power culture
    B   Role culture
    C   Task culture
    D   Existential culture

4   A project team is most likely to be a role culture. True or false?

5   What are the three types of departmentation?

6   What are the responsibilities of project managers and department heads in a matrix structure?

7   Who is an employee's boss in a matrix structure?

8   What is a business process?

9   Explain the difference between tacit and explicit knowledge

ANSWERS TO QUICK QUIZ

1   Objectives should be: **S**pecific, **M**easurable, **A**chievable, **R**esults-oriented and **T**ime-bounded.

2   Observable phenomena (behaviour, artefacts, rituals), values and beliefs, assumptions.

3   B (Role culture)

4   False – it is most likely to be a task culture.

5   Functional, product and territorial.

6   Project managers are responsible for all aspects of the project, including the schedule and the budget; department managers are responsible for their departments, as line managers.

7   Both the project coordinator and the department head. Some matrix organisations combine territorial and functional organisation.

8   A business process is a transformation converting inputs such as raw materials, people, information, managerial and technical skills and knowledge into outputs such as products, services, and profits.

9   Explicit knowledge is formal, systemised and easily shared. Tacit knowledge is personal, formalised and rooted in specific concept.

ANSWERS TO ACTIVITIES

1   An example could be:

Mission: have a healthier lifestyle

Aims: get fit and lose weight

Objective: lose a stone by March

Strategies: join local gym and exercise for one hour daily; eat more vegetables, fewer biscuits

2   Here are some hints. The army is very disciplined. Officers make decisions; behaviour between ranks is sometimes very formal. The organisation values loyalty, courage and discipline and teamwork. Symbols and artefacts include uniforms, medals, regimental badges and so on. Rituals include parades and ceremonies.

An advertising agency, with a different mission, is more fluid. Individual flair and creativity, within the commercial needs of the organisation, are expected. Artefacts may include the style of creative offices, awards or prizes and the agency logo. Rituals may include various award ceremonies, team meetings and social gatherings.

3   Zeus
Apollo
Athena
Dionysus

4   You will probably have found sales-floor departments such as: ladies' outer wear, gent's outfitting, sports goods, children's clothes, stationery, ladies' shoes, linens, furniture and carpets. Service departments might include: accounts, credit, personnel, transport and warehousing and marketing. The advantages of such specialisation are greater expertise and efficiency.

5   The correct answers are (a) functional; (b) territorial; (c) product.

6   The group has identified three major functions of their business (sales, repairs and quality control) and to main product areas (guitars and drums). They might decide to structure the business in the following ways.

(a)   Have one 'general manager' (whose responsibilities may include quality control) and three 'operatives' who share the sales and repair tasks.

(b)   Divide tasks by function: have one person in change of sales, one quality controller and two repairers (perhaps one for drums and one for guitars).

(c)   Divide tasks by product: have a two-man drums team (who share sales/repair/control tasks between them) and a similar guitar team.

Since there are only four individuals, each (we assume) capable of performing any of the functions for either of the products, they may decide to have a looser social arrangement. They may prefer to discuss who is going to do what, as and when jobs come in. A larger organisation would not have this luxury.

7   An example of a garage procedure is dealing with a client bringing their car in for repair, with logging the car in and estimating the cost of the repair. Where procedures are written down – and thus codified – competitors may copy them. The basic assets of a small garage would include the equipment used in the repair of cars, eg ramps, test equipment, its buildings and its reputation. Explicit knowledge would include car-servicing schedules and instructions describing the workings of car engines.

Chapter 02

Plans for areas of responsibility

Introduction

The functions of management include **planning** – where managers establish goals, objectives, strategies, and policies and plan to achieve the stated aims of the organisation, and **organising** where managers structure the tasks that need to be performed, and decide which department and which individuals will complete which task and when. Planning helps the organisation to define its purposes and activities. It enables performance standards to be set so that results can be compared with the standard to help managers to see how the organisation is progressing towards its goals.

Because organisations have goals they want to satisfy, they need to direct their activities by:

- Deciding what they want to achieve
- Deciding how and when to do it and who is to do it
- Checking that they do achieve what they want, by monitoring what has been achieved and comparing it with the plan
- Taking action to correct any deviation

Your objectives

After completing this chapter and Chapter 3, (which is a continuation) you should be able to:

- design plans which promote goals and objectives for own area of responsibility

- write objectives which are specific, measurable, achievable, realistic and time-based to align people and other resources in an effective and efficient way

- implement appropriate systems to achieve objectives in the most efficient way, on time, to budget and meeting organisational standards of quality

- carry out work activities meeting the operational plan through effective monitoring and control

1 PLANNING

1.1 HIERARCHY OF OBJECTIVES

It is generally much easier to perform a task if the objective or objectives to be achieved are clearly expressed. Yet frequently individuals, teams and even entire businesses attempt to make progress without having agreed and stated the performance objectives they wish to achieve. It is also possible to go to the other extreme and generate too many conflicting or contradictory objectives. This state is particularly easy to achieve in the matrix management structures common in business today, where an individual may have two 'bosses'. The aim in an organisation should therefore be to set clear objectives which are consistent throughout and can apply at all levels – from an entire enterprise to the individual.

Most writers agree with the idea that there is a hierarchy of objectives, just as there is a hierarchy of managers. At each higher level in the hierarchy the objectives are more relevant to a greater proportion of the organisation's activities so that the objectives at the top of the hierarchy are relevant to every aspect of the organisation. Plans are made at various levels in an organisation and may be stated in the form of a hierarchy. The diagram opposite illustrates the hierarchical relationship of mission, goals, objectives, strategy, tactics and operational plans.

Objectives are normally quantified statements of what the organisation actually intends to achieve.

Mission statements, however, describe a value system for the organisation and some indication of the business it is in, objectives are well defined, as the following example demonstrates.

(a)   Mission: deliver a quality service
(b)   Goal: enhance manufacturing quality
(c)   Objectives: reduce the number of defects to 1 part per million

Goals and objectives are devised to fulfil the mission. The terms are often used interchangeably: if there is a difference, objectives are more likely to be quantified, and so progress towards them is more measurable. Goals and objectives can also be said to interpret the organisation's mission to a number of different client groups or *stakeholders*, all of whom have an interest in what the organisation does.

Mission — *Mission* describes the organisation's basic function in society, in terms of the product and services it produces for its clients.

Goals — *Goals* are the intentions behind decisions or actions, the states of mind that drive individuals or organisations to do what they do

Objectives — *Objectives* are targets or standards that orientate the activities of the organisation.

Strategy — *Strategy* is a course of action, including the specification of resources required. Strategy is converted into everyday performance with policies and standards of behaviour.

Tactics — *Tactics* are the most efficient deployment of resources in an agreed strategy e.g., for road safety tactics might include random breathalyser tests and the installation of street cameras.

Operational plans — *Operational plans* are concerned with the way in which the company is to be run from day-to-day to optimise performance.

Figure 2.1: Planning hierarchy

EXAMPLE   THE CO-OP

The Co-op is a good example of the role of mission. Although it is a business organisation, its mission is not simply profit. Being owned by its suppliers/customers, rather than external shareholders, it has a wider social concern.

The Co-op has been criticised by some analysts on the grounds that it is insufficiently profitable, certainly in comparison with supermarket chains such as Tesco. The Co-op has explicit social objectives. In some cases it will retain stores which, although too small to be as profitable as a large supermarket, provide an important social function in the communities which host them. Of course, the Co-op's performance as a retailer can be improved, but judging it on the conventional basis of profitability ignores its social objectives.

As with business planning (of which it forms an integral part) the process of setting objectives can be approached from either a 'top-down' or 'bottom-up' direction. The 'top-down' approach ensures that the overall 'hierarchy of objectives' reflects the overall business objectives, whereas the 'bottom-up' direction is necessary to establish practicality and feasibility in objectives applied at a local operational level.

1.2 THE BUSINESS PLAN

If individuals and groups within an organisation are to be effective in working for the achievement of the organisation's objectives, they need to know what it is they are expected to do. Planning allows managers to identify the objectives for which they are responsible and how far they are being successful in achieving those objectives.

Planning involves decisions about:

- What to do in future
- How to do it
- When to do it
- Who should do it

Such questions are relevant at all levels of organisational activity:

(a) At a strategic level – deciding what business the organisation should be in, and what its overall objectives should be

(b) At a tactical level – deciding how it should go about achieving its overall objectives: what products it should produce, how it will organise work and so on

(c) At the operational level – deciding what needs to be done from day to day and task to task

Strategic, or long-range, planning looks at where the business wants to be in maybe two to three years time, and works out how to get it there. This will involve consideration of environmental factors, current and potential competitors, declining and emerging markets, projected technological change, possible diversification (producing new, different products or services) and forecast movements in consumer spending. In other words, long-range planning has to deal with a lot of variables and a high level of uncertainty. The strategic plan will constantly be amended in the light of new developments.

Tactical, or short-range planning takes a shorter time period, for instance a year, and decides what needs to be done within that time period to further the strategic plan. At this level, planning will look at expansion targets, market penetration, asset purchases, financing requirements, resource requirements, and any improvements that need to be made to efficiency in order to maintain and widen the gap between costs and revenues. Improvements to efficiency will then be translated into operational planning.

Operational planning represents the lowest level of planning and involves line manager, supervisory management and foreman levels in setting specific tasks. The focus is on individual tasks, for example, scheduling individual works orders through a production planning process. Whatever it is that a supervisor intends to plan for, generally he or she will need to determine the following:

- What has to be achieved – the goal or objective?
- What jobs have to be done in order to reach that goal or objective?
- What resources are needed to do the jobs that have to be done?
- What sequence of task performance is required to progress efficiently toward the goal or objective?

BPP
LEARNING MEDIA

- What kind of coordination is required?

- What has to be communicated and to whom must it be communicated?

- What has to be controlled and how must control be achieved to ensure that the plan is realised?

Planning horizon

Planning covers the long-term as well as the short-term. A planning period or time horizon is the length of time between making and implementing a planning decision. A decision to build new premises may have a time horizon of many years; a programme to develop a new product might take several years; an operating budget might span a one-year period; a production schedule might be produced weekly.

This has two main consequences.

(a)   Long-term objectives might conflict with shorter-term plans, and planners should try to reconcile the two. If a company has a short-term problem with limited funds, for example, it might be tempting to cut costs to maintain profitability – but if spending on research or marketing are ignored, the company's long-term profitability might suffer.

(a)   Plans, once formulated, should not be rigid, because the future is uncertain: plans might need to be changed if unforeseen circumstances arise. A compromise should be found between the need for flexibility (which suggests keeping plans short-term) and the need for commitment to decisions that have been made (which suggests planning over the whole of a long-term period).

1.3   PLANNING AND CONTROL CYCLE

Planning is an activity that involves decisions about ends (organisational objectives), means (plans), behaviour (policies) and results. It is an activity which must take place against the background of the organisation's environment and which must take account of the organisation's internal strengths and weaknesses.

The stages in the planning and control cycle can be shown diagrammatically, as follows:

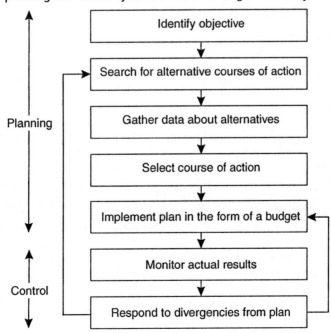

Figure 2.2: Planning process

Planning is the process of deciding what should be done. Control is the process of checking whether it has been done, and if not, doing something about it. Once the plan has been formulated and steps have been taken to carry it out, it is necessary to monitor and measure the actual results achieved. These results can then be compared to the planned results. This will show that either results are proceeding according to plan, or corrective action is necessary in order to ensure the plan is achieved.

Control is necessary because unexpected factors may arise and affect the system, so making actual results deviate from the expected results. Examples of such unpredictable factors in a business system might be:

- The entry of a powerful new competitor into the market
- An unexpected rise in labour costs
- A decline in quality standards
- A supplier going out of business
- Loss of a major customer
- New legislation affecting products
- The appearance of new technology

A good control system will provide management with rapid feedback enabling it to react appropriately to changes in the business environment.

It is as well to recognise that there always will be unpredictable factors. Given the current pace of change in finance, technology and world markets, it would be more surprising to see a long-term, or even a short-term, plan which proceeded as envisaged without any changes being made to keep it on track. It has even been argued that long-term planning is a waste of time, as the plan is bound to be overtaken by events.

An important part of planning in this regard is the consideration of contingencies. **Contingencies** are unexpected events, which may or may not happen. Contingency planning looks at how the overall plan will be affected if something unexpected happens, or if some part of the business does not proceed according to plan. As part of the contingency planning process, managers will come up with alternative solutions in response to possible problems. Contingency planning is covered in detail later in this chapter.

1.4 PURPOSES OF PLANNING AND ORGANISING

If individuals and groups within an organisation are to be effective in working for the achievement of the organisation's objectives they need to know what it is they are expected to do. Planning allows managers to identify:

(a) the objectives for which they are responsible;
(b) what actions will serve towards achieving those objectives; and
(c) how far they are being successful in achieving those objectives.

Planning and organising are important functions in an organisation for the following reasons.

(a) **Uncertainty**. Organisations cannot deal with things *ad hoc*, as they occur, without chaos. The future cannot be foreseen with certainty in any case, and even the best-laid plans will go wrong to a greater or lesser degree (which is where 'control' comes in). Nevertheless, plans and structures give some direction and predictability to the work of the organisation: in other words, they are a form of risk management.

(b) **The need for coordination**. Organisations are collections of individuals and groups (or sub-systems): each will perceive its own part of the organisation's activity, and work towards its own objectives accordingly.

Planning and organising ensures that:

(i)   sub units of the organisation know what it is they need to achieve, and when;

(ii)   work 'flows' from one process (or department) to another without holdups or clashes, and without idle time or overwork for staff and machinery;

(iii)   the resources required for a task are available where and when they are required;

(iv)   required work is being done by somebody – but not being duplicated by others, with a waste of effort;

(v)   all of the above are achieved in such a way that products/services of the required quality are available to customers at the right place, at the right price and at the right time.

FOR DISCUSSION

Suggest examples of the planning/organising needed in each of the areas given in (i) to (v) above, and what would happen if planning was not carried out.

(c)   The need for objectives. Human beings are 'purposive': they like to feel that their actions have a point. If the organisation doesn't set objectives, people will set their own, according to their own interpretation of the situation: chaos ensues. Objectives are also important in learning and motivation, so people can target and adjust their behaviour according to what they want to achieve.

1.5 MEASURES OF SUCCESS

The degree to which the goals and objectives are attained is a measure of the organisation's *effectiveness.* This term should not be confused with the *efficiency* of the organisation, which is concerned with the means employed. If inappropriate means are employed the organisation could be very efficient but totally ineffective – conversely an organisation can be very effective but have sufficient organisational slack to be able to operate inefficiently.

Efficiency

Efficiency is a term often used loosely to express the idea of 'doing things well'.

DEFINITION

Efficiency is the relationship between inputs used and outputs achieved. The fewer the inputs used to obtain a given output, the greater the efficiency. Efficiency can be expressed as: $\frac{\text{output}}{\text{input}}$

If a car does 400 miles on ten gallons of petrol it does $400 \div 10 = 40$ miles per gallon. This is a measure of its efficiency at using fuel.

Efficiency is about avoiding **waste** – of effort, time and material resources – in producing desired outputs, or achieving the organisation's goals. Efficient operation might involve:

(a)   producing no less, but no more, than the demand for the product;

(b)   avoiding spoiled or unacceptable products, according to the organisation's quality standards;

(c)   avoiding overmanning (employing more people than the task requires), or improving productivity: output (or profit, say) per employee;

(d)   avoiding unnecessary movements, operations and routines (such as paperwork, task duplications, double-checks and so on) which take time, without adding value in the process;

(e)   avoiding expense of finance and resources which add no value and earn no return.

Effectiveness

It has been argued that efficiency focuses too much on controlling the 'inputs' to the organisation's activities, and not enough on the 'outputs'. (You can improve efficiency by cutting costs instead of improving sales.)

DEFINITION

Effectiveness is the measure of how far an organisation (and its managers) achieve their output requirements, as defined by performance objectives and targets.

In other words, **effectiveness** is about 'doing the right things', not just 'doing things right'. Effectiveness-oriented managers are concerned with fulfilling objectives with regard to:

(a)   output quantity;
(b)   output quality and customer satisfaction;
(c)   added value (the value added to inputs, reflected in the sale price of the output);
(d)   innovation, or new products/services/improvements implemented.

ACTIVITY 1   (5 MINS)

Read through and tick in the relevant columns whether the statements relate to efficiency or effectiveness.

		Efficiency	Effectiveness
(a)	A customer is satisfied	☐	☐
(b)	The factory produces more cars	☐	☐
(c)	Waste has been reduced	☐	☐
(d)	Better quality products are produced	☐	☐
(e)	Ten employees were given early retirement packages	☐	☐
(f)	The company increased its dividend payment to shareholders	☐	☐

Efficiency and effectiveness require:

(a)   an idea of what outputs the organisation wants from the production system;

(b)   an idea of what inputs will be required; and

(c)   a way of monitoring and measuring performance, to ensure that it conforms to the organisation's expectations.

SIGNPOST

In essence, this is the process of planning and control.

2   MANAGEMENT BY OBJECTIVES (MBO)

2.1   ACHIEVEMENT OF ORGANISATIONAL GOALS

Management by objectives (MBO) is a scheme of planning and control that provides coordination:

- of short-term plans with longer-term plans and goals;
- of the plans (and commitment) of junior with senior management;
- of the efforts of different departments.

Successful achievement of organisational goals requires the following.

(a)   Each job is directed towards the same organisational goals. Each managerial job must be focused on the success of the business as a whole, not just one part of it.

(b)   Each manager's targets must be derived from targets of achievement for the organisation as a whole.

(c)   A manager's results must be measured in terms of their contribution to the business as a whole.

(d)   Each manager must know what his or her targets of performance are.

(e)   A manager's superior must know what to demand from the manager, and how to judge his or her performance.

Consequently, to ensure coordination, the various functional objectives must be interlocked:

(a)   *vertically* from top to bottom of the business;

(b)   *horizontally*, for example, the objectives of the production function must be linked with those of sales, warehousing, purchasing and R & D;

(c)   *overtime*. Short-term objectives can be regarded as intermediate milestones on the road towards long-term objectives.

2.2 SMART OBJECTIVES

MBO also introduced the SMART method for checking the validity of objectives. SMART is an acronym for:

- Specific
- Measurable
- Achievable
- Realistic, *and*
- Time-related.

Specific	• Is the objective precise and well defined? For example, 'Answer the phone quickly' can be said to be a precise description of behaviour, you can clearly see whether someone answers the phone or not, but there is no rate, number, percentage or frequency linked to it. So, if we add 'Answer the phone within three rings' a rate has been added and the behaviour is now much more specific.
	• Is it clear?
	• Can everyone understand it?
Measurable	• How will the individual know when the task has been completed?
	• What evidence is needed to confirm it?
	• Have you stated how you will judge whether it has been completed or not? Setting an objective that requires phone calls to be answered in three rings is fine, provided a system exists which measures whether this is actually being achieved.
Achievable	• Is it within their capabilities? They need to be stretching and agreed by the parties involved. Setting targets that are plainly ridiculous does not motivate people; it merely confirms their opinion of you as an idiot.
	• Are there sufficient resources available to enable this to happen?
	• Can it be done at all?
Realistic /relevant	• Is it possible for the individual to perform the objective?
	• How sensible is the objective in the current business context?
	• Does it fit into the overall pattern of this individual's work?
	• Example: Telling the cleaners that they 'have to increase market share over the next financial quarter' is not actually something they can do anything about – it is not relevant to them. However, asking them to reduce expenditure on cleaning materials by £50 over the next three months is entirely relevant to them. It is what they spend their budget on every day.
Time-related	• Is there a deadline – in the objective somewhere there has to be a date (Day/Month/Year) for when the task has to be started (if it's ongoing) and/or completed (if it's short term or project related)?
	• Is it feasible to meet this deadline?
	• Is it appropriate to do this work now?
	• Are there review dates?

2.3 COORDINATION

Coordination is one of the major functions of management. Each department will have its own procedures and its own priorities. It is the job of the manager to get all of these to mesh together harmoniously and move in the direction of the common purpose.

This is nowhere more apparent than in the planning process. Each department will have its own long-term and short-term goals and purposes and targets that it wants to achieve. There may also be bonus schemes tied into this. Each department will have its own set of priorities. Effective coordination will cause some of these to change, in the interests of pursuing an overall set of priorities.

As the business plan will cover all departments of the organisation, so all of the departmental plans and budgets must be coordinated, so that they are all working together to achieve the business plan. For instance, sales should be planning to sell the number of units that the production departments agreed to produce, otherwise there will be either unsold stock or unfilled orders.

At the production level, coordination will ensure that:

- Departments know what it is they need to achieve, and when

- Work 'flows' from one department to another without hold-ups or clashes, and without idle time or overwork for staff and machinery

- The resources required for a task are available where and when they are required

- There is no duplication of effort

2.4 INDIVIDUAL EFFECTIVENESS AND TIME MANAGEMENT

The aim of MBO for the individual is to provide clear direction. This is the first step in delivering managerial effectiveness. There must also be a *meeting* of objectives. The individual will have personal objectives, which need to be placed in the context of the business objectives to ensure 'goal congruence' – so that the individual can work towards personal and organisational objectives simultaneously.

From then on, the effectiveness of individuals depends on how well they organise themselves. This involves competence areas like:

- Setting priorities – the organisation's operations require proper scheduling of resources to run efficiently and avoid periods of over and under utilisation. Some activities must occur at precisely the right time, eg specific day and time slot for advertising a new product. The scheduling of tasks can also affect customer service in terms of delivery.

- Skill at marshalling and utilising the resources at one's disposal – this applies to both human and material resources. For human resources the manager has to get the best out of the available resource by leading, communicating, delegating and motivating.

- Ability to communicate – this is the major key to being efficient and effective

- Efficiency in time management – the process also starts with a hierarchy of plans and objectives based on the following questions:

- What are my long-term goals and what strategy will I employ to achieve them?

    - What are my plans for the mid term?
    - What are my daily work plans?

3 SYSTEMS, POLICIES AND PROCEDURES

3.1 PLANNING AND COORDINATION TOOLS

The tools by which planning and coordination are carried out can be categorised as follows.

Systems – a system is an agreed-upon plan or process for carrying out an activity. An operating system interfaces between the hardware, programs and data in a computer. It organises and schedules the tasks. A production plant will have a system, which determines how production is organised, who does what, when the machines are serviced, how long the shifts run etc.

In a business, the accounting system will ensure that all bookkeeping and related tasks are carried out accurately and in a timely fashion. At the next level, the management information system will provide management with the financial information needed for planning and control.

Policies – are general statements or 'understandings' that provide guidelines for management decision-making. It might be company policy, for example, to offer five-year guarantees on all products, or to promote managers from within the organisation. Policy guidelines allow managers to exercise their own discretion and freedom of choice, but within certain acceptable limits.

Procedures – are chronological sequences of actions required to perform a task. They exist at all levels but are more extensive lower down the company hierarchy, where the work is more routine. They have three main advantages:

(a)   **Efficiency** – procedures prescribe the most efficient way of doing a job.

(b)   **Routine** – procedures remove the need for the exercise of discretion or ad hoc decision-making.

(c)   **Standardisation** – this makes output more predictable and more consistent throughout the organisation.

Rules – a rule (or regulation) prescribes a specific, definite action that must be taken in a given situation. It allows no discretion – unlike a policy. For example:

(a)   'employees in department X are allowed ten minutes exactly at the end of their shift for clearing up and cleaning their work bench'

(b)   'employees with access to a telephone must not use the telephone for personal calls'.

Programmes – are coordinated groups or series of plans, which together achieve a particular objective; for instance, a company might undertake a programme of expansion, computerisation or customer care, involving different aspects and stages of planning.

Budgets – a budget is a formal statement of expected results set out in numerical terms, usually summarised in money values. It is a plan for carrying out certain activities with specified resources within a given period of time, in order to achieve certain targets.

ACTIVITY 2 (20 MINS)

Dial-a-DVD Limited offers home DVD rental service to subscribers. Subscribers choose a DVD from a catalogue, phone Dial-a-DVD Limited and the DVD is delivered by a despatch rider. The Chairman, Rajiv Bharat, says to you: 'I hope to expand the business. I've discovered a market for art movie DVDs. I've had to knock the directors' heads together to develop plans for building a distribution system: they've agreed a number of stages: for a new catalogue, market research and that sort of thing. We'll charge £4 per DVD per day including delivery. It is a premium price, but people who like that sort of movie will pay for it. We'll tell the despatch riders not to accept tips though.'

What sort of plans has Rajiv Bharat described to you?

3.2 OFFICE PROCEDURES AND SYSTEMS

Office systems and procedures are designed to allow the different administrative functions to operate effectively. This diagram shows in a simplified form the flow of funds, documentation and information in an office.

Figure 2.3: Office systems

Effective systems and procedures should ensure that:

- Relationships with customers are effectively managed
- Relationships with suppliers are effectively managed
- Office functions interrelate properly and are not duplicated

Within the overall system, which we can consider to be how each department relates to the other departments and to outside bodies, there will be sub-systems. For instance, the purchase ledger function will have its own system, which will be designed to ensure that only authorised payments are made, that no invoice ever gets paid twice and that expenses are coded to the correct accounts. Weaknesses in office procedures may be signalled by:

- Arguments over job functions
- Missing paperwork
- Disputes with customers/suppliers
- Goods not delivered

3.3 FINANCIAL CONTROL PROCEDURES

Financial control procedures exist specifically to ensure that:

- Financial transactions are properly carried out
- The assets of the business are safeguarded
- Accurate and timely management information is produced

These are some examples of financial control procedures:

- Cheques over a certain amount to need two signatories
- Authorisation limits for purchase orders
- Authorisation for petty cash and expenses claims
- Effective credit control procedures
- Computer security procedures and access levels

Weaknesses in financial control procedures may be signalled by:

- Cash or cheques going missing
- Excessive bad or doubtful debts
- Debtors not paying within credit terms
- Suppliers not being paid on time
- Unauthorised purchases being made
- Failure to produce accounts or other reports at the specified time

3.4 MANAGING RISK

Plans do not give managers control over the future.

(a) The future cannot be forecast with any certainty. You can only anticipate what is **likely** to happen in future, based on what has happened in the past, and any trends or tendencies that you can see in the pattern of past events.

(b) Unexpected, uncontrollable events happen. Computers break down, terrorists blow up buildings, suppliers go bust, transport strikes shut down operations for a day and so on.

Risk is the exposure to the possibility of such things as economic or financial loss, physical damage, injury or delay as a consequence of pursuing or not pursuing a particular course of action. It is the probability of an event and magnitude of its consequence.

Risk management is the process whereby an organisation anticipates the potential for adverse events that may lead to injury or loss and acts to avoid those events before they occur and/or to ameliorate them after they occur. As with all risk management, the key objective is to introduce measures that cost less than the potential damage, which might arise if the risks identified occurred. Specifically, risk management involves three steps: risk assessment, risk management and risk transference.

Risk assessment – all potential problems that can be thought of should be listed and broken down under headings eg, physical, human and systems or employees, computers, operating conditions and criminal activities.

Physical	Human	Systems
Fire, flood or terrorist action	Staff on strike	A computer virus which destroys all the files on the hard disk
Currency devaluation in your main trading country	Payroll theft	Accounting error due to posting a wrong amount
Power cut	Employee has heart attack	Snow breaks telephone lines

These risks should then be assessed as to the impact and damage they would cause to the business if they occurred. The risk should be quantified as far as possible, eg the failure of a particular computer on the network might result in the loss of half a day's sales and the time involved in re-keying information. The qualitative nature of the risk needs to be noted as well.

Risk management – once the potential damage has been assessed, steps are taken to minimise the damage. It is a vital element of risk management that the cost of the steps must be commensurate with the damage avoided. Management can attempt to reduce the risk through good work practices, quality specifications and standards, backup systems and contingency plans. The remaining risk may be an insurable risk.

Risk transference – ultimately, there are some areas where the risk is small in terms of its probability but high in the damage that would be incurred. An example might be earthquake damage in most of the UK, or losses arising due to fire, etc. Whilst steps can be taken to ensure the integrity of data, the most sensible way of dealing with the rest of the risk to the systems is to transfer, or share the cost via insurance or some other form of contingency plan covering the area of 'disaster recovery'.

Contingencies are unexpected and uncontrollable events that do not feature in the main plan of the organisation. However, some such events can be anticipated: managers do not expect them to happen, but acknowledge that they might happen, and consider what should be done if they do. Contingency plans are those which are prepared in advance to deal with a situation that may (or may not) arise.

All plans should be contingency plans to an extent, since planners must make room for:

(a) margins of error; time and resource estimates are only estimates;
(b) changes in the circumstances;
(c) slippage in the schedule which needs to be caught up elsewhere.

Remember that planning is part of the control system: plans may constantly have to be adjusted in order to correct or improve performance.

ACTIVITY 3 (20 MINS)

What kind of contingency plans might you want to make if you were in charge of:

(a) transferring all your transactions onto a new computer system?
(b) accomplishing a project which required all the 'people hours' you have at your disposal?
(c) organising (yet another) sales conference at an external venue

---

4 CUSTOMER ORIENTATION

4.1 MANAGING THE RELATIONSHIP WITH CLIENTS/CUSTOMERS

Management is not just about 'managing' the organisation and the people within it, it is also about 'managing' the relationship with clients, or customers. All organisations have customers, clients, patients, etc, and with the exception of some types of monopolies, the success and future of the organisation depends upon the continued goodwill of its clients. These clients may be individuals, businesses, governments or even other large organisations.

The customer is the basic reason for the existence of any business since without customers to sell to, a business cannot operate. Meeting the needs of those customers more effectively than competitors is the key to continued profitable existence for any business. Each customer who deals with an organisation should leave with a feeling of satisfaction. This outcome is important since it can lead to increased sales and/or a willingness to pay higher prices and thus lead to higher profits. If customers are satisfied they may:

- Buy again from the same supplier
- Buy more of the same item, or more expensive items
- Advise their friends to buy from the supplier

When anyone buys they take a risk. Everyone likes to feel that they get value for money. There is increased risk of dissatisfaction when buying a new product or buying from a new supplier. It is important that the supplier helps to reduce this risk for new customers so that they are more likely to become regular customers.

Customer loyalty is promoted, achieved and enhanced in several differing ways.

(a) The launch of specific initiatives aimed at engaging the customer in schemes which help to guarantee loyalty, eg the Tesco ClubCard and various SMART card offers run by retailers and others.

(b) Creating a customer proposition offering something which customers may feel they cannot refuse, eg supermarkets offering to match their prices with Tesco.

(c) Engaging the customer in a dialogue, thus ensuring that the customer feels an affinity with the product or service on offer.

Customer focus represents a major shift in marketing emphasis for many organisations, which at one time did not seem to realise that they had customers at all.

Indeed, British Telecommunications plc (BT) used to call its customers 'subscribers', and kept them diligently at arm's length; many public-sector service operations were not in any sense 'customer-focused' simply because they were monopolies, supplying services like education, housing and refuse collection to 'ratepayers' whether they wanted them or not.

In most large organisations there is a customer service department, however, departments such as these were set up primarily to deal with problems or complaints. Whilst serving a useful purpose, it should, however, be considered that with a closer management-customer relationship such departments would be much less busy.

ACTIVITY 4 (10 MINS)

Why is customer loyalty important?

4.2 CUSTOMER ORIENTATION: INTERNAL AND EXTERNAL CUSTOMERS

According to *Drucker*, customer orientation is ' the business seen from the point of view of its final result ie, from the customer's point of view.' To meet the customers' requirements means to listen to them and to respond to what they want and to what is agreed upon. But customers are not only external to the company – people outside the company who are the end users of a firm's products and services – they are also the internal customers.

DEFINITION

An **internal customer** is the person within the company who receives the work of another and then adds his or her contribution to the product or service before passing it on to someone else.

In manufacturing, the internal customer is the next person down the assembly line. In a restaurant, the chef has assistant chefs, waiters, and waitresses as internal customers and the chef must meet their requirements if the diners are to be pleased. There are two approaches to customer orientation:

(a) the market driven (reactive) approach which adapts products and services to customer expectations and preferences; and

(b) the driving markets approach which adapts customer expectations and preferences to the products and services

Figure 2.4: Approaches to customer orientation

To remain competitive today, a company must focus on quality. Product quality must encompass all aspects of a business, from superior service to turnaround time. Businesses strive to achieve quality for one main reason – customer satisfaction.

An organisation can be viewed as a series of transactions between customers and suppliers. Transfers and exchanges are observable within a team or department, and between teams, departments, divisions, or other organisational units. Therefore, every department and every person should see themselves as a customer of colleagues and a supplier to other internal customers. Viewing employees as internal customers allows the activities of the organisation to be viewed from a process management perspective. Each process within an interrelated system (and the personnel that carried out that process) is considered a customer for the preceding process as well as a supplier for the ensuing process.

Each person in the process is an important link in the chain of events. Quality failure at any stage could be catastrophic. The customer/supplier chain illustrated below shows the stages from an external customer's requirements given to a sales person, through order processing, planning and purchasing and production to dispatch and handover to the satisfied external customer.

Figure 2.5: Customer/supplier chain

4.3 QUALITY CHAIN

What constitutes a 'quality product or service' must, it seems, be related to what the customer wants. Indeed, quality would have no commercial value unless it delivered customer benefit, since the key reason for aiming to produce quality products is to derive extra sales, to establish competitive advantage through tangible and generally perceived superiority in particular product or service features.

John Oakland (1989) argues that meeting customer requirements is the main focus in a search for quality and the supplier/customer relationships are part of a series of quality chains throughout and beyond all enterprises. The quality implementation process requires that all the supplier/customer relationships within the quality chain should be treated as marketing exercises, and that each customer should be carefully consulted as to their precise requirements from the product or service with which they are to be provided.

Each link in the chain should prompt the following questions, according to Oakland.

Of customers:

- Who are my immediate customers?
- What are their true requirements?
- How do or can I find out what the requirements are?
- How can I measure my ability to meet the requirements?
- Do I have the necessary capability to meet the requirements? (If not, then what must change to improve the capability?)
- Do I continually meet the requirements? (If not, then what prevents this from happening, when the capability exists?)
- How do I monitor changes in the requirements?

Of suppliers

- Who are my immediate suppliers?
- What are my true requirements?
- How do I communicate my requirements?
- Do my suppliers have the capability to measure and meet the requirements?
- How do I inform them of changes in the requirements?

It should be noted that this focus on the customer does pose a number of problems.

(a) **Quality is subjective**

    (i) If quality is relative to customer expectations, it cannot be measured in an absolute sense.

    (ii) Different customers will want, need or expect different things from the same product-type

(b) **Quality is distinctive** – product differentiation and highly segmented modern markets mean that the precise requirements of a particular market segment will produce an equally precise and differentiated definition of quality.

(c) **Quality is dynamic** – expectations, and therefore definitions of quality, are highly dynamic: they change over time as a consequence of experience. A ratchet effect is highly likely, so that expectations will rise relatively easily, but will rarely and very reluctantly fall.

5 PRODUCT POLICY

5.1 PRODUCT DEVELOPMENT

By 'product' we mean everything that is used by a firm to provide consumer satisfaction. A product can be a physical commodity, or a service, a group of either of these, or a product-service combination.

It is important to bear in mind exactly what a product is to the consumer. It is really a package of satisfaction. The consumer's image of the product is frequently more significant than the physical description of the product itself. It is what it means to the consumer, not what it means to the seller, that is the key to product policy.

When the outputs of factories are virtually identical, and within a given price range, the conversion of an indifferent (even apathetic) potential customer into a buyer needs effort. Irrespective of whether the product is a toy, a pair of shoes, a lipstick or management consultancy, the existence of competition often means that the successful seller offers more than the actual product itself. The product must be surrounded by value satisfactions, which differentiate his product from others.

Developing your product line has to be based on a thorough understanding of the consumer, the market and all the various forces that make an impact upon them. The steps taken to achieve this are, broadly:

- appraising the products and their trends, in relation to those of competitors, as viewed by the consumer;

- analysing consumer needs and habits and evaluating them with respect to both present and possible future markets;

- preparing product specifications of performance, physical characteristics, quality level, dependability, serviceability, safety features, product identification, packaging and appearance that offers the benefits that our target market is seeking;

- formulating prices with the targets of volume and profit in mind;

- controlling product-lines by developing and administering policies, programmes and plans;

- processing product ideas to make plans for innovation;

- providing product information for manuals, advertising, etc;

- recommending design and redesigning;

- coordinating the plans and product programmes of the various chief management functions: sales, finance, production and personnel.

5.2 MARKETING RESEARCH

Marketing research is the systematic and objective search for, and analysis of, information relevant to the identification and solution of any problem in the field of marketing. It is not just obtaining information, but *involves*

- framing questions whose answers will provide data to help solve problems;
- asking questions to those best qualified to answer them;
- recording answers correctly;
- interpreting answers; and
- translating interpretations and making recommendations for marketing action.

It consists of

(a) *market research* (analysis of the market size, trends, market shares, etc);

(b) *distribution research* (analysis of present channels of distribution, warehouse and other storage locations, discount policy, transport needs, etc);

(c) *economic research* (analysis of trends including social and forecasting);

(d) *evaluation of product(s)* (customer requirements analysis, product life cycles, quality measurements, reliability); and

(e) *communication analysis* (of the media usage, suggested media combinations eg TV and newspaper advertising, etc).

Information required

Organisations need knowledge about

(a) *Consumers*

(i) Who is the customer and who is the consumer? (Not necessarily the same person.)

(ii) What do they desire in the way of satisfactions?

(iii) Where does the customer choose to purchase?

(iv) Why does he or she purchase?

(v) How does he or she go about seeking satisfaction in the market?

(b) Their own performance

(c) Activities of *competitors*

(d) Attitude of other *stakeholders*

FOR DISCUSSION

How are you at planning? How did you approach exam-revision, for example, or essay-writing? People must have told you how important it is to 'make a proper plan'. If you didn't do so – why not? Do you think managers suffer from the same difficulties?

6 ORGANISING

6.1 STRUCTURES AND SYSTEMS

Organising – or organisation – implies the establishment of structures, social arrangements, or systems, for the purposes of:

- (a) distributing **authority and responsibility** in such a way as to ensure that each task of the organisation is facilitated and controlled: that someone is both authorised to perform it and accountable for performing it;

- (b) **communication** of the information needed for the task and for control feedback;

- (c) **coordination** of resources – including people's time and effort – towards unified objectives, via a hierarchy of objectives and targets for each sub-unit of the organisation; and

- (d) the **grouping and allocation** of tasks in logical ways.

The grouping of organisational activities (into teams, departments or larger divisions) can be done in different ways. The most common are as follows.

- (a) **By function,** or specialism. Primary functions in a manufacturing company, for example, might be production, sales, finance, and general administration.

- (b) **By territory** or geographical area. This method of organisation occurs when similar activities are carried out in different locations. Water and electricity services, for example, operate region by region. Many sales departments are organised territorially, with regional sales areas.

    The main advantage of territorial departmentation is better local decision-making at the point of contact between the organisation (eg a salesman) and its customers.

- (c) **By product.** Some organisations group activities on the basis of products or product lines. Functional division of responsibility remains, but under the control of a manager with responsibility for a product, product line or brand, with authority over the personnel of different functions involved in its production, marketing and so on.

    The main advantages of product departmentation are the development of specialised product knowledge, and the coordination of functional activities.

BPP
LEARNING MEDIA

(d)   **Matrix organisation.** The new emphasis on flexibility has created a trend towards task-centred structures, such as multi-disciplinary project teams, which draw people together from different functions. Authority is divided between the members' departmental managers, and the team's product/project manager or coordinator.

SIGNPOST

Having recapped the broader implications of organising for organisation and job design, we will now look briefly at the day-to-day aspects: to whom should a manager allocate or delegate a given task.

6.2 ALLOCATING TASKS

Some decisions about division of labour will be pre-programmed by:

(a)   **organisational positions and job descriptions**, which dictate who does what (although these are becoming less rigid, in favour of flexibility and empowerment); and

(b)   **specialisms**. There may be an obvious expert to whom specialised tasks should be given: a payroll, legal or information technology expert, say.

However, other decisions will require management discretion.

(a)   Peak periods in some tasks may necessitate redistribution of staff to cope with the workload: there should be flexibility in who does, and is able to do, non-specialist tasks.

(b)   Status and staff attitudes must be considered. Flexibility in reassigning people from one job to another or varying the work they do may be hampered by an employee's perception of his own status: helping out or covering for others may be out of the question: 'I'm a secretary, not a copy typist!' etc. Task allocation must take into account people's experience and seniority – and also the fact that junior employees may want greater challenge and responsibility.

(c)   Individual abilities and temperaments differ, and work should be allocated to the best person for the job. Some staff like routine work but crack under pressure, and vice versa; some are good with computers, some with people. Planning should allow for flexibility in the event of an employee proving unfit for a task – or more able than his present tasks indicate.

6.3 ALIGN RESOURCES WITH OBJECTIVES

Resource planning involves identifying potential resources and allocating them in order that the defined and agreed corporate objectives may be achieved. At operational level the stages in resource planning are as follows.

(a)   Carrying out a *resource audit* to establish currently available or obtainable resources by category and details of any that are not available or readily obtainable.

(b)   Estimating what resources would be needed to pursue a particular strategy and deciding whether there would be enough resources to pursue it successfully.

(c)   Assigning responsibilities to managers for the acquisition, use and control of resources.

(d)   Identifying all internal and environmental factors exerting an influence on the availability and use of resources.

Some strategies can be met from existing resources, new resources, or a mixture of existing and new resources in tandem, but the objectives and strategies that cannot be met will have to be deferred until a later time, or abandoned altogether.

The situation might be explained more simply by means of a *Venn* diagram.

Johnson and Scholes suggest that there are three central questions in operational resource planning that must be resolved.

(a)   *Resource identification.* What resources will be needed to implement the strategy?

(b)   *Fit with existing resources.* An assessment must be made of the following.

   (i)   The extent to which the required resources are *already* in place.

   (ii)   The extent to which any new resources that are needed can be built on existing resources.

   (iii)   Whether there will have to be some *changes* to existing resources in order to implement the strategy.

(c)   *Fit between required resources.* An assessment must also be made, when new resources are required to implement a strategy, of how these resources can be properly integrated with each other. For example, increasing output might require more people *and* more machines, and extra resources might be needed for training.

Planning issues

Resource plans can be prepared in detail, providing organisations know what they need to achieve.

(a)   Critical success factors (CSFs) 'are those factors on which the strategy is fundamentally dependent on its success'.

(b)   Key tasks are what must be done to ensure each critical success factor is achieved.

(c)   Priorities indicate the order in which tasks are achieved.

For example, the critical success factor to run a successful mail order business may be speedy delivery. Some CSFs are generic to the whole industry, others to a particular firm: a generic CSF of a parcel delivery service is that it *should* be quicker than the normal post. Underpinning critical success factors are key tasks. If *customer care* is a CSF, then a key task, and hence a measure of performance, would include responding to enquires within a given time period. There may be a number of key tasks – but some might be more important than others, or come first in a sequence.

CSFs can be used to translate strategic objectives into performance targets and tactical plans. Here is an example.

(a) Dogger Bank plc has increased profit as a business objective.

(b) The strategy for increased profits is to increase revenue per customer.

(c) Increasing revenue per customer might not be possible unless customers buy other services, such as insurance from the bank.

  (i) The *critical success factor* will be the number of extra services sold to each customer.

  (ii) A *key task* might involve developing a customer database so that the firm can target customers within information about other services more effectively.

The relevance of CSFs to resource planning is that they indicate some idea of the resources that are needed. For example, if the key task for Dogger Bank plc is the development of a customer database, then the resources needed might include new hardware and the services of a systems analyst.

A resource plan will address critical success factors, key tasks and priorities – through one or more of the following planning tools:

- Budgets

- Financial plans

- HR plans

- Network analysis (project plan) – indicating how resources will be deployed in a particular sequence. This is especially relevant for one-off projects.

A resource plan will then be built up, containing detailed estimates of what is needed for the various activities of the business. The plan will contain mechanisms for testing its key assumptions, like demand, if they are liable to change.

Resource allocation includes estimates of the task requirements with regard to:

(a) how many people working for how many hours;
(b) machine hours;
(c) raw materials and components (allowing for a certain amount of wastage); and
(d) finance – that is, the cost of all the above.

It also includes estimates of the availability of all these resources.

(a) How many people with the required skills or experience are available (inside or outside the organisation)? What is their standard level of productivity, and could it be increased?

(b) What machinery is available, given the demands made on it by the task and by other tasks from other units? What is its standard level of productivity, and could it be increased?

(c) Is there sufficient stock of raw materials or components? If not, can they be bought in or made, and at what cost? Are they of the required specifications and quality? What is the expected usage rate of stock: when will stocks run out and need to be replenished? What is the standard wastage rate in the course of operations, and can this be reduced?

(d) How much money needs to be budgeted or allowed for, to complete the task? Is such an amount available and worth spending, for the expected results?

ACTIVITY 5 (20 MINS)

What kind of resources might a sales conference organiser have to plan for?

6.4 TIME MANAGEMENT

A manager's use of time is affected by a number of factors.

The nature of the job

A manager's job involves regular contact with other people in the organisation: it is important to control the inevitable interruptions which this causes. Other typical causes of wasted time include prolonged or unnecessary meetings, and the preparation of unnecessary paperwork (which could be replaced with a brief oral communication).

The personality of the manager

A confident and assertive manager may be better able to resist interruptions and unnecessarily lengthy contacts than one who is diffident, and finds it difficult to 'say no'. A manager may fail to delegate, and end up with a lot of routine work on his own plate. On the other hand, he may simply be disorganised or lacking in self discipline and so be comparatively idle one minute and extremely busy the next.

The influence and demands of colleagues

There will be extra demands on the manager's time if:

(a)   subordinates keep referring to the manager for decisions;

(b)   subordinates require either close supervision or a consultative style of management;

(c)   the culture of the organisation or department requires lots of communication, informal relationship-building, Management by Walking Around, an 'Open Door' availability policy and so on: this takes time.

ACTIVITY 6 (10 MINS)

Suggest two ways in which the management style of a superior may make extra demands on a manager's time.

Time management will involve the following.

(a)   **Identifying objectives** and the key tasks which are most relevant to achieving them – sorting out what the manager **must** do, from what he **could** do, and from what he would **like** to do.

(b)   **Prioritising**: assessing tasks for relative importance, amount of time required, and any deadlines or time-spans.

(c)   **Scheduling** – assigning start and end times/dates to tasks (in other words, timetabling).

(d)   **Control**: avoiding, where possible, disruption by the unexpected.

BPP
LEARNING MEDIA

ACTIVITY 7   (10 MINS)

Think about how effectively you manage time by answering these questions.

1.   Do you often miss deadlines for activities you are responsible for?

2.   Are you often late for meetings or appointments?

3.   Do you have to work late regularly to get things done?

4.   Do you feel you are constantly trying to beat the clock?

5.   Are you too busy to find time to plan?

6.   Do you seem to have more work to do than others?

7.   Have you got a good balance between time spent on study or work, with family, on yourself?

6.5   LEGAL AND REGULATORY CONTROL

Regulatory control involves the guidance, monitoring and control of organisational practices through formal mechanisms such as laws, regulations, 'watchdog' bodies and agreed Codes of Practice. These act as constraints on managerial discretion.

Laws

Laws can affect businesses in the following different ways.

(a)   *Dealings with customers* can be affected by laws on the sale of goods and services, on advertising and trade descriptions, on product safety and on shop opening hours.

(b)   *How a business treats its employees* is affected by employment legislation and trade union law, largely designed to protect employees' rights. Thus there are strict rules on the dismissal of employees and on equal opportunities.

(c)   *Dealings with shareholders* are affected by the Companies Acts, which lay down how information must be given in published accounts and what dividends may be paid.

(d)   The *criminal law* can affect companies. Some offences can be committed by companies as separate legal persons distinct from their directors and employees.

Some laws apply to all businesses. Others apply only to particular types of business. An example is the Financial Services and Markets Act 2000, which affects firms in the financial sector dealing with investments.

Businesses are also affected by laws made outside the UK. For example, anyone doing business in the USA must take account of US law. Even a UK business which has no international dealings must take account of European Union law. The EU has done many things to make the sale of goods in different countries easier, and to allow the free movement of capital and labour. Here are some examples.

(a)   Setting common standards on food labelling and hygiene

(b)   Setting common standards for information technology

(c)   Making rules to ensure that when a government needs to buy something, all EU companies have an equal chance to supply and the home country's companies are not favoured

(d)   Liberalising of capital movements, so that (for example) a UK investor can freely move money to another country and invest it in a business there

(e)   Removing of rules limiting access to financial services – it should soon be possible for insurance companies to sell their products anywhere in the EU

(f)   Ensuring mutual recognition of professional qualifications, so that (for example) a French lawyer can practise in the UK without having to re-qualify as a UK solicitor or barrister

(g)   Giving all EU citizens the right to work anywhere in the EU

Changes in the law can affect organisations in many ways. A tightening of health and safety legislation may increase costs. Premises failing to meet the higher standards could be closed down. Particularly damaging might be the imposition of a complete ban on the organisation's product, clearly made worse should they have failed to develop a product portfolio sufficiently broad to absorb such a loss. Tobacco companies are at present faced with the prospect of a ban on advertising, if not on their products.

FOR DISCUSSION

Do you think it is necessary for governments to introduce legislation in areas such as:

(a)   health and safety at work (obliging employers to provide a healthy and safe environment and procedures)?

(b)   product safety (fire-retardant materials, no asbestos, safety belts in cars, health warnings and so on)?

If so, why? If managers were free to do what they liked or thought best for the organisation, what might standards be like? Do you think that laws encourage people to do only what is required, and not more – perhaps even lowering standards to what can be got away with?

Regulation

In some areas of decision-making, regulation has increased in recent years, where it has been felt to be in the public interest.

(a)   Regulatory bodies oversee the activities of privatised utilities like BT, British Gas and the electricity and water companies. They can influence the company's pricing policy, competitive strategy (if they feel it is unfair) and so on.

(b)   The financial services industry in the City is more heavily controlled than hitherto, though much of this is self-regulation carried out by the industry itself, with its own regulatory bodies and codes of practice covering investment advice, 'insider dealing' and so on.

(c)   Codes of Practice may be agreed by industry representative bodies, or published by other bodies, like ACAS. They allow monitoring bodies, like the Commission for Racial Equality or the Advertising Standards Authority, to measure the behaviour of organisations against defined standards.

(d)   There is a body of regulations and standards covering the reporting of the financial performance of organisations and the verification of reports by auditors. For example, standards issued by the Financial Reporting Council.

Ethical obligations

Each of us has our own set of values and beliefs that we have evolved over the course of our lives through our education, experiences and upbringing. As a manager you bring with you your own concept of what is right and what is wrong. Every decision that you make, for better or for worse, is the application of these values to the question at hand. This is made more difficult by the pressures of organisational life. There are the pressures of productivity, competition and your superiors. Sometimes managers make decisions which conflict with their own or society's values because of what they see as the pressures of the business world.

Business ethics are concerned with the expectations of society, fair competition, advertising, social responsibilities and corporate behaviour (at home, as well as abroad), with how individuals interact with each other and with how organisations ought to relate to their external stakeholders and the community as a whole.

Most managers expect their organisation to develop an ethics programme or code. As with the development of other organisational programmes, it involves the input, interaction, cooperation, decision-making and ongoing commitment of many people.

There are five factors that affect ethical obligations.

(a) **The law** – this defines the minimum ethical standards in a given area of practice. For example, deceptive advertising is illegal and violators of this law are liable to large fines, court action and/or loss of goodwill. Bear in mind, however, that some unethical behaviour is not illegal, such as head hunting employees from other companies, padding expense accounts and so on.

(b) **Government regulations** – these are also fairly clear-cut outlining what is acceptable and what is not. These regulations set standards on issues such as unfair competition, unsafe products, and so on. Failure to comply with these regulations could lead to criminal charges or fines. Unfortunately, there are times when these regulations do not force ethical behaviour. In the US cyclamates (artificial sweeteners) were banned because there was evidence that they were carcinogenic. Following the ban a major food manufacturer sold 300,000 cases of cyclamate-sweetened food overseas. Similarly many banned food additives and pesticides are sold overseas, mainly to third world countries.

(c) **Industry and company ethical codes** – codes that clearly state the ethical standard a manager should follow within his or her organisation. These standard practices are usually followed if they are written down and the rules enforced. However many companies have 'unwritten' codes of practice or if written down, have no method of enforcing these rules. Generally, written codes clarify the ethical issues but leave the resolution to the individual's conscience

(d) **Social pressures** – exerted by society as a whole on a company to act in a humane, environmental and socially-conscious way.

(e) **Tension between personal standards and the goals of the organisation** – we can refer back to the example involving the sale of banned substances overseas. It is not strictly illegal, but it may be against your personal values to sell these products to unsuspecting overseas clients. What would you do if this action were a direct order from a superior? Does this take away your responsibility? As with many ethical problems there are no easy answers.

7 PROJECT MANAGEMENT

7.1 WHAT IS PROJECT MANAGEMENT?

DEFINITION

A **project** is an undertaking, often cutting across organisational and functional boundaries, and carried out to meet established goals within cost, schedule and quality objectives.

Project management is directed at a particular end: achieving specific objectives within a specific time span. It is not, like general management, directed at maintaining or improving continuous work activities.

ACTIVITY 8 (20 MINS)

See if you can think of an example of a project in each of the following areas.

(a) Building and construction.
(b) Manufacturing.
(c) Management.
(d) Research and development.

Project management therefore requires even closer attention to planning, organising and control, with regard to:

(a) **quality** – the end result should conform to specification; in other words, the project should achieve what it was meant to do;

(b) **cost** – the project should be completed without exceeding authorised expenditure (as specified in a budget) of money and other human and material resources;

(c) **time** – each stage of the project's progress must conform to schedule, so that the end result is achieved when requested or required.

7.2 PROJECT PLANNING

A project plan aims to ensure that the project objective is achieved within the requirements of quality, cost and time. This will involve:

(a) breaking the project down into manageable units of activity, and determining the sequence of, or relationships between, those units or tasks;

(b) estimating the resources (materials, money, time and so on) required for each unit;

(c) sequencing and scheduling each unit in the most appropriate way for coordinated performance.

SIGNPOST

We will now look at techniques and tools used for planning and organising interrelated and interdependent activities.

8 PROJECT PLANNING TOOLS

8.1 WORK BREAKDOWN STRUCTURE (WBS)

Breaking a project down into its component phases or stages is often the best way of:

(a) discovering exactly what work must be accomplished;
(b) determining the resources required; and
(c) sequencing and coordinating the work done.

ACTIVITY 9 (30 MINS)

Suppose you set yourself the project of cooking a dinner party for yourself and five friends.

(a)   Define the objectives of the project: devise a three course meal menu.

(b)   Estimate (roughly):

(i)   the cost and
(ii) the time it will take you to prepare.

(c)   Establish a work breakdown structure, in the form of a detailed list of things to do, for preparing your menu.

(d)   What does your WBS tell you about your cost and time estimates?

This is called establishing a work breakdown structure (WBS) for the project.

Figure 2.6 is a simple example of a **diagrammatic** work breakdown structure for a house-building project. We have only broken down two of the component stages to the second level (the foundations and the wiring), but you should get the idea. The breakdown process continues until the smallest sub-unit or task is reached, for which man and machine hours can most easily be calculated and scheduled.

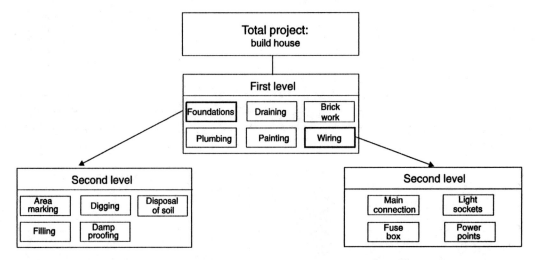

Figure 2.6: Diagrammatic work breakdown structure

SIGNPOST

Once the component activities of the project have been determined, they can be sequenced and scheduled. Here, we will show how some of the simple charts can be applied to more complex project planning.

8.2 USING CHARTS

Bar line charts

A simple project plan can be shown on a bar line or Gantt chart. Figure 2.7 is an example of a chart for a project to build a garage.

	DESCRIPTION OF WORK OR ACTIVITY	TIME (DAYS)													
		1	2	3	4	5	6	7	8	9	10	11	12	13	14
1	Excavate for foundations and services (drainage)	▭													
2	Concrete foundations			▭											
3	Build walls and soakaways for drainage					▭									
4	Construct roof									▭					
5	Fit garage doors									▭					
6	Provide services (electric)											▭			
7	Plaster												▭		
8	Decorate													▭	

Figure 2.7: Gantt chart for building a garage

This chart shows the sequence of activities to be followed, as well as the duration of each activity. You need to excavate before you can put in foundations, before you can build walls: once you've got to that stage, you can do the roof and doors together, if you have the manpower – sheltered from the elements – you can then follow the next sequence.

ACTIVITY 10   (15 MINS)

How could you, very simply, turn this chart into a work schedule?

This type of chart has the advantage of being very easy to understand. It can also be used as a progress control chart, with the lower section of each bar being completed (eg shaded in) as the activity is completed.

Linked bar charts

In order to show more clearly where the activities are dependent on each other, you might prefer to use a linked bar chart, as in Figure 2.8.

DESCRIPTION OF WORK OR ACTIVITY	TIME (DAYS)													
	1	2	3	4	5	6	7	8	9	10	11	12	13	14
Excavate for foundations and services (drainage)														
Concrete foundations														
Build walls and soakaways for drainage														
Construct roof														
Fit garage doors														
Provide services (electric)														
Plaster														
Decorate														

Figure 2.8: Linked bar chart

This shows the link between activities. In our example, the roofing and door-fitting can be done together, starting on day 9, but the door-fitting only takes one day, while the roofing takes two days – and needs to be finished before electrical wiring can be done, hopefully on day 11. The door-fitting therefore has a certain amount of leeway: it can be started late if necessary, since it does not hold up any other activity until the roofing and electrical installation are finished. This leeway is called float time, and is shown by the dotted line on the chart: the activity can be moved into the dotted area if necessary. Activities that have no float time are called critical activities: they must be completed on time in order to avoid a knock-on effect which will make the project as a whole run over time.

ACTIVITY 11 (20 MINS)

You are the site manager of the garage construction project. You have drawn up the linked bar chart above as a guide to all your on-site staff as to the order of activities and the speed of progress required to meet the customer's two-week deadline. You decide to use the chart to monitor progress. Using a different-coloured pen, you draw a line beneath the one on your plan chart to show what your team has actually accomplished.

(a) Everything takes the time it was planned to, except that on the Wednesday (day 3) the weather is too bad to work, so that concreting of the foundations actually takes three days.

(b) The door fitting takes one day, and the door-fitter is also qualified to do roofing work. His help will knock a day off the roofing schedule.

Draw the control line onto Figure 2.8. Has your project run over time?

SIGNPOST

The big advantage of such charts is that they are easily understood by all levels of staff, and without undue calculation. However they can only display a restricted amount of information, and the links between activities are fairly crude. To overcome these limitations, when planning and organising more complex projects, we use a more sophisticated technique called network analysis.

8.3 NETWORK ANALYSIS

Network analysis is a term for project planning techniques which aim to 'map' the activities in a particular project, and the relationship between them, including:

(a)   what tasks must be done before others can be started;

(b)   what tasks could be done at the same time;

(c)   what tasks must be completed on schedule if the completion date for the whole project is not to slip: the critical tasks.

These relationships and sequences are represented in a network diagram, which flows from left to right. The most commonly used form of network is called an **activity-on-arrow** diagram, because activities are represented by an arrowed line, which runs between one event (start or completion of the activity) and another. Events are depicted by a node, or circle.

Hence in the following example we map activity A, which starts at a certain point (event 1) and ends at a certain point (event 2).

Let us tackle a more complex example. Suppose your work breakdown structure comprises six activities: we will call them activities A–G.

(a)   Activities A and B can start together.

(b)   You have to have done activity B before you can do activity C.

(c)   Once activity A is completed, activities D and E can start, at the same time.

(d)   Activity F follows on from activity D.

(e)   Activity G will be completed at the same time as activity F, to end the project. However, activities C and E must be completed before G can commence.

ACTIVITY 12   (10 MINS)

Read (a)–(e) above again. Working from left to right, draw the network diagram showing activities A–G and events 1–6.

One further complication. It is a convention in network analysis that two separate activities should not start and end at the same events. If the real activities **could** start and end at the same event, this is shown on the network by inserting a **dummy activity**, represented by an extra event node with a dotted line joining it to the next event, Figure 2.9.

Incorrect

Correct

Figure 2.9: Network diagram with dummy activity

The correct version shows that activities B and C **both** have to be completed before D can begin, and the dotted line indicates that no extra activity is actually done and no extra time is taken between event 3 (completion of B) and event 4 (completion of C). The two activities therefore do start and end at the same points in the sequence, but not at the same nodes on the diagram.

Apart from pure convention, dummy activities may be needed to preserve the basic logic of the network.

ACTIVITY 13   (10 MINS)

In the network produced in the previous activity, suppose that activity G depended on the completion of activity D, as well as activities C and E. Activity F still depends on activity D alone. There is no extra time or activity involved; all you need to do is to indicate the link between activities D and G. Draw the 'dummy activity' dotted line on our network diagram, to represent this scenario.

Another use of the dummy activity is to ensure that all activities end up at a single completion event, joining in any loose events.

SIGNPOST

More information can be added to a network diagram, to describe not just what happens next, but when it should happen, and how long the whole project will take if each activity takes as long as it is supposed to. This technique is called CPA, or critical path analysis.

8.4 CRITICAL PATH ANALYSIS (CPA)

If Activity A takes three days, it is shown like this.

Let us say, building on our original A-G network, that:

Activity   A takes 3 days
              B takes 5 days
              C takes 2 days
              D takes 1 day
              E takes 6 days
              F takes 3 days
              G takes 3 days.

Our network would be as in Figure 2.10.

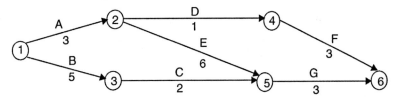

Figure 2.10: Network diagram with timings

Let us assume that you have all the resources you need to carry out the above project as drawn: in other words, you have enough workers to do activities A and B at the same time, and so on. The shortest possible time in which you can complete the project is twelve days. See if you can work out why, before reading on.

Each of the 'routes' of arrows from the first event to the last event is called a **pathway**, or **path**.

ACTIVITY 14 (20 MINS)

List all the pathways in Figure 2.10, and add up how many days each path will take to reach event 6.

The shortest possible duration for the project is twelve days. This is the duration of the longest path (AEG), not the shortest! The activities on the longest path determine the deadline for the whole project, because if one of them runs over time, the whole project will run over time. They are therefore critical activities, and the path on which they sit is called the critical path. We show the critical path on a network by drawing double or thicker lines between the events on that path.

ACTIVITY 15 (30 MINS)

Activity	Depends on activity	Duration (weeks)
A	–	5
B	–	4
C	A	2
D	B	1
E	B	5
F	B	5
G	C, D	4
H	F	3
J	F	2

Hint: all your activities should 'tie up' at event 7.

8.5 SCHEDULING USING THE CRITICAL PATH

Once you have estimated activity durations and worked out the total project time, you can start scheduling. First of all, you work forwards from event 1, working out the **earliest start date** of each activity. We show the earliest start date of an activity as follows.

Obviously, event 1 starts at 0 (on day one): the earliest possible time for C to start, given that B takes 5 days, is at the end of day 5. If we do the same exercise with all the activities in our A–G example, we get Figure 2.11.

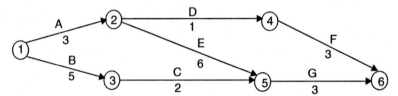

Figure 2.11: Network diagram showing start times

Note that the earliest start date for G (which has to follow A and E) is nine days. But B and C only take seven days: they can take two extra days, if necessary, without affecting the start of G.

We make this clear by next working backwards from event 6 to event 1, identifying the **latest start dates** when activities can start and still keep up with the timing set by the critical path. The earliest deadline of event six is twelve days: this is also its **latest** deadline, because it is the end of the critical path, which must not run late. Activity G takes three days, so its latest start date is 12 – 3 = 9 days: again, this is the same as its earliest start date, because G is on the critical path. Activity C takes two days, so its latest start date (if G is to start on time) is 9 – 2 = 7 days. However, its earliest start date (if B was on time) was five days: it has two days' leeway, or **float**. (Remember: activities on the critical path have no float.)

We insert the **latest** start date in the bottom quarter of the circle, as follows.

You can see just from this that Activity C can be started any time between days five and seven, giving the project manager a degree of flexibility, but that event 5 is on the critical path and must not run late!

ACTIVITY 16   (20 MINS)

Starting from event 6 and working backwards, fill in the latest start dates in Figure 7. Which activities can afford to start late, and by how much?

Attach actual dates to your days currently numbered 1 to 12, and you have a detailed and effective schedule.

8.6 WORK FLOW

A work flow process is a series of steps through which work is directed. It can be represented by a diagram composed of nodes and connectors.

Individual steps in the work flow process are called **nodes**. A start node is the first part in the process and is where a task begins. For example, if the process is technical support, the start node may involve receiving a phone call or email.

Activity nodes comprise all the steps in the workflow process between the task's acquisition and its resolution. They can involve examination, sorting and dissemination of the data involved in the task.

The stop node is the last node in a workflow process. It should be at the point where the task is resolved and is no longer a concern for the manager.

There are at least two types of workflow processes:

1. Serial processes which consist of nodes and connectors attached in a straight line.

2. Parallel processes that consist of a node that has more than one connector to send work on multiple routes, allowing two people to work on the same task at once.

8.7 LINKING WORK FLOWS

Managers seek to optimise the output by linking several operations into a scheduled workflow. This means that the output from one process becomes the input for the next. In attempting to schedule this, the manager may be faced with either great rigidity or reasonable flexibility. This will depend upon:

- the type of work;
- the evenness of work spread;
- staff quality and versatility
- timetables;
- output rates;

9 RESOURCE ALLOCATION

9.1 GANTT CHARTS

As well as plotting time to be taken (and actually taken), Gantt charts can be used to estimate the amounts of resources required for a project.

Let us take the example we have been using so far in this section. We will be starting with our final network showing earliest and latest start times for A–G, so you may like to make a clean copy of the solution to Activity 16 and keep it by you for reference.

Suppose that, in addition to the information contained on our network, we know the number of workers required to do each job, as follows.

Activity	A requires	6 workers
	B "	3 "
	C "	4 "
	D "	4 "
	E "	5 "
	F "	6 "
	G "	3 "

Suppose that we have a team of **nine** workers, each of whom is paid a fixed wage, regardless of hours worked in a week (so we want to avoid idle time if possible). Each worker is capable of working on any of the seven activities involved in the project (so we can swap them round freely if required).

Figure 2.12 shows a Gantt chart, simply plotting the various paths against the twelve-day timescale. We have assumed that activities will be started at the **earliest** start times, adding **floats** (where available) as a dotted line.

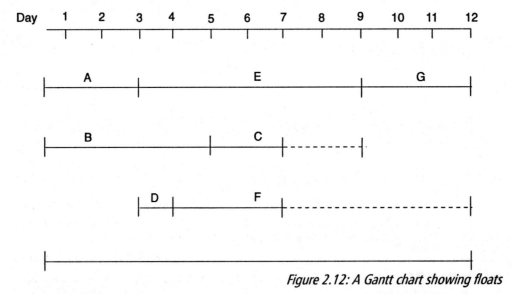

Figure 2.12: A Gantt chart showing floats

EXAMPLE   **GANTT CHART**

1   On Figure 2.12 add the **number** of workers **required**, below the line under the relevant activity letter: $\frac{A}{6}$ and so on.

2   Now, label the line at the bottom of the chart '**Workers required**'.

3   Draw a line vertically through the **start and end of each activity**, from the 'Time' line (days) to the 'Workers required' line. With each activity beginning or ending, the number of workers required will change.

4   In your first section of the 'Workers required' line, which extends between days 0 and 3, A and B are going on simultaneously. Mark 'AB' above this section of the line.

5   Activities A and B require six and three workers respectively: that is, nine workers. Mark '9' below the 'AB' on the 'Workers required' line.

6   Keep going until you have completed all segments of the 'Workers required' line.

ANSWER

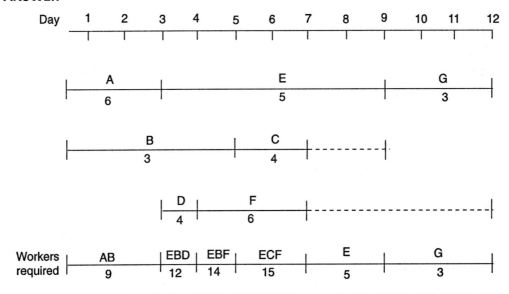

From the answer to the above activity, you may note that on days 6 and 7 you need as many as fifteen workers though you only have nine. On days 8–12, you would have most of your team sitting about twiddling their thumbs. What are you going to do?

Let's look at the really busy period of days 4–7. Can you see any activities that **need** not be done during that period? We know that the path DF is **not** on the critical path. It takes four days, and need not finish until day 12: we have a full five-day float. If we leave DF until its last possible start time (day 9), we are taking pressure off the busy period. Our Gantt chart would be redrawn as in Figure 2.13.

Figure 2.13: The final Gantt chart

The project can be completed without hiring any additional labour, and without running late. Good job! You can keep shuffling non-critical activities and re-calculating worker requirements like this until you are satisfied you have found the best solution. If there is too little float time at convenient stages to allow you do this, you may have to:

(a)   reschedule the project to find the **minimum excess demand for labour,** and hire in extra labour for those times; **or**

(b)   move critical activities as well as non-critical ones (thereby lengthening the project) to avoid excess demand for labour. The same method should be used to find the **minimum extension of the project's duration** required.

9.2 COST SCHEDULING

Cost estimating

It is usually not possible to say with certainty what the costs of a project will be, but some idea will be required in advance so that costs can be monitored and controlled. Estimates of costs can be based on rough guesswork (a 'ballpark' estimate), comparison with similar projects in the past, or the initial plans for the project (a 'feasibility' estimate).

The work breakdown structure will clearly be useful in devising estimates because it enables the project manager to compile a complete list of items that will attract expenditure. **Estimation forms** can be designed, based on the WBS, with columns for labour, materials, components and so on for each of the work units or tasks. This ensures that no items are forgotten, and speeds up the process of estimating, where jobs are routine or similar in type.

Cost scheduling

Costs can be scheduled, in exactly the same way as labour requirements.

(a)   Draw a bar chart for the project.

(b)   Estimate the cost of each activity.

(c)   Divide by the duration of the activity to get the cost of the activity per week (or other appropriate time unit).

(d)   Work out the cost of all activities going on in a given week: ie a total cost per week of the project.

For ease of cash-flow, the project manager may need to restrict cash outflows in any week. As with labour requirements, he may be able to do this by rescheduling tasks which have a float.

It may, however, be more important simply to keep within the planned amount for the total expense on the project. And even then, it may be preferable to spend extra finance on a project to stop it running over time.

FOR DISCUSSION

In what kinds of project would you consider the time deadlines more important than the expenditure budget? And vice versa? (What projects do you know of which have gone way over budget, or late? Look out for examples in the press.)

ACTIVITY 17   (20 MINS)

Find your answer to Activity 9 – your WBS for a dinner party menu.

(a)   Make up a cost estimate, based on your WBS. Draw a column marked B for budget, down the right-hand side of your list, and enter your estimated amounts for each task.

(b)   Go out and find out what it would actually cost, and write down each amount in a column marked A for actual, next to your Budget column.

How was your estimating? If you gave your dinner party, you might have written down what you really paid for your ingredients in the Actual column. You could monitor how you were doing, compared to your budget. This is called budgetary control: another useful management technique!

SIGNPOST

It should be clear from our discussion of 'estimates' that project planning is inexact and uncertain: the project manager does not have a crystal ball to tell him how long an activity will take, how much it will cost or how successful it will be. Finally, in this chapter, we look briefly at this problem of uncertainty, and how it can be planned for.

10   FLEXIBLE PLANNING

10.1 ALLOWING FOR DELAYS

As we have already discussed, activities which are not on the critical path are non-critical, and can, within limits, **start later** and/or **take longer**, without holding up the completion time of the project as a whole. This slack time is called the activity's **float**. It allows unexpected delays to be absorbed and resources to be diverted, to avoid the late start of critical activities.

SIGNPOST

What happens if your critical activities are threatened with delays, though, and the final deadline simply cannot be extended?

10.2 CRASH TIMES

The crash time is the **minimum** time an activity can take to be completed. Crashing often involves the use of extra resources.

Job X takes one worker $1^1/_2$ days – say, twelve working hours. The worker gets paid £10 per hour, so the cost of the job is £120. If the project manager needs Job X completed at the end of a single day, (s)he might ask the worker to do four hours' overtime to complete the twelve hours work in a single working day. However, the overtime rate of pay is £15 per hour. So the crash cost is (8 hours @ £10) + (4 hours @ £15) = £140.

There would be no point crashing non-critical jobs, because you would not shorten the overall project duration or affect the critical path by doing so. However, crashing can be used to shorten the critical path itself, if necessary, to:

(a)   catch up with delays; or
(b)   shorten the project duration for any reason.

You may have noted that, in most cases, we are still only talking about estimated job times or durations. What happens if you get those wrong in the first place? One answer is to take account of uncertainty and contingencies at the estimating stage. A well-known technique for doing this is PERT.

10.3 PERT

Programme Evaluation and Review Technique (PERT) recognises that the activity durations in the network are in fact uncertain. Instead of one estimate of each activity time, three estimates are used.

- The **most likely** duration of the activity, given what is known about it (which we will call m)

- The **most optimistic** (shortest) estimate, assuming that all goes well (o)

- The **most pessimistic** (longest) estimate, assuming that things that are likely to go wrong will go wrong (p)

These can be converted into a 'mean' (or middle) estimate, which takes into account the small chance that things will go entirely well or entirely badly. The mean time is calculated using the formula:

$$\frac{o+4m+p}{6}$$

As an example, here are some more data!

Activity	Must be preceded by activity	Optimistic (o) days	Most likely (m) days	Pessimistic (p) days
A	–	5	10	15
B	A	16	18	26
C	–	15	20	31
D	–	8	18	28

The mean times for each activity are as follows.

Activity	(o + 4m + p)	÷ 6 =	Mean time
A	5 + 40 + 15 = 60		10 days
B	16 + 72 + 26 = 114		19 days
C	15 + 80 + 31 = 126		21 days
D	8 + 72 + 28 = 108		18 days

ACTIVITY 18   (20 MINS)

Draw the network for A–D, using the mean times. Include earliest start and latest start times, and show where the critical path is.

Other calculations can be made using PERT, including the probability that a job will overrun by a given time. Because of their complexity, PERT systems are often run on computers, which generate the planning and control data required.

PERT is frequently used where there are a number of possible contingencies which would affect the project duration. Construction projects, for example, need to allow for delays due to unfavourable weather.

CHAPTER ROUNDUP

- Plans are made a various level in an organisation and my be stated in the form of a hierarchy showing the relationship of mission, goals, objectives, strategy, tactics and operational plans.

- Planning takes place at strategic, tactical and operational levels.

- Planning is the process of deciding what should be done, by whom, when and how. It is essential for coordination and control and for the management of risk and uncertainty.

- Customer focus concentrates an organisation's efforts on the customer to provide satisfaction and delight.

- Customer care and service help provide a competitive advantage.

- Customer retention is important because it can be expensive to attract and retain new customers.

- The total cost of customer care has various elements.

- The heart of quality programmes is the need to define, research and respond to customer need.

- Project management is directed at a particular end, achieving specific objectives within a limited time span.

- Regulatory control involves the guidance, monitoring and control of organisational practices through formal mechanisms such as laws, regulations, 'watchdog' bodies and agreed Codes of Practice

- Project planning and organisation involves

    - breaking the project into units (work breakdown structure)
    - determining the sequence and/or relationships between those units
    - estimating the resources required for each unit
    - scheduling time and allocating resources for each unit.

- Popular techniques for project planning include:

    - network analysis (including critical path analysis) and
    - Gantt charts.

- Network analysis aims to 'map' the relationships and dependencies of tasks in a project. The critical path is the longest path on the network, representing the shortest possible completion time of the project: if any activity on the critical path runs late, the project will run late. Non-critical activities may have some 'slack' time within which they can be extended without having a knock-on effect on the project duration: this is called a float.

- Estimating costs and job times is not an accurate science. One technique for taking uncertainty into account is Programme Evaluation and Review Technique (PERT) which calculates a mean time for each activity using most likely, optimistic and pessimistic estimates.

? QUICK QUIZ

1   What is a strategic plan?

2   Why is control a necessary part of planning?

3   What is contingency planning?

4   What does coordination achieve?

5   If a customer suddenly went bankrupt owing the business a large sum of money from six months ago, which system would not have been operating effectively?

6   What are satisfied customers likely to do?

7   Give some examples of costs associated with attracting new customers.

8   What does customer care aim to achieve?

9   What are business ethics concerned with?

10 What is a work breakdown structure, and what can it be used for?

11 What are (a) a critical activity and (b) a float?

12 What is depicted by (a) nodes, (b) arrowed lines and (c) thick arrowed lines, in a network diagram?

13 In what circumstances might you add a 'dummy activity' to a network diagram?

14 Is the critical path the shortest or longest line from start to end of the project network?

15 If you know how many workers are required for each job, and all team members can do all jobs, how might you go about scheduling your manpower in an efficient manner?

16 What is a 'crash time' and why might you not want to 'crash' a non-critical activity?

17 What is the mathematical formula for calculating a mean time for a job whose duration is uncertain?

ANSWERS TO QUICK QUIZ

1. A long-term plan, taking account of known environmental factors, which formulates long-range goals for the business and works out how to achieve them.

2. Because only through feedback from an effective control system can managers know whether or not the plan is being carried out.

3. Planning for unforeseen developments.

4. Coordination gets all departments working in the same direction, by substituting overall for individual priorities.

5. This would be a serious failure of the credit control system.

6. Buy again, buy more, recommend to friends.

7. Advertising; salesforce time; credit checks; agent commission; initial discounts.

8. To close the gap between customers' expectations and their experience.

9. Business ethics are concerned with the expectations of society, fair competition, advertising, social responsibilities and corporate behaviour (at home, as well as abroad), with how individuals interact with each other and with how organisations ought to relate to their external stakeholders and the community as a whole.

10. It breaks a project down into its component phases or stages. It can be used to discover what work is needed and what resources are required and for sequencing and coordinating.

11. (a) Events
    (b) Activities
    (c) Critical activities

12. When two activities could start and end at the same event.

13. (a) One that must be completed on time.
    (b) The amount of leeway there is for completion of the activity.

14. Longest.

15. Using a Gantt chart.

16. It is the minimum time to complete an activity. Crashing a non-critical activity would not affect the critical path or shorten the overall project time.

17. $\dfrac{o + 4m + p}{6}$

ANSWERS TO ACTIVITIES

1   The statements fit the following categories.

Efficiency = b, c, e.

Effectiveness = a, d, f.

Statement (e) is an example of increased efficiency because fewer employees (inputs) are needed. Other interpretations are possible however.

2   The plans Dial-a-DVD Limited propose are a strategy to exploit the 'art movie' market segment. A programme for the build-up of the distribution. The £4 charge is a tactic or policy. The 'no-tips' plan is a rule or regulation.

3   Contingency plans for the situations given would include the following.

(a)   New systems may have 'bugs', or be unfamiliar to operators. A good contingency plan would be running the old system in parallel with the new one for a trial period.

(b)   People get sick, or need holidays, or have problems getting to work during transport strikes, or go on strike themselves. You may have contingency plans to do with pre-notifying holidays, or laid-on transport in the event of transport strikes. A general contingency plan would be a temporary staff agency on standby to provide replacement/overflow staff.

(c)   Again, transport may cause unexpected problems, or there could be an upset such as the venue being double-booked, the key speaker falling ill, or overhead projectors not working. Alternative transport/speaker/venue might be pre-planned, and back-up visual aids equipment (such as a flip-chart) on hand. You can't anticipate everything!

4   Here are some suggestions.

(a)   It means that regular customers will support the supplier. It will be difficult for competitors to attract customers away from their favoured supplier.

(b)   Regular customers provide reliable income and turnover

(c)   It is possible to build a rapport with customers over time. This helps the supplier understand their needs more easily, thus making the marketing process more straightforward.

(d)   Customer loyalty is also a source of goodwill. It will enhance the supplier organisation's image and can be a source of very potent advertising in that customers may recommend the supplier to their friends or colleagues.

5   Resources for the sales conference will include the conference centre; equipment (overhead projectors etc); staffing of the conference centre; time of speakers; materials such as paper and slides; telephone and fax facilities; refreshments – and so on.

6   A superior may interfere too much in the manager's job and want constant reports: very disruptive. (Tact in warding off such attention can be a valuable attribute.) On the other hand, if the superior delegates too much, the manager's workload may be excessive.

7   If you answered yes to any of 1 to 6 and no to question 7, then you need to improve your time management. If you answered more than five of them this way, then time management must be a priority, particularly while you are trying to find time to study.

8   You will have come up with your own ideas for different projects: here are some suggestions.

(a)   Construction of a motorway extension, say, or the Channel Tunnel.

(b)   Limited-edition production of a car, for example, or one-off tailor-made products.

(c)   Implementation of a computer system, say, or mounting a trade exhibition or conference.

(d)   Ironing out bugs in a system or product, completing a market research survey and so on.

Check that your own examples have a beginning, an end, and goals.

9   The answer will depend on your menu, but your WBS may include stages such as: the purchasing of the various ingredients; washing, peeling and chopping vegetables (if any); mixing ingredients; cooking and/or preparing each dish; laying the table and preparing plates and utensils and so on. Your WBS should give you a fairly clear idea of what ingredients, in what quantities, you will need to buy: a more accurate cost estimate than trying to judge the cost of the meal as a whole. The same is true of the timetable, with the added advantage that it provides the basis for an action checklist and schedule for preparation.

10   To turn Figure 2.7 into a work schedule, you could put the days of the week across the top instead of the number of days given. So the excavations should take up Monday and Tuesday, the foundations start on Wednesday and so on.

11   The control line added to Figure 2.8 yields the result shown here.

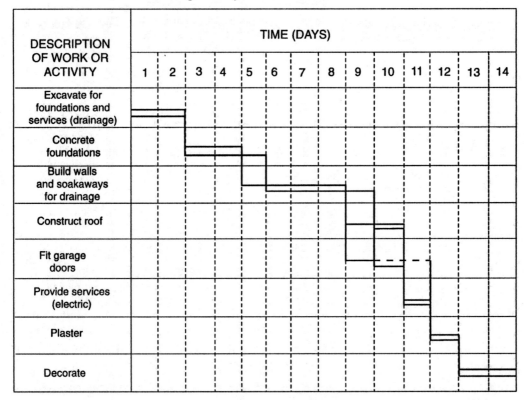

You've made up your lost day of concreting because you had the float time on the door-fitting and were able to divert the door person to the roofing.

12.

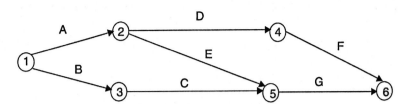

13   You should draw a dotted line from event 4 to 5.

14   There are three paths, as follows.

ADF   = 3 + 1 + 3 days   = 7 days
AEG   = 3 + 6 + 3 days   = 12 days
BCG   = 5 + 2 + 3 days   = 10 days

15

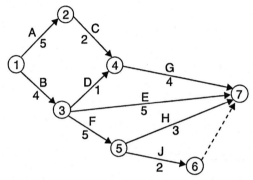

The paths are   ACG   = 5 + 2 + 4   = 11 weeks
                     BDG   = 4 + 1 + 4   = 9 weeks
                     BE   = 4 + 5   = 9 weeks
                     BFH   = 4 + 5 + 3   = 12 weeks
                     BFJ Dummy = 4 + 5 + 2 + 0   = 11 weeks

BFH is the longest (and therefore the critical) path: the shortest time in which the project can be completed.

16

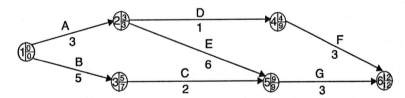

Activity C: anytime between days 5 and 7 (a 2-day float)
Activity F: anytime between days 4 and 9 (a 5-day float)

17   Did you totally underestimate your budget, and have to spend your food allowance for the next three weeks?

18

Operational plans

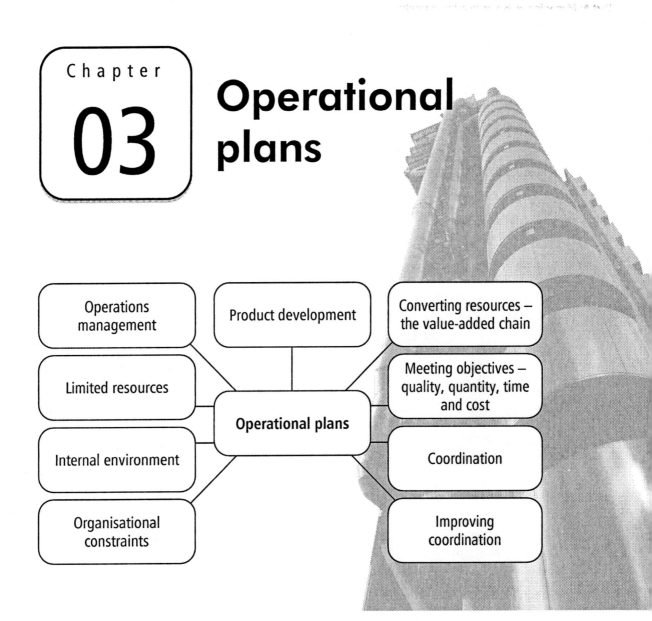

- Operations management
- Product development
- Converting resources – the value-added chain
- Limited resources
- **Operational plans**
- Meeting objectives – quality, quantity, time and cost
- Internal environment
- Coordination
- Organisational constraints
- Improving coordination

Introduction

It is generally easier to perform a task if the objectives to be achieved are clearly expressed. This is especially important where the operational plans of an enterprise are involved, so as to ensure that the organisation's strategic purpose is supported by operational work. Production and operations management is used not only to describe factory environments, but applies to all organisations including, for example, schools and banks. It is the application of techniques to the design and operation of any system that transforms inputs into finished goods and services. Many of the techniques are applicable to service industries as well as manufacturing. Value chain analysis assesses how the business adds value to the resources it obtains, and how it delivers these resources to service customers. Just-in-Time (JIT) scheduling is a method used to reduce inventory costs and Statistical Process Control (SPC) is the continuous monitoring and charting of a process while it is operating, to warn when the process is moving away from predetermined limits.

Coordination ensures that within any organisation (as a whole) departments, sections and individuals must all be organised in such a fashion as to ensure that the overall objectives of the organisation are attained and each department, section and individual makes a valid contribution. This must all be done within the organisational constraints and limitations that apply.

Your objectives

After completing this chapter you should be able to:

- Prepare and agree implementation plans which translate strategic targets into practical efficient and effective actions

- Carry out work activities meeting the operational plan through effective monitoring and control

- Implement appropriate systems to achieve objectives and goals of the plan in the most effective and efficient way, on time and to budget and to meet organisational standards of quality

1 OPERATIONS MANAGEMENT

1.1 THE IMPORTANCE OF OPERATIONS

One of the major areas in any organisation is production and operations management. The objectives, premises and strategies determine the search for and the selection of the product or service.

The term 'operations management' refers to the activities required to produce and deliver a service as well as a physical product. Production management used to be associated solely with the manufacture of goods but its expansion to operations management means that it now includes purchasing, warehousing and transportation – dealing with all the operations from the procurement of raw materials through various activities until the product is available to the buyer.

Operations are the link between the strategy and the customer and also between the different functions. The organisation's mission is only really meaningful if, at operational level, the mission is embodied in policies and behaviour standards.

The design of an operations system requires decisions on the location of facilities, the process to be used, the quantity to be produced and the quality of the product.

1.2 OPERATIONS MANAGEMENT AS A SYSTEM

The production function plans, organises, directs and controls the necessary activities to provide products and services.

Figure 3.1: Operations management as a system

In the model shown above the inputs include the needs of the customers, information, technology, labour and management and the fixed and variable assets that are relevant to the transformation process. Managers and workers use the information and physical factors to produce the outputs. The transformation process incorporates planning, operating and controlling the system. There are many tools and techniques available to facilitate this process. The model also shows that external factors such as safety regulations and legal and ethical issues influence operations.

1.3 RELATIONSHIPS WITH OTHER FUNCTIONS

Longer-term decisions, particularly relating to design and the innovation of improved products, cannot be taken by the production department alone; its activities must be integrated with other functions in the firm.

- **Product design** is coordinated with **R&D**. Production should advise R&D as to the consequences of particular designs for the manufacturing process.

- **Job design** will involve consultation with **human resources** specialists.

- The **marketing department** will detail expected selling quantities, timings, advertising expenditure and sales force activities.

- The **human resources department** will be involved in managing the work force.

- The **finance department** might indicate the resources available for new equipment.

1.4 STANDARDS AND PROCEDURES

Standards and procedures assist the manager with the planning and control of work.

Policies are general guidelines for management decision-making.

Company policies might be, for example:

- to offer five-year guarantees on all products sold and to give money back to customers with valid complaints;

- to promote managers from within the organisation, wherever possible, instead of recruiting managers to senior positions from outside;

- to encourage all recruits to certain jobs within the organisation to work towards obtaining an appropriate professional qualification;

- to be price-competitive in the market;

- that employees in the purchasing department should decline gifts from suppliers (subject, perhaps, to certain exceptions or purchase limits).

Procedures are a logical sequence of required actions for performing a certain task. Procedures exist at all levels of management; even a board of directors will have procedures for the conduct of board meetings. However, they become more numerous, onerous and extensive lower down in an organisation's hierarchy. The advantages of procedures for routine work are as follows.

- Procedures should prescribe the most *efficient* way of getting a job done.

- The absence of any need for the exercise of *discretion* in routine tasks.

- Staff will find jobs easier to do when they are familiar with established procedures.

- *Standardisation* of work. Prescribed procedures ensure that a task of a certain type will be done in the same way throughout the organisation.

- *Continuity.* The work will be done the same way even when a different person starts in a job or takes over from the previous holder.

- A written record of required procedures can be kept in a *procedures manual.* People unfamiliar with how a job should be done can learn quickly and easily by referring to the manual.

- They reduce the likelihood of *inter-departmental friction.* For example, work done by the warehousing department of a factory will affect the work of the sales force, delivery and distribution department and production department. The warehousing department will require documentation about sales orders from the sales force. It will issue delivery instructions to the delivery crews. By having established procedures, disputes between departments about who should do what, and when, and how, should be avoided.

A **rule** is a specific, definite course of action that must be taken in a given situation. Unlike a procedure, it does not set out the sequence or chronology of events. For example, the following are rules, but not procedures:

- employees in department X are allowed ten minutes exactly at the end of their shift for clearing up and cleaning their work-bench;

- employees with access to a telephone must not use the telephone for personal calls.

Rules allow no deviations or exceptions, unlike policies which are general guidelines allowing the exercise of some management discretion.

2 PRODUCT DEVELOPMENT

2.1 DESIGN AND DEVELOPMENT

Product development is the process of creating a new product to be sold by an enterprise to its customers.

- *Design* refers to those activities involved in creating the styling, look and feel of the product, deciding on the product's mechanical architecture, selecting materials and processes, and engineering the various components necessary to make the product work.

- *Development* refers collectively to the entire process of identifying a market opportunity, creating a product to appeal to the identified market, and finally, testing, modifying and refining the product until it is ready for production. A product can be any item from a book, musical composition, or information service, to an engineered product such as a computer, hair dryer, or washing machine.

The impetus for a new product normally comes from a perceived market opportunity or from the development of a new technology.

- With a market-pull product, the company first determines that sales could be increased if a new product were designed to appeal to a particular segment of its customers. Engineering is then asked to determine the technical feasibility of the new product idea.

- With a technology-push product, a technical breakthrough opens the way for a new product and marketing then attempts to determine the idea's prospects in the marketplace.

With either scenario, manufacturing is responsible for estimating the cost of building the prospective new product, and their estimations are used to project a selling price and estimate the potential profit for the company.

2.2 ESTABLISHING SPECIFICATIONS

During the development stage, the needs of the target market are identified, competitive products are reviewed, product specifications are defined, an economic analysis is done, and the development project is outlined.

- *Identify customer needs* – through interviews with potential purchasers, focus groups, and by observing similar products in use, researchers identify customer needs. Customer needs and product specifications are organised into a hierarchical list with a comparative rating value given to each need and specification.

- *Analyse competitive products* – an analysis of competitive products is part of the process of establishing target specifications. Rather than beginning from scratch and re-inventing the wheel with each new project, traditionally, the evolution of design builds on the successes and failures of prior work.

- *Establish target and final specifications* – based on customers' needs and reviews of competitive products, the team establishes the target specifications of the prospective new product. Target specifications are essentially a wish list tempered by known technical constraints. Final specifications are the result of tradeoffs made between technical feasibility, expected service life, projected selling price, and the financial limitations of the development project. With a new luggage product, for example, consumers may want a product that is lightweight, inexpensive, attractive, and with the ability to expand to carry varying amounts of luggage. Unfortunately, the mechanism needed for the expandable feature will increase the selling price, add weight to the product, and introduce a mechanism that has the potential for failure. Consequently, the team must choose between a heavier, more costly product and one that does not have the expandable feature. When product attributes are in conflict, or when the technical challenge or higher selling price of a particular feature outweighs its benefits, the specification may be dropped or modified in favour of other benefits.

Once the development plan is approved, marketing may begin to develop ideas for additional product options and add-ons, or perhaps an extended product family. Designers and engineers develop the product architecture in detail, and manufacturing determines which components should be made and which should be purchased, and identifies the necessary suppliers. Detail design, or design-for-manufacture, is the stage wherein the necessary engineering is done for every component of the product. During this phase, each part is identified and engineered. Tolerances, materials, and finishes are defined, and the design is documented with drawings or computer files.

3 CONVERTING RESOURCES – THE VALUE-ADDED CHAIN

3.1 PRODUCTION

Production can be defined as the activity of transforming raw materials or components into finished products. Before production commences, production policies must be known and then the processes of manufacture, machine requirements, factory layout, storage and handling systems, skills required in the workforce and the method of training can be determined. These policies are largely determined by the nature of the work. The types of production are:

- Job production (or unit production) – output of single product to specific requirements (eg suit or ship). Demand is difficult to forecast, and generally production schedules can be prepared only when the customer's order arrives

- Batch production – output of a batch or quantity of a product (eg furniture). There is repetition, but not continuous production. Production is often for stock.

- Mass production – output of products of a uniform and standardised nature – production is continuous and carried out by specialised units (eg cars).

- Process (flow) production – continuous production of products of a more or less identical nature eg oil refinery

The production function plans, organises, directs and controls the necessary activities to provide products and services.

DEFINITION

Activities are the means by which a firm creates value in its products. (They are sometimes referred to as.)

They procure inputs and process them, adding value to them in some way, to generate outputs for customers. Activities incur costs, and, in combination with other activities, provide a product or service that earns revenue.

Activity	Example
Obtain inputs to the production 'system', such as plant facilities, materials and labour	Inputs: timber, screws, nails, adhesives, varnish, stain, templates, cutting tools, carpenters
Adding of value The activities below occupy most of the production manager's attention: Scheduling jobs on machines Assigning labour to jobs Controlling the quality of production and/or service delivery	Operations: sawing, sanding, assembly and finishing
Improving methods of work	
Managing materials and equipment, to avoid waste	
Create outputs, ie finished products and services	Outputs: tables, chairs, cabinets etc.

Intermediate activities in all three processes include processing, inspection and storage. The linkages in the process are usually provided by information. For example the stock control system will detail movements in and out of the warehouse. To control operations, a variety of records are required.

3.2 VALUE-ADDED CHAINS

The *value chain* model of corporate activities, developed by Michael Porter, provides a bird's-eye view of an organisation's operations. *Competitive advantage*, says Porter, arises out of the way in which firms *organise and perform activities*; that is how an organisation uses its inputs and transforms them into outputs for which customers are prepared to pay.

Activity

Before we go any further, keep in mind that in Porter's analysis, business *activities* are *not* the same as business *functions*.

(a) *Functions* are the familiar departments of a business such as the production function, or the finance function, and reflect the formal organisation structure.

(b) *Activities* are what actually goes on: the work that is done. A single activity can involve work by a number of functions in sequence or concurrently.

An example should make this clear. An organisation needs many inputs of resources from the environment to function. The activity of obtaining these resources can be called procurement. However, the procurement activity may involve more than one function or department. Consider raw materials. The purchasing function may negotiate the best price and delivery terms but the production or design functions will provide the specification and the quality manager may oversee acceptance. The finance function will deal with payment, in consultation with purchasing, and if there is any dispute the legal department may be involved.

'Firms create value for their buyers by performing these activities.' Let us explain this point by using the example of a *restaurant*. A restaurant's activities can be divided into buying food, cooking it, and serving it (to customers). There is no reason, in theory, why the customers should not do all these things themselves, at home. The customer however, is prepared to pay for someone else to do all this. The customer also pays more than the cost of the food, wages and so on. The ultimate value a firm creates is measured by the amount customers are willing to pay for its products or services above the cost of carrying out value activities. A firm is profitable if the realised value to customers exceeds the collective cost of performing the activities.

There are two points to note here.

(a) Customers *purchase 'value'*, which they measure by comparing a firm's products and services with similar offerings by competitors.

(b) The business *creates 'value'* by carrying out its activities either more efficiently than other businesses, or combined in such a way as to provide a unique product or service.

ACTIVITY 1 (10 MINS)

Outline different ways in which the restaurant can create value

---

Activities that add value do not stop at the organisation's boundaries. For example, when a restaurant serves a meal, the quality of the ingredients – although the cook chooses them – is determined by the producer (grower). The producer has also added value, and success in producing ingredients of good quality is as important to the customer's ultimate satisfaction as the skills of the chef. Porter (in *Competitive Advantage*) analysed the various activities of an organisation into a *value chain.*

DEFINITION

Value chain. 'The sequence of business activities by which, in the perspective of the end user, value is added to the products or services produced by an organisation'

Figure 3.2: Value chain

The margin is the excess the customer is prepared to pay over the cost to the firm of obtaining resource inputs and providing value activities. It represents the value created by the value activities and by the management of the linkages between them.

Primary activities are those directly related with production, sales, marketing, delivery and services. The diagram shows five primary activities.

	Comment
Inbound logistics	Receiving, handling and storing inputs to the production system, including warehousing, transport and stock control.
Operations	Convert resource inputs into a final product. Resource inputs are not only materials. People are a resource especially in service industries.
Outbound logistics	Storing the product and its distribution to customers, including packaging, testing, warehousing and delivering.
Marketing and sales	Informing customers about the product, persuading them to buy it, and enabling them to do so. This includes advertising, promotion and selling.
After sales service	Installing products, repairing them, upgrading them, providing spare parts and servicing them.

Support activities provide purchased inputs, human resources, technology and infrastructural functions to support the primary activities. You will recognise them all as aspects of administration.

	Comment
Procurement	Acquire the resource inputs to the primary activities, particularly the purchase of materials, subcomponents and equipment.
Technology development	Product design, improving processes and/or resource utilisation. 'Technology' is used in the sense of apparatus, techniques and work organisation.
HR management	Recruiting, training, developing and rewarding people.
Management planning	Planning, finance and quality control: Porter believes they are crucially important to an organisation's strategic capability in all primary activities.

Analysing the value chain helps managers to decide how individual activities might be changed to reduce costs of operation or to improve the value of the organisation's offerings. Such changes will increase 'margin' – the residual value created by what customers pay minus the organising costs. For example, a clothes manufacturer may spend large amounts on:

- buying good quality raw materials (inbound logistics)

- hand-finishing garments (operations)

- building a successful brand image (marketing)

- running its own fleet of delivery trucks in order to deliver finished clothes quickly to customers (outbound logistics).

All of these should add value to the product, allowing the company to charge a premium for its clothes. Another clothes manufacturer may:

- reduce the cost of its raw materials by buying in cheaper supplies from abroad (inbound logistics)

- making all its clothes by machinery running 24 hours a day (operations)

- delaying distribution until delivery trucks can be filled with garments for a particular request (outbound logistics).

All of these should allow the company to be able to gain economies of scale and be able to sell clothes at a cheaper price than its rivals.

ACTIVITY 2 (10 MINS)

A lawn mower manufacturer has introduced some technologically advanced methods to its production but still needs to make improvements.

Use Porter's value chain analysis to decide how individual activities might be changed to reduce costs of operation or to improve the value of the organisation's offerings.

Linkages connect the interdependent elements of the value chain together. They occur when one element of the value chain affects the costs or effectiveness of another.

Here are some examples.

(a) More costly product design or better quality production might reduce the need for after-sales service.

(b) To deliver on time requires smooth functioning of operations, outbound logistics and service activities such as installation.

3.3 VALUE SYSTEM

A company's value chain is not bounded by a company's borders. It is connected to what *Porter* describes as a *value system*.

Figure 3.3: Value system

As well as managing its own value chain, a firm can secure competitive advantage by good administration of the linkages with its suppliers and customers. A company can create competitive advantage by making best use of these links and this means considering the value chains of these suppliers and customers.

ACTIVITY 3 (10 MINS)

Sana Sounds is a small record company. Representatives from Sana Sounds scour music clubs for new bands to promote. Once a band has signed a contract (with Sana Sounds), it makes a recording. The recording process is subcontracted to one of a number of recording studio firms which Sana Sounds uses regularly. (At the moment Sana Sounds is not large enough to invest in its own equipment and studios.) Sana Sounds also subcontracts the production of records and

CDs to a number of manufacturing companies. Sana Sounds then distributes the disks to selected stores, and engages in any promotional activities required.

What would you say were the activities in Sana Sound's *value chain?*

A firm's value chain is not always easy to identify nor are the linkages between the different elements. However, it is an important analytical tool because it helps people to:

(a) see the business as a whole;
(b) identify potential sources of competitive advantage.

3.4 PURCHASING AND INBOUND LOGISTICS

Purchasing – is generally taken to mean the procurement of the supplies for the enterprise. The buyer will study commodities, sources of supply, systems and procedures, inventory problems and market trends, methods of delivery, whether maximum discounts are being earned and the amount and use of waste materials.

The process carries many risks: materials may be purchased at too high a price, or of the wrong quality or too great a quantity, which may lead to obsolescence and loss of interest on capital. Too little purchased may mean production delays, which would also have an effect on the organisation's profits.

The purchasing mix includes quantity, quality, price and delivery. The right materials should be in the right place at the right time and at the right price.

- **Quantity** – the size and timing of the purchases will depend on delays in production as a result of stock shortages and the costs of holding the stock in terms of capital tied up, deterioration, pilferage, insurance and obsolescence.

- **Quality** – if this is very important for the manufacturing process detailed specifications of goods required and tolerances accepted must be prepared. When the goods are received there must be a system to ensure conformity with the specifications. As we have already noted in a previous chapter, some suppliers guarantee the quality of goods supplied and allow the customer access while the goods are being manufactured.   This is usually done through supplier quality assurance (SQA) officers, who control the specification of the goods supplied.

- **Price** – should represent the best value considering the quality, delivery and urgency of order.

- **Delivery** – involves the supplier's lead-time and reliability.

Purchasing policy may be concerned with:

- whether to buy when required – limiting the purchases to minimum requirements

- whether to buy on contract on a medium- or long-term basis – assuring continuity of supply in very important flow production

- speculative or bargain buying – where material is bought with the hope of future price rises.

Security of supplies is so important to some concerns that they have integrated backwards eg, tea producers buying tea plantations.

Inbound logistics – are the activities concerned with receiving, storing and handling raw material inputs and assets. Once the raw materials are purchased, they must be managed like any other resource. This includes stock control and security.

3.5 STOCK LEVELS

Most businesses, whatever their size, will be concerned with the problem of which items to have in stock, and how much of each item should be kept.

The principal reasons why a business needs to hold stock are:

- it acts as a buffer in times when there is an unusually high rate of consumption

- it enables the business to take advantage of quantity discounts by buying in bulk

- the business can take advantage of seasonal and other price fluctuations (eg buying oil in the summer when it is cheaper)

- any delay in production caused by lack of parts is kept to a minimum, so production processes will flow smoothly and efficiently

- it may be necessary to hold stock for a technical reason, for example whisky must be matured.

Irrespective of the nature of the business, a certain amount of stock will always need to be held. However, holding stock costs money, and the principal 'trade-off' in a stockholding situation is between the costs of acquiring and storing stocks on the one hand and the level of service that the company wishes to provide on the other hand.

The total cost of holding stock consists of the following.

- The purchase price (as affected by discounts)
- Holding costs
- Reorder costs
- Shortage costs
- Systems costs

The aim of a stock control system is to maintain the quantities of stocks held by a company at a level that optimises some predetermined management criterion (eg minimising costs incurred by the business).

There are obviously disadvantages in holding either too much or too little stock, and the problem is to balance these disadvantages against the benefits obtained.

There are two main types of stock control systems:

In a **reorder level system**, a replenishment order of fixed size is placed when the stock level falls to the fixed reorder level. Thus a fixed quantity is ordered at variable intervals of time.

In a **periodic review system** the stock levels are reviewed at fixed points in time, when the quantity to be ordered is decided. By this method variable quantities are ordered at fixed time intervals.

The economic order quantity (EOQ) approach to determining inventory levels works reasonably well when demand is predictable and fairly constant throughout the year ie, no seasonal patterns. However, where demand is likely to be intermittent, resulting in excesses at some times and inventory shortages at other times, EOQ does not work very well. The system that performs better under these circumstances is the just-in-time system.

3.6 JUST-IN-TIME

This technique, where the supplier delivers the components and parts to the production line 'just in time' to be assembled, has revolutionised the acquisition of resources, with a resultant reduction in costs (of stock) or improvement in lead times.

Just-in-time (JIT) techniques are an example of long-linked technologies which have the effect of increasing technological interdependence by removing slack from the system.

DEFINITION

A system whose objective is to produce or to procure products or components as they are required by a customer or for use, rather than for stock. A just-in-time system is a 'pull' system, which responds to demand, in contrast to a 'push' system, in which stocks act as buffers between the different elements of the system, such as purchasing, production and sales.

(a) **Just-in-time production.** A production system which is driven by demand for finished products whereby each component on a production line is produced only when needed for the next stage.

(b) **Just-in-time purchasing.** A purchasing system in which material purchases are contracted so that the receipt and usage of material, to the maximum extent possible, coincide.

JIT emerged from criticisms of traditional responses to the problems of improving manufacturing capacity and reducing unit costs of production. These traditional responses include the techniques given below.

- Longer production runs
- Economic batch quantities
- Fewer products in the product range
- More overtime
- Reduced time spent on preventive maintenance, to keep production flowing

In general terms, longer production runs and large batch sizes should mean less disruption, better capacity utilisation and lower unit costs.

However, JIT techniques and stockless production challenge traditional views of manufacture.

- Its principles include greater flexibility in production, and matching production to meet demand.

- This in turn means shorter batch production runs and a greater product variety.

- There will be much smaller stocks of finished goods, because output is being matched more closely to demand.

- Production systems must therefore be reliable and prompt, without unforeseen delays and breakdowns. Machinery must be kept fully main-tained, and so **preventive maintenance** is an important aspect of production.

The most obvious physical manifestation of JIT is a small warehouse. In other words, there are few raw materials stocks, as these are only purchased when needed. There are few finished goods stocks, as effort is not expended on production that is not required.

JIT aims to eliminate all **non-value-added costs**. Value is only added while a product is actually being processed. Whilst it is being inspected for quality, moving from one part of the factory to another, waiting for further processing and held in store, value is not being added. Non value-added activities (or **diversionary** activities) should therefore be eliminated.

ACTIVITY 4 (2 MINS)

Which of the following is a value-added activity?

A   Setting up a machine so that it drills holes of a certain size
B   Repairing faulty production work
C   Painting a car, if the organisation manufactures cars
D   Storing materials

Problems associated with JIT

JIT should not be seen as a panacea for all the endemic problems associated with Western manufacturing. It might not even be appropriate in all circumstances.

(a)   It is not always easy to predict patterns of demand.
(b)   JIT makes the organisation far more vulnerable to disruptions in the supply chain.

3.7   IMPACT OF JIT

JIT has a significant impact on departmental interdependence, and indeed on the interdependence between different companies in the **supply chain**. This is because there is no slack and no buffer stock. JIT massively increases the need for standardisation of quality, as there is no space for waste, and coordination of deliveries. As a result, firms are establishing long-term relationships with their suppliers.

ACTIVITY 5 (5 MINS)

Batch sizes within a JIT manufacturing environment may well be smaller than those associated with traditional manufacturing systems.

What costs might be associated with this feature of JIT?

1   Increased set-up costs

2   Opportunity cost of lost production capacity as machinery and the workforce reorganise for a different product

3   Additional materials handling costs

4   Increased administrative costs

A   None of the above
B   1, 2, 3 and 4
C   1 only
D   2 and 3 only

4 MEETING OBJECTIVES – QUALITY, QUANTITY, TIME AND COST

4.1 OPERATING AND CONTROLLING THE SYSTEM

Operating the system requires setting up an organisation structure, staffing the positions and training the people. Managers are needed who can provide the leadership to carry out the activities necessary to produce the desired products or services. The aim is to obtain the best productivity ratio within a time period and conforming to quality specifications.

Controlling operations requires setting performance criteria, measuring performance against them and taking action to correct unwanted deviations. Control covers production, product quality, reliability, inventory levels and workforce performance.

Output control relies upon the ability to identify specific tasks having a measurable output or criterion of overall achievement – for example, an end product, a part manufactured to agreed standards, batch production or a sub-assembly. Once outputs or criteria for achievement have been identified, management can specify output standards and targets. Rewards and sanctions can be related to performance levels expressed in output terms.

Time and money, budgets and schedules are the most basic resources within which every operation must operate. Measurement can be based on the actual start or finish times of critical activities and (especially for a project) the completion of milestones, or the timing of acceptance tests. Operation control charts use budget and schedule plans to report cumulative time and cost so that variances can be calculated. *Performance* is also monitored, by:

- inspection
- progress reviews (at regular stages)
- quality testing
- financial audit

A control limit signifies the deviation of a critical success factor that has gone beyond acceptable limits. Control limits are set to assess the severity of deviations and deviations that are larger than a predetermined value are used to trigger corrective action.

Corrective action can be taken, if deficiencies are not self-correcting. Falling behind schedule, perhaps because of some circumstance unforeseen at the planning stage, might require the rescheduling of the operation or a change in resource configuration.

4.2 BALANCING THE OBJECTIVES

There are likely to be many objectives for the operation, which include completing the required output within a timescale and within budget; maintaining a high level of technical quality; conforming to all applicable legislation and codes; reflecting the customer's scope, standards and other requirements; incorporating applicable professional standards and practice; being responsive; maintaining an excellent working relationship with members of the value chain and others involved in the production; and continuously striving for technical excellence.

These objectives must be expressed in quantitative and qualitative measures by which the proper completion of an operation can be judged.

The four elements – cost, time, quantity and quality – should be considered together, because the optimum performance typically involves a trade-off of several dimensions, specifically what is done (scope and quality) versus the resources used to do the work (time and cost). Scope involves both stated needs (requirements or 'deliverables') and unstated needs ('expectations'). Quality involves both 'built-in' quality (internal and/or less readily noticeable aspects) and 'inspected' quality (visible and/or noticeable aspects).

Consider the performance of a department where there is a plan to improve cost-effectiveness by simply reducing costs; it may be possible to do this to some extent without affecting either the time taken, the output or the quality performance. At some stage, however, further cost reduction will either affect the ability of the department to fulfil its purpose or alternatively reduce the quality or quantity of output to a point where it is not acceptable.

4.3 QUANTITY OBJECTIVES

Output performance objectives set for some individuals, teams and departments are relatively easy to measure. They may be sales revenue, manufacturing output, or the number of deliveries made, for example. For other support activities it is perhaps easiest to judge output by the volume of service supplied to 'internal customers' – a concept widely used in quality programmes. A personnel and training department's output may be measured in terms of recruitment activity, the number of training days delivered or some similar measurement of activity.

4.4 COST OBJECTIVES

Similarly, the cost-effectiveness or efficiency objective associated with the output objective is often easy to express, although again the measurement may be done in many different ways. It may, for instance, be expressed as total cost, or cost per unit of activity, or percentage usage (the sort of measure that reflects the efficiency with which assets are used – eg use of a machine or vehicle).

Expenditure (cost) measures – start with the establishment of budgets that refer to actual versus planned costs as outlined in the objectives. As the operation/production progresses, decisions regarding procurement, design, development, deployment etc, will be assessed with respect to their impact on expenditures. Actual expenditures will be compared to a baseline, and any variances will be reported to management for corrective action.

4.5 TIME OBJECTIVES

Schedule (time) performance measures – refer to the timely completion of the output of an operation as compared to a baseline schedule defined in the manufacturing/ production plan. The schedules will identify all of the operation's stages, phases, and activities assigned to various employees or teams mapping them to a timeline that measures key milestones (dates) that are used to keep track of work progress. Avoiding schedule slippage is a key objective.

4.6 QUALITY OBJECTIVES

The most difficult measure to express in numerical terms is usually quality.

(a) **Functional quality** – refers to the quality or correctness of the products and/or services features/functions delivered as a result of the operation. It can be measured by comparing the quality or correctness of the baseline product and services features/functions to the proposed deliverables. It can also be measured using the number of product and service change requests made, approved, and effectively implemented or the number of critical, serious, and non-critical defects outstanding and resolved on a weekly basis.

The customer will at some point perceive a product or service as being unacceptable if the quality declines. But the point at which that occurs depends on both the individual customer and the particular circumstances that he or she has experienced, In an organisation the ability of an individual or a department to delivery a satisfactory service is often dependent on the quality of supply of an *internal* service eg, credit controllers' ability to manage debt will be badly affected if they are served by poor quality debtor systems where the latest cash receipts have not been entered. They will lose confidence if the data is not accurate and will be less effective. More importantly, both they and the firm will lose credibility with customers if they chase payments, which have already been made.

(b) **Technical quality performance** – refers to the technical infrastructure that provides the foundation for product and service delivery. In the case of an IT operation, such indicators as system availability, downtime, problem resolution, and response time and network utilisation would measure technical quality performance.

(c) **Issue management performance** – refers to the identification and resolution of issues or exceptions that are impacting the successful delivery of the operation. Issues can be related to communications, human resources, contracts, product/service features and functions etc. The purpose of issue management is to ensure that all matters requiring resolution, decisions or direction are addressed as soon as possible to avoid negative consequences on operational objectives and deliverables.

4.7 QUALITY CONTROL

Quality control is the process of ensuring that goods and services are produced in accordance with specifications. The major objective of quality control is to see that the organisation lives up to the standards it has set for itself.

For many operations it is accepted that it is not possible to achieve perfection in products because of the variations in raw material quality, operating skills, different types of machines used, wear and tear, etc. but quality control attempts to ascertain the amount of variation from perfect that can be expected in any operation. If the expected variation is acceptable according to engineering requirements, then production must be established within controlled limits and if the actual variation is too great then corrective action must be taken to bring it within acceptable limits.

Quality control is concerned with trying to make sure that a product is manufactured, or a service is provided, to meet certain design specifications. It is aimed at preventing the manufacture of defective items or the provision of defective services.

BPP
LEARNING MEDIA

This means:

- establishing standards of quality

- establishing procedures or production methods to ensure that these required standards are met in an agreed proportion of cases

- monitoring actual quality

- taking control action when actual quality falls below standard.

4.8   STATISTICAL PROCESS CONTROL

Statistical process control (SPC) is the continuous monitoring and charting of a process while it is operating, to warn when the process is moving away from predetermined limits. The goal of an SPC programme should be to minimise and eliminate if possible these variations and to operate a process such that it has the capability to produce product within a customers' specification or better.

Data obtained, manually or automatically, at the time of processing can be plotted graphically in order to provide a visual record of the performance of a process. Critical dimensions or other characteristics are measured. A typical control chart is shown in the diagram below. The horizontal axis is either time or a cumulative output volume. The vertical axis is a measure of a critical characteristic of the component such as its length or diameter. Typically the upper and lower control limits will be three standard deviations away from the mean.

Figure 3.4: Quality control chart

The objective value of the characteristic being measured is plotted as a horizontal line. An analysis of past output will indicate the amount of random variation expected for the type of process being used. From this the standard deviation of the process from the mean (expected value) can be measured. Further horizontal lines can then be drawn on the graph at positions representing 2 and 3 standard deviations above and below the objective line. These values are derived from an analysis of the process and are control limits. It is expected that 67% of values will lie between ± 2 standard deviations hence within that part of the chart that lies between the warning limits. 99.75% will lie between ± 3 standard deviations and lie within the action limits. A control chart shows the limits within which output is expected. All points outside the control limits should be investigated and corrected.

As actual output is produced the value of the chosen dimension is plotted. This will show both random and gradual variations and also any deviations. Some output can be expected to be beyond the 2 standard deviation control limits. These are known are 'warning limits'.

Some output of this type is not a problem since it is expected but successive values in this region indicate a problem that needs to be corrected. Virtually no output should occur beyond the 3 standard deviations limits. These are known as 'action limits'. If such values occur this indicates that the process is out of control and action is required to correct it.

SPC covers a wider range of topics:

- It can be used to process data to optimise plant performance. In its simplest form it is looking at the standard deviation of controlled variables and how close they are to the plant tolerance limits, and seeing if they can be pushed closer, making the plant more productive.

- It is an aspect of Total Quality Management (TQM), which is a way of managing a business to ensure complete customer satisfaction internally and externally. If the expected variation is acceptable according to engineering requirements, then production must be established within controlled limits and if the actual variation is too great then corrective action must be taken to bring it within acceptable limits.

- It can be used to control buffer stocks or inventories. These are an accumulation of stock, usually raw materials, for use in case of supply problems, or cash-flow difficulties that prevent purchase of new stock. A buffer stock, or safety stock, is an insurance against unexpected problems, but excessive hoarding ties up assets and limits supplies of the resource to other companies. The use of just-in-time techniques has reduced the requirement for buffer stock.

- It can involve the use of charts to record and monitor the accuracy of the physical dimensions of products. Representational samples of an output manufacturing process may be taken daily or even hourly, and faults in the process which are revealed may be fairly simple to correct by adjusting the appropriate machinery. If output exceeds the control limits consistently then more urgent management action would be required because this could indicate some inadequacy in production methods or quality of raw materials and components. It could even be due to inefficiency in production or excessively tight tolerances in the first place.

- Control charts can also be applied to the inspection of raw materials received from suppliers in order to confirm that the supplier is supplying materials, which conform to the size and standard specified in the purchase contract.

BPP
LEARNING MEDIA

5 COORDINATION

5.1 ORGANISATION

Up to now in this study guide the term 'organisation' has been broadly used. Another interpretation of this term may be made if organisation is regarded as being the coordination of all the procedures, systems and functions within that organisation.

Coordination is one of the major functions of management. Each department will have its own procedures and its own priorities. It is the job of the manager to get all of these to mesh together harmoniously and move in the direction of the common purpose.

This is nowhere more apparent than in the planning process. Each department will have its own long-term and short-term goals and purposes, and targets that it wants to achieve. There may also be bonus schemes tied into this. Each department will have its own set of priorities. Effective coordination will cause some of these to change, in the interests of pursuing an overall set of priorities.

As the business plan will cover all departments of the organisation, so all of the departmental plans and budgets must be coordinated, so that they are all working together to achieve the business plan. For instance, sales should be planning to sell the number of units that the production departments agreed to produce, otherwise there will be either unsold stock or unfilled orders.

At the production level, coordination will ensure that:

- Departments know what it is they need to achieve, and when

- Work 'flows' from one department to another without holdups or clashes, and without idle time or overwork for staff and machinery

- The resources required for a task are available where and when they are required

- There is no duplication of effort

DEFINITION

To **coordinate** is 'to plan, or take action to improve, the inter-relationships (especially of timing and methods of communication) between a number of various activities, which contribute to the achievement of a single objective, so that they do not conflict and the objective is achieved with a minimal expenditure of time and effort.'

(Dictionary of Management)

5.2 FORMAL AND INFORMAL TYPES OF COORDINATION

Many organisations endeavour to set up formal systems of coordination to ensure that individuals, groups and functions work effectively with each other and that the parts, although existing individually, operate in harmony. This is usually attained by the setting of an overall organisational goal, which is broken down into supporting objectives for individuals, groups and functional areas. This is important – it is of little value to have a stock control system that appears to work for both raw materials and finished goods and an apparently efficient production department system if the two functional areas are not coordinated. If the right type of raw materials cannot be issued to the production department at the right time then however efficient the production department may be internally it will not be able to contribute effectively to the organisation as a whole. In turn such failure will mean that the production department will be unable to furnish the stores section with the required quantity of finished units to meet customers' orders. Formal systems of coordination are required to ensure that the goals of the organisation are achieved and not hampered.

It is to the credit of many individuals within organisations that they recognise instinctively the relationship between different procedures, systems and functional areas and implement them. This is usually achieved without formal modes, within small groups and sections where, having identified the goals of the particular group/section, the group/section leader and individuals devise suitable and logical ways of attaining the required goals. This is normally achieved informally whilst the coordination of a number of groups or sections requires attention of a more formal nature.

5.3 THE IMPORTANCE OF COORDINATION

Remember that we defined the purpose of organisations as 'the controlled performance to achieve collective goals'. This is, in essence, what coordination involves. Coordination is important because:

(a) the organisation is a collection of individuals and groups, each with their own interests and goals; these must be given a unified, common direction if the organisation as a whole is to achieve its objectives;

(b) the organisation's activities involve a variety of:

(i) people;
(ii) tasks;
(iii) resources; and
(iv) technologies

all of these will have to be at the right place, at the right time, working in the right way, if smooth operations are to be maintained;

BPP
LEARNING MEDIA

(c) some activities of the organisation will be dependent on the successful and timely completion of other activities (as we saw in network analysis): someone needs to ensure that such interrelationships are taken into account in the overall activity of the organisation;

(d) some activities of the organisation will be higher priority than others: someone needs to ensure that there is an overall balance between urgent/ high-priority activities and routine activities, on which the organisation nevertheless depends;

(e) resources (human, material and financial) are limited, and possibly scarce. Different units in the organisation are, in effect, in competition for their 'slice' of the resources available. Someone has to balance their demands and the organisation's priorities to ensure that overall, resources are used efficiently and effectively in pursuit of the organisation's goals.

FOR DISCUSSION

Think about a team sport you know well – say, football. What would happen if you had:

(a) no positions for each of the players to adopt?

(b) no team strategy?

(c) no team purpose – if, say, prizes were awarded to individual goal scorers, and there were no such thing as a team win?

(d) nobody in charge of providing kit, the ball, the playing field or the referee on a regular basis?

5.4 WHAT NEEDS COORDINATING?

From the above, we can see that, broadly, managers coordinate:

(a) the **timing** of activities, so that their inter-relationships are controlled without wasted time or bottlenecks;

(b) the **direction** or **purpose** of activities, so that units of the organisation work towards common objectives, and the relative priority of activities are balanced;

(c) the **resources** (human, financial and material) required for activities, so that each sub-unit of the organisation is able to do what it should, when it should.

ACTIVITY 6 (20 MINS)

(a) Can you immediately think of some techniques we have already discussed which might help a business in each of these areas?

(b) Give an example of a problem arising from failure to coordinate in each of these areas.

5.5 SYMPTOMS OF POOR COORDINATION

A manager might be alerted to problems of coordination by the following tell-tale signs.

(a) Complaints from clients, customers and other external parties, indicating that products are not being supplied on time, or that they have been given different information by different departments of the organisation.

(b)   Production problems, with alternating overloads and idle time, and associated problems with labour resourcing and production costs. (The equivalent for service organisations might be missed deadlines or commitments to customers, internal paperwork failing to reach the right people at the right time and so on.)

(c)   Persistent conflict within and between departments, especially the placing of blame for problems, and empire-building and power games in place of cooperation.

(d)   Lack of communication between units of the organisation.

(e)   Appeals to rules and red tape to try to give the appearance of integrated activity.

5.6   CAUSES OF POOR COORDINATION

Some of the major causes of poor coordination are as follows.

(a)   **Poor communication** – both vertically and horizontally – so that units do not know what they are supposed to be doing, or what other units are doing, or how the two are meant to be related.

(b)   **Inadequate planning and control**, so that unit objectives are not clearly understood, and/or integrated with those of other units, within overall objectives.

(c)   **Weak organisation structure,** which does not make the inter-relationships between units clear, or link them via the chain of command. This problem will be particularly acute where the organisation's task requires interdependent input across the boundaries of departments and functions.

(d)   **Interpersonal and/or interdepartmental conflict**. Power and resources are limited in organisations, and there is frequently competition, rivalry, jealousies, the guarding of 'territory' and information and so on, to protect the interests of individuals and groups. This kind of activity is known as organisational politics.

(e)   **Differences** between the cultures and tasks of different units. These may be differences in:

(i)   the time pressures a unit works under;

(ii)   the leadership style of the units' managers;

(iii)   the technology used by the units;

(iv)   the methods of working adopted by the units;

(v)   the culture or values of the units;

and so on.

ACTIVITY 7   (20 MINS)

Give an example of each of the types of difference between cultures and tasks of different units suggested above, which might cause problems of coordination.

---

6 IMPROVING COORDINATION

6.1 MANAGEMENT STRATEGIES

Maintaining and improving communication

Communication is essential for coordination, ensuring that:

(a)   the inter-relationship of activities and plans is understood;

(b)   variations from plan in one activity are notified to, and taken into account by, other units;

(c)   conflict and organisational politics are not allowed to develop, to obstruct the common goals of the organisation.

Managers should give attention to horizontal, as well as vertical, communication.

ACTIVITY 8	(10 MINS)

Suggest three ways in which a manager might encourage horizontal communication.

Planning

Systematic planning and control is essential for coordination. Tasks need to be sequenced and scheduled in a way that:

(a)   balances their relative urgency and priority;

(b)   takes into account their inter-relationships and the dependency of one task on another;

(c)   allows resources to be rationally allocated on the basis of priorities and overall objectives; *and*

(d)   allows the plans and schedules of each unit to be integrated with those of other units, towards the organisation's overall objectives.

Controlling conflict

Managers should try to create conditions in which individuals and departments are able to cooperate instead of conflict.

Direct supervision

The manager occupies a coordinating role within his or her own section, as the central person responsible for all the work of the group: issuing instructions, monitoring performance and so on.

6.2 STRUCTURES AND MECHANISMS

As well as using the coordinating function of managers, an organisation can aid coordination through its structures and various formal mechanisms.

Organisation structure

The organisation structure may be designed to provide:

(a) a **coordinating level of management**. Just as the individual manager acts as the 'lynchpin' of coordination for his own unit, so he has a superior who is responsible for coordinating his work with that of other units, see the diagram below;

Figure 3.5: Organisation structure

(b) **liaison or integration officers** – for example, project coordinators, client liaison managers and so on. These posts essentially encourage communication;

(c) **multi-disciplinary teams,** committees, project groups and so on. These are matrix structures, including representation from all departments involved in a given task or activity, with a coordinating authority (a project manager, say) crossing functional boundaries.

Standardisation

Standardisation is an important mechanism for coordinating work at the operational level: it involves getting people to do things the same way, or with the same results. This adds reliability, or predictability, to work processes, allowing them to be more closely coordinated and controlled.

(a) **Standardisation of work processes** is possible for routine tasks, where the actual content of the task is specified or programmed. For example, think about the assembly instructions for a model or piece of furniture, or the operation of a video recorder: the task is designed to be done in the same way, regardless of who is doing it. Standardisation of forms and documents is another important aid to consistency and coordination.

(b) **Standardisation of output** is possible for more complex tasks, where discretion is needed in performing the work. The organisation may set standards for design, quality, cost and so on, so that its product or service is consistent, regardless of who does the work and how.

(c) **Standardisation by skill and knowledge** is possible for complex and varied work, which nevertheless requires a certain standard of performance. So, for example, a hospital sets standard requirements for the qualifications of its doctors, as an accountancy firm does for its accountants and so on.

EXAMPLE   **MCDONALD'S**

McDonald's fast food restaurants are highly standardised in terms of work processes and outputs. This helps them to control consistency of food quality and specification in their outlets spread worldwide. McDonald's management want a Big Mac bought in Sydney or Stockholm to be the same; this can only be achieved through tight controls on standardisation.

FOR DISCUSSION

How well coordinated is the course you are on? (Consider how 'smooth' your timetable is: clashes? bottlenecks? idle time? How consistent is the teaching and course material? Is there a course leader or coordinator, and what is his or her function?)

7   ORGANISATIONAL CONSTRAINTS

7.1   CONSTRAINTS ON MANAGEMENT

In putting forward theories and techniques for managing activities, it is all too easy to give the impression that managers are in a position to make any and all decisions they think necessary to achieve their objectives, bounded only by the scope of their authority within the organisation. Of course, this isn't really so. We have already touched on the uncertainty of forecasting and planning the future; the impossibility of gathering all relevant information; the fact that power and resources are limited; the need for compromise in interpersonal relations and in business decisions alike; the importance – and unpredictability – of human behaviour at work. All these factors act as constraints on the individual manager's right and ability to manage people and activities as (s)he sees fit, or even in the most effective way possible (in an ideal world ...). This section aims to draw together all those threads.

7.2 EXTERNAL STAKEHOLDERS

Stakeholders are people or groups who have a 'stake' or interest in the activities and performance of an organisation and who impose certain obligations on its management. The external stakeholders of the organisation include:

(a) **its owners or shareholders** – the organisation, and its management, have a primary responsibility to look after the owners' interests and to secure them a return on their financial investment in the organisation; the shareholders of a public company have the right to vote on organisational issues in an Annual General Meeting and any General Meetings that may be called: ultimately, the shareholders have the say in what the organisation does and how it should be managed;

(b) **its customers** – the organisation's customers depend on it for the goods and services they need, and for the safety, value and honest marketing of those goods and services; in a free market economy, however, customers have the choice to accept or reject an organisation's offerings, and this gives them power: organisations need to tailor their products and their image to the values and wants of the market, if they are to survive competition;

ACTIVITY 9 (20 MINS)

What sort of issues have consumer organisations focused on in the attempt to influence businesses to protect buyers' interests and values? Suggest four examples that you are aware of.

(c) **the community, or society as a whole** – society depends on businesses for employment, investment, social responsibility (eg towards the environment) and so on. It also provides the organisation with labour, with potential customers and with a reputation which may affect the organisation's position in the market, so managers need to consider whether their decisions will be socially acceptable.

In relation to external stakeholders, an organisation has:

(a) obligations or responsibilities, which it may undertake voluntarily, but which do not form a part of its internal guidance or control mechanisms; for example, value for money, charitable donations, generous wages and so on; and

(b) boundaries or constraints on its managers' freedom to act as they see fit. For example, government legislation (on pollution, health and safety at work and redundancy), regulation (on financial reporting) and agreements with a trade union.

7.3 PEST FACTORS

A useful acronym, widely used in the UK to describe the external environment of organisations, is PEST: Political-legal, Economic, Socio-cultural and Technological factors.

7.4 THE POLITICAL-LEGAL ENVIRONMENT

Political-legal factors which managers must take into account include the following.

(a) Law and regulation, as discussed above.

(b) The power of the government, as the nation's largest supplier, employer, customer and investor. (Consider the effect of a change of government policy on defence for the defence industry, say).

BPP
LEARNING MEDIA

(c)   Political events at home and abroad. There may be trading sanctions imposed on states (as was the case with South Africa, Iraq and Serbia) by the international community. A war or change of regime can harm industries (as happened to airlines during the Gulf War) or build them (as in the opening up of commerce in Eastern Europe after the collapse of communism).

(d)   Government economic policy – for example, on public spending, borrowing and taxation (**fiscal** policy) and on interest and exchange rates and control of the money supply (**monetary** policy). Businesses are affected by taxation, and by monetary policy: high interest rates, for example, increase the cost of investment and depress consumer spending.

(e)   Government industrial policy – for example, encouraging exports (by subsidies or promotion), sponsorship of businesses in depressed regions, protection of domestic industry (duty on imported goods) and so on.

(f)   Government social and foreign policy – on education and training of the workforce, trade promotion overseas, obligations towards the EU and so on.

7.5 THE ECONOMIC ENVIRONMENT

An organisation is affected by overall economic conditions, as these influence:

(a)   the demand for its products; *and*
(b)   the cost of its supplies.

In times of boom and increased demand and consumption, the overall planning problem will be to identify the demand. Conversely, in times of recession, the emphasis will be on cost-effectiveness, continuing profitability, survival and competition.

A company's immediate regional geographical environment is also important. It might be located in a growth area full of modern thriving industry, such as Milton Keynes; or it may be located in an area of urban decay. The economic future of the area will affect wages, availability of labour, the disposable income of local consumers, the provision of roads and other services and so on.

7.6 THE SOCIO-CULTURAL ENVIRONMENT

DEFINITION

Demography is the analysis of statistics on birth and death rates, sex and age distributions, ethnic groups and geographical movements within a population.

Social and cultural influences on management decisions include the following.

(a)   **Demography,** or demographics; that is, population trends.

Conditions and changes in the local and/or national population can affect:

(i)   the availability of labour of the age and skills required by the organisation in its operating area; and

(ii)   the demand for its products and services in particular areas (eg if population is declining or growing) or by particular groups (eg an increasing proportion of the population of a certain ethnic group, or over retirement age).

(b)   **Culture**: the beliefs and values, attitudes, customs, language and tastes of a given society or social group.

(i) Organisations need to adapt their products, marketing approach and corporate image to the values of a given group. Language and other cultural barriers may have to be overcome, especially if the organisation is operating internationally. (The custom of giving gifts to business contacts is embedded in some cultures, for example – but would be called bribery in other places!)

EXAMPLE   COCA-COLA

In the 1980s, Coca-Cola decided to change its flavour to compete with Pepsi. Market research, taste tests and so forth elicited positive responses to the change, and so the new formulation was introduced. A small group of consumers vociferously opposed the change; and this opposition spread suddenly and rapidly like an epidemic, forcing Coca-Cola to re-introduce the old formula. It seemed that some consumers perceived Coke to symbolise 'American values', so changing the formula appeared to be an assault on them.

(ii) Organisations need to adapt their management styles and practices to the values prevailing in the culture from which they draw their workforce.

ACTIVITY 10   (15 MINS)

Give three examples of:

(a) products tailored to a particular cultural market; *and*
(b) employment and management practice influenced by culture.

7.7 THE TECHNOLOGICAL ENVIRONMENT

Technology is not just **apparatus** (ie tools and machines), but also **technique** (skills and procedures for the use of tools and machines) and **organisation** (the social and work structure of tasks).

Technological **change** is extremely rapid, and organisations must constantly adapt to it. Technology can affect the management of organisations by:

(a) **presenting opportunities and threats in the market for the organisation's goods and services** – compact discs, satellite dishes and home computers are 'in'; records, typewriters and heavy wooden-framed tennis rackets are 'out';

(b) **changing the possibilities for how products are made** – (for example, using computer-aided design and robots) – **and services are provided** (for example, cashpoint machines instead of bank tellers);

(c) **changing the way in which labour is utilised** – technology has facilitated the delayering and downsizing of organisation structures, and created a much more knowledge-based workforce.

In general, managers will be constrained to adopt new technology – especially if the organisation's competitors have done so – in order to cut costs, enhance quality, innovate and so on.

Apart from the PEST factors, which affect all organisations, a business organisation faces competition.

7.8 THE COMPETITIVE ENVIRONMENT

Business organisations compete for customers and for labour – and the price of competitive failure may be the collapse of the business. The need to compete may constrain managers to:

(a) maintain or improve the quality of products/services;

(b) control the price charged for products/services;

(c) pay more to secure a reliable supply of high-quality materials from suppliers (particularly in specialised areas);

(d) pay more for selling, advertising, promotion, sponsorship and so on;

(e) pay higher wages, salaries and benefits;

(f) implement attractive human resource practices to attract skilled labour: welfare, training, workplace crèche or whatever.

These constraints will be particularly acute if there is a new or strengthening competitor in the market.

8 INTERNAL ENVIRONMENT

8.1 INTERNAL STAKEHOLDERS

The internal stakeholders of an organisation are its members or employees.

FOR DISCUSSION

Why do employees have a 'stake' in the organisation? What kind of things do they need or want from it?

The needs, wants and expectations of the employees will act as a constraint on management decision-making because the organisation may be concerned:

(a) to harness the energy and committed cooperation of its employees;

(b) not to lose skilled and experienced employees to competitors;

(c) to maintain a reputation as a responsible or generous employer, to secure a future pool of labour.

ACTIVITY 11 (20 MINS)

Give five examples of managerial decisions which might require careful thought because of their potential effects on the morale and attitudes of employees.

8.2 ORGANISATION

The freedom of individual managers to make decisions as they see fit will be constrained by organisational factors such as the following.

(a) **The scope and amount of authority delegated to them**: their 'territory' and power within the organisation. A manager can only manage activities for which (s)he is responsible and has authority.

(b) **Plans, programmes, procedures, rules and so on**, which may already be in place. A manager is rarely able to plan activities and work methods from scratch: systems will have been developed for most routine sequences of activity. Managers often have to stick to plans and expenditure budgets which have been determined (with varying degrees of consultation) by more senior officials.

(c) **The existing organisation structure**. An individual manager is rarely able to organise work and workers from scratch. There may be no experience of multi-disciplinary teamworking to build on, for example, or departmental boundaries and job demarcation lines may be too firmly fixed to change.

(d) **The demand for coordination**. As we noted earlier, some tasks depend on others and have to be scheduled accordingly, and some processes and outputs need standardising in order to maintain coordination and consistency. An individual manager cannot make decisions for his or her own unit without reference to the requirements of the organisation system as a whole.

(e) **Organisation culture**. An individual manager is unlikely to be able to choose his or her own style of communication, motivation and management in general, without reference to the culture of the unit or organisation as a whole. A manager who does not 'fit' the organisational 'style' rarely lasts long.

9 LIMITED RESOURCES

BPP LEARNING MEDIA

9.1 MONEY

Money, and the infinite variety of things it represents, is always limited and tightly controlled in organisations. Money allocated to different units represents cost to the organisation, whose financial objectives are likely to be profitability, return on investment and so on: in other words, to **maximise earnings** and **minimise costs**.

Individual unit budgets for expenditure are components of the overall organisational budget – like slices of a cake. A great deal of the politics and conflict within organisations is concerned with competing for bigger slices of the cake!

Limited financial resources therefore constrain managerial decision-making because:

(a) a limited budget can only be stretched so far, and the manager may not be able to obtain or retain all the other resources – quality materials, extra labour, new equipment and so on – that (s)he would want;

(b) a manager may be tempted to spend up to the allocated budget, even though it is not required, so as not to have the allocation reduced next time round.

9.2 TIME

You may not have thought about it, but time is a limited resource.

(a) There are only so many working hours available. If these are not sufficient to accomplish everything a manager wishes, (s)he will be constrained to:

    (i) find extra labour or machine capacity, to cover the excess workload in the time available; or

    (ii) eliminate, or simplify, tasks or 'cut corners' in order to get high-priority work done with the existing workforce; or

    (iii) allow work to run late, and adjust the work plan for the knock-on effects.

(b) Deadlines may be imposed by customer requirements or internal coordination. Deadlines get closer: they make time both a limited and an increasingly scarce resource. Compromises of cost or quality may have to be made to meet deadlines.

(c) Time for information-gathering and decision-making is also limited. This may constrain managers to make decisions which seem riskier or less informed than they might be, or which have not been subject to as much consultation with team members as the manager's style might otherwise dictate.

9.3 INFORMATION

Information is a limited resource for several reasons.

(a) Time and money for gathering it may be limited.

(b) There is a limit to how much a person can take in and use effectively.

(c) Some information is simply not obtainable with any certainty – for example, how people are going to react, or what is going to happen tomorrow!

(d) 'Information is power', and individuals and units in organisations tend to hoard it if they think it will give them extra influence or a competitive edge over others.

Limited information constrains the management of activities because:

(a)   decisions have to be taken on the basis of what is known: the full range of possible options can never be known, and a certain degree of uncertainty and inaccuracy remains;

(b)   it is not possible to predict the outcome of all decisions and actions, nor the contingencies that might affect them. Changes in the PEST, competitive or physical environment of an organisation cannot always be foreseen and planned for.

If **management** information is not made available to a manager – for example, the objectives and results of the organisation, or the attitudes of employees – then the ability of the manager to make effective decisions will clearly be impaired.

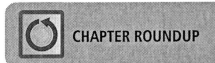

CHAPTER ROUNDUP

- Operations management can be described as a system. The inputs include the needs of the customers, information, technology, labour and management and the fixed and variable assets that are relevant to the transformation process. Managers and workers use the information and physical factors to produce the outputs. The transformation process incorporates planning, operating and controlling the system.

- Policies are general guidelines for management decision-making. Procedures are a logical sequence of required actions for performing a certain task and rules are specific, definite courses of action that must be taken in a given situation.

- Production can be defined as the activity of transforming raw materials or components into finished products.

- The value chain is a sequence of business activities by which, in the perspective of the end user, value is added to the products or services produced by an organisation

- Primary activities are those directly related with production, sales, marketing, delivery and services.

- Support activities provide purchased inputs, human resources, technology and infrastructural functions to support the primary activities.

- Linkages connect the interdependent elements of the value chain together. They occur when one element of the value chain affects the costs or effectiveness of another.

- JIT or zero inventory was conceived to ensure the inventory has only what is needed, when it is needed.

- The four objectives – cost, time, quantity and quality – should be considered together, because the optimum performance typically involves a trade-off of several dimensions, specifically what is done (scope and quality) versus the resources used to do the work (time and cost).

- Quality control is the process of ensuring that goods and services are produced in accordance with specifications. The major objective of quality control is to see that the organisation lives up to the standards it has set for itself.

- Statistical process control (SPC) is the continuous monitoring and charting of a process while it is operating, to warn when the process is moving away from predetermined limits.

- Coordination is one of the major functions of management. Each department will have its own procedures and its own priorities. It is the job of the manager to get all of these to mesh together harmoniously and move in the direction of the common purpose.

QUICK QUIZ

1   Give an example of a procedure for the board of directors.

2   What does product development include?

3   How does job production differ from process production?

4   List the five primary activities in the value chain model.

5   How can performance be monitored?

6   Give three reasons why coordination is necessary.

7   Give three examples of the symptoms of poor coordination.

8   List the main causes of poor coordination.

9   Why is (a) communication and (b) planning helpful to coordination?

10   What can be 'standardised' in order to coordinate activities at an operational level?

11   List the main external stakeholders of an organisation.

12   Give three examples of (a) political and (b) cultural factors.

13   How does (a) organisation structure, (b) coordination and (c) organisation culture constrain management discretion?

14   What resources do managers compete for in organisations?

ANSWERS TO QUICK QUIZ

1   The conduct of board meetings will be set out as a procedure for the board of directors.

2   Development refers collectively to the entire process of identifying a market opportunity, creating a product to appeal to the identified market, and finally, testing, modifying and refining the product until it is ready for production.

3   Job production (or unit production) is the output of a single product to specific requirements (eg suit or ship) whereas process (flow) production is continuous production of products of a more or less identical nature, eg oil refinery.

4   Inbound logistics
Operations
Outbound logistics
Marketing and sales
After-sales service

5   Measurement can be based on the actual start or finish times of critical activities and (especially for a project) the completion of milestones, or the timing of acceptance tests. Operation control charts use budget and schedule plans to report cumulative time and cost so that variances can be calculated. Performance can also be monitored by inspection, progress reviews (at regular stages), quality testing and financial audit.

6   There must be a common direction for the organisation to achieve its goals; coordination also helps to maintain smooth operations and to balance high priority work with routine tasks.

7   Complaints, production problems, persistent conflict.

8   Poor communication
Inadequate planning and control
Weak organisation structure
Interpersonal and/or interdepartmental conflict
Differences between the cultures and tasks of different units

9   (a)   Communication ensures that the inter-relationship of activities and plans is understood, that variations are notified and that conflict is not allowed to develop.

    (b)   Planning prioritises, understands the dependency of one task on another, allows resources to be rationally allocated and integrates, plans and schedules.

10 Work processes, output, design, quality cost, skill and knowledge.

11 External stakeholders include owners and shareholders, customers, the community or society as a whole.

12 (a)   Trading sanctions, war, change of regime.
    (b)   Beliefs and values, attitudes and customs.

13 (a)   Managers can only manage activities for which they are responsible and have authority.

    (b)   Decisions are not possible without considering the requirements of the organisation system as a whole.

    (c)   Decisions must 'fit in' to the organisational 'style'.

14 Money, time and information.

ANSWERS TO ACTIVITIES

1   The restaurant has a number of choices as to how to create value.

(a)   It can become more efficient, by automating the production of food, as in a fast food chain.

(b)   The chef can develop commercial relationships with growers, so he or she can obtain the best quality fresh produce.

(c)   The chef can specialise in a particular type of cuisine (eg Nepalese, Korean).

(d)   The restaurant can be sumptuously decorated for those customers who value 'atmosphere' and a sense of occasion, in addition to a restaurant's purely gastronomic pleasures.

(e)   The restaurant can serve a particular type of customer (eg celebrities).

Each of these options is a way of organising the activities of buying, cooking and serving food in a way that customers will value.

2   The first step is to outline the primary activities that may be a source of advantage. Then link these to the support activities, showing how each of them cuts across all of the primary activities.

HR management	Training	Stable workforce Quality of work		Retention of best salespeople	Training service staff
Procurement		Highest quality components	Best located warehouse		Quality parts replacement
Technology development	Material handling and sorting	Unique product features	Special purpose vehicles	Engineering support	Advanced servicing techniques
Firm infrastructure	Reduced damage	Low defect rates	Quick order processing	Extensive credit to buyers	Rapid installation Service quality
	Inbound logistics	Operations	Outbound logistics	Marketing and sales	Service

Primary activities

The technology development activity at the lawn mower manufacturer, shown in the diagram, indicates material handling and sorting adding value at the inbound logistics stage. Other sources of potential advantage are sought with the unique product features at the operations stage, special purpose delivery vehicles at the outbound logistics stage and engineering support and servicing techniques in the marketing, sales and service stages.

3   Sana Sounds is involved in the record industry from start to finish. Although recording and CD manufacture are contracted out to external suppliers, this makes no difference to the fact that these activities are part of Sana Sounds' own value chain. Sana Sounds earns its money by managing the whole set of activities. If the company grows then perhaps it will acquire its own recording studios. The purpose of this exercise has been to drive the point home that a *value chain of activities* is not the same as an *organisation's business functions.*

4   The correct answer is C. The other activities are non-value-adding activities.

5   The correct answer is B.

6   Coordination techniques, and problems that might arise if an organisation does not coordinate, include the following

(a)   Timing: scheduling, network analysis, Gantt charts.

Direction: planning and goal-setting, priority-setting, work breakdown, network analysis.

Resources: network analysis, resource allocation charts, budgets.

(b)   Timing: the costing department is 'behind' in its analysis of production employees' time sheets, leaving the payroll department without the information required to prepare and pay the wages.

Direction: the marketing department is trying to sell an 'upmarket' image of the product, while the production department is trying to increase profits by cutting down on 'frills' and packaging.

Resources: the organisation does not have enough trained staff to cope with a peak work period; there are insufficient components in store to complete a given production order on time.

7   Differences between culture and tasks might cause coordination problems for the reasons below.

(a)   The implementation of a computer system (devised over a period of months or years) by a project group, in an operational department with tight time schedules for ongoing work.

(b)   The manager of one unit may inform his team of decisions, while the manager of the other consults her team, resulting in different approaches. The clash of style may also prevent effective communication between the two managers.

(c)   Incompatible computer systems in two departments, preventing them from sharing information easily.

(d)   Two departments using different forms for the same purpose, making it difficult to share data, and encouraging different approaches (eg different criteria in staff assessment forms), which may become sources of conflict.

(e)   One unit dedicated to serving the customer at all costs, another dedicated to saving costs, and never mind the customer!

8   Horizontal communication might be beneficial if a manager encouraged in the following ways.

(a)   Not discouraging informal communication at work – even encouraging it, by providing an environment where people can talk during breaks and so on.

(b)   Teambuilding and empowerment, so that people do not see themselves as individuals in competition with other individuals, but as teams who must communicate freely in order to do their jobs.

(c)   Appointing team members to interdisciplinary or joint team meetings, so that they can exchange information with people at the same level but in different areas of the organisation.

9   Aspects of business activity on which consumer organisations have focused include:

(a)   Dangerous products and by-products (such as cigarettes and car exhaust emission)

(b)   Dishonest marketing or promotion; in the UK there is legislation designed to deal with this kind of abuse

(c)   The abuse of political and economic power by organisations (for example, ignoring international sanctions or trading with regimes with poor human rights records)

(d)   The availability of information. Consumers are anxious, for example, to be informed of any artificial additives in foodstuffs

10   (a)   Cultural products include: kosher food (to the Jewish community); magazines specifically for men or women; low premium car insurance for mature drivers; cosmetics tested without cruelty to animals, for the 'green' market – eg Body Shop.

(b)   Employment practices affected by culture include: work hours to allow for religious holidays and observances; separate facilities and offices to differentiate managers and workers (not a cultural norm in Japan, for example); the extension of benefits previously given to 'spouses' of employees to 'partners' – for example, by British Airways.

11   Managerial decisions requiring special care about morale and employee attitudes include, for example: office relocation; redundancies; change in work practices (eg introducing shiftworking); cut in benefits; cancellation of holidays in busy periods.

04 Quality

Introduction

In recent years quality has become the key in determining many organisations' positions in respect of their competitive advantage. Unfortunately, quality is difficult to define because it has a wide range of meanings, covering a wide range of businesses and processes.

Quality control is concerned with maintaining quality standards. The process goes through a cycle of establishing standards and procedures, monitoring actual quality and taking control action when actual quality falls below standard. Quality assurance, however, is the term used where a supplier guarantees the quality of goods supplied and allows the customer access while the goods are being manufactured. Total quality management is the term given to programmes that seek to ensure that goods are produced and services are supplied of the highest quality.

Your objectives

After completing this chapter you should be able to:

*   Define resources, tools and systems required to support business process

*   Design systems to manage and monitor quality to standards specified by the organisation

*   Demonstrate a quality culture to ensure continuous monitoring, evaluation and development of the process

1   QUALITY SYSTEMS

1.1   THE IMPORTANCE OF QUALITY IN A BUSINESS ENVIRONMENT

The modern business environment is remarkably different from the business environment of a decade or so ago. One change has been the **switch in emphasis away from quantity towards quality**. Consumers and **customers** have become **more sophisticated and discerning** in their requirements. They are no longer satisfied with accepting the late delivery of the same old unreliable products from an organisation which does not appear to care for its customers. They want new products, superior on-time delivery performance and an immediate response to their requests. Many organisations are therefore turning to quality to help them to survive the competitive modern business environment.

1.2   WHAT IS QUALITY?

DEFINITION

Quality has been defined by Ken Holmes (*Total Quality Management*) as 'the totality of features and characteristics of a product or service which bears on its ability to meet stated or implied needs.'

In ordinary language, quality implies some degree of excellence or superiority. In an industrial context, it is defined in a much more functional way. Here, quality is more concerned with 'fitness for purpose', and quality management (or control) is about ensuring that products or services conform to specifications.

Juran defines quality as 'fitness for use', which in fact includes two elements.

(a) *Quality of design*, which can include the customer satisfactions built into the product.

(b) *Quality of conformance*, in other words a lack of defects in the finished goods

Quality must be considered from the viewpoint of both the consumer and the producer (or service provider).

The **consumer** – according to Deming the consumer is the most important part of the production line. Quality should be aimed at the needs of the consumer, present and future. This is driven by what the consumer wants and will pay for.

The **producer** – the product should be designed to meet or exceed the customer's expectations. Once a product has been properly designed the role of operations' managers is to ensure that the product actually produced meet the design specifications. This is done through product design, process design, process control and **conformance to specifications.**

Product design

- Assess customer needs
- Design a product to meet those needs at the least cost
- Involve customers, suppliers and manufacturing personnel
- SET – product specification*s*

Process design

- Process must be designed to meet final product design specification
- Design process while product is being designed to avoid inefficiencies in production or the need to redesign the product
- SET – process limits

Process control

- Ensure that the process actually produces a product that meets specifications
- This will happen if the process was designed correctly and if it is kept in control
- Keep the process within limits

ACTIVITY 1 (10 MINS)

The boss of Acme Umbrellas Ltd believes that customers want robust umbrellas, so he makes one *entirely* out of titanium (even the canopy) apart from some gold decoration. 'It is a bit heavy I suppose', he says, showing an example, 'but it's *perfectly* made, look at the gold pins and look at the perfect, flawless finish. Why don't people want it?'

1.3 QUALITY SYSTEMS

Quality systems include all activities that contribute to quality, directly or indirectly. Product quality depends on many variables, such as the calibre of the components or materials used; type of equipment used in design, production, handling, installation, testing and shipping; the equipment calibration and maintenance procedures employed; the training and experience of production and supervisory personnel; the level of 'workmanship'; and sometimes the environmental conditions (temperature, humidity, level of dust particles) in the area where the product is produced.

A Quality Management System (QMS) is the organised structure of responsibilities, activities, resources and events that together provide procedures and methods of implementation to ensure the capability of an organisation to meet quality requirements. To achieve this a QMS needs to be capable of:

- demonstrating continuous improvement
- preventing non-conformity
- assisting self-evaluation.

This QMS will consist of the documented rules, procedures and instructions prepared in accordance with agreed standards. These are stated in the quality manual as well as the associated core processes, procedures and work instructions. The document hierarchy is shown below.

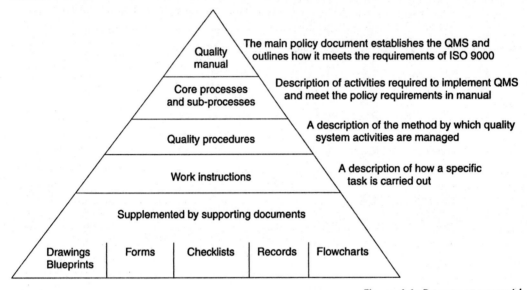

Figure 4.1: Document pyramid

1.4 QUALITY STANDARDS

ISO 9000 is intended to establish, document and maintain a system for ensuring the output quality of a process. It is the generic term for a series of five international standards (ISO 9000, 9001, 9002, 9003, and 9004) sponsored by the International Organisation for Standardisation (ISO), and created to standardise quality management systems for manufacturing and service industries worldwide. Each standard addresses a different aspect of quality assurance, depending on the needs of the user. ISO 9000 does not dictate the quality of *individual* goods and services, but aims to ensure that quality management *systems* of a suitable standard are in place. The standard does not cover every quality issue; it deals with quality systems. While it provides feedback about performance, it cannot guarantee that control action is taken; it is 'an indicator of potential, not of achievement'.

The ISO 9000 Standard Series is almost directly parallel to the British standard BS-5750 and is also identical, in most respects, to the European standard, EN-29000 and the American standard, Q9000. ISO 9000 certification is a tangible expression of a firm's commitment to quality that is internationally understood and accepted.

To gain certification an organisation:

- Prepares a quality manual which sets out the company's policy and procedures on quality assurance

- An assessor will visit the client company and review the facility's quality manual to ensure that it meets the standard and audit the firm's processes to ensure that the system documented in the quality manual is in place and that it is effective.

- The certificate is issued if approval is given. ISO 9000 will increasingly influence the choice of suppliers. Customers wish to avoid the cost of inspecting goods inwards.

- Once certification is obtained, the certifying body conducts audits of the facility once a year and oversees changes and evolutions of the facility's quality system to ensure that it continues to meet the requirements of the standard. ISO 9000 certification is a continuous process, and approval can be withdrawn.

1.5 THE QUALITY HIERARCHY

Methods of achieving quality have evolved over the years.

- Originally craftsmen individually crafted quality into the products they produced. People purchased products based on the craftsman's reputation, or 'hallmark'. The producer knew the customer directly

- Craftsmanship declined after the Industrial Revolution and volume became the goal of choice. The focus was on designing and building products for mass consumption and limiting customer choices. Quality control is maintained by inspecting and detecting bad products

- Things began to change around 1950. Japan was rebuilding and looking for markets for their products. To compete they combined low prices with improved quality. They developed new manufacturing and management techniques – a major innovation was statistical process control.

- During this time a new system was evolving based on the prevention of non-conforming products. Mistakes were not considered inevitable and could be prevented. They would be analysed and eliminated. This prevention of non-conformances is the basic concept of Quality Assurance that is promoted by ISO 9000.

- TQM was introduced to allow potential customers to determine what to design and build. Higher quality could be obtained by focusing on preventing problems and continuously reducing variability in all organisational processes.

Figure 4.2: The quality hierarchy

2 QUALITY CONTROL (QC)

2.1 INSPECTION

In the past quality control meant *inspection* of finished output or goods inward. Quality was assured at the *end* of the process, often by specialised quality control staff. Inspection is concerned with looking at products that have been made, supplies that have been delivered and services that have been provided, to establish whether they have been up to specification. It is a technique of *identifying* when defective items are being produced at an unacceptable level. Inspection is usually carried out at three main points:

(a) receiving inspection for raw materials and bought out components;
(b) floor or process inspection; and
(c) final inspection or testing.

The problems with this inspection approach are as follows.

(a) The inspection process itself does not 'add value': if it could be guaranteed that no defective items were produced, there would be no need for a separate inspection function.

(b) The production of substandard products wastes raw materials, machine time, and human effort.

(c) The inspection department takes up space, and has to be paid.

(d) The production of defects is not compatible with newer production techniques such as just-in-time: there is no time for inspection.

(e) Working capital is tied up in stocks that cannot be sold.

2.2 QUALITY CONTROL AND QUALITY STANDARDS

Quality control is concerned with maintaining quality standards. There are usually procedures to check quality of bought-in materials, work-in-progress and finished goods.

In the past, failure to screen quality successfully has resulted in rejections, re-work and scrap, all of which add to manufacturing costs. Modern trends in industry of competition, mass production and increasing standards of quality requirements have resulted in a thorough reappraisal of the problem and two important points have emerged:

1. It is necessary to single out and remove the causes for poor quality goods before production instead of waiting for the end result. Many companies have instigated 'zero defects' programmes following the Japanese practice of eradicating poor quality as early in the chain as possible and insisting on strict quality adherence at every stage – as Crosby points out in his book *Quality is Free*, this is cost effective since customer complaints etc. reduce dramatically.

2. The coordination of all activities from the preparation of the specification, through to the purchasing and inspection functions and right up to the function of delivery of the finished product, is essential.

It is accepted that it is not possible to achieve perfection in products because of the variations in raw material quality, operating skills, different types of machines used, wear and tear, etc. but quality control attempts to ascertain the amount of variation from perfect that can be expected in any operation. If this variation is acceptable according to engineering requirements, then production must be established within controlled limits and if the variation is too great then corrective action must be taken to bring it within acceptable limits.

2.3 QUALITY CONTROL AND INSPECTION

A distinction should be made between quality control and inspection.

(a) Quality control involves setting controls for the process of manufacture or service delivery. It is aimed at preventing the manufacture of defective items or the provision of defective services. The procedure is:

    (i) establishing standards of quality for a product or service;

    (ii) establishing procedures or production methods to ensure that these required standards of quality are met in a suitably high proportion of cases;

    (iii) monitoring actual quality; *and*

    (iv) taking control action when actual quality falls below standard.

(b) Inspection is a technique of identifying when defective items are being produced at an unacceptable level. Inspection is usually carried out at three main points.

    (i) Receiving inspection – for raw materials and purchased components
    (ii) Floor or process inspection for WIP
    (iii) Final inspection or testing for finished goods

EXAMPLE   **THE POSTAL SERVICE**

The postal service might establish a standard that 90% of first-class letters will be delivered on the day after they are posted, and 99% will be delivered within two days of posting.

- Procedures would have to be established for ensuring that these standards could be met (eg frequency of collections, automated letter sorting, frequency of deliveries and number of staff employed etc).

- Actual performance could be monitored, perhaps by taking samples from time to time of letters that are posted and delivered.

- If the quality standard is not being achieved, the management of the postal service could take control action (eg employ more postmen or advertise again the use of postcodes) or reduce the standard of quality of the service being provided.

2.4 ADVANTAGES OF QUALITY CONTROL

The advantages lie in the fact that quality control identifies why faulty work is being produced and the quantity of faulty work produced. Action taken as a result can reduce scrap and the amount of necessary re-work. It shows where a design modification could raise efficiency in manufacture. It minimises the chances of poor materials being processed.

The important factor is that quality control must be applied during processing and not after. The most effective areas where control can be usefully applied in most enterprises are:

- goods inwards;

- inspection at the supplier's business to see the type of plant and the methods used;

- inspection of all new tools and plant;

- inspection of the first part completed at each stage;

- the first part produced at each stage should be inspected;

- inspection should take place between processes;

- a final check should be made at the end of the production line and any minor adjustments made.

It is as much a fault to produce goods of too high a quality as goods of poor quality. The requirements of the customers must be borne in mind and the sales department and market research can advise on this. They will be aware of competitor's prices and qualities and a decision must be taken whether or not to increase quality. To increase quality means increasing costs and at what point will the quality be more than the customer can afford?

3   QUALITY ASSURANCE (QA)

3.1 ACCEPTABLE STANDARD

Quality assurance is about designing a process of which the end result is guaranteed to be of an acceptable standard, because of the checks that have been made along the way. It goes beyond inspection and quality control to embrace the whole organisation in trying to ensure that the quality of the product/service is of the required standard. In order to fulfil this objective, a company should have clear policies on quality together with precise and measurable objectives. In this way all employees will know exactly what is required in terms of product quality. Policies on quality will depend upon what standards the market requires. This means that effective quality assurance depends upon reliable market research to ascertain what the quality requirements of the customer are.

Obviously, the position and sector within the market will dictate the level of quality required. Having established the quality standards, the initiative is upon the operational department management to ensure that the standards are complied with.

3.2 SUPPLIER QUALITY ASSURANCE (SQA)

Supplier quality assurance (SQA) is the term used where a supplier guarantees the quality of goods supplied and allows the customer access while the goods are being manufactured. This is usually done through SQA officers, who control the specification of the goods supplied. Usually, the customer and supplier agree inspection procedures and quality control standards and checks are made to ensure that they are being adhered to.

- The customer can almost eliminate goods inwards inspection and items can be directed straight to production. This can give large savings in cost and time in flow production, and can facilitate JIT production.

- The supplier produces to the customer's requirement, thereby reducing rejects and the cost of producing substitutes.

Suppliers' quality assurance schemes are being used increasingly, particularly where extensive sub-contracting work is carried out, for example in the motor industries. One such scheme is BS EN ISO 9000 (formerly BS 5750) certification. This is a nationally promoted standard, only awarded after audit and inspection of a company's operations. A company that gains registration has a certificate testifying that it is operating to a structure of written policies and procedures which are designed to ensure that it can consistently deliver a product or service to meet customer requirements. The British Standards Institution is the largest of the certification bodies.

Some companies follow Japanese practice and use supervisors, work people or quality circles to control suppliers' quality. These representatives or the SQA officer may enter the supplier's plant, to verify that production is to the correct specification, working tolerances, material and labour standards. For example, the Ministry of Defence would reserve the right to ensure that defence contractors produce to specification, since defective work could mean the failure of a multi-million pound aircraft, loss of trained pilots and possibly ground crew as well as damage to civilian life and property. Likewise, a weapons system failure could have disastrous consequences.

One great advantage of SQA is that it may render possible reduction of the in-house quality control headcount, since there will be no need to check incoming materials or sub-assemblies or components. Statistical quality control through sampling techniques is commonly used to reduce costs and production interruptions.

ACTIVITY 2 (10 MINS)

Does your organisation have BS EN ISO 9000 certification? Do its competitors? Would it be worthwhile for your organisation to gain certification? If not, why not?

3.3 QUALITY ASSURANCE OF GOODS INWARDS

The quality of output depends on the quality of input materials, and so quality control should include procedures for acceptance and inspection of goods inwards and measurement of rejects. Each supplier can be given a 'rating' for the quality of the goods they tend to supply, and preference with purchase orders can be given to well-rated suppliers. This method is referred to as 'vendor rating'.

Where a quality assurance scheme is in place the supplier guarantees the quality of goods supplied and allows the customers' inspectors access while the items are being manufactured. The onus is on the supplier to carry out the necessary quality checks, or face cancellation of the contract.

3.4 INSPECTION OF OUTPUT

This will take place at various key stages in the production process and will provide a continual check that the production process is under control. The aim of inspection is *not* really to sort out the bad products from the good ones after the work has been done. The aim is to satisfy management that quality control in production is being maintained.

The inspection of samples rather than 100% testing of all items will keep inspection costs down, and smaller samples will be less costly to inspect than larger samples. The greater the confidence in the reliability of production methods and process control, the smaller the samples will be.

3.5 STATISTICAL PROCESS CONTROL (SPC)

Statistical process control (SPC) is a method of monitoring processes and process variation. The purpose is to identify causes for process variations and resolve them. Process variables may include rework, scrap, inconsistent raw materials, and downtime on equipment. It is used to monitor the consistency of processes used to manufacture a product as designed. No matter how good or bad the design, SPC can ensure that the product is being manufactured as designed and intended. Thus, SPC will not improve a poorly designed product's reliability, but can be used to maintain the consistency of how the product is made and, therefore, of the manufactured product itself and its as-designed reliability.

Statistical quality control refers to using statistical techniques for measuring and improving the *quality* of processes and includes SPC in addition to other techniques, such as sampling plans, experimental design, variation reduction, process capability analysis, and process improvement plans. A primary tool used for SPC is the control chart, a graphical representation of certain descriptive statistics for specific quantitative measurements of the manufacturing process.

A typical control chart is shown below. The horizontal axis on the graph is time, the vertical axis is the physical dimension of the product in appropriate units. Above and below the level of the expected dimension of the product are the control limits. The graph shows inner warning limits and outer action limits although in many cases only one limit is used. The limits are set such a distance from the expected dimension that a value outside the limits is very unlikely to have occurred by chance and consequently the size of the deviation from the expected dimension indicates that something may have gone wrong with the manufacturing process. Normally, the values plotted on the chart would be the mean of a small sample taken at regular points in time.

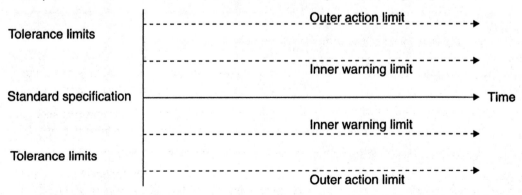

Figure 4.3: Quality control chart

Representational samples of an output manufacturing process may be taken daily or even every hour, and faults in the manufacturing process which are revealed may be fairly simple to correct by adjusting the appropriate machinery.

If output exceeds the control limits consistently, more urgent management action would be called for, because this would indicate a systematic fault such as those below.

- Inefficiency in production, by labour or the machines
- Inadequacy in production methods
- Inadequate quality of raw materials and components
- Excessively tight tolerances in the first place

The ultimate goal of SPC is the reduction of variation.

4 TOTAL QUALITY MANAGEMENT (TQM)

DEFINITION

ISO 8402:1994 defines **total quality management** (TQM) as a management approach of an organisation centred on quality, based on the participation of all its members and aiming at long-term success. This is achieved through customer satisfaction and benefits to all members of the organisation and to society.

In other words, TQM is a philosophy for managing an organisation in a way that enables it to meet stakeholder needs and expectations efficiently and effectively, without compromising ethical values.

4.1 TQM PHILOSOPHY

The basic principles for the Total Quality Management (TQM) philosophy of doing business are to satisfy the customer, satisfy the supplier, and continuously improve the business processes.

TQM is a management philosophy that seeks to integrate all organisational functions (marketing, finance, design, engineering, production, customer service etc) to focus on meeting customer needs and organisational objectives. It views organisations as a collection of processes.

It maintains that organisations must strive to continuously improve these processes by incorporating the knowledge and experiences of workers. The simple objective of TQM is to 'Do the right things, right the first time, every time.' Every mistake, delay and misunderstanding, directly costs the organisation money through wasted time and effort, including time taken in pacifying customers. The lost potential for future sales because of poor customer service must also be taken into account.

(a) The first and major TQM principle is to **satisfy the customer** – the person who pays for the product or service. Customers want to get their money's worth from a product or service they purchase. A company that seeks to satisfy the customer by providing them with value for what they buy and with the quality they expect will get more repeat business, referral business, and reduced complaints and service expenses. Some top companies not only provide quality products, but they also give extra service to make their customers feel important and valued.

Often in a company, there is a chain of customers, each improving a product and passing it along until it is finally sold to the external customer. Each worker must not only seek to satisfy the immediate internal customer, but he or she must look up the chain to try to satisfy the ultimate customer.

(b) A second TQM principle is to **satisfy the supplier**, which is the person or organisation from whom you are purchasing goods or services. A company must look to satisfy their external suppliers by providing them with clear instructions and requirements and then paying them fairly and on time. It is only in the company's best interest that its suppliers provide it with quality goods or services, if the company hopes to provide quality goods or services to its external customers.

A manager must try to keep his or her workers happy and productive by providing good task instructions, the tools they need to do their job and good working conditions. The manager must also reward the workers with praise and good pay. The reason to do this is to get more productivity out of the workers, as well as to retain the good workers.

One area of satisfying the internal suppler is by empowering the workers. This means to allow them to make decisions on things that they can control. This not only takes the burden off the manager, but it also motivates these internal suppliers to do better work. Empowerment therefore has two key aspects.

(i) Allowing workers to have the freedom to decide how to do the necessary work, using the skills they possess and acquiring new skills as necessary to be an effective team member.

(ii) Making workers responsible for achieving production targets and for quality control.

(c) The third principle of TQM is **continuous improvement**. Management can never be satisfied with the method used, because there can always be improvements. The aim should be to 'get it more right next time'. Certainly, the competition is improving, so it is very necessary to strive to keep ahead of the game. Some companies have tried to improve by making employees work harder. This may be counter-productive, especially if the process itself is flawed. For example, trying to increase worker output on a defective machine may result in more defective parts. Examining the source of problems and delays and then improving them is what is needed. Often the process has bottlenecks that are the real cause of the problem. These must be removed.

Workers are often a source of continuous improvements. They can provide suggestions on how to improve a process and eliminate waste or unnecessary work.

4.2 TOOLS AND TECHNIQUES

There are a number of approaches to take towards adopting the TQM philosophy. The teachings of Deming, Juran, Taguchi, Ishikawa, Imai, Oakland etc can all help an organisation realign itself and embrace the TQM philosophy. However, there is no single methodology, only a collection of tools and techniques. Examples of tools include:

- flowcharting
- statistical process control (SPC)
- Pareto analysis
- cause and effect diagrams
- employee and customer surveys

Examples of techniques include:

- benchmarking
- cost of quality
- quality function deployment
- failure mode effects analysis
- design of experiments

Measurements – after using the tools and techniques an organisation needs to establish the degree of improvement. Any number of techniques can be used for this including self-assessment, audits and SPC.

TQM initiatives have been prone to failure because of common mistakes. These include:

- allowing external forces and events to drive a TQM initiative

- an overwhelming desire for quality awards and certificates

- organising and perceiving TQM activities as separate from day-to-day work responsibilities

- treating TQM as an add-on with little attention given to the required changes in organisation and culture

- senior management underestimating the necessary commitment to TQM

4.3 DESIGN FOR QUALITY

A TQM environment aims to get it right first time, and this means that **quality, not faults, must be designed into the organisation's products, services and operations from the outset.**

Quality control happens at various stages in the process of designing a product or service.

(a) At the **product design stage**, quality control means trying to design a product or service so that its specifications provide a suitable balance between price and quality (of sales and delivery, as well as manufacture), which will make the product or service competitive.

(b) **Production engineering** is the **process of designing the methods for making a product** (or service) **to the design specification**. It sets out to make production methods as efficient as possible, and to avoid the manufacture of sub-standard items.

(c) **Information systems** should be designed to get the required information to the right person at the right time; **distribution systems** should be designed to get the right item to the right person at the right time; and so on.

As well as physical products, quality also applies to service businesses such as banks and restaurants. Quality issues arise in a number of areas.

- Customer expectations
- The process by which the service is delivered
- The attitudes and demeanour of the people giving the service
- The environment of the service encounter

4.4 QUALITY CIRCLES

A quality circle is a group of employees who meet regularly to discuss problems of quality and quality control in their area of work, and perhaps to suggest ways of improving it. The main aim is to be able to offer management:

(a) ideas connected with improvement and recommendation;
(b) possible solutions and suggestions;
(c) organising the implementation of the ideas and solutions

Quality circles have emerged as a mechanism to develop and utilise the tremendous potential of people for improvement in product quality and productivity. The development of quality circles allows the process of decision-making to start at shop floor level, with the ordinary worker encouraged to comment and make suggestions, as well as being allowed to put them into practice. Circle members experience the responsibility for ensuring quality, and have the power to exercise verbal complaint. General productivity is considered as well as reduced frustration and grievances and reduced labour turnover. Quality circles may be applied at any level of organisational activity, being used to cover all aspects and could conceivably involve all employees.

The benefits arising from the use of quality circles are substantial:

- improved quality leading to greater customer satisfaction;

- greater motivation of employees;

- improved productivity;

- shop floor understand and share management/customers problems;

- a spirit of seeking improvements is generated;

- employees become more aware of opportunities for improvement because of training, in areas outside quality circles.

4.5 CONTINUOUS IMPROVEMENT

Quality management is not a one-off process, but is the continual examination and improvement of existing processes. The idea of continuous improvement might appear to go against the law of diminishing returns, in that it might be arguable that there is a limit beyond which there is no point in pursuing any further improvements.

Advocates of continuous improvement, however, believe that this 'law' does not always apply. Remember, that continuous improvement does not only apply to the finished product, but also to the processes which give rise to it.

- It is not easy to determine where diminishing returns set in.

- A philosophy of continuous improvement ensures that management are not *complacent,* which can be a cultural disaster.

- Customer needs change, so a philosophy of continuous improvement enables these changes to be taken into account in the normal course of events.

- New technologies or materials might be developed, enabling cost savings or design improvements.

- Rarely do businesses know every possible fact about the production process. Continuous improvement encourages experimentation and a scientific approach to production.

- It is a way of tapping employees' knowledge.

- Reducing *variability* is a key issue for quality

- Improvement on a continual, step-by-step basis is more prudent in some cases than changing everything at once.

Holmes proposes an eight-stage model for improving quality.

Step 1   **Find out the problems** (eg from customer and employees).

Step 2   **Select action targets** from the number of improvement projects identified in Step 1, on the basis of cost, safety, importance and feasibility with current resources.

Step 3   **Collect data** about the problem.

Step 4   **Analyse data** by a variety of techniques to assess common factors behind the data, to tease out any hidden messages the data might contain.

Step 5   **Identify possible causes** (eg using brainstorming sessions). No ideas are ruled out of order.

Step 6   **Plan improvement action**. Significant help might be required.

Step 7   **Monitor the effects of the improvement.**

Step 8   **Communicate the result.**

Reducing variability often requires improving the process itself, rather than changing the machines or adjusting them.

ACTIVITY 3 (15 MINS)

You have just overheard the following conversation. The board of a company are in a meeting and they are having a 'full and frank exchange of views' (ie a blazing row).

Chairman : Ladies and gentlemen, *please....*

Marketing director: No, he's said quite enough. Customers are our department, and all this TQM nonsense is just another, yes *another* example of those jargon-spouting boffins and bodgers in production trying to encroach on my turf! I *do* need resources. I don't need white-coated robots criticising the angles at which I fix the paper clips on to my reports!

Chairman: Ladies and gentlemen, *please.....*

Production director: No, she's said quite enough. Marketing people couldn't give one hoot, let alone two, about quality and we all know it's quality that sells the goods. Remember, when we had to abandon our solar powered torch? State of the art, state of *the art* that was, and did they try and sell it? Did they?

Chairman: Ladies and gentlemen, *please....*

Finance director: No, they've both said quite enough. If all we get out of TQM is pointless rows like this, I might as well go back and count some more beans. At least it's *meaningful and* relaxing.

Chairman: Ladies and gentlemen! No, you've all said *quite* enough. Not one of you has grasped the point. I'd better get another management consultant in with a better flipchart.

What insights do each of the above characters have into TQM?

4.6 THE POTENTIAL BENEFITS OF QUALITY PROCESSES

Glyn Thomas in *Accounting Technician* provides a useful summary of the benefits of TQM.

> 'It makes quality the central concern of the business. Too often, quality is either confused with addressing customer complaints which inevitably leads to it being viewed negatively, or is viewed as a direct measure of the product or service itself. Instead, all activities that are involved should be considered. Quality should be inherent in every facet of the business and not just a 'bolt-on extra'.

A key factor of [TQM] is that it can apply to all or parts of your business, so there may be scope for partially introducing it and then expanding it at a later date. Applied to the whole business however, it will allow a holistic approach to quality throughout the whole company and have an effect from shop floor through to ordering, sales and management.

It reduces wastage and mistakes, and therefore leads to contracts being completed on time without unnecessary remedial work. In addition, due to built-in fault-logging procedures, it is unlikely that problems will be duplicated in the future.

ACTIVITY 4 (10 MINS)

(a) What are the potential benefits of training for quality?
(b) What are the potential benefits of quality control?

5 MANAGING AND MONITORING QUALITY

5.1 ORGANISATIONAL IMPLICATIONS

Introducing TQM involves a significant shake up.

- TQM is associated with giving employees a say in the process (eg in the *quality survey)* and in getting them to suggest improvements.

- TQM implies a greater discipline to the process of production and the establishment of better linkages between the business functions.

- TQM involves new relationships with suppliers, which requires them to improve their output quality so that less effort is spent rectifying poor input. Long-term relationships with a small number of suppliers might be preferable to choosing material and sub-components on price.

- It requires both work standardisation and employee commitment.

5.2 QUALITY MANAGEMENT

Quality management suggests a concern that the organisation's products or services meet their planned level of quality and perform to specifications. Management has a duty to ensure that all tasks are completed consistently to a standard that meets the needs of the business. To achieve this they need to:

(a) set clear standards
(b) plan how to meet those standards
(c) monitor the quality achieved
(d) take action to improve quality where necessary.

Setting standards – to manage quality everyone in the organisation needs to have a clear and shared understanding of the standards required. These standards will be set after taking account of:

(a) the quality expected by the customers
(b) the costs and benefits of delivering different degrees of quality
(c) the impact of different degrees of quality on:
    (i) the customers and their needs
    (ii) contribution to departmental objectives
    (iii) employee attitude and motivation

Having decided on the standards these must be communicated to everyone concerned to ensure that the right standards are achieved. Documentation of the standards must be clear, specific, measurable and comprehensive.

Meeting the standards – having decided on appropriate quality standards management should then:

(a)   agree and document procedures and methods to meet the standards

(b)   agree and document controls to ensure that the standards will be met

(c)   agree and document responsibilities via job descriptions and terms of reference

(d)   prepare and implement training plans for employees to ensure they are familiar with the standards, procedures, controls and their responsibilities

Monitoring the quality – after the process to achieve quality has been established, an information system to monitor the quality should be set up, which can be used constructively to improve quality and work on problem areas.

Monitoring customer reaction – some sub-standard items will inevitably be produced. Checks during production will identify some bad output, but other items will reach the customer who is the ultimate judge of quality. Complaints ought to be monitored in the form of letters of complaint, returned goods, penalty discounts, claims under guarantee, or requests for visits by service engineers. Some companies actually survey customers on a regular basis.

Employees within the organisation have a huge influence on the quality of their work and to gain their commitment and support the management should:

(a)   publish the quality being achieved

(b)   meet regularly with the staff involved to discuss the quality being achieved as well as the vulnerabilities and priorities as they see them and also agree specific issues and action points for them to work on to improve quality

(c)   encourage ideas from the staff about improvements and consider introducing short-term suggestion schemes

Take action – it takes commitment to quality and excellence. *Tom Peters'* advice to managers is: 'Starting this afternoon, don't walk past a shoddy product or service without comment and action – ever again!'

In his seminars on quality he poses a situation where a brochure is going out to customers. The deadline is missed; five thousand have been printed, inserted into envelopes, addressed and sealed. They are packed and ready to take to the post office. The unit you are in charge of has a not-too-healthy cash flow. You then discover a single typo on page two, in the small print. Should you walk past it or act?

He argues that you should act and throw it out. If you knowingly ignore a tiny act of poor service or quality, you have destroyed your credibility and any possibility of moral leadership on this issue.

ACTIVITY 5 (10 MINS)

Read the following extract from an article in the *Financial Times* and then explain how the bank could monitor the impact of the initiative.

'If you telephone a Lloyds TSB call centre it rings five times before there is a reply; if the person who answers does not introduce him or herself by name during the conversation; if you are standing in a queue in a branch with more people in it than the number of tills, then something is wrong.'

'If any of these things happen then the branch is breaching standards of customer service set by the bank since last July ... the "service challenge" was launched in the bank's 1,888 branches last summer after being tested in 55 branches ...'

'Lloyds already has evidence of the impact. Customers were more satisfied with pilot branches last year than with others.'

5.3 DIFFICULTIES

Managers find some aspects of TQM particularly hard to accept.

- Social and status barriers are removed with the removal of office partitions.

- Administrative functions must now be seen as supporting the shop floor.

- The shop floor is the most important area.

- Managers are judged by their contribution to team spirit, not 'the virility of their decisions'.

- Meetings are used to gather information, not to take decisions.

- New personal skills are needed (eg the ability to listen and communicate).

- A manager's role is in supporting and training, not disciplining and restricting.

Holmes believes that managers most suited for a TQM culture will 'understand how people motivate themselves and direct this motivation towards good team results. They are concerned with achieving the goals of the team, supporting the individual members of the team, and keeping the team together'. They will 'ensure time is spent setting objectives, planning, briefing, controlling, evaluating. These activities will be conducted in a participatory or controllable way'.

5.4 CREATING A CULTURE OF IMPROVEMENT

TQM is more than just a philosophy. It is the culture of an organisation committed to total customer satisfaction through continuous improvement and in which resources, material, equipment and quality management systems are cost effectively implemented and fully utilised.

TQM is impossible to achieve when the pervasive organisational culture is hostile to it. When the basic mechanisms of an organisational culture such as language, artefacts and symbols, behavioural patterns, basic underlying assumptions and subcultures do not operate in total accord then the whole social organisation may be in trouble. In the final analysis, a receptive organisational culture is a prerequisite of total quality management.

Guiding the change process requires an understanding of the present organisational cultures, attitudes, structures and systems. Employees often have a poor attitude towards quality, as a system imposed 'from outside' by non-operational staff and as an implication of lack of trust in workers to maintain quality standards or to apply a control system with objectivity themselves. Attitudes to quality control and the management of it have, however, been undergoing changes.

- As the pace of change in the environment has increased so attention to quality and a commitment to quality standards has become a vital factor for organisational adaptation and survival.

- It is being recognised that workers can be motivated by a positive approach to quality: producing quality work is a tangible and worthwhile objective. Where responsibility for quality checking has been given to the worker himself (encouraging self-supervision), job satisfaction may be increased: it is a kind of job enrichment, and also a sign of trust and respect, because imposed controls have been removed.

- Non-aversive ways of implementing quality control have been devised. Cultural orientation (the deep 'belief' in quality, filtered down to all operatives) can be enlisted. Inter-group competition to meet and beat quality standards, for example, might be encouraged.

Problems can therefore be overcome by changing people's attitudes rather than teaching them new tricks. The key issue is to instil understanding of, and commitment to, working practices that lead to quality.

5.5 PARTICIPATION

Participation is important in TQM, especially in the process of continuous improvement, where workforce views are valued. The management task is to encourage everybody to contribute. When TQM is successful employees at every level participate in decisions affecting their work. Employee involvement practices include:

- Suggestion system – programme that elicits individual employee suggestions on improving work or the work environment.

- Survey feedback – attitude survey data are used to encourage, structure, and measure the effectiveness of employee participation.

- Quality circle – employees that meet voluntarily to identify and suggest work-related improvements.

- Quality of work-life committee – usually focuses on issues to improve organisational performance and employee work-life

- Job redesign – to increase employee performance for example, job enlargement to increase use of employee skills, broaden the variety of work performed and provide the individual with greater autonomy.

- Self-managing team – group of employees given responsibility for a product or service and empowered to make decisions about tasks and work methods.

However, the barriers to participation are numerous.

- An autocratic chief executive, who believes he or she is the sole key to the process.

- Individualism, in which people 'possess' ideas in order to take credit for them rather than share them for mutual benefit.

- Ideas of managers as leaders and directors rather than facilitators and supporters.

- Middle managers who feel their authority is threatened.

5.6 W EDWARDS DEMING

Based on his work with Japanese managers and others, Deming outlined fourteen steps that managers in any type of organisation can take to implement a total quality management programme. The key points include:

- **Create constancy of purpose** – this requires innovation, investment in research and education, continuous improvement of product and service, maintenance of equipment, furniture and fixtures, and new aids to production.

- **Cease mass production** – inspect products and services only enough to be able to identify ways to improve the process.

- **Drive out fear** and build employee trust. Managers need to create an environment where workers can express concerns with confidence.

- **Break down departmental barriers** (create win-win situations). Fostering interrelationships among departments encourages higher quality decision-making.

- **Seek long-term supplier relationships** – the lowest priced goods are not always the highest quality; choose a supplier based on its record of improvement and then make a long-term commitment to it.

- **Eliminate numerical goals**; abolish annual rating or merit systems.

- **Eliminate slogans** – they provide no value in terms of improving quality.

Deming gave a new perspective to the benefits of improving quality. This he gave in the form of a chain reaction, which is illustrated below:

Figure 4.4: The Deming chain reaction

5.7 BARRIERS TO QUALITY AND EXCELLENCE

It has been shown that it is much easier to achieve quality and excellence in a new business, where the principles are built in from the start. It is much harder to develop and improve quality and excellence in an existing company because it may be necessary to overcome a series of barriers. These barriers may be human, technical or financial.

(a) Human barriers exist because people are naturally resistant to change. Some kind of revolutionary process is usually necessary to provide the momentum and incentive for change. This transformation of attitudes needs total commitment from the top and requires one or more champions as well as involvement at all levels.

(b) Technical barriers concern the knowledge and skills that are required to plan, implement and control the best performance practices.

(c) The finance required to sustain excellence and improve quality may be yet another barrier for the company to surmount.

5.8 QUALITY AUDITS, ASSESSMENTS AND REVIEWS

Quality assessment is a process of identifying business practices, attitudes and activities that are either inhibiting or enhancing the achievement of quality improvement. The purpose of assessment is to:

- supply proof that quality improvement measures are necessary;
- provide a base for future measurement;
- build support for quality measures; and
- convince senior management that the issue is important.

The quality control function looks at the process as a continuous operation, a series of trends and rejection rates. Reports from the quality control department to management include:

(a)   analysis of defects by cause;
(b)   comparisons between processes and departments;
(c)   comparison of defect levels with previous levels and standard levels;
(d)   longer term trends in quality;
(e)   reports on customers' complaints;
(f)   developments in quality control practice; and
(g)   special reports.

Apart from receiving reports, management may also commission a quality control audit to find answers to the following questions:

(a)   What is the actual level of rejects?

(b)   Are the standards fairly set?

(c)   Are the standards achieved at the expense of excessive costs?

(d)   What is the number of customer complaints?

(e)   Has the quality control system been modified in accordance with changes in processing policies, materials and products?

(f)   What are the costs of quality control?

(g)   What is done to improve performance by eliminating causes of poor performance?

(h)   Should a personnel audit on efficiency and knowledge be carried out?

Assessments and reviews of the systems and procedures are an ongoing activity in excellent companies. The responsibility for quality control cannot be isolated as we have seen and can only be effective when it is the result of joint effort. The advantages lie in the fact that quality control points out why faulty work is being produced and the extent of it. Action taken as a result can reduce scrap and the amount of necessary re-work. It shows where a design modification could raise efficiency in manufacture. It minimises the chances of poor materials being processed.

The requirements of the customers must be continually reviewed and the sales department and market research can advise on this. They will be aware of competitors' prices and qualities and a decision must be taken whether or not to increase quality. To increase quality may mean increasing costs and establishing the point at which the customer will decide that the quality is more than he or she can afford.

6 COSTS OF QUALITY

When we talk about quality-related costs you should remember that a concern for **good quality saves money**; it is **poor quality that costs money**.

DEFINITION

Prevention costs are the costs of any action taken to investigate, prevent or reduce defects and failures.

Appraisal costs are the costs of assessing the quality achieved.

Internal failure costs are the costs arising within the organisation of failing to achieve the required level of quality.

External failure costs are the costs arising outside the organisation of failing to achieve the required level of quality (after transfer of ownership to the customer).

EXAMPLE   QUALITY-RELATED COSTS

Quality-related cost	Example
Prevention costs	Quality engineering
	Design/development of quality control/inspection equipment
	Maintenance of quality control/inspection equipment
	Administration of quality control
	Training in quality control
Appraisal costs	Acceptance testing
	Inspection of goods inwards
	Inspection costs of in-house processing
	Performance testing
Internal failure costs	Failure analysis
	Re-inspection costs
	Losses from failure of purchased items
	Losses due to lower selling prices for sub-quality goods
	Costs of reviewing product specifications after failures
External failure costs	Administration of customer complaints section
	Costs of customer service section
	Product liability costs
	Cost of repairing products returned from customers
	Cost of replacing items due to sub-standard products/marketing errors

EXAMPLE   COST OF POOR QUALITY

A manufacturer's inspection procedures indicate that one faulty item out of every 1,000 good items produced is sent to a customer. The management regards this as acceptable, as a replacement will be supplied free of charge. Unit sales are 10,000,000 per year, and each unit costs £20 to manufacture and makes a profit of £5. It is probable that every customer who buys a faulty product will return it, and will thenceforth buy a similar product from another company. The average customer buys two units a year. Marketing costs per new customer are £10 per year.

(a)   What is your best estimate of the net cost of this policy for a year?
(b)   What name(s) would you give to quality-related costs of this type?
(c)   Could the situation be improved by incurring other types of quality-related cost?

ANSWER

(a)   Presumed number of bad units delivered a year = 10,000,000/1,000 = 10,000

	£
Cost of defects 10,000 × £20	200,000
Cost of free replacement 10,000 × £20	200,000
Manufacturing cost	400,000
Marketing costs for replacement customers £10 × 10,000	100,000
Gross cost of poor quality	500,000
Less income from original sale	250,000
Net cost of poor quality	250,000

Although the cost of the original defective item is recovered, the company **does not get it right first time**. The company has still suffered the cost of the replacement and the cost of replacing the customer by marketing to new customers.

(b)   The cost of replacements is an external failure cost; the cost of defects and the new marketing costs are internal failure costs.

(c)   It appears that the manufacturer already incurs *appraisal* costs, since there are inspection procedures for goods about to be despatched. The reason(s) for the fault should be established (a further *internal failure* cost) and the extent of the problem should be more precisely ascertained (further *appraisal* costs), since it is not certain that all dissatisfied customers return their goods, though it is highly likely that their business is lost. Once this has been done it will be possible to decide whether, by spending more on *prevention,* the overall cost of poor quality can be reduced.

6.1 TRADITIONAL ACCOUNTING SYSTEMS AND THE COST OF QUALITY

Traditionally, the **costs of scrapped units, wasted materials and reworking** have been **subsumed within the costs of production** by assigning the costs of an expected level of loss (a normal loss) to the costs of good production, while **accounting for other costs of poor quality within production or marketing overheads.** So such costs are not only **considered as inevitable** but are not highlighted for management attention.

Traditional accounting reports **tend also to ignore the hidden but real costs of excessive stock levels** (held to enable faulty material to be replaced without hindering production) **and the facilities necessary for storing that stock.** The introduction of a system of **just-in-time** purchasing and manufacturing should eradicate such costs, however. A just-in-time production system is driven by demand from customers for finished products so that components on a production line are only produced when needed for the next stage of production, thereby eradicating stocks of work in progress and finished goods. In a just-in-time purchasing system, materials are not delivered until they are needed in production, thereby eradicating stock of raw materials.

To **implement a TQM programme, costs of quality** must be **highlighted separately** within accounting reports so that *all* employees are aware of the cost of poor quality.

6.2 EXPLICIT AND IMPLICIT COSTS OF QUALITY

Explicit costs of quality are those that are recorded in accounting records, to be separately highlighted with the implementation of a TQM programme.

Implicit costs of quality are not recorded in accounting records. They tend to be of two forms.

- **Opportunity costs** such as the loss of future sales to a customer dissatisfied with faulty goods

- **Costs which tend to be subsumed** within other account headings such as costs which result from the disruptions caused by stockouts due to faulty purchases

CHAPTER ROUNDUP

- Quality control happens at various stages in the process of designing a product or service.

- Quality control is aimed at preventing the manufacture of defective items or the provision of defective services. Inspection is a technique for identifying when defective items are being produced at an unacceptable level.

- The costs associated with a concern for quality are prevention costs, appraisal costs, internal failure costs and external failure costs.

- Explicit costs of quality are those that are recorded in accounting records, to be separately highlighted. Implicit costs of quality are not recorded in accounting records.

- Quality assurance procedures should not be confined to the production process but must also cover the work of sales, distribution and administration departments, the efforts of external suppliers and the reaction of external customers.

- Total quality management (TQM) is the process of applying a zero defect philosophy to the management of all resources and relationships within an organisation as a means of developing and sustaining a culture of continuous improvement which focuses on meeting customer expectations.

QUICK QUIZ

1   What are the two elements in Juran's definition of quality as 'fitness for use'?

2   How does the quality hierarchy progress?

3   What are the three main points at which inspection is usually carried out?

4   What is statistical process control?

5   What is the simple objective of TQM?

6   What are the four aspects of the process of managing quality?

7   What are internal failure costs?

8   Provide two examples of external failure costs.

ANSWERS TO QUICK QUIZ

1   The two elements are:

- quality of design
- quality of conformance

2   The quality hierarchy progresses from inspection, through quality control, quality assurance to total quality management

3
- Receiving inspection for raw materials and purchased components
- Floor or process inspection for WIP
- Final inspection or testing for finished goods

4   Statistical process control (SPC) is a method of monitoring processes and process variation. The purpose is to identify causes for process variations and resolve them.

5   The simple objective of TQM is to 'Do the right things, right the first time, every time.'

6   The costs arising within the organisation of failure to achieve the quality specified.

7   Administration of customer complaints section
Costs of customer service section
Product liability costs
Cost of repairing products returned from customers

8   Cost of providing replacement items due to sub-standard product or marketing errors.

ANSWERS TO ACTIVITIES

1   The *design quality* is poor, in that it does not meet customer requirements in an *appropriate* way. The umbrella is, however, perfectly made, so its *conformance quality* is *high*.

2   This quality standard is aimed at manufacturing companies. It is useful to some companies because it demonstrates they are in control of their business, and have proved it to a certification body. ISO 9000 registration is a good way of measuring progress and monitoring maintenance of the standard. It reduces the need for customer supplier demonstration of quality assurance procedures by its introduction and ensures that the organisation's product is compatible with EU and USA quality procedures.

There are many different reasons for implementing the standard.

(a)   Pressure from large customers
(b)   To maintain contracts with existing customers
(c)   To use the constraints of the standard to prevent scrap
(d)   To reduce auditing of the quality system by customers
(e)   To make reference to the standard on company letterhead paper
(f)   To get the kitemark symbol on the company's product
(g)   To enforce discipline on employees

3   The chairman has got the gist. All of them miss the point as to the nature of TQM. The marketing director has a point in that TQM *does* imply a blurring of functional boundaries, but the marketing director *ought* to be pleased that, if TQM is implemented, the marketing concept will be brought into product design.

       The production director still has not grasped the concept. His idea of quality is 'technical excellence' not fitness for use. The finance director ought to care, as TQM has meaningful cost implications. The row is not pointless: at least the issue is being discussed, which is a beginning.

4   (a)   The potential benefits of training for quality include improved quality of output, improved productivity and greater job satisfaction and commitment on the part of employees.

       (b)   The benefits of quality control come from savings in quality-related costs, from improvements in customer relations and hopefully (because of the quality of the final product) increased sales revenue due to increased sales demand.

5   A wide variety of answers is possible. The article goes on to explain how the bank has monitored the initiative.

       (a)   It has devised a 100 point scale showing average satisfaction with branch service.

       (b)   It conducts a 'first impressions' survey of all new customers.

       (c)   There is also a general survey carried out every six months which seeks the views of a weighted sample of 350 customers per branch.

       (d)   A survey company telephones each branch anonymously twice a month to test how staff respond to enquiries about products.

       (e)   A quarter of each branch's staff answer a monthly questionnaire about the bank's products to test their knowledge.

       (f)   Groups of employees working in teams in branches are allowed to set their own additional standards. This is to encourage participation.

       (g)   Branches that under perform are more closely watched by 24 managers who monitor the initiative.

Chapter 05

Organisational performance

Introduction

Organisational control is the process whereby an organisation ensures that it is pursuing strategies and actions that will enable it to achieve its goals. The measurement and evaluation of performance are central to control and involve posing four basic questions

- What has happened?
- Why has it happened?
- Is it going to continue?
- What are we going to do about it?

The first question can be answered by performance measurement. Management will then have to hand far more useful information than it would otherwise have in order to answer the other three questions. By finding out what has actually been happening, senior management can determine with considerable certainty which direction the company is going in and, if all is going well, continue with the good work. Or, if the performance measurements indicate that there are difficulties on the horizon, management can then make adjustments or even alter course altogether with plenty of time to spare.

Change in organisations is always the result of some external influence. Even seemingly small internal changes can be traced back to an external source. In this chapter we shall consider the environment of the organisation, specifically those influences stemming from political, economic, social and technological forces.

Your objectives

After completing this chapter you should be able to:

- Monitor systems and work activities and identify problems and opportunities for improvement

- Recommend improvements which align with the organisation's objectives and goals and which result in improvements

- Report on the wider implications of proposed changes within the organisation

1 MONITORING SYSTEMS

1.1 MONITORING AND CONTROL

Monitoring in simple terms means watching over something that is happening. Generally the word also carries a sense of warning: detecting things that are going wrong. Active monitoring systems ensure that the organisation is quickly aware of changes in the market place (competitors' actions, changes in customer tastes etc). This is probably best achieved by both formal and informal information collection methods. The organisation will keep abreast (as far as it can) of what its competitors are doing and someone will have an eye on general economic trends, the opinions of political commentators and the progress of scientific research at the *pure* as well as the *applied* stage, in addition to any more specific research work the company may itself be engaged in.

An organisation is a system, and any system must be controlled to keep it steady or enable it to change safely: each system must have a control system. Control is required because unpredictable disturbances arise and enter the system, so that actual results, the outputs of the system, deviate from the expected results or goals. Examples of disturbances in a business system would be the entry of a powerful new competitor into the market, an unexpected rise in labour costs, a decline in quality standards, the failure of a supplier to deliver promised raw materials, or the tendency of employees to stop working in order to chatter or gossip. A control system must ensure that the business is capable of surviving these disturbances by dealing with them in an appropriate manner.

BPP
LEARNING MEDIA

To have a control system, there has to be a plan, standard, budget or any other sort of target or guideline towards which the system as a whole should be aiming. Control is dependent on the receipt and processing of *information*, both to plan in the first place and to compare actual results against the plan, so as to judge what control measures, if any, are needed.

1.2 PROCESS OF CONTROL

The managerial process of controlling is the measurement and correction of performance to make sure that the enterprise objectives and the plans devised to attain them are accomplished. Control techniques and systems are essentially the same for cash, office procedures, morale or product quality. The basic control process involves three steps:

- establishing standards, ie criteria of performance
- measuring performance against these standards *and*
- correcting variations from standards and plans

1.3 FEEDBACK

Feedback is information about actual achievements. In a business organisation, it is information about actual results, produced from within the organisation (for example, management accounting control reports) with the purpose of helping with control decisions.

A feature of feedback is that it is information that is gathered by measuring the outputs of the system itself, as distinct from environmental information, which comes from outside the system. For some control systems, notably for control by senior management at a strategic planning level, control information will be gathered from both environmental sources and internal sources. For example, a company might be unable to judge the success or failure of its activities without putting them into the context of the national economy (Is it booming? Is it in recession? How high is the rate of inflation?) and its markets (How well are competitors doing? Is the number of potential customers rising or falling?).

Some form of internally generated feedback is essential if there is to be any effective monitoring within an organisation and the most common types of monitoring systems in businesses, such as budgetary control, stock control and production control systems, are all based on feedback cycles.

A **feedback system** measures the outputs of a process and then provides information regarding corrective action to the process or the inputs, after the outputs have been produced. In most management problems, because of time lags in implementing the corrective process, this is not good enough. For example, if the manager is informed in August that the administration department has overspent against budget due to a purchase in June, there is nothing that can be done.

Feed forward control will inform management of deviations in time for them to take corrective action. It is used to overcome the time lag problems often encountered by feedback systems. This type of system monitors the inputs into the process to ascertain whether the inputs are as planned; if they are not, the inputs, or perhaps the process, are changed in order to ensure the desired results. In the above example, the administration department would have to submit an estimate for the item they wish to purchase. The organisation would then have to decide whether to refuse the request or change the budget in order to allow the purchase to be made. The diagram below shows feedback/ feedforward control.

Figure 5.1: Feedback/feedforward control

1.4   CRITICAL CONTROL POINTS AND STANDARDS

Actual or expected performance is measured against standards or yardsticks. If the operation is simple, a manager might control through observation of the work being done. However, in most situations this is not possible because of the complexity of the operations and the fact that a manager has better things to do. He or she must choose critical points for special attention and monitor them to be sure that the operation is proceeding as planned. The principle of critical point control states that effective control requires attention to those factors critical to evaluating performance against plans. Managers need to select these points after asking themselves:

- what will best reflect the goals of my department?
- what will best show me when these goals are not being met?
- what will best measure critical deviations?
- what will tell me who is responsible for any failure?
- what standards will cost the least?
- for what standards is information economically available?

1.5   TAKING CORRECTIVE ACTION

Where these are critical deviations from the plan, the action to be taken will vary from organisation to organisation according to the managerial style employed and the structure adopted.

A problem analysis exercise will be carried out, which will cover the following issues.

- Why are current methods and working practices used?

- What problems are restricting the effectiveness of the current system and the reasons for their existence?

- Are alternative methods available to achieve the same or better results?

- What changes can be introduced?

- What performance criteria are required from the system and how they can be measured?

It must be appreciated that some failures to attain standards are symptomatic of more fundamental causes and that tinkering with the system may not lead to any real improvement. Changes in standards and overall objectives should not be ruled out.

2 PERFORMANCE MEASUREMENT

2.1 WHAT IS EVALUATED?

Performance measurement aims to establish how well something or somebody is doing in relation to the planned activity and desired results. It is a vital part of control and generates the results, which are fed back for comparison with objectives. The 'something' may be a machine, a factory, a subsidiary company or an organisation as a whole. The 'somebody' may be an individual employee, a manager, or a group of people.

Performance measurement is a highly topical issue at present. The factors that have given rise to this interest include the following.

(a)   The move away from the traditional emphasis on increasing volume and reducing costs towards a focus on quality and customer satisfaction.

(b)   Increasingly competitive world markets, requiring a 'world class' response.

(c)   Recognition that the way to achieve (a) and (b) is through the empowerment of those who have most direct control over the product or service, so that responsibility is devolved as far down the line as possible.

(d)   The impact of advanced manufacturing technology and information technology on methods of working.

(e)   The opportunities presented by activity based approaches to management.

(f)   A government intent on achieving excellence and value for money in the public sector through target setting and performance evaluation.

A typical business requires performance measurement in the following areas.

(a)   In terms of its relations with external parties, that is its customers or market, suppliers and competitors

(b)   Across the organisation as a whole (divisional performance measurement)

(c)   *Within* each of the main sub-divisions of the business

(d)   At the level of individual activities

Three possible points of reference for measurement are profitability, activity and productivity.

(a)   *Profitability.* Profit has two components: cost and income. All parts of an organisation and all activities within it incur costs, and so their success needs to be judged in relation to cost. Only some parts of an organisation receive income, and their success should be judged in terms of both cost and income.

(b)   *Activity.* All parts of an organisation are also engaged in activities that cause costs. Activity measures could include the number of:

(i)   orders received from customers, a measure of the effectiveness of marketing

(ii)   deliveries made, a measure of the effectiveness of distribution

(iii) production runs achieved by a particular factory

(iv)   machine breakdowns attended to by the repairs and maintenance department.

Each of these items could be measured in terms of physical numbers, monetary value, or time spent.

(c)   *Productivity.* This is the quantity of the product or service produced in relation to the resources put in, for example so many units produced per hour, or per employee, or per tonne of material. It defines how *efficiently* resources are being used. The dividing line between productivity and activity is thin, because every activity could be said to have some 'product'. The concept of value is important for assessing activities: that is, to what extent do they add value to the overall output of the organisation?

ACTIVITY 1   (10 MINS)

An invoicing assistant works in a department with three colleagues. She is paid £18,000 per annum. The department typically handles 10,000 invoices per week. One morning she spends half-an-hour on the phone to her grandfather, who lives in Australia, at the company's expense. The cost of the call proves to be £32.

Required

From this scenario identify as many different performance measures as possible, explaining what each is intended to measure. Make any further assumptions you wish.

2.2   QUALITY MEASURES – IMPORTANCE OF PREVENTION RATHER THAN CORRECTION

The **cost of quality** attempts to provide a single measure of all the costs of ensuring a product meets specifications as well as the costs incurred because of the failure of the product to meet specifications. These costs can be classified into four categories, *prevention, appraisal, internal failure* and *external failure.*

Prevention costs – are incurred in order to prevent the production of non-conforming products. They include costs of:

- designing and administering a quality assurance programme.
- development of improved production processes.
- equipment to produce higher quality products.
- ensuring supply of quality raw materials and component parts.
- tooling, calibration and preventative maintenance programmes.

Appraisal costs – are incurred to identify those products that do not meet specification before the product leaves the factory. They include cost of:

- inspecting and testing programmes for purchases, work in process and finished goods.
- quality audits and statistical quality control programmes.
- field-testing.

Internal failure costs – are the costs incurred to rework defective products before the product is delivered to customers. These include cost of:

- scrap, repair and rework.
- downtime associated with trouble-shooting a process.
- discounts on sale of seconds.

External failure costs – are the costs incurred when defective products reach the customer. They include:

- Cost of handling customer complaints and claims.
- Warranty and replacement costs.
- Product liability costs.
- Loss of customer goodwill.

The *quality of a service* could be measured by the level of complaints or by favourable reaction. The quality of a training course, for example, could be monitored by asking trainees to complete an assessment form when the course has finished. The training manager's performance could be assessed on the basis of the responses. It would be far more difficult to measure actual achievement in terms of improved performance, as there are so many other variables involved.

Management may be surprised to learn how much is spent on quality-related costs. Because of the importance of prevention rather than correction, there may be high payoffs from shifting quality costs from the last three categories to the prevention category.

2.3 PROFIT AND OTHER OBJECTIVES

A traditional view has been that a desire to achieve greater profitability often entails a sacrifice in some other aspect of performance. One obvious example is quality: if cheaper materials are used to make a product or less highly trained workers deliver a service, money will be saved (increasing profits), but quality will fall. It is now widely recognised that economising on quality has an adverse effect in the longer term.

In other cases there may not be a clear link between an objective and the profitability objective. A company may aim to improve working conditions for its staff, and measure its success in terms of the cost of improved facilities, falls in staff turnover, or absenteeism and so on. Some of the successes are directly contrary to profitability, while others can only with difficulty be linked to extra productivity.

A third example is where a company aims to fulfil its social and moral responsibilities, for example by incurring costs to make a manufacturing process more environmentally friendly or by keeping a loss-making facility open so as not to cause undesirable unemployment in a depressed area.

2.4 CRITICAL SUCCESS FACTORS

Some CSFs that cover both financial and non-financial criteria are outlined below.

Sphere of activity	Critical factors
Marketing	Sales volume
	Market share
	Gross margins
Production	Capacity utilisation
	Quality standards
Logistics	Capacity utilisation
	Level of service

2.5 SYSTEM RESOURCE APPROACH

An effective organisation is one which does the right things and is thus able to satisfy the needs of its client group. However, effectiveness is often difficult to measure.

The system resource model bears some relationship to the systems approach, which views an organisation as a system, which obtains inputs and processes them into outputs. System resource effectiveness covers the ability to do the following.

(a) *Obtain scarce and valued resources from the environment.* Oil companies need to secure oil reserves. So, for an oil company indicators of future success are the volume of reserves.

(b) *Sustain day-to-day activities.* An example is the UK's voluntary blood donor scheme.

(c) *Respond to environmental changes and sustain the environment.* Business organisations which fail to ensure they have the ability to remain in business *in future* are not effective.

At first sight, this might seem a rather bizarre way of measuring effectiveness. However, effectiveness in obtaining resources *now* might be essential in meeting clients' needs *in future*. Consider the following example.

Parents often judge prospective schools in part on their academic record (eg proportion of 'A' GCSE and 'A level' passes obtained, number of ex-pupils going to university etc). A school, which attracts the right pupils, will find it easier to meet these exacting targets: attracting the right mix of pupils is a measure of success. It is a vicious circle. Similarly, the ability to attract a high quality teaching staff indicates effectiveness.

Obviously, there are many better ways of measuring organisation effectiveness – but in cases where *outputs* are hard to measure quantitatively, this approach is all there is.

2.6 INTERNAL PROCESS APPROACH

The internal process approach really refers to efficiency and the internal workings of the organisation, rather than effectiveness as we have defined it. However, it assumes that *because* the organisation is healthy and efficient in its internal processes, *therefore* it is effective. Internal efficiency and health is an outward sign of organisational effectiveness in meeting client needs.

There are problems with this approach:

(a) *Ignores customers.* You could run a factory making asbestos ceiling tiles with incredible efficiency and a deeply satisfied workforce: but customers' needs are not satisfied.

(b) *Ignores strategy.* Concentration on internal processes is never enough; you might want to be close to your customer – but is this the *right* customer, and, furthermore, does the customer value the relationship as much as you do?

(c) *Assumes status quo.* Managers may not be *objective* judges of internal health. The soft systems approach suggests that managers are 'actors' in a problem situation with their own objectives and perspectives.

(d) *Ignores environment.* The organisation's relationship with the environment is not addressed by this approach.

Possible performance indicators include:

(a) Ratio of inputs to outputs, in other words, economic *efficiency* in the use of scarce resources (eg revenue per employee, units of output per labour hour).

(b) Strong corporate culture.

(c) Team spirit, loyalty etc.

(d) Good communications, horizontally and vertically, and between workers and management.

(e) Swift, flexible decision-making.

(f) Reward systems that encourage optimum performance.

(g) Successful resolution of conflicts in favour of the overall well-being of the organisation.

(h) Quality.

2.7 THE GOAL APPROACH

The 'goal approach' measures 'effectiveness' by comparing the actual performance of the business with its *stated* objectives and goals. It is quite easy to use and it is possible, for example, to use output measures as measures of effectiveness.

(a) Profitability
(b) Growth
(c) Market share
(d) Innovation
(e) Staff turnover (as a measure of employee satisfaction)
(f) Quality, as measured.

If the goals and objectives are congruent with the organisation's purpose, then reaching them can indicate that an organisation is effective. But there are problems.

(a) *Comparisons.* Organisations do not exist in isolation. Their output effectiveness can only be realistically measured in comparison with *other* organisations.

(b) Effectiveness can only be measured across a *wide* variety of indicators. There may have to be *trade-offs* between them.

(c) *Subverting the goal setting process.* Managers may set goals which they can *easily* achieve.

(d)   *Measurability does not equal significance.* There may be a bias towards goals that can be *measured.* Not all the aspects of effectiveness can be easily measured. In a service organisation, it is hard to measure staff courtesy, although this is vitally important for organisation effectiveness.

(e)   *'What gets measured gets managed'.* Managers may only *care* about what is measured, to the detriment of other aspects of performance.

Finally, we must assume that the objectives chosen are the right ones, and that they do stand in successfully for effectiveness. And here is the nub of the problem. *Who* decides what is *effective?*

(a)   For a *business*, the issue is reasonably clear cuts shareholders have the ultimate say, as the business is run on their behalf.

(b)   For other organisations, this is not so easy to determine.

2.8 THE STAKEHOLDER VIEW APPROACH

The stakeholder view is a way of looking at an organisation that holds that many different groups of people have an interest in what the organisation does. From their various perspectives they have different objectives, which they would like to see the organisation fulfil. There are three broad types of stakeholder in an organisation, as follows.

(a)   Internal stakeholders (employees, management).
(b)   Connected stakeholders (shareholders, customers, suppliers, financiers).
(c)   External stakeholders (the community, government, pressure groups).

The *ecology model of effectiveness* brings the issues of stakeholders into the foreground by identifying the extent to which the organisation *depends* (or is reliant) on a stakeholder group at *any particular time.* For example, a firm with persistent *cash-flow problems* might depend on its *bankers* to provide it with money to stay in business at all.

In the long-term, any firm depends on its customers. Their strategic importance will vary depending on:

(a)   *customer bargaining power* in the industry as a whole;

(b)   the *relationship of customers* to the firm. For example, much of the defence industry depends on the procurement decisions of a small number of government officials.

The *degree of dependence or reliance* can be analysed according to these criteria.

(a)   *Disruption.* Can the stakeholder disrupt the organisation's plans or operations (eg a bank withdrawing overdraft facilities)?

(b)   *Replacement.* Can the firm replace the relationship (eg find another bank)?

(c)   *Uncertainty.* Does the stakeholder cause uncertainty in the firm's plans? A firm with healthy positive cash-flows and large cash balances need not worry about its bank's attitude to a fixed asset investment. A firm which has to borrow money might be concerned about the bank's attitude.

In this model, measuring organisational effectiveness depends on identifying:

(a)   the key stakeholders
(b)   the degree of dependence
(c)   the goals of each stakeholder group
(d)   potential conflicts between them
(e)   the organisation's ability to satisfy key stakeholder groups

2.9 THE COMPETING VALUES APPROACH

The *competing values* approach suggests that organisational goals and performance indicators are defined by top and middle managers. However, different groups of managers have different sets of priorities.

These can be modelled on two dimensions.

(a) *Organisational focus*

    (i)   *External.* This group of managers are focused on the environment and the organisation's well-being within it.

    (ii)   *Internal.* Managers with an internal focus are concerned with internal issues such as efficiency or employee well-being.

(b) *Organisation structure*

    (i)   *Stability.* Managers who favour stability prefer an ordered environment, with top-down control, as in a bureaucracy, or any organisation run according to classical or scientific management principles.

    (ii)   *Flexibility.*

The key issue is that different groups of managers are concerned about different things. For example, the marketing manager will have the external, customer focus, whereas a production manager will have an internal focus. In some organisations, marketing managers have more power than production managers. In others, the reverse is true.

In practice, an organisation contains features of *all* approaches in different degrees. Employees cannot be ignored, even if managers are more concerned with customers. Much depends on the *values* of the senior executives and key decision-makers in the organisation. Currently, many managers are emphasising flexibility and responsiveness.

3 PERFORMANCE MEASURES

3.1 QUANTITATIVE AND QUALITATIVE PERFORMANCE MEASURES

It is possible to distinguish between *quantitative* information, which is capable of being expressed in numbers, and *qualitative* information, which can only be expressed in numerical terms with difficulty.

An example of a quantitative performance measure is 'You have been late for work *twice* this week and it's only Tuesday!' An example of a qualitative performance measure is 'My bed is *very* comfortable'.

The first measure is likely to find its way into a staff appraisal report. The second would feature in a bed manufacturer's customer satisfaction survey. Both are indicators of whether their subjects are doing as good a job as they are required to do.

Qualitative measures are by nature subjective and judgmental but this does not mean that they are not valuable. They are especially valuable when they are derived from several different sources because then they can be expressed in a mixture of quantitative and qualitative terms which is more meaningful overall: 'seven out of ten customers think our beds are very comfortable' is a *quantitative* measure of customer satisfaction as well as a *qualitative* measure of the perceived performance of the beds. (But it does not mean that only 70% of the total beds produced are comfortable, nor that each bed is 70% comfortable and 30% uncomfortable: 'very' is the measure of comfort.)

3.2 FINANCIAL PERFORMANCE MEASURES

Financial measures (or *monetary* measures) are very familiar to you if you read the business pages of a quality newspaper. Here are some examples, accompanied by comments from a single page of the *Financial Times*.

(a) *Profit* is the commonest measure of all. Profit maximisation is usually cited as the main objective of most business organisations: 'ICI increased pre-tax profits to £233m'; 'General Motors ... yesterday reported better-than-expected first-quarter net income of $513 (£333m) ... Earnings improved $680m from the first quarter of last year when GM lost $167m.'

(b) *Revenue*: 'the US businesses contributed £113.9m of total group turnover of £409m'.

(c) *Costs*: 'Sterling's fall benefited pre-tax profits by about £50m while savings from the cost-cutting programme instituted...[last year]...were running at around £100m a quarter'; 'The group interest charge rose from £48m to £61m'.

(d) *Share price*: 'The group's shares rose 31p to 1278p despite the market's fall'.

(e) *Cash-flow*: 'Cash-flow was also continuing to improve, with cash and marketable securities totalling $8.4bn on March 31, up from $8bn at December 31'.

The important point to note here is that the monetary amounts stated are only given meaning in relation to something else. Profits are higher than last year's; revenue for one part of the business is so much compared with the total for the group; costs are at a lower level, in keeping with a planned reduction and in the light of changing economic conditions; share price is relative to the market; cashflow has improved compared with last quarter's.

We can generalise the above and give a list of yardsticks against which financial results are usually placed so as to become measures.

- Budgeted sales, costs and profits

- Standards in a standard costing system

- The trend over time (last year/this year, say)

- The results of other parts of the business

- The results of other businesses

- The economy in general

- Future potential (for example, the performance of a new business may be judged in terms of nearness to breaking even).

3.3 NON-MONETARY MEASURES

The term non-monetary (or more commonly 'non-financial') needs care. It means *either* 'quantitative (but not in money quantities)' *or* 'qualitative', and we suggest that you use these more precise terms.

Quantitative non-monetary measures are either expressed in units other than money, such as units of product, hours or weight, or in a relative form such as percentages, ratios and indices.

Ratios – are a useful way of measuring performance for a number of reasons.

(a) It is easier to look at changes over time by comparing ratios in one time period with the corresponding ratios for periods in the past.

(b) Ratios are often easier to understand than absolute measures of physical quantities or money values. For example, it is easier to understand that 'productivity in March was 94%' than 'there was an adverse labour efficiency variance in March of £3,600'.

(c) Ratios relate one item to another, and so help to put performance into context. For example the profit/sales ratio sets profit in the context of how much has been earned per £1 of sales, and so shows how wide or narrow profit margins are.

(d) Ratios can be used as targets. In particular, targets can be set for ROI, profit/sales, asset turnover, capacity fill and productivity. Managers will then take decisions that will enable them to achieve their targets.

(e) Ratios provide a way of summarising an organisation's results, and comparing them with similar organisations. For example:

(i) the results of one investment centre or profit centre can be compared directly with the results of another by means of ratio analysis;

(ii) the results of one company can be compared with the results of similar companies.

Percentages – a percentage expresses one number as a proportion of another and gives meaning to absolute numbers. Examples are as follows.

(a) *Market share.* A company may aim to achieve a 25% share of the total market for its product, and measure both its marketing department and the quality of the product against this.

(b) *Capacity levels* are usually measured in this way. 'Factory A is working at 20% below full capacity' is an example which indicates relative inefficiency.

(c) *Wastage* is sometimes expressed in percentage terms. 'Normal loss' may be 10%, a measure of *in*efficiency.

(d) *Staff turnover* is often measured in this way. In the catering industry for example, staff turnover is typically greater than 100%, and so a hotel with a lower percentage could take this as an indicator both of the experience of its staff and of how well it is treating them.

4 OPERATIONAL PERFORMANCE INDICATORS

4.1 FINANCIAL AND NON-FINANCIAL INDICATORS

SIGNPOST

In this section we are going to look mainly at performance measurement under conventional headings: sales, material, labour and overheads. These are financial terms and we shall be considering what you may think of as financial measures such as standard costs and variances.

You will by now appreciate that financial measures do not convey the full picture of a company's performance, especially in a modern manufacturing environment.

'In today's worldwide competitive environment companies are competing in terms of product quality, delivery, reliability, after-sales service and customer satisfaction. None of these variables is directly measured by the traditional responsibility accounting system, despite the fact that they represent the major goals of world-class manufacturing companies.'

Many companies are discovering the usefulness of quantitative and qualitative non-financial indicators (NFIs) such as the following.

(a) Quality
(b) Number of customer complaints and warranty claims
(c) Lead times
(d) Rework
(e) Delivery to time
(f) Non-productive hours
(g) System (machine) down time, and so on

Unlike traditional variance reports, measures such as these can be provided quickly for managers, per shift or on a daily or even hourly basis as required. They are likely to be easy to calculate, and easier for non-financial managers to understand and therefore to use effectively.

4.2 PERFORMANCE MEASURES FOR SALES – A CUSTOMER-FOCUSED CULTURE

Traditionally sales performance is measured in terms of price and volume variances, and also perhaps a sales mix variance. Other possible measures include revenue targets and target market share.

These are all highly valid measures and there is no reason to suppose that they will not remain the principal measures for sales. They may, of course, be analysed in some detail: by country, by region, by individual products, by salesperson and so on.

However, in organisations with a customer-focused culture the basic information 'Turnover is up by 14%' can be supplemented by a host of other indicators.

(a) *Customer rejects/returns: total sales.* This ratio helps to monitor customer satisfaction, providing a check on the efficiency of quality control procedures.

(b) *Deliveries late: deliveries on schedule.* This ratio can be applied both to sales made to customers and to receipts from suppliers. When applied to customers it provides an indication of the efficiency of production and production scheduling. The term 'cycle time' is used in this context: total cycle time is the length of time between receipt of an order and delivery of the product.

(c) *Flexibility* measures indicate how well able a company is to respond to customers' requirements, not only in terms of delivering the goods on time, but also in terms of speed of launching new products and changing old procedures to meet market needs.

(d) *Number of people served and speed of service,* in a shop or a bank for example. If it takes too long to reach the point of sale, future sales are liable to be lost.

(e) *Customer satisfaction.* You have probably filled in questionnaires in fast-food restaurants or on aeroplanes without realising that you were completing a customer attitude survey for input to the organisation's management information system. Horngren cites the 'Customer Satisfaction Target' used by Holiday Inns where information is measured by evaluating scores (A – F) on guest inspection cards and imposing a limit of 0.457 guest complaint letters per 1,000 room-nights sold.

(f) *Marketing* measures might include number of sales per enquiry, amount of new business brought in, share by sales territory of the organisation's total market share and so on.

(g) *Customer profitability analysis*

In certain circumstances a useful approach to performance evaluation may be the analysis of profitability by customer or customer group. Profitability can vary widely between different customers because various overhead costs are, to some extent, variable and 'customer-driven'. These overheads include:

- discounts;
- sales force (eg telesales are cheaper and more time-efficient than a field sales force);
- quality control (some customers demand higher quality);
- merchandising;
- distribution (full-pallet transactions are cheaper than breaking bulk);
- promotions;
- financing costs;
- enquiries.

The task of customer profitability analysis is to relate these variabilities in cost to individual customers or customer groups. Managers can use this information to check whether individual customers are actually profitable to sell to, and to assess whether profitability can be improved for any customer by switching effort from one type of overhead activity to another, or by reducing spending on some overhead activities.

Customer profitability analysis can provide valuable management accounting information.

(a) It helps a firm to identify unprofitable customers as well as unprofitable products.

(b) It draws attention to the *three* ways of improving profitability, both for individual customers and so for products in total. These are:

(i) productivity improvements to reduce product costs;

(ii) higher sales volumes to customers, to increase total contribution;

(iii) more efficient use of 'overhead' resources to improve customer profitability.

4.3 PERFORMANCE MEASURES FOR MATERIALS

Traditional measures are standard costs for materials, and price and particularly usage variances. Many traditional systems also analyse wastage, although as we have seen elsewhere, wastage is to some extent *encouraged* by systems that regard a certain level of loss as 'normal' and acceptable. Other relevant measures include the following.

(a) *Stock turnover.* This is a traditional measure, but a particularly relevant one in a Just-in-Time production environment, where the aim is to minimise all stocks.

(b) *Physical qualities* of materials may be crucially important to the final product, and if so the performance of materials should be measured. They may have to demonstrate a certain degree of smoothness, hardness, pliability, or stickiness; they may have to be a consistent shade of a certain colour or a consistent smell. Do they retain their shape, or do some get misshapen in transit or during production?

4.4 PERFORMANCE MEASURES FOR PEOPLE

Labour costs are traditionally reported by rate and efficiency variances against standards. Many other staff-related measures have already been mentioned such as sales per salesperson; almost any aspect of an organisation's performance can be measured in terms of the different individuals or groups who actually do the job.

Qualitative measures of labour performance concentrate on matters such as ability to communicate, interpersonal relationships with colleagues, customers' impressions ('so and so was extremely helpful/rude'), and levels of skills attained. Some matters are extremely difficult to measure, notably staff morale, but attempts can be made.

4.5 PERFORMANCE MEASURES FOR OVERHEADS

Apart from standards for variable overheads and efficiency variances, a variety of time-based measures are available. Here are just two examples.

(a) *Machine down time: total machine hours.* This ratio could be used to monitor machine availability and can provide a measure of machine usage and efficiency.

(b) *Value added time: production cycle time.* Value added time is the direct production time during which the product is being made and value is therefore being added. The production cycle time includes non-value-added times such as set-up time, downtime, idle time etc. The optimum ratio is 100%, but in practice this optimum will not be achieved. A high ratio will help a company to satisfy customer orders more quickly.

Overhead expenses may also be measurable in qualitative terms: is the light adequate? Is the office or factory warm enough? Does the general state of cleanliness detract from workers' performance?

4.6 THE BALANCED SCORECARD

A technique which has been developed to integrate the various features of corporate success is the **balanced scorecard**, developed by Kaplan and Norton.

It can be defined as 'a set of measures that gives top managers a fast but comprehensive view of the business'. The balanced scorecard includes financial measures that tell the results of actions already taken and it complements these with operational measures on customer satisfaction, internal processes, and the organisation's innovation and improvement activities – operational measure that are the drivers of future financial performance.'

The reason for using such a system is that 'traditional financial accounting measures like return on investment and earnings per share can give misleading signals for continuous improvement and innovation – activities today's competitive environment demands'.

The balanced scorecard allows managers to look at the business from four important perspectives:

Financial perspective: reflecting how the business looks to shareholders and typically would include familiar measures such as asset turnover and earnings per share.

Customer perspective: how the business looks to customers, indicated by market share and customer satisfaction for example.

Internal business processes: pointing to what the organisation must excel at, response times and product quality for instance.

Innovation and learning: focusing on the ability to change and improve and will be reflected in employee attitudes and morale, organisational culture and so forth.

(a) **Financial perspective** – from the financial perspective, the question to be asked is: 'How do we appear to shareholders?' Financial performance indicators indicate 'whether the company's strategies, implementation, and execution are contributing to bottom line management.'

(b) **Customer perspective** – 'How do customers see us?' Given that many company mission statements identify customer satisfaction as a key corporate goal, the balanced scorecard translates this into specific measures. Customer concerns fall into four categories.

(i) *Time.* Lead time is the time it takes a firm to meet customer needs from receiving an order to delivering the product.

(ii) *Quality.* Quality measures not only include defect levels – although these should be minimised by TQM – but accuracy in forecasting.

(iii) *Performance* of the product. (How often does the photocopier break down?)

(iv) *Service.* How long will it take a problem to be rectified? (If the photocopier breaks down, how long will it take the maintenance engineer to arrive?)

(c) **Internal business perspective**

Findings from the customer's perspective need to be translated into the actions the firm must take to meet these expectations.

(i) The internal business perspective identifies the business processes that have the greatest impact on customer satisfaction, such as quality and employee skills.

(ii) Companies should also attempt to identify and measure their distinctive competences and the critical technologies they need to ensure continued leadership. Which processes should they excel at?

(iii) To achieve these goals, performance measures must relate to employee behaviour, to tie in the strategic direction with employee action.

(iv) An information system is necessary to enable executives to measure performance. An *executive information system* enables managers to drill down into lower level information.

(d) **Innovation and learning perspective**. The question is 'Can we continue to improve and create value?' Whilst the customer and internal process perspectives identify the *current* parameters for competitive success, the company needs to learn and to innovate to satisfy *future* needs. This might be one of the hardest items to measure. Examples of measures might be these.

(i) How long does it take to develop new products?

(ii) How quickly does the firm climb the experience curve to manufacture new products?

(iii) What percentage of revenue comes from new products?

(iv) How many suggestions are made by staff and are acted upon?

(v) What are staff attitudes? Some firms believe that employee motivation and successful communication are necessary for organisational learning.

(vi) Depending on circumstances, the company can identify measures for training and long-term investment.

Continuous improvement measures might also be relevant here.

An example of how a balanced scorecard might appear is offered below.

Financial – How do we look to our shareholders?	**Process** – What must we excel at?
• Return on capital employed	• Hours with customer on new work
• Cash-flow	• Tender success rate
• Project profitability	• Rework
• Profit forecast reliability	• Safety incident index
• Sales backlog	• Project performance index

Customer – How do our customers see us?	**Innovation and Learning** – Can we continue to improve and create value?
• Pricing index	• Percent revenue from new projects
• Customer ranking survey	• Rate of improvement index
• Customer satisfaction index	• Staff attitude survey
• Market share	• Number of employee suggestions
	• Revenue per employee

In each perspective, sets of measures are chosen that both provide the appropriate balance as well as capturing the cause and effect relations inherent in a coordinated strategy. For example if Return on capital employed (ROCE) was the prime financial measure, then to increase that indicator would require retention and loyalty of customers so customer loyalty would be measured as the cause of high ROCE. Perhaps for the customers, the key determinant of their loyalty might be on time delivery that would be the driver of customer loyalty. To achieve on time delivery, quality and cycle time would have to be improved, which in turn would require an increase in employee skills.

ACTIVITY 2 (20 MINS)

Draw up a balanced scorecard for the organisation for which you work.

5 TYPES OF CHANGE

Organisational change can be initiated deliberately by managers, it can evolve slowly within a department, it can be imposed by specific changes in policy or procedures or it can arise through external pressures. The forces for change may come from:

- the environment external to the organisation
- changes in technology
- changes in structure
- changes in culture

5.1 ENVIRONMENTAL CHANGE

Environmental change can affect the strategy, structure or culture of an organisation. It may affect a combination of them all. Environmental changes are sometimes dramatic, such as a sudden change in public opinion, but it is more frequently the case that changes are insidious and gradual. Organisations which communicate effectively with their environment are well placed to become aware of changes as they occur. Organisations that have become insular may take longer to pick up on such changes.

SIGNPOST

Pressure for change can come from a variety of sources – political, economic, social and technological.

Social pressures for change. There are many examples of changes brought about by social pressures for change.

EXAMPLE   CHANGE THROUGH SOCIAL PRESSURE

Green issues

Recent changes in the awareness of the public concerning the potential destruction of various parts of the flora or fauna of our planet have had an impact on many industries. In some of these both the products made and the production processes have had to be changed. For example, paper production may now be from sustainable forests, and canned tuna may be caught by methods that are dolphin friendly.

The National Health Service

The National Health Service has undergone major changes in terms of waiting times and clients' expectations of level of service. While some of this change can be attributed to changes in government policy (political pressures), it is the pressure from the population that has increased the impetus for change.

Communication is important in enabling social pressure for change to grow and to have an effect. Effective communication within the organisations concerned is essential to enable these changes to occur. It is also the case that growth in worldwide communication has increased the social pressures themselves.

ACTIVITY 3   (20 MINS)

Make a list of four products or industries which have been forced to change in the last ten years as a result of social pressures

In each case, give the reason for the change and indicate in what direction the changes have been made.

SIGNPOST

Social and political pressures are often interrelated. Here we focus on the effects of political pressures emanating from outside the UK.

Political pressures for change. European directives have considerable effect on the way UK organisations are run, especially as many UK companies now have links outside this country. The integration process that is occurring between EU member states in respect of working conditions within organisations is forcing many established firms to rethink their staff management policies.

ACTIVITY 4 (60 MINS + research)

In the 1990s the European Union issued a directive concerning works councils. Although the UK has not become party to the Maastricht Treaty from which this directive stems, the directive has had implications for UK firms. For the purpose of this activity, assume that the directive is equally valid in the UK as in other European countries.

The directive instructs that all organisations over a specified size (based on number of employees) must set up works councils through which employees will be kept informed of anything affecting them (directly or indirectly) and at which employees can have their say over working conditions. The works councils will not deal with remuneration matters or other subjects covered by existing collective bargaining agreements.

Write a short essay (500-1000 words) on how you think this directive changed the emphasis of communication within UK organisations.

For organisations to be successful in introducing these changes in a beneficial way, there must be effective communication between all those involved.

Economic pressures for change. External competition has always been a driving force behind changes in product design and innovation of new products. However, in the economic climate of the recent past, there has been even greater pressure on organisations to find ways to change and to adapt to fierce competition. One of the ways some organisations have achieved this is by the use of **strategic alliances**, where firms work together to enhance their competitive advantages. An example of a very successful strategic alliance is that of the *One World* alliance that brings together twelve of the world's biggest airlines, including American Airlines, British Airways, Cathay Pacific and Qantas. The alliance allows them to offer an integrated service, including code-sharing, and the common use of passenger terminals. However, strategic alliances are not always so successful. One example is the alliance between Apple and Hewlett Packard in 2004 and 2005. This alliance was driven by two factors.

(a) **HP would become not just a player in the online music race, but a leader.** As part of the alliance, HP consumer PCs and notebooks were preinstalled with Apple's iTunes jukebox software and an easy-reference desktop icon to point consumers directly to the iTunes Music Store, ensuring a simple, seamless music experience. HP would gain newfound independence from Microsoft and a significant advantage over Dell Computer, which sells its own music players only online.

(b) **Apple would receive cash for every HP-iPod sold without having to do any of the 'heavy lifting'** (marketing, distribution, etc) – thus increasing their market share in a cost-effective way. They would also get their software on the Windows desktop, where an alias to an application is worth its weight in gold. Also, Apple would further strengthen the open standard audio format that iTunes runs on.

The reality was not as bright as hoped. HP received new stock well after Apple had already released it, and they were not able to customise the stock from Apple as much as they had wanted. As a result, HP were never really able to share in the iPod phenonemon in a significant way, and terminated the agreement after a mere 18 months.

FOR DISCUSSION

Discuss the following statement in groups.

Increasing competitive pressure will result in greater openness in communications between rivals. The eventual outcome will be such close alliance that each sector of the market will become an effective monopoly.

SIGNPOST

One of the greatest recent changes in the environment of organisations is in the area of technological advances. Technological changes have also had impacts on the strategy, structure and culture of organisations.

5.2 TECHNOLOGICAL CHANGE

Technology has had an impact on the whole strategy of organisations. The globalisation of organisations would have been impossible without present day means and methods of communications. Similarly, the concept of selling to a customer you never see would have remained a small niche market if technological innovation had not allowed television and internet shopping. The growing interest of the UK food retailing industry in the concept of home shopping is testament to the viability of such changes.

The use of IT-based data collection systems to determine where there are areas of waste has allowed organisations to realise their ambitions to cut costs. This represents a change in the values of the organisation and thus a change in its culture.

Improved communications technology has helped to improve partnership relationships with suppliers to such an extent that raw materials and components can now be delivered exactly when they are needed. This reduces the need for manufacturers to hold large stocks and thus saves money. This is one of the few areas when it is easy to quantify the benefits of highly developed and effective communications systems.

ACTIVITY 5 (15 MINS)

How has improved communications technology facilitated the expansion of the global organisation? Make a list of the factors you consider to be important.

ACTIVITY 6
(45 MINS)

Robert and Son is a small factory producing components for the electrical industry. Their system of production has for many years taken the form of a series of production lines, with each line producing a different sub-section of the finished component.

The development of new technology, which partly automates the production of the subsections, now means that it is possible to increase the production capacity. The old system required a large factory floor to house the production lines and a final assembly line where the components were put together and packaged. The new technology reduces the amount of space required, so that all operations can be housed in one building. The production manager has put forward two separate layout plans for the 'new look' plant as shown in Figures 2 and 3 opposite. Figure 1 shows the existing layout.

Based on what you know about communications, draw up an advantages and disadvantages list for each of the three layouts. Make a final decision as to which layout to choose. Give reasons for your choice.

Figure 1: Existing layout

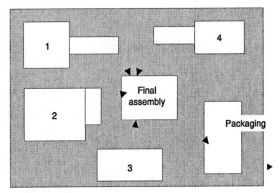

Figure 2: Possible new layout (a)

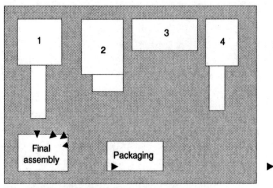

Note: This system is expected to reduce
work in progress

Figure 3: Possible new layout (b)

5.3 CHANGES IN WORKING PRACTICES

Changes in working practices can be a simple as introducing a new information collection form or as complex as transferring from a paper to computer-based system. However great or small the change, communication plays its part in its introduction and ultimate success.

Effective communication will:

(a) allay fear and suspicion about the motivation for the change;
(b) involve the workforce and gain their commitment;
(c) highlight potential problems;
(d) ensure that the change is appropriate;
(e) encourage feedback regarding unexpected side effects of the change;
(f) monitor the results of the change;
(g) facilitate the adaptation of the original plans.

SIGNPOST

We concentrate here on three contemporary and far reaching changes to working practices – downsizing, outsourcing and outworking.

Downsizing

DEFINITION

Downsizing: the term used to describe the contraction of an organisation so that it concentrates on its core activities.

De-layering: the removal of one or more layers of middle management, accompanied by the devolving of responsibility and authority further down the organisation structure.

It is important to note the distinction between downsizing and de-layering. Although they are quite separate concepts, both can have similar effects on the motivation of the workforce, although within differing groups of workers. If communications are poor, the workforce do not understand the strategy that is being followed and the only effect they see is redundancies. This undermines their security and their commitment to the organisation, and, in turn, their performance is likely to suffer.

Effective communications can reduce these effects and actively generate a stronger commitment to the change from those workers who remain after the process is complete.

ACTIVITY 7 (25 MINS)

You are the chief executive officer of a large group of companies. You have decided that, in order to consolidate your business with a view to expansion of your core activities in the future, you must sell off some of your smaller enterprises. Make a list of who you think you should communicate with in your environment to ensure that this will be a positive action for your company. Give reasons for communicating with each individual, group or organisation on your list.

Outsourcing

DEFINITION

Outsourcing: the term used to describe the process of employing outside contractors to perform tasks which, although not core activities of the organisation, were formerly performed in-house. Examples can be cleaning, security, legal work and occupational health.

Outsourcing is often the result of downsizing and, as such, can encounter the same problems. Effective communication is especially important to ensure that the outsourced service is to the same standard, or better, and at lower cost than that previously provided in house. Partnership relationships are required with these service providers, and effective communications are the only way to achieve these. (There can be other influencing factors, but without effective communications they will not ensure success.) A great deal of outsourcing has been carried out in public sector organisations, especially as a result of compulsory competitive tendering.

ACTIVITY 8 (25 MINS)

Consider the following:

(a)   A local hospital
(b)   The council for your locality

Make a list of any activities associated with the above which are outsourced.

Make a second list of activities that you think could be outsourced.

Outworking

DEFINITION

Outworking: the term used to describe a formerly office-based function being carried out primarily from the home of the job holder. This form of working has become popular in the financial services and data processing industries. The effects on the organisation are (a) to reduce overheads on expensive office accommodation and (b) to access the pool of (predominantly) female labour who have child care commitments that prevent them from taking office-based work. Outworking should not be confused with outsourcing.

The advent of the home computer and advances in telecommunications have facilitated the move towards home working. Critics of this working method claim that it will be a passing phase, as the effects of lack of communication on the worker become more evident. However, advances in all technological communication methods mean that the only area that cannot be satisfied is that of face-to-face personal interaction with others. While there is debate as to the importance of interpersonal communication on the performance of the worker, it is clear that it does play a part in job satisfaction and motivation. It remains to be seen whether communications can be so carefully structured and facilitated as to remove this problem.

5.4 CONTINUAL IMPROVEMENT CULTURE

Continual improvement is a type of change that is focused on increasing the effectiveness and/or efficiency of an organisation to fulfil its policy and objectives. It is far more than a set of techniques and for many organisations it involves a radical change in attitudes. A continual improvement culture requires the commitment of the organisation's leaders. Clearly, there can be no continual improvement or business strategy without the direct commitment and involvement of the leadership. Organisations which practice continual improvement are truly focused on continually enhancing customer and stakeholder value. The defence of the status quo, and resistance to innovation, cannot be treated as normal management behaviour. A fear of reprisals for reporting problems has to be replaced by congratulating staff for identifying an opportunity to improve. People will be encouraged to share their knowledge and experience in the search for greater collective success.

We have already noted (in Chapter 4) its relationship with TQM and ISO 9000. Continual improvement is one aspect of a TQM philosophy. It can also be an element of an ISO 9000 quality system. ISO 9000:2000 will in fact include requirements for continual improvement. However, continual improvement is not limited to quality initiatives. It can apply to improvement in business strategy, business results, customer, and employee and supplier relationships.

It should focus on enablers such as leadership, communication, resources, organisation structure, people and processes and lead to better results such as price, cost, productivity, time to market, delivery, responsiveness, profit and customer and employee satisfaction.

There are three types of improvement.

1   Continuous improvement is gradual never-ending change

2   Continual improvement is incremental change

3   Breakthroughs are improvements but in one giant leap – a step change that tends to arise out of chance discoveries and could take years before being made

All managerial activity is either directed at control or improvement. Managers are either devoting their efforts at maintaining performance, preventing change or creating change, breakthrough or improvement. If businesses stand still they will lose their competitive edge, so improvements must be made to keep pace and stay in business.

Every system, programme or project should have provision for an improvement cycle. Therefore when an objective has been achieved, work should commence on identifying better ways of doing it.

There are ten steps to undertaking continual improvement.

1   Determine current performance

2   Establish a need to improve

3   Obtain commitment and define the improvement objective

4   Organise the diagnostic resources

5   Carry out research and analysis to discover the cause of current performance

6   Define and test solutions that will accomplish the improvement objective

7   Produce improvement plans which specify how and by whom the changes will be implemented

8   Identify and overcome any resistance to the change

9   Implement the change

10   Put in place controls to hold new levels of performance and repeat step one

6   MANAGING CHANGE

6.1   FRAMEWORK FOR MANAGING CHANGE

A framework for managing change will involve:

- continually looking for areas where improvements can be made
- assessing the benefits against any problems caused by the changes
- consulting with all concerned to get them to agree to the changes
- implementing your plans for change
- evaluating whether improvements have been achieved.

It can be helpful to take four steps to ensure that you manage change effectively:

1   Ensure that everyone understands why change is necessary. If people are dissatisfied with the way that things are, they will be more likely to welcome change.

2   Show those affected how things will be better in the future.

3   Ensure that they understand the plan.

4   Try to ensure that there can be no way of going back to previous ways of doing things: ensure that only new forms are available, that computer systems reflect the new way of working, and that procedures work smoother under the new system than the old.

6.2 IDENTIFYING OPPORTUNITIES FOR IMPROVEMENT

To keep up to date with developments in your sector you must make sure you monitor and evaluate your operations continuously – always looking for areas where improvements can be made, getting relevant, valid, reliable information from various sources on developments in materials, equipment, technology and processes and taking appropriate action. You can then use the information to identify opportunities for growth, improvements in procedures or improvements in quality, using your experience of previous improvements to help identify new ones. By identifying any obstacles to change, appropriate measures can be taken to alleviate any problems that may prevent improvements being made.

6.3 ASSESSING THE BENEFITS AND PROBLEMS OF CHANGE

Make sure you have sufficient, reliable information on both current and proposed services, products and systems to allow you to make a reliable assessment using qualitative and quantitative techniques to assess the advantages and disadvantages of current and proposed services, products and systems.

The implications of introducing changes will be assessed – changes may affect cash flow, working practices and conditions, health and safety, team morale, supply and distribution networks and customer loyalty. You can look at how realistic previous assessments turned out to be and use these to modify your current assessment.

You will then be in a position to present your recommendations to the appropriate people – make your recommendations to senior managers or specialists in a way that helps them make a decision and in time to allow the decision to be put into effect. In the light of responses you get from senior managers and specialists you can make appropriate alterations to your recommendations.

6.4 PROPOSING THE INTRODUCTION OF CHANGE

Presenting the plans on projected change involves communicating the changes, and the anticipated benefits for your organisation and for individuals, to team members, colleagues, senior managers and others in order to gain their support. Negotiations will be conducted in a spirit of goodwill to make sure you retain people's support and find mutually acceptable ways of settling any disputes. It may be necessary to make compromises to accommodate other priorities, but make sure these compromises are consistent with your organisation's strategy, objectives and practices.

You need to reach an agreement in line with your organisation's strategy and revise your implementation plans accordingly. It is advisable to keep complete and accurate records of negotiations and agreements so that they are available for others to refer to if necessary.

Where you could not secure the changes you anticipated, tell those affected in a positive manner; sometimes you are disappointed in not being able to obtain the changes you wanted due to other organisational priorities; explain the reasons for this in a way which maintains people's morale and motivation. Encourage all relevant people to understand and participate in the changes – explain the changes and their effects to people, and gain their support.

6.5 PLANNING CHANGE

When planning change it helps to get people involved – giving them the chance to comment on the proposed change and help in the planning. Clear and accurate information should be provided to let those affected know about the proposed change in time for them to prepare effectively. This will help you make the case for change and you can give a clear and convincing rationale for the change and support this with sound evidence.

BPP
LEARNING MEDIA

You may identify potential obstacles to change so must find effective ways of avoiding or overcoming these obstacles before developing the plan for the change. The plan will include:

- the rationale
- the aim and objectives of the change
- how it will be implemented
- who will be involved and their individual roles
- the resources required
- the time scale
- how the plan will be monitored
- how you will know that the change has been successful.

Once you have worked out the details of your plan, the next stage is to decide whether it will work and its impact. Often you may find that a plan may have unexpected effects, either positive or negative.

You may also find that when you cost the plan, and compare this against the benefits achieved, that the plan is simply not worth carrying out. This can be frustrating after the hard work of detailed planning, however it is much better to find this out now than when you have invested time, resources and personal standing in the success of the plan. Evaluating the plan now gives you the opportunity to either investigate other options that might be more successful, or to accept that no plan is needed or should be carried out.

6.6 IMPLEMENTING CHANGE

You should now be in a position to present details of implementation plans to all concerned. Make sure that you brief everyone involved, or affected by, the changes on their role in the changes and the possible impact on their area. Encourage people to seek clarification, check on their understanding of their role and encourage them to ask questions.

A systematic approach should be established, for planning and implementing changes.

Step 1   **Determine** need or desire for change in a particular area.

Step 2   Prepare a tentative **plan**.

Brainstorming sessions a good idea, since alternatives for change should be considered (Lippitt 1981)

Step 3   Analyse **probable reactions** to the change.

Step 4   Make a **final decision** from the choice of alternative options.

Decision taken either by group problem-solving (participative) or by manager on his own (coercive)

Step 5   Establish a **timetable** for change.

- 'Coerced' changes can probably be implemented faster, without time for discussions.

- Speed of implementation that is achievable will depend on the likely reactions of the people affected (all in favour, half in favour, all against etc).

- Identify those in favour of the change, and perhaps set up a pilot programme involving them. Talk with the others who resist the change.

Step 6   **Communicate** the plan for change.

This is really a continuous process, beginning at Step 1 and going through to Step 7.

Step 7   **Implement** the change. **Review** the change.

Continuous evaluation and modifications

6.7 PLAN EVALUATION

At this stage you can monitor the changes – checking to see that the changes have been implemented according to plan and that they result in the improvements anticipated. You can also modify the way you implement changes to cope with unforeseen problems.

It is important to keep clear and accurate records of your monitoring and evaluation activities and the results. They will help you to review the change process – the whole process of identifying, assessing, negotiating, agreeing, implementing and evaluating change; note ways of doing it better next time and make appropriate recommendations to senior managers, colleagues and specialists.

There are a number of ways in which you can evaluate your plan:

Cost/benefit analysis

This is probably one of the simplest ways of evaluating a plan. During the implementing process above you should have carried out an analysis of the costs involved with each activity within the plan. Simply add up these costs, and compare them with the expected benefits.

Cost/benefit analysis is a strategy evaluation technique often used in the public sector, where many of the costs and benefits of a project are intangible.

(a)   The project and its overall objectives are defined.

(b)   The costs and benefits are analysed in detail. It is not always easy to put a value on social costs. For example, a new road might result in excessive noise for local residents. They can be asked how much, in principle, they would be able and prepared to pay to move to a quieter dwelling. This gives a very rough estimate of the value of tranquillity.

(c)   The net benefits for the project are estimated, if possible. A road might reduce journey times, and so save money. These are compared with costs, and the project is appraised by:

      (i)   discounted cash-flow methods such as Net Present Value (NPV) and Internal Rate of Return (IRR);

      (ii)   cost/benefit ratios.

PMI – 'Plus/Minus/Implications'

Once you have carried out a cost/benefit analysis, you may find it useful to mix its financial information with an assessment of the intangible or non-financial aspects of the decision. An effective way of doing this is with a PMI analysis. To use the technique, draw up a table with three columns headed Plus, Minus and Implications. Within the table write down all the positive points of following the course of action, all the negatives, and all the interesting implications and possible outcomes.

If the decision is still not obvious, you can then score the table to show the importance of individual items. The total score should show whether it is worth implementing the decision. A strongly positive score shows that an action should be taken, a strongly negative score that it should be avoided.

Force field analysis

Similar to PMI, force field analysis helps you to get a good overall view of all the forces for and against the change that you want to implement.

This allows you to see where you can make adjustments that will make the plan more likely to succeed. By carrying out the analysis you can plan to strengthen the forces supporting a decision, and reduce the impact of opposition to it. To carry out a force field analysis, follow these steps.

(a)   List all forces for change in one column, and all forces against change in another column.

(b)   Assign a score to each force, from 1 (weak) to 5 (strong).

(c)   Draw a diagram showing the forces for and against change. Show the size of each force as a number next to it.

For example, imagine that you are a manager deciding whether to install new manufacturing equipment in your factory. You might draw up a force field analysis like the one in below:

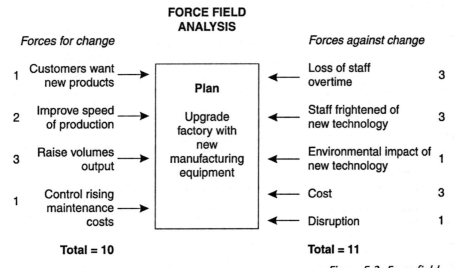

Figure 5.2: Force field analysis

Once you have carried out an analysis, you can decide whether your project is viable. In the example above, you might initially question whether it is worth going ahead with the plan. Where you have already decided to carry out a project, force field analysis can help you to work out how to improve its probability of success. Here you have two choices:

*   To reduce the strength of the forces opposing a project, or
*   To increase the forces pushing a project

Often the most elegant solution is the first: just trying to force change through may cause its own problems. People can be uncooperative if change is forced on them. If you had to implement the project in the example above, the analysis might suggest a number of changes to the initial plan:

*   By training staff (increase cost by 1) you could eliminate fear of technology (reduce fear by 2)

*   It would be useful to show staff that change is necessary for business survival (new force in favour, +2)

*   Staff could be shown that new machines would introduce variety and interest to their jobs (new force, +1)

*   You could raise wages to reflect new productivity (cost +1, loss of overtime, –2)

- Slightly different machines with filters to eliminate pollution could be installed (environmental impact, −1)

These changes would swing the balance from 11:10 (against the plan), to 8:13 (in favour of the plan).

Cash-flow forecasts and break-even analysis

Where a decision has mainly financial implications, such as in business and marketing planning, preparation of a cash flow forecast can be extremely useful. It allows you to assess the effect of time on costs and revenue, and it also helps in assessing the size of the greatest negative and positive cash-flows associated with a plan, and provides the basis for accurate break-even analysis. When it is set up on a spreadsheet package, a good cash-flow forecast also functions as an effective model of the plan, allowing the effect of variance in assumptions to be examined.

Risk analysis & contingency planning

All of the above analyses broadly assume that the plan functions correctly. None of them assess the risks associated with carrying the plan out and the potential costs should those risks damage the plan. Risk management involves three stages.

(a)   *Risk assessment* requires the identification and quantification of risks. They must then be categorised in terms of potential loss. The importance of some attempt to *quantify* potential loss in financial terms is that this is a measure against which the cost of safeguards can be assessed.

(b)   *Risk minimisation*

   (i)   Selection of counter-measures. Insignificant risks may not justify the cost of setting up and operating controls.

   (ii)   Implementation of counter-measures

   (iii)   Draw up contingency plans (eg backup if counter-measures are ineffective)

   Scenario analysis is a technique whereby descriptions of a number of possible loss-causing events are circulated to the relevant functional managers who assess which are the most probable. Security measures are taken against any events that are thought likely to result in loss.

(c)   *Risk transfer (insurance)*It is impossible to eliminate all risk. Risks that cannot be covered by security measures should be insured against, so that at least the financial consequences are not too severe.

A contingency plan sets out what needs to be done to restore normality after something has gone wrong. The plan needs to provide for:

(a)   standby procedures so that some operations can be performed while normal services are disrupted;

(b)   recovery procedures once the cause of the problem has been addressed;

(c)   the personnel management policies to ensure that (a) and (b) above are implemented properly.

6.8 WIDER IMPLICATIONS OF CHANGE

It is important to ensure that you do not rely exclusively on the results of numeric analysis as the basis of your plan evaluation. Many factors that are important to the evaluation of your plans cannot practically be quantified. These factors include:

(a) **Ethical considerations** – this should include an assessment of likely changes in public ethics over the lifetime of the plan.

(b) **Shareholders** – how will the shareholders, owners, or trustees of the organisation view the plan?

(c) **Members/employees** – what effects will the plan have on members or employees? Should these effects stand in the way of improving efficiency?

(d) **Customers** – will the plan change the way in which your organisation's customers view it? Will this affect their likelihood of reordering?

(e) **Suppliers** – how will your plan affect relations with suppliers?

(f) **Public relations** – will the plan have a positive or negative effect on your organisations relations with the public, press and politicians?

(g) **Environment** – will it enhance or damage the environment?

Any analysis of your plan must be tempered by common sense. It is much better to change a beautifully crafted plan that analysis shows will not work than deal with the consequences after a failed attempt at implementation.

7 BUSINESS PROCESS RE-ENGINEERING

DEFINITION

Business process re-engineering: 'the fundamental rethinking and radical redesign of business processes to achieve dramatic improvements in critical contemporary measures of performance, such as cost, quality, service and speed.'   (*Hammer and Champy*)

Investment in technology can be wasted if the fundamental processes of the business remain unaltered. In other words, the apparatus might change and even the techniques, but not the organisation behind it. This might be a reason why, despite all the investments in information technology, the productivity of office workers has not matched the dramatic improvements in manufacturing productivity of recent years.

Business process re-engineering (BPR), is also known as process innovation and core process re-design.

7.1 DEVELOPMENT

The concept of BPR was originally formulated in 1990 by Michael Hammer in a seminal article for the *Harvard Business Review.* He contended that: 'In a time of rapidly changing technologies and ever-shorter product life cycles, product development often proceeds at a glacial pace. In an age of the customer, order fulfilment has high error rates and customer enquiries go unanswered for weeks.

In a period when asset utilisation is critical, inventory levels exceed many months of demand. The usual methods of boosting performance – process rationalisation and automation – have not yielded the dramatic improvements companies need. In particular, heavy investments in information technology have delivered disappointing results – largely because companies tend to use technology to mechanise old ways of doing business. They leave the existing processes intact and use computers simply to speed them up.'

7.2 HOW IT WORKS

The chief BPR tool is a clean sheet of paper. Re-engineers start from the future and work backwards. They are unconstrained by existing methods, people or departments. In effect, they ask, 'If we were a new company, how would we run the place?' Re-engineers ask two fundamental questions about everything that happens in organisations: 'Why?' and 'What if?'. Only when they receive satisfactory answers to these questions do they then begin to explore better ways of doing things. The critical questions they then ask are:

• What is done?	• Why do it?
• How is it done?	• Why do it that way?
• Where is it done?	• Why do it there?
• When is it done?	• Why do it then?
• Who does it?	• Why that person?

7.3 PROCESSES

By process which Hammer and Champy mean 'a collection of activities that takes one or more kinds of input and creates an output that is of value to the customer.' For example, order fulfilment is a process that takes an order as its input and results in the delivery of the ordered goods. Part of this process is the manufacture of the goods, but under BPR the aim of manufacturing is not merely to **make** the goods. Manufacturing should aim to **deliver** the goods that were **ordered**, and any aspect of the manufacturing process that hinders this aim should be re-engineered. The first question to ask might be 'Do they need to be manufactured at all?'

A **re-engineered process** has certain characteristics.

- Often several jobs are combined into one.
- Workers make decisions.
- The steps in the process are performed in a natural order.
- The same process has different versions depending on the market, or the inputs etc.
- Work is performed where it makes most sense.
- Checks and controls are reduced.
- Reconciliation is minimised.
- A case manager provides a single point of contact.
- The advantages of centralised and decentralised operations are combined.

7.4 PRINCIPLES OF BPR

Hammer presents seven principles for BPR.

(a) Processes should be designed to achieve a **desired outcome** rather than focusing on **existing tasks**.

(b) Personnel who **use the output from a process should perform the process**. For example, a company could set up a database of approved suppliers; this would allow personnel who actually require supplies to order them themselves, perhaps using on-line technology, thereby eliminating the need for a separate purchasing function.

(c) Information processing should be included in the work which produces the information. This **eliminates the differentiation between information gathering and information processing**.

(d) **Geographically dispersed resources should be treated as if they are centralised**. This allows the benefits of centralisation to be obtained, for example, economies of scale through central negotiation of supply contracts, without losing the benefits of decentralisation, such as flexibility and responsiveness.

(e) **Parallel activities should be linked rather than integrated**. This would involve, for example, coordination between teams working on different aspects of a single process.

(f) **'Doers' should be allowed to be self-managing**. The traditional distinction between workers and managers can be abolished: decision aids such as expert systems can be provided where they are required.

(g) **Information should be captured once, at source**. Electronic distribution of information makes this possible.

7.5 CHARACTERISTICS

Because of its strong links to overall strategic planning, BPR cannot be planned meticulously and accomplished in small and cautious steps.

- It tends to be an **all-or-nothing proposition**, often with an uncertain result. It is therefore a **high risk** undertaking and not worth attempting unless there is a pressing need to rethink what the organisation is doing overall or in a major area.

- Many organisations trying BPR do not achieve good results because they **fail to think it through**, do not engage **hearts and minds** sufficiently, act on **bad advice or cannot override established departmental/functional power groups** which have a vested interest in the *status quo*, or in incremental change rather than radical revolution.

- Business process re-engineering has received a great deal of attention in the UK over the last couple of years and there are now concerns that it has been promoted to such an extent that it has become misunderstood. According to a recent independent study of 100 European companies, the Cobra report, BPR has become allied in managers minds with narrow targets such as reductions in staff numbers and cost-cutting measures.

- Champy suggests that management itself should be re-engineered. Managers are not, according to Champy, used to thinking in systems terms, so, instead of looking at the whole picture (which might affect their own jobs), they tend to seize on individual aspects of the organisation, such as re-engineering of processes.

EXAMPLE

BPR

A company employs 25 staff to perform the standard accounting task of matching goods received notes with orders and then with invoices. A process review established that 50% of employees' time was spent trying to match the 20% of document sets that do not agree.

One way of improving the situation would be to computerise the existing process to facilitate matching. This would help, but BPR would go further.

A BPR approach may question why any incorrect orders are accepted. To enable incorrect orders to be identified before being accepted, all orders could first be entered into a computerised database. When goods arrive, they either agree to goods that have been ordered (as recorded in the database) or they don't.

Goods that agree to an order are accepted and paid for. Goods that are not agreed are sent back to the supplier. Time is not wasted trying to sort out unmatched documents.

Gains would include staff time saved, quicker payment for suppliers, lower inventory costs, and lower investment in working capital.

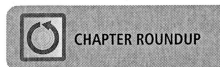

CHAPTER ROUNDUP

- By monitoring the system, managers can identify deviations from the plan and introduce alternatives.

- Performance measurement is highly fashionable because of market pressures and because information technology makes it possible.

- Measurement can take place at various levels ranging from external comparisons to reports on individual activities. Profitability is often a key objective but other 'success factors' are also critical.

- An imaginative approach to performance measurement is becoming a necessity in the modern business environment, and many businesses now recognise the need to supplement traditional financial measures like standard costs with other indicators.

- The balanced scorecard allows managers to look at the business from four important perspectives: financial, customer, internal business and innovation and learning.

- Continual improvement is a type of change that is focused on increasing the effectiveness and/or efficiency of an organisation to fulfil its policy and objectives.

- By identifying any obstacles to change, appropriate measures can be taken to alleviate any problems that may prevent improvements being made.

- Management sometimes must introduce change to the organisation. A variety of forces will promote or resist the change. Force field analysis is a way of identifying these factors.

- Where you have already decided to carry out a project, force field analysis can help you to work out how to improve its probability of success. Here you have two choices to:
    - reduce the strength of the forces opposing a project, *or*
    - increase the forces pushing a project

- A contingency plan sets out what needs to be done to restore normality after something has gone wrong.

- BPR is the fundamental rethinking and radical redesign of business processes to achieve dramatic improvements in critical contemporary measures of performance such as cost, quality, service and speed. The aim of the process is to reorganise business around processes rather than around functions or departments. BPR reorganises workflows, eliminating waste.

QUICK QUIZ

1	What general issues govern the approach to performance evaluation?
2	What is productivity?
3	List seven financial yardsticks.
4	What are the advantages of ratios in performance measurement?
5	List five traditional measures of sales performance.
6	List the four perspectives of the balanced scorecard.
7	What external factors can give rise to the need for change?
8	Define 'outworking'.
9	List the differences between outworking and outsourcing
10	What is a scenario analysis?

ANSWERS TO QUICK QUIZ

1 • What is evaluated?

   • Who decides what constitutes 'performance' and whether it is good or bad?

   • Does an organisation have a single unambiguous purpose which can be translated into specific goals?

   • Are the measures that will be used quantitative and qualitative?

2 This is the quantity of the product or service produced in relation to the resources put in, for example so many units produced per hour, or per employee, or per tonne of material. It defines how efficiently resources are being used.

3 (a) Budgeted sales, costs and profits
   (b) Standards in a standard costing system
   (c) The trend over time (last year/this year, say)
   (d) The results of other parts of the business
   (e) The results of other businesses
   (f) The economy in general
   (g) Future potential

4 Ratios are a useful way of measuring performance.

   • it is easier to look at changes over time by comparing ratios in one time period with the corresponding ratios for periods in the past.

   • it is easier to understand than absolute measures or physical quantities or money values.

   • can be used as targets.

   • can provide a way of summarising an organisation's results, and comparing them with similar organisations.

5 Customer rejects/returns, Deliveries late: deliveries on schedule, Flexibility, Number of people served and speed of service, Number of people served and speed of service.

6 The balanced scorecard allows managers to look at the business from four important perspectives: customer; financial; internal business; and innovation and learning.

7 Any change in the environment of the organisation – political, social, technological or economic.

8 Outworking is when a job is done from home rather than from an office.

9 Outworkers are (a) employed directly by the organisation, (b) may perform core activities and are usually individuals. Outsourcing is the practice of contracting out work; such work is usually peripheral or a support activity and is often contracted out to another organisation.

10 Scenario analysis is a technique whereby descriptions of a number of possible loss-causing events are circulated to the relevant functional managers who assess which are the most probable.

ANSWERS TO ACTIVITIES

1   Invoices per employee per week: 2,500 (activity)
Invoices per employee per day: 2,500/5 =500 (activity)
Staff cost per invoice: £0.14 (cost/profitability)
Invoices per hour: 2,500/7 = 71.4 (productivity)
Cost of idle time: £32 + £4.94 = £36.94 (cost/profitability)
You may have thought of other measures and probably have slight rounding differences.

2   This will depend on your own organisation.

3   Here are four products/industries that have been forced to change in the fast ten years.
You may have thought of other equally valid examples.

   (a)   The major players in the retail food industry have had to change the focus of their
product ranges as a result of pressure from consumers to reduce prices. They have
done this by introducing 'own brand' labels.

   (b)   Building societies have found that they cannot compete against the range of
services provided by high street banks, and have thus changed from the traditional
mutual society.

   (c)   Lucozade became less fashionable as concern regarding the sugar contents of food
and drink grew. The target market of the drink changed away from the wider
consumer towards the young and sporting fraternity.

   (d)   Fewer fur coats are now sold in the UK as a result of social pressures regarding
animal cruelty.

4   Your essay should include the following points.

   (a)   Works councils could raise the awareness of management regarding the
importance of communication with their workforce.

   (b)   The workforce could begin to feel that their views are important.

   (c)   Adversarial relationships between workers and management should begin to be
broken down.

   (d)   Greater commitment towards the organisation may result.

   (e)   No change may occur in attitudes.

   (f)   Works councils may be 'window dressing' with no substance or commitment from
management.

   (g)   Adversarial relationships could be created between works council and unions.

   (h)   Union power could be further decreased.

5   Technology has facilitated the expansion of the global organisation by:

   (a)   speeding up the communication process;
   (b)   increasing the ability to coordinate activities;
   (c)   facilitating data collection to raise awareness of customers' needs;
   (d)   allowing standardisation of response;
   (e)   enabling decision making to be better informed.

6   The relative merits of the two possible new layouts are as follows.

	Advantages	Disadvantages
Present layout (Figure 1)	Logical sequence to production Production lines do not interfere with each other	Cost of larger premises Communication difficult between production lines Isolation from final assembly stops workers from feeling part of the final product Communication difficult along assembly lines
Layout (a) (Figure 2)	Savings on space Less work-in-progress Central final assembly gives all workers a feeling of completing the product Communication between all workers easier 'Shorter' and 'fatter' production lines make communication and team building easier	All workers will be affected by disruption to one area, even if only mentally
Layout (b) (Figure 3)		Lines 3 and 4 are more isolated from final assembly Communication between lines 3 and 4 and final assembly more difficult

Based on these factors, your choice of layout should be layout (a) (Figure 2.) The reasons are that communications are easier, work-in-progress is reduced, team spirit is facilitated and there is a lower cost from the size of the facilities.

7   You could have included the following in your list.

(a)   Trade unions – Effective communications with unions can avoid misinterpretation of your actions and the militant reaction that often accompanies such misunderstandings.

(b)   Shareholders, including the money markets in general if a Plc is involved -you may need the agreement of shareholders in order to carry out your strategy. Failure to have your reasons for change understood may result in the strategy being seen as a symptom of financial difficulties. The effects of this on share prices would be detrimental to the proposed sale.

(c)   The media – much of the potential misinterpretation can be averted if regular accurate information is communicated to the media.

Note. The activity asked for communication with your environment, so your answer should not include internal communication, such as with the workforce.

8   Your lists could have included the following:

(a)   Hospital: security, cleaning services, laundry, sterilisation of instruments, non-emergency transport, portering.

(b)   Council: gardening, refuse collection, street lighting, house and footpath maintenance, snow clearance and road gritting, library services, the running of any leisure facility.

Chapter 06

Health and safety in the workplace

Introduction

Health and safety at work are important for several reasons.

- Employees should be protected from pain and suffering. (Obvious – we hope!)

- An employer has legal obligations for the health and safety of employees.

- Accidents and illness cost the employer money.

- The company's image in the market-place (to which it sells goods and services, and from which it recruits labour and buys in other resources) will suffer if its health and safety record is bad.

This chapter looks at the law and best practice relating to health and safety at work.

Your objectives

After completing this chapter you should be able to:

- Carry out risk assessments as required by legislation, regulation and organisational requirements ensuring appropriate action is taken.

- Demonstrate that health and safety regulations and legislation applicable in specific work situations are correctly and effectively applied.

- Carry out a systematic review of organisational health and safety policies and procedures in order to ensure they are effective and compliant.

- Carry out practical application of health and safety policies and procedures in the workplace.

1 HEALTH AND SAFETY LEGISLATION

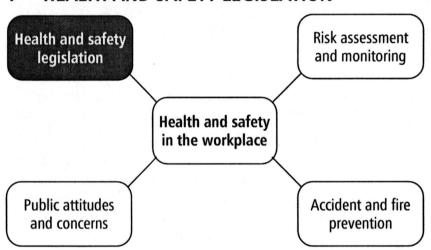

In 1972, a Royal Commission on Safety and Health at Work reported that unnecessarily large numbers of days were being lost each year through industrial accidents, injuries and diseases, because of the 'attitudes, capabilities and performance of people and the efficiency of the organisational systems within which they work'. Since then, major legislation has been brought into effect in the UK, most notably:

(a)   Health and Safety at Work Act 1974;

(b)   the regulations introduced in January 1993 implementing EU directives on Health and Safety.

Some of the most important regulations are as follows.

- Reporting of Injuries, Diseases and Dangerous Occurrences Regulations 1995
- The Health and Safety (First Aid) Regulations 1981
- The Noise at Work Regulations 1989
- The Control of Substances Hazardous to Health Regulations 2002
- The Manual Handling Operations Regulations 1992
- The Workplace (Health, Safety and Welfare) Regulations 1992
- The Provision and Use of Work Equipment Regulations 1998
- The Health and Safety (Display Screen Equipment) Regulations 1992
- The Management of Health and Safety at Work Regulations 1999
- The Personal Protective Equipment at Work Regulations 1992

We will not be able to cover their provisions in detail here. Just be aware that the framework for personnel policy in the area of health and safety is extensive and detailed!

SIGNPOST

We will begin by looking at the major legal landmarks in the area of health and safety at work. This legislation is refreshingly practical, with lots of measures to be taken and procedures to be put in place. Like other legal provisions we have discussed, the 'law is a floor': remember that these are minimum standards, not a description of best practice.

1.1 THE HEALTH AND SAFETY AT WORK ACT 1974

In the UK, the Health and Safety at Work Act 1974 provides for the introduction of a system of approved codes of practice, prepared in consultation with industry. Thus an employee, whatever his/her employment, should find that his/her work is covered by an appropriate code of practice.

Employers also have **specific** duties under the 1974 Act.

(a) All systems (work practices) must be safe.

(b) The work environment must be safe and healthy (well-lit, warm, ventilated and hygienic).

(c) All plant and equipment must be kept up to the necessary standard (with guards on machines and so on).

In addition, information, instruction, training and supervision should be directed towards safe working practices. Employers must consult with **safety representatives** appointed by a recognised trade union, and appoint a **safety committee** to monitor safety policy, if asked to do so. Safety policy and measures should be clearly **communicated in writing** to all staff.

The **employee** also has a duty:

(a) to take reasonable care of himself/herself and others;

(b) to allow the employer to carry out his or her duties (including enforcing safety rules); and

(c) not to interfere intentionally or recklessly with any machinery or equipment.

FOR DISCUSSION

'A baby was put on a social services "at risk" register', reported The Times in February 1992, 'after his father, a roofer, took him to work up ladders in a sling fixed to his back.' The story continues:

After a two-hour hearing it was decided to place the boy in his godparents' care while his father goes to work. Putting [the child] on a register will allow social workers to ensure the child remains grounded. [The roofer] said that his wife... a bank clerk... was happy with the outcome.

'But I intend to fight this decision in the European Court', he said 'I should be allowed to raise my son as I want to.'

Who do you think is responsible for a person's safety? Should people be allowed to take risks if they 'want to'? Or should measures be taken to protect them 'for their own good'?

1.2 THE MANAGEMENT OF HEALTH AND SAFETY AT WORK REGULATIONS 1999

Under the Management of Health and Safety at Work Regulations 1999 employers now have the following additional general duties.

(a)   They must carry out risk assessment, generally in writing, of all work hazards. Assessment should be continuous.

(b)   They must introduce controls to reduce risks.

(c)   They must assess the risks to anyone else affected by their work activities.

(d)   They must share hazard and risk information with other employers, including those on adjoining premises, other site occupiers and all subcontractors coming onto the premises.

(e)   They should revise safety policies in the light of the above, or initiate safety policies if none were in place previously.

(f)   They must identify employees who are especially at risk.

(g)   They must provide fresh and appropriate training in safety matters.

(h)   They must provide information to employees (including temps) about health and safety.

(i)   They must employ competent safety and health advisers.

Employees are also given an additional duty under the 1999 regulations to inform their employer of any situation which may be a danger. This does not reduce the employer's responsibilities in any way, however, because his/her risk assessment programme should have spotted the hazard in any case.

Under the **Health and Safety (Consultation with Employees) Regulations 1996**, employers must consult all of their employees on health and safety matters (such as the planning of health and safety training, any change in equipment or procedures which may substantially affect their health and safety at work or the health and safety consequences of introducing new technology). This involves giving information to employees *and* listening to and taking account of what they say before any health and safety decisions are taken.

1.3 THE WORKPLACE (HEALTH, SAFETY AND WELFARE) REGULATIONS 1992

In replacing many older pieces of law including parts of the Factories Act 1961 and the Offices, Shops and Railway Premises Act, 1963, the Workplace (Health, Safety and Welfare) Regulations 1992 cover many aspects of health, safety and welfare in the workplace. The Regulations set general requirements in:

(a)   The working environment including: temperature; ventilation; lighting including emergency lighting; room dimensions; suitability of workstations and seating; and outdoor workstations (eg weather protection).

(b)   Safety including: safe passage of pedestrians and vehicles, windows and skylights (safe opening, closing and cleaning); glazed doors and partitions (use of safe material and marking); doors, gates and escalators (safety devices); floors (their construction, obstruction slipping and tripping hazards); falls from heights and into dangerous substances; and falling objects.

(c)   Facilities including: toilets, washing, eating and changing facilities; clothing storage, seating, rest areas (and arrangements in them for non-smokers); and rest facilities; cleanliness; and removal of waste materials.

(d)   Housekeeping including maintenance of the workplace, its equipment and facilities; cleanliness and removal of waste materials.

Guidance on the implementation of the Regulations is given in an Approved Code of Practice 17.

To augment the above the Home Office is preparing regulations with regard to fire precautions in the workplace. Assessments will have to be made of risks to persons in case of fire leading to the drawing up of emergency plans and establishing reasonable means of escape. Fire fighting and detection equipment will have to be provided and maintained and persons in the workplace instructed and trained.

1.4 HEALTH AND SAFETY (DISPLAY SCREEN EQUIPMENT) REGULATIONS 1992

The *Financial Times* reported in October 1991 that RSI accounted for more than half of all work-related injuries in the USA and that in Australia it had reached almost epidemic proportions. Disorders seem to arise from poor equipment, environment and posture, which lead to muscles being starved of oxygen, the build up of waste products in the body and the compression of nerves.

DEFINITION

Repetitive strain injury (RSI) is the term for various complaints associated with sustained computer use, frequently including back ache, eye strain and stiffness or muscular problems of the neck, shoulders, arms or hands.

Although the Health and Safety Executive issued helpful guidelines on working with VDUs some time ago these did not have legal force, and employers remained free to ignore the problem. However, under the Health and Safety (Display Screen Equipment) Regulations 1992, any new workstations put into service have to meet new requirements and existing workstations had to be adapted to comply or be replaced by the end of 1996.

The main provisions of the directive are as follows. (You might like to check them off, if you are a regular VDU user yourself.)

(a)   **VDUs**: these must not flicker, must be free from glare, and must swivel and tilt.

(b)   **Keyboards**: must also tilt and be free from glare; the workspace in front of them must be 'sufficient' for the operators to rest their forearms.

(c)   **Desks**: these must be free from glare; there must be enough space to allow 'flexible' arrangement of all equipment and documents. Measurements are not specified.

(d)   **Chairs**: the seat must be adjustable in height, and the back in height and angle; footrests must be made available if required.

(e)   **Lighting**: there must be 'appropriate contrast' between the screen and its background; windows must have some form of blinds.

(f)   **Heat and humidity** levels must be 'adequate' on the one hand and not uncomfortable on the other.

(g)   **Radiation**, for example from computer screens, must be reduced to negligible levels.

(h)   **Breaks**: screen work must be 'periodically interrupted by breaks or changes in activity'.

(i)   **Eyesight**: the employer must offer free eyesight testing at regular intervals and provide any special glasses that may be needed for screen work.

(j)   **Consultation**: employees must be consulted about health and safety measures.

(k)   **Training**: training in the proper use of equipment must be provided.

1.5 WORKING TIME REGULATIONS

The Working Time Regulations, which apply to all workers, including the majority of agency workers and freelancers, came into force in October 1998 but were amended, with effect from 1 August 2003, to extend cover to other sectors eg, all workers in rail transport, that were not included previously. Also, from 1 August 2004, doctors in training were subject to weekly working time limits, to be phased in as follows:

- 58 hours from 1 August 2004 to 31 July 2007;
- 56 hours from 1 August 2007 to 31 July 2009; *and*
- 48 hours from 1 August 2009.

The basic rights and protections that the Regulations provide are:

- a limit of an average of 48 hours a week which a worker can be required to work (though workers can choose to work more if they want to).

- a limit of an average of eight hours work in 24 which night workers can be required to work.

- a right for night workers to receive free health assessments.

- a right to eleven hours rest a day.

- a right to a day off each week.

- a right to an in-work rest break if the working day is longer than six hours.

- a right to 5.6 weeks' paid leave per year.

The rights of young workers – those aged between 16 and 18 – differ in the following ways:

- a limit of eight hours working time a day and 40 hours a week
- not to work between 10pm and 6am or 11pm and 7am (except in certain circumstances)
- twelve hours' rest between each working day
- two days' weekly rest and a 30-minute in-work rest break when working longer than four-and-a-half hours.

ACTIVITY 1 (60 MINS)

Look at your own college (or workplace) from a health and safety perspective. Compare the provisions outlined in the regulations above with what you see within your college/workplace. Make a note of areas where health and safety provisions may fall short of requirements.

1.6 SMOKE-FREE LEGISLATION

The smoke-free law has been introduced to protect employees and the public from the harmful effects of secondhand smoke. Five sets of regulations set out the detail of the legislation that applies to England:

1. **The Smokefree (Premises and Enforcement) Regulations 2006.** On 1 July 2007, the smoke-free law was introduced. It is now against the law to smoke in virtually all 'enclosed' and 'substantially enclosed' public places and workplaces.

Fig 1.
Example of substantially enclosed premises ✗

Fig 2.
Example of non-substantially enclosed premises ✓

    Premises are considered **'enclosed'** if they have a ceiling or roof and (except for doors, windows or passageways) are wholly enclosed either on a permanent or temporary basis. a

    Premises are considered **'substantially enclosed'** if they have a ceiling or roof, but have an opening in the walls, which is less than half the total area of the walls. The area of the opening does not include doors, windows or any other fittings that can be opened or shut. Staff smoking rooms and indoor smoking areas are not allowed, so anyone who wants to smoke has to go outside

2. **The Smoke free (Exemptions and Vehicles) Regulations 2007.** Public transport and work vehicles used by more than one person must be smoke-free at all times.

    Guest accommodation: operators are free to allow smoking in designated guest bedrooms, provided that they meet certain minimum requirements. Smoking is not permitted in common parts or corridors and the exemption only applies to guest bedrooms – you cannot designate a smoking lounge in a hotel, for example. The regulations also state that staff cannot smoke in these rooms as smoking at work is banned

Private accommodation: the ban does not apply to private accommodation, such as company flats, unless the premises as a whole or a room within it is used solely for working in and is shared with other workers. This is particularly relevant for traditional 'over the shop' accommodation as it depends upon how the premises are used as to whether smoking is permitted.

3. **The Smoke free (Penalties and Discounted Amounts) Regulations 2007** set out the levels of penalties for offences under smoke-free legislation.

   Local councils are responsible for enforcing the law in England. Those who do not comply with the smoke-free law are committing a criminal offence. Most offences are handled by means of a fixed penalty notice:

   - Smoking in a smoke-free place £30 fixed penalty notice

   - Failure to display no-smoking sign £150 fixed penalty notice

   - Failing to prevent smoking in a smoke free place fine of up to £2500

4. **The Smoke free (Vehicle Operators and Penalty Notices) Regulations 2007** set out the responsibility on vehicle operators to prevent smoking in smoke-free vehicles and the form for fixed penalty notices.

5. **The Smoke free (Signs) Regulations 2007** set out the requirements for no-smoking signs required under smoke-free legislation.

The operator/manager is required to ensure that there is at least one 'no smoking' display sign at the entry to the premises which meets minimum signage requirements – flat, rectangular sign at least A5 in size, displaying the 'no smoking' symbol and carrying the words 'No smoking. It is against the law to smoke in these premises'

1.7 FURTHER HEALTH AND SAFETY REGULATIONS

Other regulations that apply to the workplace include:

- **The Health and Safety (First Aid) Regulations 1981** require employers to provide adequate and appropriate equipment, facilities and personnel to enable first aid to be given to employees if they are injured or become ill at work. The minimum contents that should be found in a first aid box, for example, consist of dressings (plasters) and bandages of various sizes.

- **The Health and Safety (Young Persons) Regulations 1997** require employers to take into account the lack of experience, absence of awareness of existing or potential risks and/or the relative immaturity of young employees (aged under 18) when assessing the risks to their health and safety.

- **The Health and Safety (Safety Signs and Signals) Regulations 1996** describe the safety signs and signals that should be provided in the workplace, how they should be used and also require employers to instruct employees on their use and meaning.

2 RISK ASSESSMENT AND MONITORING

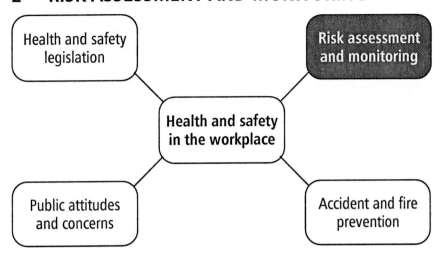

2.1 WHAT IS RISK ASSESSMENT?

Risk assessment is a legal requirement under Regulation 3 of the Management of Health and Safety at Work Regulations 1999. This regulation seeks to ensure that the hazards are identified and assessed by a 'competent person' and action taken to minimise the likelihood of them being realised. This person must have a sound knowledge of the working environment/activity involved, be able to recognise hazards and understand how to minimise the level of risk. Appropriate staff should be trained in how to carry out risk assessments.

DEFINITION

Hazard – is something with the potential to cause harm. It could be a substance, a piece of machinery, an activity, the building itself or the method of work;

Risk – is the chance, high or low, that somebody will be harmed by the hazard.

2.2 ASSESSING THE RISK

The Health and Safety Executive devised a logical sequence called 'five steps to Risk assessment'.

Step 1   Look for the hazards

Step 2   Decide who might be harmed and how

Step 3   Evaluate the risks and decide whether the existing precautions are adequate or more needs to be done

Step 4   Record your findings, inform affected employees

Step 5   Review your assessment on a regular basis or whenever something changes and revise if necessary

Step 1 Look for the hazards

- Take a look at the workplace, for example awkward corners, a jutting drawer of the filing cabinet and how machinery is used. Consider the accident book; are there any accidents that could have been prevented? Be realistic and look for the obvious. In an office, is the filing stored on a high shelf? How do people place and retrieve the files? How heavy are they? How secure is the shelf?

- In a warehouse, do you know the maximum weights you can safely stack? Do employees observe them? How do they stack?

- Look at potentially dangerous substances. Do you have the safety data sheets, or manufacturer's instructions in the event of an accident?

- Look for hazards that could cause injury or affect several people. It is important to ask and involve all employees, as they know what happens on a day-to-day basis.

Step 2 Decide who might be harmed and how

Consider how many people might be harmed and how severe the worst-case scenario would be. The more people in danger and the more serious the accident, the more important the controls become. Include specific groups of people such as young workers, trainees, or pregnant women; they may need extra consideration.

Step 3 Evaluate the risks

Each hazard has the potential to cause harm. Once the hazards are identified a decision must be made on the likelihood of them being realised. This means:

- considering who may be harmed

- considering how likely it is that harm will arise

- considering how severe the injury may be

- considering whether or not existing procedures to avoid harm are sufficient and if not, recommending further action (control measures) to minimise the level of risk

There are many ways to evaluate the level of a risk. Risk level or rating is considered to be determined by two factors – first, the likelihood or frequency that a mishap will occur and, second, the severity of the consequence or outcome of the event. To aid the judgement of the level of the risk, the following simple procedure is appropriate. The likelihood and severity of a hazard occurring are judged separately in terms of three categories.

Severity

This is the measure of the harm or damage as a result of a hazard affecting one or more persons. The three levels of severity can be shown as:

A	Death
	Major injury or disabling illness
	Major damage or major loss to property/equipment
B	Significant but non-disabling injury
	Damage to property/equipment
C	Minor injury
	Moderate damage to property/equipment

Likelihood/frequency

This is an estimation based on all available facts of the chance that a hazard will actually occur and result in injury or damage.

1	Extremely likely to occur – probable within a month
2	Frequent – possible within a year Often likely to occur
3	Unlikely or remotely possible. Slight chance of occurring

Risk rating

Risk	A	B	C
1	Unacceptable – must receive immediate attention to remove/reduce risk	Urgent – must receive attention as soon as possible to reduce hazard or risk	Must receive attention to check if hazard or risk can be reduced and that systems are satisfactory
2	Urgent – must receive attention as soon as possible to reduce hazard or risk	Should receive attention to check if hazard or risk can be reduced and that procedures are satisfactory	Low priority
3	Must receive attention to check if hazard or risk can be reduced and that systems are satisfactory	Low priority	Low priority

Many activities in the workplace are covered by regulations, such as dangerous machinery, hazardous substances, manual handling, etc. A check must be made on whether the organisation is doing what the law requires. Have industry guides, good trade practice and standards been put in place?

The aim is to eliminate (if possible) and certainly reduce the risk of the hazard occurring. The law states that management must do what is reasonably practicable to make the work safe.

- Draw up a **priority action list**, with hazards that have the potential to cause the greatest harm and for the highest number of people at the top of the list.

- Look at ways to **eliminate the hazard** altogether. If that is not possible look to control the hazards so that the chance of them being realised is minimised.

- Ensure that the **controls** have suitably reduced the risk and have not created another hazard.

- **Appoint somebody** as responsible for ensuring that the action is carried out and provide a target date for completion. All of these details must be recorded. The section manager should ensure that the recommendations have been put into place.

When controlling risks follow the principles below:

- try a less risky option, eg change from using a hazardous substance to an alternative that is less hazardous;

- prevent access to the hazard (for example, by guarding or restricting access to qualified staff);

- organise work to reduce exposure to the hazard;

- issue personal protective equipment, but make sure it does not pose a second hazard;

- provide welfare facilities for example, washing facilities for removing contamination.

It need not be expensive; installing a mirror around a blind corner or putting non-slip mats on a slippery floor are inexpensive precautions, or arranging for fire drills, to test the organisation's fire precautions. Failure to take simple precautions can cost a lot of money if an accident does happen.

Step 4 Record your findings

If you employ five or more people, you must record your significant findings and keep the written record in an easily retrievable format as proof for visiting inspectors or any civil liability action. It helps to demonstrate you have done what the law asks you to. Staff may also find it useful to refer to the document.

What will be recorded:

- the hazards connected with your work
- the harm if the hazard were to be realised
- who and how many people might be affected
- action taken to minimise the hazard by controlling the risk

The information arising from the risk assessment must be shared with the appropriate persons. For example if violence is identified as a hazard for staff, then the procedures and if appropriate the training for dealing with violent persons must be delivered. In other words the persons likely to be affected by the hazards must be instructed in the findings and recommendations of the risk assessment

Step 5 Review and revision

Anything that introduces a hazard must trigger a review of the risk assessment. For example, if new machinery is purchased or if there is a change in a process or procedure, then the risk assessment must be reviewed. New hazards must be considered in their own right and, again, everything must be done to minimise or eliminate the risk.

It is good practice to review the assessment on a regular basis to check for new hazards and see if the control measures are still effective. All staff should be involved as they often work with the hazards on a regular basis.

An overview of the process is shown in the diagram below.

Figure 6.1: Health and safety assessment risk

2.3 BENEFITS OF RISK ASSESSMENT

Apart from identifying the measures needed to comply with health and safety legislation, the main benefit of risk assessment is improved standards of health and safety for staff, service users and members of the public. Other reasons to use risk assessment include:

- Reduce accidents/injuries/fatalities
- Increase standards and efficiency
- Helps to recognise, manage and control risk
- Improved employee/employer relations
- Improved use of resources
- Fewer compensation claims
- Reduced insurance claims
- Reduction in the costs of:
  - absenteeism
  - cover for absent employees
  - loss of productivity

2.4 MONITORING HEALTH AND SAFETY

A monitoring programme for health and safety will identify existing and potential hazards and provide recommendations for appropriate corrective action. Monitoring is a pro-active action to ensure workplace health and safety is obtained. A number of monitoring methods are used – inspections and audits, benchmarking, and accident/incident reports. If performed correctly, and with sufficient frequency, health and safety inspections will help to reduce the risk of accidents and injuries, and save lives. Health and safety monitoring/inspections are essential in order to:

- Identify hazards
- Set standards and related procedures
- Establish controls
- Monitor effectiveness

All employees should be encouraged to report unsafe working conditions to their supervisor or health and safety representative, to have the situation promptly investigated and appropriate action taken. A number of monitoring methods are used – inspections and audits, benchmarking, and accident/incident reports.

Inspections

Safety inspections should be carried out to locate and define faults in the system that allow incidents to occur. They may be carried out as a comprehensive audit, working through a checklist; or by using random spot checks, regular checks of particular risk points, or statutory inspections of particular areas, such as lifts, hoists, boilers or pipelines. It is essential that checklists used in the inspection process should identify corrective action to be taken, and allocate responsibility for that action. There should be reporting systems and control procedures to ensure that inspections are taking place and that findings are being acted on. Safety managers will compile their own lists of relevant safety deficiencies whilst on safety inspection tours. The checklist will include:

- **Fire/emergency evacuation procedures**. The manager will check that records of employee training are kept, signage is clear and up to date, fire extinguishers are present and correct, provisions for assisting disabled persons in emergencies are in place, fire alarms are tested weekly and can be heard and are understood by all employees and a fire practice is carried out at least annually.

- **Housekeeping** – checks will cover the cleanliness and accessibility of work areas, the availability of drinking water, the safety of the equipment and storage facilities, the adequacy of the welfare facilities, the suitability of the lighting, heating and ventilation and the control of any environmental hazards that have been identified. Where ladders or towers are used they must be used correctly and maintenance checks carried out and recorded at annual intervals.

- **Electrical hazards** – all portable appliances should be tested annually for safety. Checks should identify damage to cables/extension leads, etc. and make sure they are safely routed and do not create a trip hazard.

- **Machinery** – all dangerous parts should be guarded, machinery instructions should be clear and on display, and a systematic maintenance programme should exist with records kept in a log book, which is readily available for scrutiny.

ACTIVITY 2 (10 MINS)

A scene from everyday office life is shown below. Note down anything that strikes you as being dangerous about this working environment.

Audits

A safety audit is an independent, systematic examination of safety systems within each area of the organisation. All aspects of safety are checked against predetermined criteria and each category given a marked assessment. From this, an overall assessment of effectiveness is calculated, which provides managers with a benchmark of their safety performance. However, because such an audit is by necessity of limited scope, it is not highly detailed, nor is it meant to be unnecessarily critical. The purpose of the report is therefore to highlight and encourage good practice, while at the same time pointing out obvious shortcomings that require attention. In this way the overall 'safety culture' of an area can be assessed within the wider context.

Safety audits give a measure of the 'health' of every area within the organisation at a specific point in time. Part of the assessment will be looking to ascertain what level of follow-up action has taken place as a result of the routine inspections.

Benchmarking

Health and safety benchmarking is a planned process by which an organisation compares its health and safety processes and performance with others to learn how to:

- reduce accidents and ill-health;
- improve compliance with health and safety law; *and/or*
- cut compliance costs.

Benchmarking is not just about comparing data or copying competitors. It is more about continuously learning from others, learning more about your organisation's strengths and weaknesses in the process, and then acting on the lessons learned. This is what leads to real improvement.

Accident/incident reports

Written records not only provide evidence that proper monitoring of safety is an integral part of normal procedures, but also record what actions have taken place. This is invaluable should an incident occur which involves investigation by an external agency, eg HSE, insurance company etc.

SIGNPOST

In addition to legislation, you need to be aware of helpful guidance on health and safety from other sources. The instruction manual to a piece of equipment or machinery, for example, makes all the difference between a help and a hazard. The Health and Safety Commission issues helpful booklets on matters such as working with VDUs, smoking and alcohol. But there is no substitute for common sense: care in handling chemicals, lifting heavy objects, operating machinery, moving around the workplace (and playing practical jokes) is part of every employee's own 'Safety Policy'. We will now look at some practical measures and requirements for accident and fire prevention in the workplace.

3   ACCIDENT AND FIRE PREVENTION

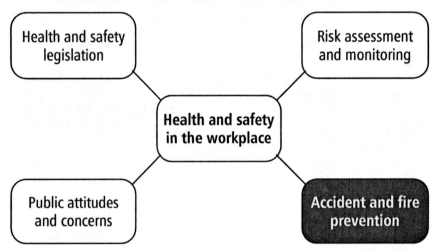

3.1 ACCIDENTS

Apart from obviously dangerous equipment in factories, there are many hazards to be found in the modern working environment. Many accidents could be avoided by the simple application of common sense and consideration by employer and employee, and by safety consciousness encouraged or enforced by a widely acceptable and well publicised **safety policy**.

ACTIVITY 3   (10 MINS)

What would you expect to be the most common causes of injury in the workplace? List at least five hazards or risky behaviours.

The **cost** of accidents to the employer consists of:

(a)   time lost by the injured employee;

(b)   time lost by other employees whose work is interrupted by the accident;

(c)   time lost by supervision, management and technical staff as a result of the accident;

(d)   a proportion of the cost of first aid materials, or even medical staff;

(e)   the cost of disruption to operations at work;

(f)   the cost of any damage and repairs and modification to the equipment;

(g)   the cost of any compensation payments or fines resulting from legal action;

(h)   the costs associated with increased insurance premiums;

(i)   reduced output from the injured employee on return to work;

(j)   the cost of possible reduced morale, increased absenteeism, increased labour turnover among employees;

(k)   the cost of recruiting and training a replacement for the injured worker.

Employers may also be liable to employees in tort if the employee is injured as a result of either:

(a)   the employer's failure to take reasonable care in providing safe premises and plant, a safe system of work and competent fellow employees; or

(b)   the employer's breach of a statutory duty – say, to fence dangerous machinery.

Although the injured employee's damages may be reduced if the injury was partly a consequence of his/her own contributory negligence, due allowance is made for ordinary human failings, such as inattentiveness, tiredness and so on.

3.2 ACCIDENT PREVENTION

The prevention of illness or accidents requires efforts on the part of employers, including workplace design, communication of health and safety policies and procedures, training and so on. Some of the steps which might be taken to reduce the frequency and severity of accidents are as follows.

(a)   Developing a safety consciousness among staff and workers and encouraging departmental pride in a good safety record.

(b)   Developing effective consultative participation between management, workers and unions so that safety and health rules can be accepted and followed.

(c)   Giving adequate instruction in safety rules and measures as part of the training of new and transferred workers, or where working methods or speeds of operation are changed.

(d)   Materials handling, a major cause of accidents, should be minimised and designed as far as possible for safe working and operation.

(e)   Ensuring a satisfactory standard from the safety angle for both basic plant and auxiliary fittings such as guards and other devices.

(f)   Good maintenance – apart from making sound job repairs, temporary expedients to keep production going should not prejudice safety.

(g)   In general, the appropriate code of practice for the industry/work environment should be implemented in full.

3.3 ACCIDENT REPORTING

An accident report is a management tool, designed to:

(a)   identify problems; and

(b)   indicate corrective action.

Recurring accidents may suggest the need for special investigation, but only more serious incidents will have to be followed-up in depth. Follow-up should be clearly aimed at preventing recurrence – not placing blame.

The drawing below shows the format of a **typical accident book,** which should by law be kept by any organisation which employs more than ten people. (The one used by your organisation may be laid out differently, or it might consist of loose-leaf sheets.)

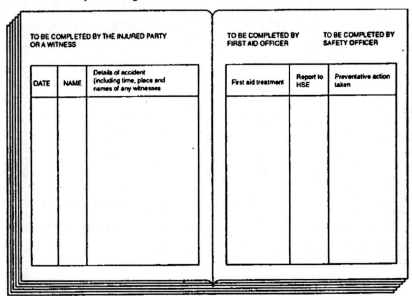

The **Reporting of Injuries, Diseases and Dangerous Occurrences Regulations 1995** (RIDDOR 95) require employers to do the following.

(a)   Notify the environmental health authority or the Health and Safety Executive **immediately** if one of the following occurs.

(i)   There is an accident connected with work and either an employee or self-employed person working on the premises is killed or suffers a major injury (including as a result of physical violence) or a member of the public is killed or taken to hospital.

(ii)   There is a dangerous occurrence.

(b)   Send a completed **Accident report form** to do the following.

(i)   Confirm within ten days a telephone report of an accident or dangerous occurrence (as described in (a) above).

(ii)   Notify, within ten days of the accident, any injury which stops someone doing their normal job for more than three days.

(iii)   Report certain work-related diseases.

HSE
Health & Safety Executive

Health and Safety at Work etc Act 1974
The Reporting of Injuries, Diseases and Dangerous Occurrences Regulations 1995

Report of an injury or dangerous occurrence

Filling in this form
This form must be filled in by an employer or other responsible person.

Part A

About you
1 What is your full name?

2 What is your job title?

3 What is your telephone number?

About your organisation
4 What is the name of your organisation?

5 What is its address and postcode?

6 What type of work does your organisation do?

Part B

About the incident
1 On what date did the incident happen?

/ /

2 At what time did the incident happen?
(Please use the 24-hour clock eg 0600)

3 Did the incident happen at the above address?

Yes [ ] Go to question 4

No [ ] Where did the incident happen?

[ ] elsewhere in your organisation - give the name, address and postcode

[ ] at someone else's premises - give the name, address and postcode

[ ] in a public place - give the details of where it happened

If you do not know the postcode, what is the name of the local authority?

4 In which department, or where on the premises, did the incident happen?

Part C

About the injured person
If you are reporting a dangerous occurrence, go to Part F.
If more than one person was injured in the same incident, please attach the details asked for in Part C and Part D for each injured person.
1 What is their full name?

2 What is their home address and postcode?

3 What is their home phone number?

4 How old are they?

5 Are they
[ ] male?
[ ] female?

6 What is their job title?

7 Was the injured person (tick only one box)
[ ] one of your employees?

[ ] on a training scheme? Give details:

[ ] on work experience?

[ ] employed by someone else? Give details of the employer:

[ ] self-employed and at work?

[ ] a member of the public?

Part D

About the injury
1 What was the injury? (eg fracture, laceration)

2 What part of the body was injured?

3 Was the injury (tick the one box that applies)

☐ a fatality?

☐ a major injury or condition? (see accompanying notes)

☐ an injury to an employee or self-employed person which prevented them doing their normal work for more than 3 days?

☐ an injury to a member of the public which meant they had to be taken from the scene of the accident to a hospital for treatment?

4 Did the injured person (tick all the boxes that apply)

☐ became unconscious?

☐ need resuscitation?

☐ remain in hospital for more than 24 hours?

☐ none of the above?

Part E

About the kind of accident

Please tick the one box that best describes what happened, then go to part G.

☐ Contact with moving machinery or material being machined

☐ Hit by a moving, flying or falling object

☐ Hit by a moving vehicle

☐ Hit by something fixed or stationary

☐ Injured while handling, lifting or carrying

☐ Slipped, tripped or fell on the same level

☐ Fell from a height
How high was the fall?

☐ [_____] metres

☐ Trapped by something collapsing

☐ Drowned or asphyxiated

☐ Exposed to, or in contact with, a harmful substance

☐ Exposed to fire

☐ Exposed to an explosion

☐ Contact with electricity or an electrical discharge

☐ Injured by an animal

☐ Physically assaulted by a person

☐ Another kind of accident (describe it in part G)

Part F

Dangerous occurrences

Enter the number of the dangerous occurrence you are reporting. (The numbers are given in the Regulations and in the notes which accompany this form.)

[_____]

Part G

Describing what happened

Give as much detail as you can. For instance

* the name of any substance involved
* the name and type of any machinery involved
* the events that led to the incident
* the part played by any people.

If it was a personal injury, give details of what the person was doing. Describe any action that has since been taken to prevent a similar incident. Use a separate piece of paper if you need to.

☐☐☐☐ [_____]

Part H

Your signature

[_____]

Date

[__ / __ / __]

Where to send the form

Please send it to the Enforcing Authority for the place where it happened. If you do not know the Enforcing Authority, send it to the nearest HSE office.

For official use

Client number [_____] Location number [_____] Event number [_____] ☐ INV REP ☐ Y ☐ N

DEFINITION

Major injuries include things such as fractures other than to fingers, thumbs or toes; amputation; temporary or permanent loss of sight and any other injury which results in the person being admitted to hospital for more than 24 hours.

Dangerous occurrences are 'near misses' that might well have caused major injuries. They include the collapse of a load bearing part of a lift, electrical short circuit or overload causing fire or explosion, the malfunction of breathing apparatus while in use of during testing immediately before use, and many others.

Notifiable diseases include certain poisonings, occupational asthma, asbestosis, hepatitis and many others.

The standard for the notification of injuries and dangerous occurrences is reproduced on previous pages.

ACTIVITY 4   (30 MINS)

Look back at the scene from everyday office life in Activity 2.

Adopt the role of each of the three workers shown and, assuming that you have by now had one of the many accidents possible in this working environment, fill out a report in the Accident Book shown below.

Accident book

Full name, address and occupation of injured person (1)	Signature of injured person or other person making this entry* (2)	Date when entry made (3)	Date and time of accident (4)	Room/place in which accident happened (5)	Cause and nature of injury † (6)
1					
2					
3					
4					
5					
6					
7					
8					
9					
10					

* If the entry is made by some person acting on behalf of the employee, the address and occupation of that person must also be given

† State clearly the work or process being performed at the time of the accident

3.4 FIRE SAFETY AND PREVENTION

The main provisions of the **Fire Precautions Act 1971** are that:

(a)   there must be adequate means of escape kept free from obstructions;

(b)   all doors out of the building must be capable of opening from the inside;

(c)   all employees should know the fire alarm system;

(d)   there must be an effective and regularly tested fire alarm system;

(e)   there must be fire-fighting equipment easily available and in working order.

Specialised buildings are covered by other legislation such as the Fire Safety and Safety of Places of Sport Act 1987. European legislation was implemented in the **Fire Precautions (Workplace) Regulations 1997** which came into force in December 1997. These regulations require employers to:

(a)   provide the appropriate number of fire extinguishers and other means for fighting fire;

(b)   install fire detectors and fire alarm systems where necessary.

(c)   take whatever measures are necessary for fighting fire (eg the drawing up of a suitable emergency plan of action) and nominate a sufficient number of workers to implement these measure and ensure that they are adequately trained and equipped to carry out their responsibilities;

(d)   provide adequate emergency routes and exits for everyone to escape quickly and safely;

(e)   ensure that equipment and facilities provided to protect workers from the dangers of fire are regularly maintained and any faults found are rectified as quickly as possible.

Apart from **fire precautions** – which are designed to protect employees in the event of a fire – there must be measures for **fire prevention**: that is, to stop it happening! The main causes of fire in industry and commerce tend to be associated with electrical appliances and installations, and smoking is a major source of fires in business premises. The Fire Protection Association (of the UK) suggests the following guidelines for fire prevention and control:

(a)   management should accept that fire prevention policies and practices must be established and reviewed regularly;

(b)   management should be aware of the possible effects and consequences of fires, in terms of loss of buildings, plant and output, damage to records, effects on customers and workers etc;

(c)   fire risks should be identified, particularly as regards sources of ignition, presence of combustible materials, and the means by which fires can spread;

(d)   the responsibility for fire prevention should be established;

(e)   a fire officer should be appointed;

(f)   a fire prevention drill should be established and practised.

The Fire Protection Association provides detailed guidelines for fire prevention, and checklists for use in assessing the adequacy of existing procedures and in designing new procedures.

ACTIVITY 5 (60 MINS)

Do you know what to do if fire breaks out in your college/workplace? Would you recognise the sound of a smoke alarm or fire alarm for what it was? Where is the nearest fire extinguisher? Is it safe to use a water extinguisher for any sort of fire? How do you set off the alarm? Where is the nearest fire exit? Should you leave doors open or shut? Does anybody know you are in the building? If you are not in the building does anybody think that you are?

Find out the answers to these questions!

3.5 HEALTH AND SAFETY POLICY

In order to enhance safety awareness, promote good practice and comply with legal obligations, many employers have a health and safety policy for their staff. Such a policy might have the following features.

(a) Statement of principles.

(b) Detail of safety procedures.

(c) Compliance with the law (eg in siting of fire extinguishers, fire exits) should be enforced.

(d) Detailed instructions should be made available as to how to use equipment.

(e) Training requirements should be identified (eg no person who has not been on a particular training course can use the equipment), as part of the context of human resource planning.

(f) Committees of safety experts, line managers and employees can discuss issues of health and safety. There is no reason for example why safety issues should not be brought up for discussion in a firm's quality circles.

SIGNPOST

Safety policy must be implemented in detailed practice (such as fire drills and equipment checking) but it is less likely to be consistently observed if senior managers fail to set a good example, to discipline breaches of policy, or to reward health and safety suggestions. The aim is to create a culture in which health and safety are key values.

3.6 A CULTURE OF HEALTH AND SAFETY

Charles Hampden-Turner (in his book *Corporate Culture*) notes that attitudes to safety can be part of a corporate **culture**. He quotes the example of a firm called (for reasons of confidentiality) **Western Oil**.

BPP
LEARNING MEDIA

EXAMPLE   WESTERN OIL

Western Oil had a bad safety record. 'Initially, safety was totally at odds with the main cultural values of productivity (management's interests) and maintenance of a macho image (the worker's culture)... . Western Oil had a culture which put safety in conflict with other corporate values.' In particular, the problem was with its long-distance truck drivers (who in the USA have a culture of solitary independence and self reliance). They sometimes drove recklessly with loads large enough to inundate a small town. The company instituted Operation Integrity to improve safety in a lasting way, changing the policies and drawing on the existing features of the culture but using them in a different way.

The culture had five dilemmas.

(a)   **Safety-first versus macho-individualism**. Truckers see themselves as 'fearless pioneers of the unconventional lifestyle... . "Be careful boys!" is hardly a plea likely to go down well with this particular group'. Instead of trying to control the drivers, the firm recommended that they become road safety consultants (or design consultants). Their advice was sought on improving the system. This had the advantage that 'by making drivers critics of the system their roles as outsiders were preserved and promoted'. It tried to tap their heroism as promoters of public safety.

(b)   **Safety everywhere versus safety specialists**. Western Oil could have hired more specialist staff. However, instead, the company promoted cross-functional safety teams from existing parts of the business, for example to help in designing depots and thinking of ways to reduce hazards.

(c)   **Safety as cost versus productivity as benefit**. 'If the drivers raced from station to station to win their bonus, accidents were bound to occur... . The safety engineers rarely spoke to the line manager in charge of the delivery schedules. The unreconciled dilemma between safety and productivity had been evaded at management level and passed down the hierarchy until drivers were subjected to two incompatible injunctions, work fast and work safely.' To deal with this problem, safety would be built into the reward system.

(d)   **Long-term safety versus short-term steering**. The device of recording 'unsafe' acts in operations enabled them to be monitored by cross-functional teams, so that the causes of accidents could be identified and reduced.

(e)   **Personal responsibility versus collective protection**. It was felt that if 'safety' was seen as a form of management policing it would never be accepted. The habit of management 'blaming the victim' had to stop. Instead, if one employee reported another to the safety teams, the person who was reported would be free of official sanction. Peer pressure was seen to be a better enforcer of safety than the management hierarchy.

In many companies, considerations of health and safety are not tied up so intimately and obviously with reward systems and other policies. Nor do health and safety issues relate directly to work. However, from this example, we can learn:

(a)   the importance of management practice in ensuring safety;
(b)   safety (like total quality) is everyone's responsibility;
(c)   culture and structures can either enhance or undermine safety policies.

Copies of legislation are readily available from the government and the Health and Safety Executive. Various companies produce newsletters on the issue to keep managers regularly informed. There is no real excuse for management ignorance in this matter.

FOR DISCUSSION

What are the cultural values in your nation, local community and organisation that:

(a)   promote health and safety? *and*

(b)   promote risk-taking and ill-health?

The diagram below shows a systematic approach to health and safety.

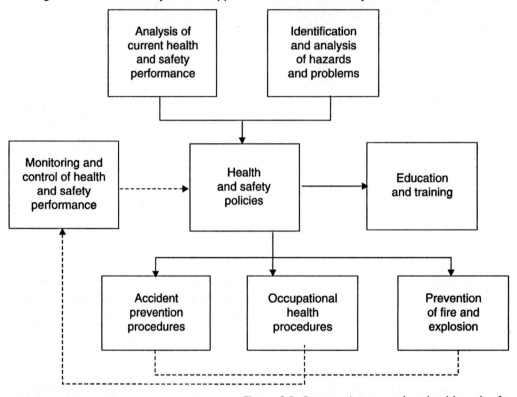

Figure 6.2: Systematic approach to health and safety

SIGNPOST

Finally, let us look at some health hazards that have recently started to cause concern.

4   PUBLIC ATTITUDES AND CONCERNS

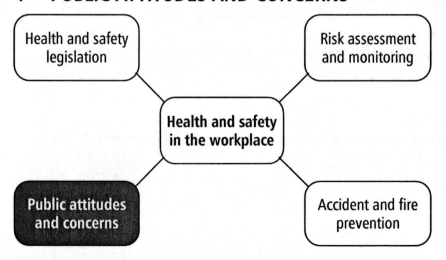

BPP
LEARNING MEDIA

4.1 GENERAL CONCERNS

Many hazards in the workplace are obvious: noise, heat, vibration, odours, poor housekeeping, chemicals, dangerous goods, manual handling and hazards associated with tools or machinery.

There are also hazards in the workplace that are less obvious; these could be called *hidden hazards*. They include:

- workplace stress
- workplace bullying
- alcohol and drug misuse.

These hidden hazards may *directly* affect a person's physical or mental health, causing illness or disease. They may *indirectly* put other people at risk of a workplace incident or accident, caused by inattention, fatigue, depression, physical illness or bad judgment.

A hidden hazard may exist by itself or it may develop with other hidden hazards. For instance, a person who is under constant and significant pressure may become stressed. They might release their stress by bullying someone else, or may turn to alcohol or other drugs to cope. A victim of bullying in turn becomes stressed – and so the effect can spread throughout the workplace.

Just as employers are required to manage physical hazards in the workplace, they also need to reduce or remove the risk these hidden hazards pose to workplace health and safety.

4.2 WORKPLACE STRESS

Stress is a term that is often loosely used to describe feelings of tension or exhaustion - usually associated with too much, or overly demanding, work. In fact, stress is the product of demands made on an individual's physical and mental energies: monotony, feelings of failure or insecurity are sources of stress, as much as the conventionally considered factors of pressure, overwork etc. It is worth remembering, too, that demands on an individual's energies may be stimulating as well as harmful: many people work well under pressure, and even require some form of stress to bring out their best performance. Excessive stress, however, can be damaging, and may be called 'strain'. This is why we talk about stress management, not 'elimination': it is a question of keeping stress to 'helpful' proportions and avenues.

Symptoms of stress (strain)

Harmful stress, or 'strain', can be identified by its effects on the individual and his performance.

(a) *Nervous tension.* This may manifest itself in various ways: irritability and increased sensitivity, preoccupation with details, a polarised perspective on the issues at hand, sleeplessness, etc. Various physical symptoms – e.g. skin and digestive disorders – are also believed to be 'stress-related'.

(b) *Withdrawal.* This is essentially a defence mechanism, which may manifest itself as unusual quietness and reluctance to communicate, or as physical withdrawal i.e. absenteeism, poor time keeping, or even leaving the organisation.

(c) *Low morale:* low confidence, dissatisfaction, expression of frustration or hopelessness etc.

(d) Signs that the individual is *repressing the problem, or* trying to deny it. Forced cheerfulness, boisterous playfulness, excessive drinking etc may indicate this. Irritability outside work (if noticed by the manager) may point to transference of the problem to the non-work environment.

The problem is exacerbated because some people tend to hide their problems.

Warning signs that somebody is suffering from excessive stress can include the following – but of course this will depend on each case.

- A decline in work quality
- Absenteeism
- Regular personal emergencies
- Psychosomatic illnesses such as headaches and stomach cramps
- Use of alcohol while at work
- Persistent failure to do simple things like paperwork
- Making destructive comments or acting in a withdrawn manner in meetings
- Consistently denigrating colleagues
- Active sabotage

It is worth noting that some of these symptoms – drinking, absenteeism etc – may or may not be correctly identified with stress: there are many other possible causes of such problems, both at work (eg lack of motivation) and outside (personal problems). The same is true of physical symptoms such as headaches and stomach pains: these are not invariably correlated with personal stress. Arguably some symptoms (eg alcoholism) might be causes of stress.

The workplace factors that can cause stress include the following.

(a) **Role conflict** – this means the conflict experienced from the various roles played at work – for example the conflicting roles of boss and friend, new supervisor and ex-workmate.

(b) **Role ambiguity** – this means uncertainty about your role in your own mind and the minds of those with whom you come into contact. There is often particular uncertainty about how your work will be evaluated, how much responsibility you have and what others expect of you.

(c) **Role overload/underload** – this means having to do too much work or work which is too hard, or too little work or work which is too easy, boring and repetitive.

(d) **Responsibility for others** – higher stress is suffered by those who are accountable for success and the performance and welfare of other people.

(e) **Lack of social support** – isolation and lack of social support increases stress.

(f) **Uncertainty** – lack of control over decisions, which affect you is also a problem.

(g) **High levels of public contact** – especially if there are risks of verbal/physical confrontation, or exposure to physical or emotional suffering.

(h) **Poor interpersonal relationships** and personality clashes.

4.3 WORKPLACE BULLYING

Workplace bullying is also known as 'workplace harassment' or 'mobbing'. It can be defined as a 'persistent, unwelcome, intrusive behaviour of one or more individuals whose actions prevent others from fulfilling their duties.' Workplace bullying includes:

- persistent and repeatedly aggressive behaviour that makes someone feel victimised, intimidated or humiliated.

- any physical abuse.

- repeated verbal abuse, including yelling, screaming, personal comments, offensive language, sarcasm.

- inappropriately and unreasonably vindictive, offensive, cruel or malicious behaviour.
- gender or racial discrimination, sexual harassment.
- having your personal belongings, tools or equipment hidden or tampered with.
- initiation practices.

The bully can be an employer, peer, subordinate, or even client or supplier. The typical bully uses aggression and violence to compensate for overwhelming feelings of inadequacy. Some bullies suffer from mental health disorders but most lack self-discipline, the ability to pursue long-term goals, or to work in a team.

Bullying is a traumatic, stressful experience that often results in the mental breakdown and otherwise ill health of the victim. Physical and mental health problems, fatigue, low functioning, and even suicide are common. The victims can no longer be productive at work and are sometimes forced to resign.

Harassment is unlawful under the Equality Act 2010 if it is connected with a person's; age, sex, disability, gender, whether they are married or have a civil partnership, pregnancy or maternity, race, religion and sexual orientation.

Individual responsibilities

Every employee has a personal responsibility to:

- ensure they understand the nature of harassment and bullying;
- be aware of how their behaviour may affect others, and to uphold the standards of behaviour set within the organisation;
- work within the policy guidelines;
- be aware of bullying and challenge unacceptable behaviour where appropriate.

Management responsibilities – Managers have a particular responsibility to ensure that bullying does not occur within their areas and, if it does, to deal with it swiftly and sensitively. Complaints of bullying should be taken seriously and investigated thoroughly. Confidentiality (as far as possible) should be adhered to and victimisation as a result of making a complaint, or witnessing an incident, must not be tolerated. An individual wishing to make formal complaints of bullying should do so through the grievance procedure.

4.4 ALCOHOL AND DRUG MISUSE

All employers and managers should be aware of the problem of drugs and alcohol in the workplace – the effect on individual employees and the potential costs for employers, associated with absenteeism, poor performance, incidents of dishonesty and theft and company image. Substances that can be misused include:

- alcohol (the most commonly misused drug)
- prescription and non-prescription medication
- illegal drugs
- solvents used as inhalants
- tobacco.

A research document published by the Health Education Authority showed that 90% of the 123 Personnel Directors of large UK organisations surveyed considered that alcohol consumption was a problem for their organisation. Employers need to be aware of the employment law implications of employees taking drugs and their responsibilities when trying to determine if there is a drugs related problem.

Keith Hellawell, former Chief Constable of West Yorkshire police has said that employers should have anti-drugs policies in the workplace and should recognise that drug taking and alcohol abuse is a problem. He also believes that 'Safety sensitive' professions, such as police forces, should introduce mandatory drugs testing.

Employers have a general duty under Section 2 of Health and Safety at Work etc Act 1974 to ensure the health, safety and welfare at work of their employees. They also have a duty under the Management of Health and Safety at Work Regulations 1999 to assess the risks to the health and safety of employees. If the employer knowingly allows an employee under the influence of drugs to continue working and his/her behaviour places himself/herself or other employees at risk then the employer could be prosecuted.

Employers also have a duty to third parties under Section 3(1) of Health and Safety at Work etc Act 1974. This states that employers must conduct their employees in a way which ensures, so far as is reasonably practicable, that people who are affected by the operation of those employees are not exposed to health and safety risks. There is a potential criminal liability for all employers who knowingly allow or at the very least tolerate, the use of controlled drugs on company premises under the Misuse of Drugs Act 1971.

Some employees are subject to specific laws covering drug testing, such as offshore oil workers and those working in transport systems – guards, drivers, conductors and signalmen.

ACTIVITY 6 (15 MINS)

Since we have broadened our awareness of what constitutes a potential threat to health and safety, take some time to think about what other issues personnel policies might cover? Suggest five areas for consideration. (If you are currently employed, check your organisation's manual on health and safety.)

CHAPTER ROUNDUP

- The major piece of legislation covering health and safety at work is the Health and Safety at Work Act 1974, which places duties on both employers and employees.

- Regulations under the Act and under EU directives place additional responsibilities regarding health and safety on employers.

- Machine safety, fire prevention, chemicals' handling and so on are obvious areas for attention. However, the average workplace contains many potential hazards, and working conditions (including stress, VDU use and long working hours) can jeopardise health. Detailed safety policies must be formulated and communicated to all staff. It is also important to create a culture in which health and safety are a priority.

QUICK QUIZ

1   Give reasons for the importance of health and safety at work.

2   What are the duties placed on an employee by the HASAW Act 1974?

3   Outline the powers of safety committees.

4   What additional duties have been placed on employers by recent regulations?

5   Explain the term Repetitive Strain Injury.

6   What does the cost of accidents to an employer consist of?

7   What preventive action could be taken to reduce the possibility of illness or accidents at the workplace?

8   What are the main causes of fire in the workplace?

9   What are the major work-related causes of stress?

ANSWERS TO QUICK QUIZ

1   To protect employees from pain and suffering; legal obligations; the cost of workplace accidents; to improve the company's image.

2   To take reasonable care of self and others; to allow employers to carry out their duties; not to interfere with machinery/equipment.

3   Safety committees can insist that the employer produces a written statement of safety measures and consults with safety representatives.

4   Risk assessment; risk control; information on risks and hazards; revise and initiate safety policies; identify 'at risk' employees; training; competence of advisers.

5   A syndrome involving back ache, eye strain, stiffness in the neck, shoulders, arms and hands.

6   Time lost by employees and management; cost of first aid and staff; cost of disrupted work.

7   Safety consciousness; consultation and participation; adequate instruction; minimal materials handling; safety devices on machines; good maintenance; codes of practice.

8   Electrical appliances and installations; smoking.

9   Job demands; role conflict; role ambiguity; role overload and underload; responsibility for others; lack of social support; non-participation in decision making.

ANSWERS TO ACTIVITIES

1   Obviously we do not know the shortcomings of safety measures at your college or work place. Your answer will depend on your following the checklist and identifying what you see in your informal inspection. If you do spot anything which you think might represent a health and safety risk, you should report it to your course tutor or your boss in the first instance.

2   You should have spotted the following hazards

(a)   Heavy object on high shelf.
(b)   Standing on swivel chair.
(c)   Lifting heavy object incorrectly.
(d)   Open drawers blocking passageway.
(e)   Trailing wires.
(f)   Electric bar fire.
(g)   Smouldering cigarette unattended.
(h)   Overfull waste bin.
(i)   Overloaded socket.
(j)   Carrying too many cups of hot liquid.
(k)   Dangerous invoice 'spike'.

If you can see others, you are probably right.

3   (a)   Slippery or poorly maintained floors.
    (b)   Frayed carpets.
    (c)   Trailing electric leads.
    (d)   Obstacles in gangways.
    (e)   Standing on chairs (particularly swivel chairs!) to reach high shelving.
    (f)   Staircases used as storage facilities.
    (g)   Lifting heavy items without bending properly.
    (h)   Removing the safety guard on a machine to free a blockage.

4

Accident book

	Full name, address and occupation of injured person (1)	Signature of injured person or other person making this entry* (2)	Date when entry made (3)	Date and time of accident (4)	Room/place in which accident happened (5)	Cause and nature of injury † (6)
1	TIM SMILEY 22 SPRING ROAD, LONDON OFFICE MANAGER	Tim Smiley	14/9/2000	10/9/2000 17.00	OFFICE FLIT POWDER CO	CAUGHT RIGHT HAND ON INVOICE SPIKE. NEEDED STITCHES
2	FRANCES FINLEY 14 SILVER ST, LONDON DATA ENTRY CLERK	Fran Finley	15 Nov 2000	8 Nov 2000	OFFICE FLIT POWDER CO	TRIPPED ON TRAILING WIRE AND SPRAINED ANKLE
3	FINBAR MCINTOSH 151 QUEEN STREET, LONDON PROGRAMMER	Finbar McIntosh	29 Nov 2000	24 Nov 2000	OFFICE FLIT'S	FELL OFF CHAIR WHILE GETTING EQUIP OFF SHELF - BROKE ARM
4						
5						
6						
7						
8						
9						
10						

* If the entry is made by some person acting on behalf of the employee, the address and occupation of that person must also be given
† State clearly the work or process being performed at the time of the accident

5   This answer is specific to your college/workplace. As an interesting additional piece of learning, though, note how difficult or easy it was to **find out** about fire prevention and safety measures in the organisation.

6   Some areas you might have thought of include:

     (a)   alcohol on the premises;

     (b)   drug taking (including prescription drugs) on the premises;

     (c)   horse play and practical jokes;

     (d)   noise (or 'acoustic shock'), particularly from headset use.

     (e)   workplace behaviour: running, throwing things, etc;

     (f)   tiredness (dangerous objects, dust, slippery objects etc).

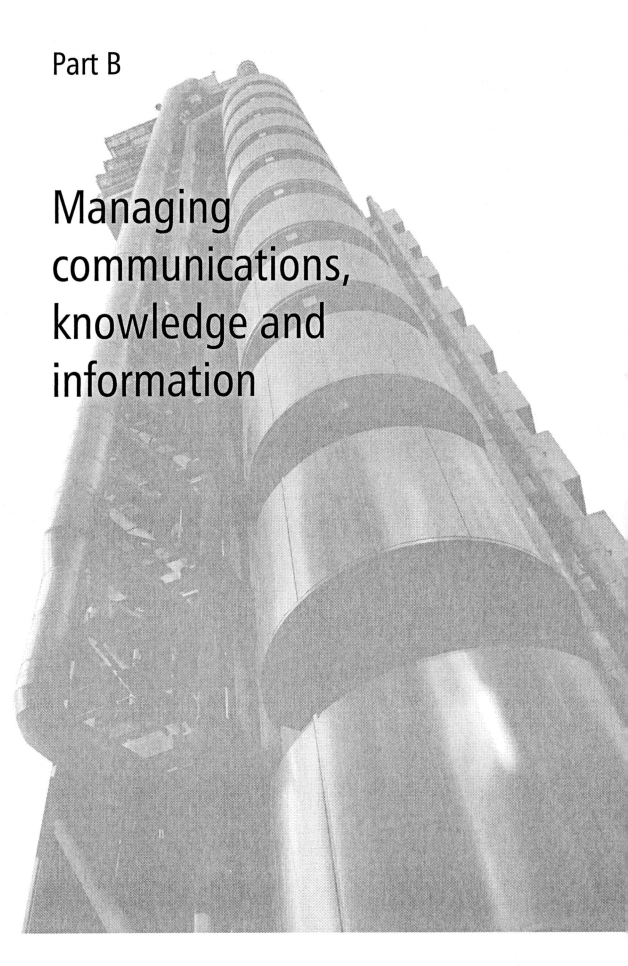

Part B

Managing communications, knowledge and information

Chapter

07 Information and knowledge needs

Introduction

In this chapter we introduce the concept of an information system. We start with the information requirements of the modern organisation and consider various aspects of the use of information systems to address corporate needs and make decisions.

The information system of an organisation is essential to allow the day-to-day activities to take place. Management and staff need information for decision-making. We describe the different types of decisions that are made within organisations and demonstrate how these dictate the type of information and information system required by the decision-makers.

Relationships are critical to success; so often, knowing the right person to ask is as valuable as knowing the answer yourself, if not more so. Being well connected is the ultimate source of personal effectiveness and advantage. And it is now a case of shared success – with what you can give being as important as what you get out of your networking success.

Personal networking provides a straightforward approach to building and working within networks. It delivers a practical guide to creating the kind of network that you need, and becoming a natural and effective networked communicator.

Your objectives

After completing this chapter you should be able to:

- Understand how to assess information and knowledge needs
- Discuss the range of decisions to be taken
- Examine the information and knowledge needed to ensure effective decision taking
- Justify recommendations for improvement
- Identify stakeholders for a decision-making process
- Make contact with those identified and develop business relationships
- Involve those identified in decision making as appropriate
- Design strategies for improvement

1 BUSINESS DATA, INFORMATION AND KNOWLEDGE

1.1 DATA AND INFORMATION

Information and communication are the means by which the activities of an organisation are coordinated. Information is sometimes said to be processed data. In normal everyday speech, the term 'data' and 'information' are often used interchangeably, as meaning the same thing. However, there are stricter definitions of the two terms, which make an important distinction between them.

> **DEFINITION**
>
> **Data** is the complete range of raw facts and measurements eg, letters, numbers, symbols, sounds and/or images, relating to events in the organisation or its environment. Data is collected and then processed into information.
>
> **Information** is data that has been processed ie, organised and arranged into a form that people can understand and use.

1.2 KNOWLEDGE

Knowledge is commonly distinguished from data and information. Data represents observations or facts out of context, and therefore not directly meaningful. Information results from placing data within some meaningful context, often in the form of a message.

DEFINITION

Knowledge is information within people's minds.

Knowledge management describes the process of collecting, storing and using the knowledge held within an organisation.

Knowledge Work Systems (KWS) are information systems that facilitate the creation and integration of new knowledge into an organisation.

Knowledge workers are people whose jobs consist primarily of creating new information and knowledge. They are often members of a profession such as doctors, engineers, authors, lawyers and scientists.

We have come to believe that knowledge is based on the meaningfully organised accumulation of information (messages) through experience, communication or inference. General knowledge is broad, often publicly available, and independent of particular events. Specific knowledge, in contrast, is context-specific. Knowledge can be viewed both as a *thing* to be stored and manipulated and as a *process* of simultaneously knowing and acting – that is, applying expertise. As a practical matter, organisations need to manage knowledge both as object *and* process.

1.3 RANGE OF PURPOSES

An organisation is composed of resources – people, materials, machines and money – and the activities it carries out to achieve its objectives. Information is necessary to convert these resources for use in the organisation's activities.

Often when data is processed the information is communicated immediately to the person who wishes to use it. If it is kept for later use it must be stored and then retrieved when required.

Organisations require information for a range of purposes. These can be categorised as follows.

- **Planning** – requires knowledge of the available resources, possible time scales and the likely outcome under alternative scenarios. Information is required that helps decision-making and how to implement decisions taken.

- **Monitoring and controlling** – once a plan is implemented, its actual performance must be controlled. Information is required to assess whether activities are proceeding as planned or whether there is some unexpected deviation from plan. It may consequently be necessary to take some form of corrective action.

- **Recording transactions** – information about each transaction or event is required. Reasons include:
  - Documentation of transactions can be used as evidence in a case of dispute
  - There may be a legal requirement to record transactions eg, for accounting and audit purposes
  - Operational information can be built up, allowing control action to be taken.

- **Performance measurement** – comparisons against budget or plan can be made. This may involve the collection of information on e.g., costs, revenues, volumes, time scales and profitability.

- **Decision-making** – just as decision-making can be analysed into three levels, so information necessary to make decisions within an organisation can be analysed in the same way.

ACTIVITY 1 (10 MINS)

Information is often required by people outside the organisation for making judgements and decisions relating to an organisation. Give four examples of decisions which may be taken by outsiders.

2 DECISION-MAKING

2.1 DECISIONS

A decision is a choice whereby a person forms a conclusion about a situation. Within an organisation, it is the point at which plans, policies and objectives are translated into concrete actions. Planning leads to decisions guided by company policy and objectives and implies the selection from alternative objectives, policies, procedures and programmes. The purpose of decision-making is to direct human behaviour towards a future goal. If there were no alternatives, there would be no need for a decision.

2.2 TYPES OF DECISIONS

Drucker distinguishes between 'tactical' and 'strategic' decisions. We will be examining these in the next section. Other classifications include a division between organisational and personal decisions:

    (a)   **Organisational decisions** are those made in the role of an official of the company and reflect company policy.

    (b)   **Personal decisions** refer to those made by a manager as an individual and cannot be delegated.

Another classification is between *basic* and *routine* decisions:

    (a)   **Basic decisions** are long-range in scope, e.g. the location of factory in a Development Area, or deciding what product to make. Wrong decisions on these matters can be costly.

    (b)   **Routine decisions** are made repetitively and need little thought.

Decisions may be classified as:

(a)   **structured** – they are programmed eg, stock re-ordering

(b)   **unstructured** – 'fuzzy' complex problems with no clear cut solutions eg, introducing a new product line

(c)   **semi-structured** – some standard procedures are applied, but also some individual judgement eg, production scheduling

A final, similar, classification by H A Simon distinguishes between programmed and unprogrammed decisions:

(a)   Automatic decision-making in a computerised control system means that the elements of some (or all) of the factors needed to make the decision have been programmed into the computer, thus allowing the computer to choose 'automatically'. Programmed decisions are routine and repetitive eg, re-ordering stock, and have procedures set up to deal with them. Risks involved are not high and they therefore can be more easily delegated.

(b)   Any decision that requires management judgement will be a non-programmed decision, so that automatic decision-making would not be appropriate. Unprogrammed decisions are new and non-repetitive, where risks involved are high and they cannot easily be assessed in numerical terms. There are many courses of action possible and decisions made will mean a greater expenditure of resources.

2.3   MANAGEMENT DECISION-MAKING

Within an organisation, different types of decision are taken at different levels. Senior management will be involved in decisions that affect the business as a whole; decisions that affect only one aspect of the business will be delegated to lower levels of management. As we explained in Chapter 2 planning and control decisions are taken at the strategic, tactical and operational levels of organisational activity.

Strategic planning is a process of deciding on objectives of the organisation, on changes in these objectives, on the resources used to attain these objectives and on the policies that are to govern the acquisition, use and disposition of these resources. Strategic decision-making:

*   is medium- to long-term
*   involves high levels of uncertainty and risk (the future is unpredictable)
*   involves situations that may not recur
*   deals with complex issues

Tactical planning/control (also called management control) means ensuring that resources are obtained and used effectively and efficiently in the accomplishment of the organisation's objectives.

*   Efficiency means that resources input to a process produce the optimum (maximum) amount of outputs.

*   Effectiveness means that the resources are used to achieve the desired ends.

Tactical decisions are routine, usually contain few alternatives and relate to the economic use of resources.

Operational control ensures that specific tasks are carried out effectively and efficiently. It focuses on individual tasks, and is carried out within the strictly defined guidelines issued by strategic planning and tactical control decisions. Managers at this level decide what needs to be done from day to day and task to task

It may help to clarify the above to consider it in terms of how well **structured** the problem situation is. Examples of unstructured and structured decisions at the different levels of management are shown in the following table.

Decision level	Structured	Semi-structured	Unstructured
Operational	Stock control procedures	Selection of new supplier	Hiring supervisor
Tactical	Selection of products to discount	Allocation of budget	Expanding into a new design
Strategic	Major investment decisions	Entry to new market; new product line	Reorganisation of whole company

2.4 DECISION MAKING AND DECISION-TAKING

Poulton (1982) distinguishes decision-making from decision-taking. Decision-makers are all those who have an interest (active or passive) in a particular decision. Decision-takers are 'those charged with reaching decisions and making specific commitments'. Decision-making, therefore, comprises the whole process (e.g., problem identification, analysis, discussion, negotiation) that involves decision-makers up to the point at which the issue is decided. Decision-taking is the function or activity of the responsible authority, as in the case of a manager deciding on a course of action.

Identifying stakeholders and examining their respective interests in the issue – in other words stakeholder analysis – is an essential part of the overall decision-making process. Satisfying stakeholders is a complicated task that begins with including their involvement in the process. The steps involved in stakeholder analysis are shown in the following diagram.

Stakeholders may have multiple and overlapping interests, so not all stakeholders will be obvious at first. To accommodate this situation we might ask the initial group of stakeholders to identify other groups who they think should be included. After we include additional stakeholders, we can reassess their interests. This will give an idea of how different groups interact and what role they will play in decision-making.

Customers and final consumers will want the product or service to live up to expectations and expect a quick response to any complaints and replacements for any defective items. For example, if an organisation wishes to follow a strategy that increases the quality of a product at the same time as increasing the price, there may be problems with both existing and potential new customers. Existing customers may not be willing to pay more for the product, while new customers are not attracted to a product that they still view as being of low quality.

Suppliers are generally concerned with being paid promptly for goods and services delivered and receiving regular repayments of any capital provided (eg banks). For example, if an organisation wishes to follow a strategy that improves working capital management by paying suppliers late, existing suppliers may decide to stop supplying the organisation, leading to the increased cost of finding new suppliers.

A robust communications and stakeholder involvement programme includes communicating with and engaging stakeholders before making final decisions on significant changes so that you can determine stakeholder response and incorporate stakeholder considerations into planning. Stakeholders have a wealth of relevant experience and knowledge to contribute. Feedback is also considered when making decisions and stakeholders are told how the input was used. If stakeholders feel that their suggestions are ignored or dismissed, the process can be undermined and future communications can be unproductive.

Stakeholder involvement is most effective when it encourages stakeholders to describe their underlying concerns and issues. Establishing a common ground can facilitate the resolution of difficult issues.

Below are some advantages that come with collaboration in decision-making.

- All parties have a chance to be part of the solution

- Businesses gain public approval and trust for dealing with their less powerful adversaries in a reasonable manner and considering alternative options

- Problems are handled more effectively when information is available to all parties

- Long-term working relationships are formed, which aid in the resolution of future problems/issues

2.5 STRATEGIES FOR IMPROVEMENT

Managers should develop consistently effective strategies and systematic approaches to negotiations. **Problem-solving** and **decision-making** will dramatically improve their personal effectiveness and the productivity of their organisations. Most models of problem solving and decision making include at least four phases:

1   An input phase in which a problem is perceived and an attempt is made to understand the situation or problem

2   A processing phase in which alternatives are generated and evaluated and a solution is selected

3   An output phase which includes planning for and implementing the solution

4   A review phase in which the solution is evaluated and modifications are made, if necessary

Most researchers describe the problem-solving/decision-making process as beginning with the perception of a gap and ending with the implementation and evaluation of a solution to fill that gap. Each phase of the process includes specific steps to be completed before moving to the next phase.

One of the many models of decision-making is the **5-step process** for decision-making

Step 1   Identify the issue – outline the objectives that a successful decision should address.

Step 2   **Determine the alternatives** – think outside the box for creative alternatives. Innovative choices often lead to a higher quality solution. The preferred alternative is chosen based on careful analysis and the actual decision is made.

Step 3   **Evaluate available alternatives** – choose the best alternative. This third step is probably the most important. Examine factors that would impact a particular decision and also determine what implications a particular decision might have. Write down the pros and cons of each alternative (consider cost, time, ethical issues, goals etc.). Is it congruent with your values or the values of your organisation?

Step 4   **Implement the decision** – take action. Just as important as making the correct decision is implementing it wisely and thoroughly. Address just what will be done to implement the solution, when it will be done, and who will do it. A successful decision is rendered useless when it is not carefully executed.

Step 5 **Follow up and feedback** – part of good decision-making is giving it time to work. Make sure you review the outcomes and reflect upon the success of the decision and what was learned from the situation. If the problem or issue is still not solved or new problems arise, make the necessary changes and evaluate the outcomes

Strategies to improve this process include:

- Understanding power in organisations and knowing how to form and use coalitions strategically to build power.

- Developing the ability to influence outcomes even when you lack might.

- Framing decisions – structuring problems to reach appropriate solutions.

- Assessing uncertainty – recognising and avoiding common pitfalls in decision-making.

- Seeking information – asking the most informative questions.

- Negotiating hard with integrity.

- Balancing assertiveness and empathy in negotiations.

- Managing joint decision making among 20 or more people.

- Using creative problem solving as a negotiation technique.

- Developing action plans—assessing individual negotiating and decision making skills and developing plans to improve job performance.

- Knowing how to assess your decision making skills and develop plans to improve your performance.

- Understanding how different negotiation tactics improve or impede beneficial agreements.

ACTIVITY 2 (5 MINS)

Consider management decisions as they affect work in a purchase ledger department. Classify each of the following three decisions according to the three types of decision identified above.

(a) The payment cycle will be extended by five days to improve cash-flow.

(b) On receipt of an invoice, the purchase order form and goods received note relating to the order must be checked to the invoice. Specified details must be checked, and the invoice stamped to show that the checks have been carried out fully and satisfactorily.

(c) Suppliers who supply over £50,000 worth of goods per annum will be asked to join the company's EDI network.

---

3   THE TYPES OF INFORMATION AND KNOWLEDGE

3.1   TYPES OF MANAGEMENT INFORMATION REQUIRED

A manager needs to know, basically, three things:

1   What are his resources? (Finance, stocks of raw materials, spare machine capacity, labour availability, the balance of expenditure remaining for a certain budget, target date for completion of a job.)

2   At what rate are his resources being consumed? (How fast is his labour force working, how quickly are raw materials being used up, how quickly are other expenses being incurred, how quickly is available finance being consumed?)

3   How well are the resources being used? (How well are his objectives being met?)

A manager uses resources in the light of information given to him. The board of a company decides how much of available funds should be allocated to any particular activity, and the same problem faces the manager of a factory or department, or even a foreman (ie which machines should he use, which men should he put on certain jobs etc). Having used information to decide what should be done, a manager then needs feedback (or else control information from the environment) to decide how well it is being done.

3.2   LEVELS OF INFORMATION

Information *within* an organisation (as distinct from information provided by an organisation to external users, such as shareholders, the general public, pressure groups, competitors, suppliers, customers etc) can be analysed into three levels.

(a)   **Strategic information** – is mainly used by directors and senior managers to plan the organisation's overall objectives and strategy and to measure whether these are being achieved. The characteristics of strategic information are as follows:

(i)   derived from internal and external sources
(ii)   summarised at a high level
(iii)   relevant to the long-term
(iv)   deals with whole organisation
(v)   often prepared on an *ad hoc* basis

Such information includes overall profitability, the profitability of different segments of the business, future market prospects, the availability and cost of raising new funds, total cash needs, total manning levels and capital equipment needs etc.

Much of this information must come from environmental sources, although internally generated information will always be used. Strategic information will be used for the management decision-making previously described as *strategic planning.*

(b) **Tactical information** – is used by managers at all levels, but mainly at the middle level for tactical planning and management control activities, such as pricing, purchasing, distribution and stocking. These managers require information and instructions from the strategic level of management and information from the operational level of management. Tactical management are able to adopt a management-by-exception approach, needing only summary reports from subordinates. As a rule, information is forwarded by tactical to strategic management, in summary report format, to assist decision-making.

A large proportion of the information used at this level will be generated from within the organisation (ie as feedback) and is likely to have an accounting emphasis.

Tactical information is usually prepared regularly – perhaps weekly, or monthly (whereas strategic information is communicated irregularly) and it is used for the decision-making previously referred to as 'management control'. The information would also be in a summarised form, but detailed enough to allow for tactical planning of resources and manpower.

Such information includes productivity measurements (output per man hour or per machine hour) budgetary control or variance analysis reports, and cash-flow forecasts, manning levels and profit results within a particular department of the organisation, stock levels and labour turnover statistics within a department, short-term purchasing requirements etc.

(c) **Operational information** is used by 'front-line' managers such as foremen or head clerks to ensure that specific tasks are planned and carried out properly within a factory or office etc. In the payroll office, for example, operational information relating to day-rate labour will include the hours worked each week by each employee, his rate of pay per hour, details of his deductions, and for the purpose of wages analysis, details of the time each man spent on individual jobs during the week. In this example, the information is required weekly, but more urgent operational information, such as the amount of raw materials being input to a production process, may be required daily, hourly, or in the case of automated production, second by second. Other examples of operational information include:

(i) listings of debtors and creditors
(ii) listings of customer complaints
(iii) machine output statistics
(iv) delivery schedules, etc

Operational information relates to the level of decision-making previously referred to as operational control. The characteristics are as follows:

(i) derived entirely from internal sources
(ii) highly detailed
(iii) relates to immediate/short-term
(iv) task-specific
(v) prepared frequently, routinely

The amount of detail provided in information is likely to vary with the purpose for which it is needed, and operational information is likely to go into much more detail than tactical information, which in turn will be more detailed than strategic information.

What is information to one level of management or one department may be raw data (needing to be processed) to another. A foreman, for example, will check the output of each of the men or machines within the area of his responsibility but his superior may only wish to know about the performance of the section as a whole.

ACTIVITY 3 (5 MINS)

What type of information are the following examples?

- listings of debtors and creditors
- payroll details
- raw materials requirements and usage
- listings of customer complaints
- machine output statistics

3.3 INFORMATION IN DIFFERENT SECTORS

Organisations can be divided into four sectors – manufacturing, service and public sectors and not for profit/charities.

Manufacturing – organisations are influenced by the need to make and monitor profit. Examples of information requirements at the strategic, tactical and operational level include:

- **Strategic level**: future demand estimates, new product development plans and competitor analysis

- **Tactical level**: information on variance analysis and stock turnover

- **Operational level**: material and labour used and stock levels

Service – increased customer and results orientation for all sectors lead to similar information requirements with activities measured in similar ways. Examples of information requirements at the strategic, tactical and operational level include:

- **Strategic level**: forecast sales growth, profitability and market share

- **Tactical level**: resource use and customer satisfaction rating

- **Operational level**: customer waiting time and individual customer feedback.

Public – information requirements depend on objectives chosen. Information may compare actual performance with standards, targets, indices and activities over time as trends. Examples include:

- **Strategic level**: population demographics and expected government policy

- **Tactical level**: average class sizes and per cent of reported crime solved

- **Operational level**: staff timesheets and student daily attendance records

Not for profit/charities – performance is usually assessed in terms of economy, efficiency and effectiveness. A key measure for charities is the amount spent on the cause rather than on administration or advertising. Examples of information requirements:

- **Strategic level**: activities of other charities and public attitudes

- **Tactical level**: percentage of revenue spent on admin, and average donation

- **Operational level**: donations, banking documentation and households approached and collected from.

3.4 PAST, PRESENT AND FUTURE INFORMATION

Another useful categorisation of information is between past, present and future information.

(a) **Past information**. This is **record keeping**, the storing of information about what has been done or what has happened in the past. This historical information will subsequently be used again at some time in the future. Much past information is information of a transaction processing nature.

    (i) In the case of a company, there is a statutory requirement of the Companies Act for a company to maintain proper accounting records of past transactions.

    (ii) Records that are kept of past transactions might be used to generate further routine operations at a later date. For example, a record of a sale to a customer, and details of the invoice sent out, will be kept, and if the customer does not pay on time, a statement or reminder will be sent out, chasing payment.

(b) **Present information**. This is information about what is happening now, so that decisions can be taken about what, if anything, to do next. Present information is therefore most readily associated with **control information**, which is the feedback in a management information system.

(c) **Future information**. This is **forecasting information** about what is expected to happen in the future. It is most readily associated with planning decisions, possibly for a budget, but also for longer-term strategic information. Future information is also likely to include a significant proportion of environmental information, because the future of any organisation will not be secure unless it continues to adapt to changes in its environment.

Past information should be the most accurate of the three categories, and future information the least accurate of the three. The degree of accuracy expected from information should therefore vary according to whether it is past, present or future.

3.5 QUANTITATIVE AND QUALITATIVE INFORMATION

Quantitative information consists of measurable information – hard facts, numbers, weights and measures, percentages, statistics, estimates, specifications.

Methods of gathering this type of information focus on numbers and frequencies rather than on meaning and experience. Examples of quantitative methods of gathering information include surveys, laboratory experiments, questionnaires, psychometric tests and consulting and analysing records. They provide information that is easy to analyse statistically and fairly reliable.

Qualitative information is difficult (or even impossible) to measure in quantitative terms. It consists of facts about opinions, preferences and perceptions. Examples of qualitative information may be employee morale, motivation, customer loyalty, goodwill or attitudes of the general public.

Methods of gathering this type of information were originally developed in the social sciences to enable researchers to study social and cultural phenomena. Examples of qualitative methods are: case study research, participant observation, interviews and questionnaires, analysing documents and texts produced by others, and the information gatherer's own impressions and reactions.

To assist management decision-making, an attempt may be made to provide a quantitative evaluation of qualitative 'phenomena'. For example, accountants may try to evaluate:

- goodwill for the purpose of agreeing the sale price of a business;
- the cost of poor employee morale, in terms of labour turnover (and the cost of training, etc or low productivity);
- the cost of poor motivation, in terms of lost output and profits.

In certain areas progress has been made in **creating** quantitative information, ie in measuring qualitative information. For example:

- **uncertainty**, which inevitably surrounds any decision, can be measured in terms of sensitivity analysis, probability distributions or a 'margin of safety';
- **attitudes** can be measured according to their strength.' For example, a scale of 0–6 might be used to quantify the motivation of employees, with 0 representing poor morale and 6 high morale.

Quantitative information is preferred to qualitative information because it can be built into mathematical models and formulae. Mathematical computer models (such as financial planning models, operation research models and simulation models) that are used extensively by management require some method of quantifying 'variables' in the situation under review.

Qualitative information depends on the experience and judgement of a manager, whereas quantitative information simply depends on the accuracy of the measured data and the assumptions used in a mathematical formula or a computer model.

When qualitative factors will influence a decision, the manager should either:

- use his or her **judgment** in reaching the final decision, trying to balance quantitative and qualitative factors;
- use a technique, if one is available in the organisation, for converting qualitative values into quantitative values, and making the decision on the strength of estimated quantified costs and benefits. This is the principle underlying so-called 'cost-benefit analysis' or CBA, which is sometimes used by a government to make decisions (eg about road-building) by putting money values to **social** costs and benefits.

3.6 KNOWLEDGE

There are different kinds of knowledge. Johnson and Lundvall (2001) distinguish between:

- Know **how**: the ability to do something
- Know **what**: knowledge about facts
- Know **why**: knowledge about principle and laws
- Know **who**: knowledge about who knows what

Other distinctions are between tacit and explicit knowledge, generic and specific knowledge, individual (or personal) knowledge and collective knowledge. Generic knowledge is knowledge that can be widely applied, in contrast to specific knowledge. Scientific knowledge is an example of generic knowledge. A useful way of labelling combinations of such knowledge is done as follows:

	Individual	Collective
Explicit	Embrained knowledge	Encoded knowledge
Tacit	Embodied knowledge	Embedded knowledge

- **Embrained knowledge** can be obtained through formal education and training, in other words, 'learning-by studying'.

- **Embodied knowledge** is based on hands-on-experience and 'learning-by-doing'.

- **Encoded knowledge** is knowledge that is codified and stored in blueprints, recipes, written rules and procedures. It is collective-explicit.

- **Embedded knowledge** is the collective form of tacit knowledge residing in organisational routines, practices, policies, values and the shared beliefs.

3.7 TACIT AND EXPLICIT KNOWLEDGE

- **Explicit** – this is formal and standardised and can be easily shared and communicated. For example, knowing the basics of how to drive a car is explicit. You could explain it to someone else.

- **Tacit** – is personal and rooted in a specific context. Once you learn how to drive a car and have been doing it for some time, you develop certain techniques (and bad habits) and driving becomes second nature. However, this phase is more difficult to articulate.

When we speak of 'knowledge', most people assume that this refers to knowledge that is written in books and discussed in classrooms and conference rooms, a form referred to as 'explicit' knowledge. But knowledge is in:

- Presentations, reports, journals
- Patents and licences
- Databases, software
- Libraries, archives and catalogues
- Manuals, policy documents and memos
- Individual ability, memory, know-how and experience
- Teams, communities, groups and networks
- Meetings, training materials and management information.

Tacit knowledge is subconsciously understood and applied, developed from direct experience and action, and usually shared through highly interactive conversation, story-telling and shared experience. It is tacit knowledge that enables us to recognise the correct 'feel' eg, the right way to hold and use a hammer or a kitchen knife. It is tacit knowledge that is critical to producing a desired outcome when the task is complex. Hence, we recognise that tacit knowledge is involved in a task when we are reduced to trying to explain the 'feel' of something, particularly the way that it feels when it feels 'right'. In many cases, this feel eludes all of our attempts to describe it, and so success in tacit domains comes, ultimately, to a matter of doing it.

Explicit knowledge, in contrast, is easier to identify, can be stored as a written procedure or as a process in a computer system and is re-usable in a consistent and repeatable manner – for decision-making and/or exercising judgement. Therefore, although more abstract, it can be more easily codified, documented, transferred or shared.

Knowledge *about* something is called **declarative knowledge**. A shared, explicit understanding of concepts, categories, and descriptors lays the foundation for effective communication and knowledge sharing in organisations. Knowledge of *how* something occurs or is performed is called **procedural knowledge**. Shared explicit procedural knowledge lays a foundation for efficiently coordinated action in organisations. Knowledge *why* something occurs is called **causal knowledge**. Shared explicit causal knowledge, often in the form of organisational stories, enables organisations to coordinate strategy for achieving goals or outcomes.

Using these two types of knowledge – tacit and explicit, we can see that there could be four ways of acquiring or creating knowledge:

(a) **Explicit to explicit** – is the standard way that management information is created and amalgamated eg, monthly sales figures.

(b) **Tacit to tacit** – the data capture skills eg, keying in the invoice details from different suppliers, can be transferred to a trainee while sitting next to someone who has been doing it for a while.

(c) **Tacit to explicit** – this is where the knowledge can be articulated to another person and understanding takes place.

(d) **Explicit to tacit** – individuals take in the knowledge and it becomes a part of their expertise ie, internalised. Experience and learning enables individuals to make connections between events and to increase their knowledge and understanding of certain situations.

To ensure than the interchanges between individual tacit and shared explicit knowledge take place, tacit knowledge has to be tapped and articulated.

3.8 KNOWLEDGE, OPINION AND POLICY

Most organisations would admit to having two types of knowledge shared:

(a) Book knowledge – facts, general regulations, statutes, or published works.

(b) Practical knowledge, which can be further classified into one of the following three categories:

(i) Personal opinion – individual opinion not necessary representing best practices. For example: 'I believe that we should check the credit ratings for every customer order.'

(ii) Personal suggestion – personal recommended solution to a problem or issue. For example: 'You might want to talk to the people in the head office.'

(iii) Institutional/organisational policy – knowledge related to what an institution currently practices or has practiced in the past. For example: 'In our company, all of our customers have limits placed on the value of each order. For our new customers, credit checking is a pre-requisite to making their first credit order.

Institutional policy is probably the most common type of knowledge shared, closely followed by personal opinion.

3.9 KNOWLEDGE SHARING

The two main motivating factors that encourage knowledge sharing are the desire to improve the profession/department/organisation and reciprocity,

The desire to improve the profession, or to improve customer care, proceeds informally and naturally in most organisations.

With reciprocity, most people would admit that they felt obligated to help others by sharing what they know because they had received help at some point in the past from other members of the group/department. Reciprocity can also work the other way. Instead of people sharing knowledge as a way to fulfil an obligation, some people share knowledge in the expectation of getting help in return - a sort of down-payment for an expected later payback.

A non-competitive environment plays an important role in supporting and sustaining the sharing of knowledge. Traditionally, organisations have rewarded their employees based on their individual performance and know-how. In such situations, it is expected that individuals will attempt to build up and defend their own store of knowledge rather than share with others Members of team-based organisations are less likely to hoard knowledge because there is no competition among them in terms of promotion or reward. People are more willing to share things when they have no ulterior motives.

4   THE SOURCES OF DATA AND INFORMATION

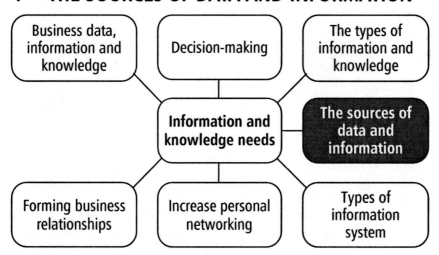

4.1 INTERNAL AND EXTERNAL DATA

Internal information is necessary for all management levels, in every function in the organisation. It will relate to activities or transactions performed within the organisation, such as administrative tasks, the production of products and services, or the sale of those products. Often these activities generate costs and revenues and so a lot of the internal data collected will be quantitative.

The internal sources include:

- The **accounting ledgers**, which are used for predicting future events eg, budgeting and analysing the stock control system eg, speed of delivery, quality of supplies

- **Personnel and payroll systems** are used for costing a project and ascertaining the availability and rate of pay of levels of staff and also for keeping detailed records of time spent on various activities

- **Production departments** are a source of information on machine capacity, fuel consumption, work in progress, maintenance requirements and the movement of people

- **Marketing departments** provide information on opinions and buying habits of customers and potential customers.

Gathering data/information from inside the organisation involves:

- establishing a system for collecting or measuring data eg, measuring output, sales, costs, cash receipts and payments, asset purchases, stock turnover etc. In other words, there must be established procedures for what data is collected – how frequently, by whom and by what method – and how it is processed and filed and communicated;

- relying to some extent on the informal communication lines between managers and staff eg, word of mouth and conversations at meetings.

Knowing the source helps the user to compensate for systematic bias. If for example the managing director of an organisation receives a sales forecast from the sales director and another from the finance director, knowledge of the two individuals involved will allow adjustments to be made to the data. In doing so, the managing director would probably consider their personal biases and those placed upon them by their positions within the firm.

External information emanates from official and unofficial sources, the latter having to be assessed for reliability. It concerns such matters as official areas (tax, regulations, etc), the economy, suppliers and customers.

There are a wide range of sources including the government, consultants, newspapers and magazines, the Internet and other electronic sources such as Reuters.

4.2 FORMAL AND INFORMAL INFORMATION

Obtaining information from outside the organisation may be formal or informal. Formal sources include statements from the organisation's officials, published documents and company advertising. Informal sources include rumours, meetings with suppliers or customers and reports compiled for personal use.

Informal gathering of data/information from outside sources goes on all the time, consciously or unconsciously, because we all learn what is going on in the world from newspapers, television or radio.

The formal collection of data from outside sources may be entrusted to particular individuals within the organisation. For example:

- a tax specialist within the organisation will be expected to gather facts about changes in tax law and determine whether it will affect the organisation;

- a responsible person will need to obtain data about any new legislation relating to health and safety at work or employment regulations. For example, companies registering under the Data Protection Act should appoint a data registration officer with the responsibility for finding out the procedure for keeping personal details on computer;

- research and development work needs someone to coordinate data on similar work being done by other companies;

- market research is undertaken by specialists to find out about the opinions and buying attitudes of potential customers.

ACTIVITY 4	**(5 MINS)**

What sort of data is collected by staff in a purchasing department?

4.3 PRIMARY AND SECONDARY DATA

Organisations frequently need to make use of data obtained outside the organisation itself. For example:

- a survey may have been commissioned to determine customer satisfaction with service arrangements in a large store;

- when determining the number of potential customers for a product, data on the size and the characteristics of a section of the population is useful;

- if a company is to remain successful and competitive, details on the activities (sales, reinvestment, etc.) of its competitors are necessary.

This data will fall into the categories of primary and secondary data.

Primary data – any data that is used solely for the purpose for which it was collected is termed primary data. Some problems can only be solved by collecting primary data and this involves carrying out an inquiry or survey.

Businesses are particularly interested in *market research* surveys. The ideal survey will cover 100 per cent of the items to be surveyed. In practice, a *sample* of this total may be used. The Census of Population in the UK is based on 100 per cent of the population. Other surveys must decide upon a suitable size of the sample to be used and also upon the methods of collection of the information.

Secondary data – is data that is taken from some other source is called secondary data. An important distinction is made here since information collected for one purpose by a company and then, at a later date, used again for another purpose would no longer be primary data. Internal sources of secondary information include:

Accounts department	• Procedures manual
	• Management accounts – balance sheets
	• Financial data
Sales and marketing department	• Sales reports by region
	• Sales by customer and product
	• Competitor intelligence
	• Market prospects and reports
	• Customer complaints
	• Marketing research reports
Production and operations	• Operations data
	• Efficiency and capacity detail
	• Process flow charts
	• Input prices

Human resources	• Number of employees
	• Training programmes
	• Staff turnover details
	• Details of pay

External sources of secondary information include:

- Books

- Journals and articles

- The Internet is an excellent source of secondary data if used with care. For example, you can use a search engine that will bring up websites of interest. Your Internet service provider may also refer you to magazines and on-line newspapers.

- Government agencies are good sources of economic and other statistical information. Most countries have an agency that provides national statistics.

- Regulatory bodies and industry associations – there are many quasi-government and other public sector bodies that can provide data on particular industry sectors.

Statistics compiled from secondary data are termed secondary statistics. For example, the government publish tables of unemployment figures (these are secondary data): when this *data* is used for calculations, they are termed secondary *statistics*.

Government statistics are widely available and are produced to measure the effects of their policies and the effect external factors have on them. Trends can also be noted and this assists future planning. The Central Statistical Office coordinates the government's statistical services.

ACTIVITY 5 (15 MINS)

Give an explanation of primary and secondary information with a quantitative and qualitative example for each.

4.4 OFFICIAL AND UNOFFICIAL SECONDARY SOURCES

We can loosely divide secondary data sources into two categories: *official* and *unofficial*. Official secondary data comprise all information collected, processed and made available by legally constituted organisations, primarily by government departments and statutory authorities. Official statistics abound in all developed societies. Governments collect data about their operations, usually for valid reasons, such as for efficient long- and short-term planning.

Unofficial secondary data comprises all other forms of secondary information sources. Examples include:

- **Private research results** – many organisations and private consultants generate potentially useful secondary data. The major problem is access: the commercial confidentiality that is usually thought to attach to such material means that they are rarely available for public scrutiny.

- **Research reports, research papers, textbooks** – academic research and publication forms a major body of secondary data sources.

- **Opinion polls** – the process of collecting public opinion via surveys and questionnaires has been developed to a high level of sophistication in recent decades, and the results of such surveys (if made public) can be an important contextual source.

- **Market research** – like opinion polls, most market research is carried out by private organisations on behalf of specific clients. Depending on the requirements of the client, the results of such surveys may or may not be made public. The commercial orientation of most surveys tends to limit their general applicability.

- **Online databases** – may range from bibliographic information to census data.

- **Anecdote/hearsay** – making due allowance for exaggeration and hyperbole, we will sometimes find that we need to use anecdotal information. Such sources are obviously best used as 'back-up' to other, perhaps more reliable, sources; there may be occasions when they are the only source open to us.

4.5 CUSTOMERS AND OTHER STAKEHOLDERS

Very often the most valuable knowledge that an organisation has is in the heads of its people, and those of its stakeholders, especially customers. However, people 'walk', so forward looking companies continually to seek ways of locking it in to their organisation.

The two complementary approaches are:

- Converting it to a more explicit form – in documents, processes, databases etc. This is often referred to as 'decanting the human capital into the structural capital of an organisation'. It is also called the 'Western tendency' since it is the main emphasis of many European and US knowledge programmes.

- Enhancing tacit knowledge flow through better human interaction, such that the knowledge is diffused around the organisation and not held in the heads of a few. In Japan various 'socialisation' activities support this kind of knowledge flow that by its very nature also sparks the generation of new ideas and knowledge. Add some basic elements of good human resource management, including a stimulating environment, personal development plans, motivation and suitable reward and recognition systems (such as knowledge sharing awards and stock options), then there is less chance of the best knowledge workers wanting to leave.

5 TYPES OF INFORMATION SYSTEM

A modern organisation requires a wide range of systems to hold, process and analyse information. So far we have talked a good deal about the need to gather and analyse *information* without stopping to consider how that information can be organised. An overall strategy or any of its component strategies could be undermined by an inadequate or non-existent information strategy. We will now examine several information technology systems that deliver information to different levels in the organisation.

5.1 TRANSACTION PROCESSING SYSTEMS

Transaction processing systems (TPS), or data processing systems, are the lowest level in an organisation's use of information systems, serving the operational level and supporting highly structured decisions.

They are used for routine tasks in which data items or transactions must be processed so that operations can continue. Handling sales orders, purchase orders, payroll items and stock records are typical examples. Transactions processing systems provide the raw material that is often used more extensively by management information systems, databases or decision support systems. In other words:

(a)   Transaction processing systems might be used to produce management information, such as reports on cumulative sales figures to date, total amounts owed to suppliers or owed by debtors and so on.

(b)   However, the main purpose of transaction processing systems is as an integral part of day-to-day operations.

5.2 KNOWLEDGE WORK SYSTEMS (KWS)

Knowledge work means creating new knowledge or information by research, experimentation and investigation into existing trends and products. There are many different areas of knowledge work, and each one can be supported by its own collection of knowledge work systems (KWS).

Examples are shown in the following table.

Areas of knowledge work	Examples
Knowledge distribution	Office automation systems (OAS)
Knowledge sharing	Group collaboration systems eg, groupware, intranets and extranets
Knowledge creation	Knowledge work systems • Computer-aided design (CAD) • Virtual reality
Knowledge capture and codification	Artificial intelligence systems Expert systems

Groupware

Groupware is a term used to describe software that provides functions for the use of collaborative work groups.

Typically, groups using groupware are small project-oriented teams that have important tasks and tight deadlines Perhaps the best-known groupware product at present is Lotus Notes.

Features might include the following.

(a)   A scheduler allowing users to keep track of their schedule and plan meetings with others.

(b)   An address book.

(c)   'To do' lists.

(d)   A journal, used to record interactions with important contacts, record items (such as e-mail messages) and files that are significant to the user, and record activities of all types and track them all without having to remember where each one was saved.

(e)   A jotter for jotting down notes as quick reminders of questions, ideas, and so on.

(f)   File sharing and distribution utilities.

There are clearly advantages in having information such as this available from the desktop at the touch of a button, rather than relying on scraps of paper, address books, and corporate telephone directories. However, it is when groupware is used to share information with colleagues that it comes into its own. Here are some of the features that may be found.

(a)   Messaging, comprising an e-mail in-box which is used to send and receive messages from the office, home, or the road and routing facilities, enabling users to send a message to a single person, send it sequentially to a number of people (who may add to it or comment on it before passing it on), or sending it to everyone at once.

(b)   Access to an information database, and customisable 'views' of the information held on it, which can be used to standardise the way information is viewed in a workgroup.

(c)   Group scheduling, to keep track of colleagues' itineraries. Microsoft Exchange Server, for instance, offers a 'Meeting Wizard' which can consult the diaries of everyone needed to attend a meeting and automatically work out when they will be available, which venues are free, and what resources are required.

(d)   Public folders. These collect, organise, and share files with others on the team or across the organisation.

5.3   MANAGEMENT INFORMATION SYSTEM (MIS)

A management information system (MIS) converts data from internal and external sources into information, and communicates that information in an appropriate form to managers at all levels. This enables them to make timely and effective decisions for planning, directing and controlling the activities for which they are responsible.

An MIS provides regular formal information gleaned from normal commercial data. For example, an MIS might provide information on the following.

(a)   **Product information**. Online, categorised information at the fingertips.

(b)   **Sales ledger**. Information will be immediately available relating to customer turnover and payment records. Trend analysis will identify customers whose business is growing or has fallen away.

(c)   **Marketing**. As enquiries and sales arise, the MIS can summarise this data to assist in forward planning. Customer satisfaction can be measured by post-purchase surveys and questionnaires. This information will be processed by the MIS and summarised for use by the management, both in report and graphical form.

(d)   **Supplier information**. Information such as amount spent with each supplier, and reliability indicators (cancellations by the supplier, satisfaction of the customers) will prove useful when negotiating and making strategic decisions.

(e)   **Accounting**. Because the transactions of the company are on the system, information will be available to trial balance stage of the nominal ledger. This will be available to the accounts department with comparable budget and prior year information, through drill down enquiry and also available in report formats.

(f) **Modelling**. Key data from the above areas can be combined into reports, possibly via spreadsheets, the create strategic and 'what if' models.

While a *management information system* (MIS) may not, in principle, be able to provide all the information used by management, it should however be sufficiently flexible to enable management to incorporate unpredictable, informal or unstructured information into decision-making processes. For example, many decisions are made with the help of financial models such as spreadsheets, so that the effect of new situations can be estimated easily.

Operational level MIS

Operational decisions are essentially small-scale and programmed, and operational information is often highly formal and quantitative. Many operational decisions can be incorporated into routine computer processing, for example allowing a sale subject to a credit limit. Most MIS are used at operational level for processing transactions, updating files and so forth.

Tactical level MIS

A variety of systems can be used at tactical level, and there may be a greater reliance on:

(a) exception reporting;
(b) informal systems;
(c) investigation and analysis of data acquired at operational level;
(d) externally generated data.

The MIS at tactical level will interact with the same systems as that at operational level, and in fact tactical information may be generated in the same processing operation as operational level information. For example, tactical level information comparing actual costs incurred to budget can be produced by a system in which those costs are recorded. Functional MIS at tactical level are typically related to other functional MIS. Information from the sales MIS will affect the financial accounting system, for example.

Strategic level MIS

At strategic level the information system is likely to be informal, in the sense that it is not possible always to quantify or program strategic information, and much of the information might come from environmental sources. The MIS will provide summary level data from transactions processing. Human judgement is used more often at this level, as many strategic decisions cannot be programmed.

Highly sophisticated *enterprise resource planning* systems such as SAP are used at this level. They may in fact be essential, depending on the complexity of the undertaking and the degree of competition. *Executive information systems* (EIS) are discussed below.

EXAMPLE
THE FINANCE SUBSYSTEM

In a finance subsystem, the operational level would deal with cash receipts and payments, bank reconciliations and so forth. The tactical level would deal with cash-flow forecasts and working capital management. Strategic level financial issues are likely to be integrated with the organisation's commercial strategy, but may relate to the most appropriate source of finance.

5.4 DECISION SUPPORT SYSTEMS

Decision support systems (DSS) have the potential to integrate data, methods, models, and other tools, within a framework that explicitly addresses the process of making decisions. They are used by management to help in making decisions on issues that are unstructured, with high levels of uncertainty about the true nature of the problem, the various responses which management could undertake or the likely impact of those actions.

- Decision support systems are intended to provide a wide range of alternative information gathering and analytical tools with a major emphasis upon flexibility and user-friendliness.

- DSS include a range of systems, from fairly simple information models based on spreadsheets to expert systems.

Decision support systems *do not make decisions*. The objective is to allow the manager to consider a number of alternatives and evaluate them under a variety of potential conditions. A key element in the usefulness of these systems is their ability to function interactively.

5.5 EXECUTIVE INFORMATION SYSTEM (EIS)

An EIS – sometimes called Executive Support Systems (ESS) – is an information system for senior managers, which gives them easy access to key internal and external data. It is designed to be easy to use. An EIS is likely to have the following features.

(a)   Provision of summary-level data captured from the organisation's main systems.

(b)   A facility that allows the executive to 'drill-down' from summaries of information to supporting detail.

(c)   Data manipulation facilities like comparison with budget or prior year data and trend analysis.

(d)   Graphics, for user-friendly presentation of data.

(e)   A template system. This will mean that the same type of data, for example sales figures, is presented in the same format, irrespective of changes in the volume of information required.

An EIS summarises and tracks strategically critical information from the MIS and DSS and includes data from external sources eg, competitors, legislation and databases such as Reuters. The basic design philosophy of EIS is that they should be easy to use as they may be consulted during a meeting.

The significance of an EIS is that it is not only a tool for analysis, but also a tool for *interrogating* data.

5.6 EXPERT SYSTEMS

Expert systems are computer programs that allow users to benefit from expert knowledge, information advice. An expert system holds a large amount of specialised data, for example on legal, engineering or medical information, or tax matters. The user keys in the known facts, perhaps responding to cues from the system if more data are required and the system then provides an expert solution or advice.

(a)   A user without a legal background can obtain guidance on the law without having to consult a solicitor – for example, on property purchase matters, or for company law guidance.

(b)   A user without much tax knowledge could consult an expert system for taxation for guidance on particular matters of tax.

(c)   As a non-business example, doctors can use an expert medical system to arrive at a diagnosis.

(d)   Banks use expert systems to assess the credit-worthiness of loan applicants.

ACTIVITY 6   **(5 MINS)**

What do you consider is the importance of some of the management information systems discussed above for organisation hierarchy?

6   INCREASE PERSONAL NETWORKING

6.1   PERSONAL NETWORKING

Personal networking begins with family and friends, co-workers and people we socialise with and then everyone they know. Through these connections, trustworthy relationships are developed that generate information, referrals, advice, support, energy, and much more. However, the true value of personal networking is found through the movement beyond one's immediate network and exploiting other people's networks, perhaps far removed from one's own.

Networking is based on good will between people. Research that has been done into networking practice in business shows that in terms of good will from other people:

- 10% of the people you know will actively help you, no matter what

- 80% are not particularly interested in your personal development, but would be willing to help if you take the initiative

- 10% of the people who know you don't like you and will actively hold you back or try to stop you.

Networking is one of the most beneficial ways for people to help each other develop their ideas and professional careers. It increases the opportunity for people to talk with each other and share ideas, information and resources and can serve to enhance both the personal and professional aspects of one's life. Building a strong network requires the effort of everyone involved.

Effective networking requires people to:

- effectively communicate
- keep pace with developments and trends in their fields
- be prepared and willing to share information
- keep in touch with others
- nurture friendships and relationships
- listen carefully and show interest in what others are saying
- exhibit curiosity – ask questions
- continue to learn – it is a life-long process
- stay visible – attend industry and community functions

Once you begin to make contacts you may find that you will become part of a group, meeting together to develop mutual interests or communicating via email and the Internet.

6.2 STAKEHOLDERS AND USEFUL CONTACTS

Networking means staying in touch with organisations and key individuals who can affect your work or help you to achieve your goals. It can serve many purposes and help you to:

1. Build alliances that will strengthen your work
2. Stay in touch with developments in your area of work
3. Get access to information that will help your work
4. Influence other organisations to take up and support your issues
5. Influence individual decision-makers

Networking is about connections. In the business sense, it is nothing more complicated than working out ways to get other people to send you business, based on word of mouth or direct introduction.

DEFINITION

Networking is consciously developing contacts in an effort to increase the number of referrals you get for your business.

Contacts are people with whom you have developed, or are developing, an ongoing relationship of trust and mutual respect, specifically regarding business matters.

Referrals are the recommendation of a business to a person who knows the prospective customer well enough to have developed some level of established trust.

Stakeholders can be internal (top management, line managers, functional heads, service and support workers) or external (regulators, environmental and legal entities, the general public). They are clients, project managers and teams, contractors and subcontractors, distributors and suppliers, and everyone else with a stake in an outcome.

This is how to arrange to meet with others who may be interested:

- Send e-mails to appropriate discussion lists.
- To colleagues.
- To people in other organisations.
- Ask if anyone is interested in meeting locally.
- On which dates they would like to meet.
- Will they forward the e-mail to anyone who might be interested?

Networking organisations can provide access to members in a wide range of fields and give you the ability to pursue additional areas of business.

Because of the careful selection of people accepted for membership, you will find that you never want for access to the best services and products available in your area. If a member cannot supply what you need, there is a high degree of likelihood that he or she can refer you to someone who can supply just about any thing you need.

6.3 INTERNAL AND EXTERNAL CONTACTS

Networking includes interaction with outsiders and socialising/politicking inside and outside the organisation; routine communication activities include exchanging information and handling paperwork; traditional management activities consist of planning, decision making and controlling; and human resource management includes motivating/reinforcing, disciplining/ punishing, managing conflict, staffing and training/developing.

Networking in the sense that we use the word here is a deliberate, planned process. It involves the open exchange of leads and introductions. It is a completely honest process.

Where and how you network can add value professionally and personally:

- Professional contacts
- Information sources
- Friends

Potentially you can network anywhere – socially, locally, at work, nationally and within the profession. Virtual networks are also important via promotional literature, e-mail discussion lists and newsletters

Network at work – reception staff are the first point of contact in the organisation. They are very important people to network with. You can also network:

- Informally, over lunch or a coffee
- Formally, in your professional capacity
- In person
- By phone
- E-mail
- Greet and meet
- Walk and talk

Network via the canteen and the works sociable club. Every so often let the people you support know that you are there, what you do and what you can do for them.

All new staff should have an induction, ensure staff know:

- Where you work
- When you are available
- What you can do for them (even for simple queries)

Networking outside of your workplace includes:

- networking with other professional groups that are relevant to your work

- attending social events away from work. They are a good opportunity to network and enjoy yourself at the same time

- being interested in the professional bodies that relate to you at work and your organisation

6.4 DIRECT OR VIA MEDIA

The most fundamental act of networking occurs when you give someone a referral or get a referral from someone based on the relationship of trust that has been built between the two of you. That connection is a simple network. And that is, in the end, all that is involved in even the most sophisticated networks. People exchanging connections, or leads, based on trust.

Networking can be done anywhere that two or more people get together. It is important to be aware of what is appropriate in the setting. Sometimes a direct approach is appropriate, others it is more acceptable to simply ask a person what they do and ask them for a business card 'in case I run into anyone who could use your services.'

Professional networking groups exist to create an exchange of leads between members. They are structured to ensure that this is effective for all the members.

The basic concept is simple. The group meets at regular times at a specific place, usually once a month or once a week. Each member tells the group exactly what would be their best customer/contact, and they keep an eye out for possible leads for the other members during the course of the week. At each meeting they exchange leads.

These groups are the best source for referrals. They limit membership, in most cases, to one person from any specific profession. This alone makes for a more certain result. The better groups also check carefully to make sure that prospective members are businesses operated with integrity and a good record of customer satisfaction. And they require a fee for membership. While the fees aren't usually anything huge, they do discourage the curiosity seekers.

What this all means is that you can be confident in the quality of work that will be done for someone when you refer them to a member of the group. Since each member has the same level of assurance, it is easier for them to send people to you.

Social networking is the latest hot application to hit the Internet world. Basically, it is a kind of search engine for people and relationships, and is based on the theory that 'a friend of my friend is my friend'. The concept revolves around connections – who you know, what you know, and who knows you.

There are also several business-oriented social networking websites available. LinkedIn.com, for example, allows you to search for people, send them messages and invite them to be added your list of contacts. On Ryze.com, you set up your own networking homepage, and you can contact other members directly. At Tribe.net, you can join a public 'tribe' or be invited to join a private 'tribe.' The idea is to find links between people and create trustworthy paths for contacting others, all in an effort to increase efficiency in establishing business contacts and cut down on cold calling.

6.5 FORMAL AND INFORMAL NETWORKING PROSPECTS

Although we are looking at networking as it applies to business, it is a practice that can cover a lot of ground. In its simplest form, networking simply means making connections to make exchanges easier. This can be social, personal, professional, or even technical.

In the professional setting, networking is getting to know people and businesses, and developing trust and communication to make the process of business easier and more profitable. This usually involves the exchange of 'leads', or referrals to potential customers, between businesses.

This can be by formal agreement, as happens in a networking group, or through the development of personal contacts over the course of time.

Identifying networking prospects among your friends, neighbours and acquaintances can pay off. They may have a useful contact in an industry you are interested in.

6.6 RELATING AND INTERACTING TRUST AND CONFIDENTIALITY

Effective business networking is the linking together of individuals who, through trust and relationship building, become walking, talking advertisements for one another.

- Keep in mind that networking is about being genuine and authentic, building trust and relationships, and seeing how you can help others.

- Ask yourself what your goals are in participating in networking meetings so that you will pick groups that will help you get what you are looking for. Some meetings are based more on learning, making contacts, and/or volunteering rather than on strictly making business connections.

- Visit as many groups as possible that spark your interest. Notice the tone and attitude of the group. Do the people sound supportive of one another? Does the leadership appear competent? Many groups will allow you to visit a couple of times before joining.

- Hold volunteer positions in organisations. This is a great way to stay visible and give back to groups that have helped you.

- Ask open-ended questions in networking conversations. This means questions that ask who, what, where, when, and how as opposed to those that can be answered with a simple yes or no. This form of questioning opens up the discussion and shows listeners that you are interested in them.

- Become known as a powerful resource for others. When you are known as a strong resource, people remember to turn to you for suggestions, ideas, names of other people, etc. This keeps you visible to them.

- Have a clear understanding of what you do and why, for whom, and what makes your doing it special or different from others doing the same thing. In order to get referrals, you must first have a clear understanding of what you do that you can easily articulate to others.

- Be able to articulate what you are looking for and how others may help you. Too often people in conversations ask, 'How may I help you?' and no immediate answer comes to mind.

- Follow through quickly and efficiently on referrals you are given. When people give you referrals, your actions are a reflection on them. Remember, there are three sides to every referral. Your side, as the person who is being trusted by both to arrange a good match. The customer's side, since they are trusting you to get them someone to handle a problem for them – the right way the first time. And of course the other businessperson's side, since they are expecting that this customer will pay on time and not create more problems than the job is worth. Respect and honour that and your referrals will grow.

- Call those you meet who may benefit from what you do and vice versa. Express that you enjoyed meeting them, and ask if you could get together and share ideas.

- Never talk about something shared in confidence. If you have a reputation for discretion, your network will grow.

- Share the credit with other individuals who helped you earn it. When others congratulate you, mention your colleague's contribution. Write letters of appreciation to his or her boss.

Remember that networking should have a purpose and should be with people who have the same interests as your organisation, or decision makers who can affect your work.

7 FORMING BUSINESS RELATIONSHIPS

7.1 STAKEHOLDER CONTACTS

Stakeholders have been defined as 'any group or individual who can affect or is affected by the achievement of the firm's objectives.'

- Primary stakeholders have interests that are directly linked to the fortunes of a company. They typically include shareholders and investors, employees, customers, suppliers, and residents of the communities where the company operates.

- Secondary stakeholders have an indirect influence on an organisation or are less directly affected by its activities. They include the media and pressure groups, regulators, competitors, and others that form the social ecology of an organisation.

Building relationships with clients, stakeholders and organisational members means following through on commitments, respecting confidentiality, and demonstrating an interest in their work-related issues and activities. **Collaborative relationships** with stakeholders can increase an organisation's stability in a turbulent environment and enhance its control over changing circumstances. For example, suppliers will be more likely to show optimal responsiveness to company needs (as well as flexibility in demanding payment in times when cash-flow is limited) if there is a trusting relationship. Similarly, if a company has a good working relationship with the community, it is more likely to get cooperation when it comes to expanding facilities or engaging in activities that will affect the community. When a company establishes collaborative relationships with stakeholder groups it is much like the process individuals go through to find and develop lasting interpersonal relationships. We decide what we want from a relationship, consider how our existing relationships measure up or fall short, and decide whether there is some obvious gap.

Establishing powerful collaborative relationships is not easy or quick. Time is needed for people to get to know one another, build trust, deal with organisational issues, negotiate agreements, and manage the logistics of working together.

Partners must clarify their expectations ('What's in it for me?'); they must develop structures, roles, and responsibilities that work for everyone; and they must establish milestones to evaluate progress.

People must also be willing to learn from each other and have the skills to communicate effectively. Communication ground rules should be set early in the process to create a safe environment within which individuals feel free to express their views.

But where can you find network contacts? Start with Websites of customers, suppliers, professional associations, trade magazines or companies in your target industry. You will eventually find lists of people who can help you.

Networking should be an ongoing and systematic part of your work. Networking is not just diplomacy and public relations – it should be meaningful communication and cooperation between organisations with shared interests.

There are many different ways to network. Some of the methods are informal or form part of your normal work; others are part of setting up a networking system. The following are some examples:

- Send your newsletters and information pamphlets to organisations and individuals you want to network with.

- Get to know key people in organisations that share your interests and talk to them regularly about common issues and problems.

- Attend the meetings, AGMs and events of other organisations.

- Attend political and community events where key organisations and decision-makers will be present.

- Attend conferences, seminars, consultation meetings, etc. Make sure your organisation is represented by someone who can speak for and raise the profile of your organisation. Lots of informal networking happens at these events.

- Offer support and advice to other organisations when you can and ask for it when you need it.

- Use your skills, contacts and expertise to help key decision-makers and organisations – networking happens naturally when you work together.

- Always have copies of your brochures and contact details so that you can hand it out to any useful contacts you meet.

- Use email and the Internet to network with national or international organisations who are working on similar issues.

7.2 RELATIONSHIPS WITH CUSTOMERS

Relationship marketing is grounded in the idea of establishing a learning relationship with customers. At the lower end, building a relationship can create cross-selling opportunities that may make the overall relationship profitable. For example, some retail banks have tried selling credit cards to less profitable customers. In determining which customers are worth the cost of long-term relationships, it is useful to consider their lifetime value. This depends on:

- Current profitability computed at the customer level

- The propensity of those customers to stay loyal

- Expected revenues and costs of servicing such customers over the lifetime of the relationship

Building relationships makes most sense for customers whose lifetime value to the company is the highest. Thus, building relationships should focus on customers who are currently the most profitable, likely to be the most profitable in the future, or likely to remain with the company for the foreseeable future and have acceptable levels of profitability. The goal of relationship management is to increase customer satisfaction and to minimise any problems. By engaging in 'smarter' relationships, a company can learn customers' preferences and develop trust. Every contact point with the customer can be seen as a chance to record information and learn preferences. Complaints and errors must be recorded, not just fixed and forgotten. Contact with customers in every medium, whether over the Internet, through a call centre, or through personal contact, is recorded and centralised. Many companies are beginning to achieve this goal by using customer relationship management (CRM) software. Data, once collected, can be used to customise service. In addition, the database can be analysed to detect patterns that can suggest better ways to serve customers in general. A key aspect of this dialogue is to learn and record preferences. There are two ways to determine customers' preferences: transparently and collaboratively.

Discovering preferences transparently means that the marketer learns the customers' needs without actually involving them. For example, the Ritz Carlton Hotel makes a point of observing the choices that guests make and recording them. If a guest requests extra pillows, then extra pillows will be provided every time that person visits. At upmarket retailers, personal shoppers will record customers' preferences in sizes, styles, brands, colours and price ranges and notify them when new merchandise appears or help them choose accessories.

7.3 SUPPLIER RELATIONSHIPS

An organisation and its suppliers are interdependent and a mutually beneficial relationship enhances the ability of both to create value.

Key benefits include:

- Increased ability to create value for both parties.
- Flexibility and speed of joint responses to changing market or customer needs and expectations.
- Optimisation of costs and resources.

Applying the principles of mutually beneficial supplier relationships typically leads to:

- Establishing relationships that balance short-term gains with long-term considerations.
- Pooling of expertise and resources with partners.
- Identifying and selecting key suppliers.
- Clear and open communication.
- Sharing information and future plans.
- Establishing joint development and improvement activities.
- Inspiring, encouraging and recognising improvements and achievements by suppliers

Tight bonds between companies and their key suppliers have been created in many industries.

For example, IKEA, the Swedish furniture retailer, commits to long-term relationships with its suppliers, and helps the suppliers to improve their products by leasing them equipment, providing technical assistance, and helping to find sources of raw materials.

CHAPTER ROUNDUP

- Organisations require information for recording transactions, measuring performance, making decisions, planning and controlling.

- An organisation's information requirements will be influenced by the sector they operate in.

- Information may be strategic, tactical or operational.

- There are many systems available to hold, process and analyse information. Examples include ESS, DSS, KWS, OAS and TPS.

- An information system should be designed to obtain information from all relevant sources – both internal and external.

- Effective information systems are vital at all levels of an organisation to assist in decision-making.

- Decision support systems allow managers to consider a number of alternatives and evaluate them under a variety of potential conditions.

- Executive information systems have summary level data, more detailed levels, data manipulation and analysis facilities, graphics and templates.

- Expert systems are computer programs that allow users to benefit from expert knowledge and information.

- Networking – is consciously developing contacts in an effort to increase the number of referrals you get for your business.

- Networking should be an ongoing and systematic part of your work. Networking is not just diplomacy and public relations – it should be meaningful communication and cooperation between organisations with shared interests.

- Relationship marketing is grounded in the idea of establishing a learning relationship with customers.

QUICK QUIZ

1   Give a brief definition of knowledge.
2   Distinguish between strategic, tactical and operational information.
3   Give two examples of strategic, tactical and operational information relevant to an organisation operating in the manufacturing sector.
4   Which is easier to measure – qualitative information or quantitative information?
5   What are the two types of knowledge?
6   Decision support systems are used for routine decisions. TRUE or FALSE?
7   What are decision support systems used for?
8   What are some applications of expert systems?
9   Give three examples of primary stakeholders and three examples of secondary stakeholders.

ANSWERS TO QUICK QUIZ

1   Knowledge is information within people's minds.

2   Strategic information is used to plan the objectives of the organisation. Tactical information is used for management control activities and operational information is used to ensure that specific tasks are executed properly.

3   Two examples of strategic information:

(a)   Communication of corporate objectives to the management of the business expressed in terms of profit targets and measures of wealth such as earnings per share.

(b)   Communicating information on strategy for future acquisitions of companies in different fields as a hedge against risk.

Two examples of tactical information:

(a)   A twelve-month budget of sales analysed by product group.

(b)   A manufacturing plan for the next twelve months.

Two examples of operational information:

(a)   An 'aged' analysis of debts showing all customers whose deliveries have been stopped pending settlement of overdue balance.

(b)   A list of all purchase orders outstanding with the financial evaluation of total purchase order commitment.

4   Qualitative information is difficult (or even impossible) to measure in quantitative terms.

5   Tacit and explicit.

6   False.

7   A decision-support system (DSS) is normally an interactive system that helps people make decisions, use judgement and work in ill-defined areas.

It supports decision-making in semi-structured and unstructured situations and provides information, models, or tools for manipulating and/or analysing information.

It enables managers to focus on the real business problems, by automating the process of gathering, summarising and analysing information relevant to a particular decision area, and enables one-off ad hoc problem situations to be resolved.

Its most likely usage is in the area of producing information to aid in tactical decision-making.

8   The ES will be used for:

- diagnosing problems
- strategic planning
- internal control planning
- maintaining strategies.

The system is able to make complex and unstructured decisions. It can offer managers advice and explanation, and is able to integrate with other systems such as MIS, DSS and EIS.

Examples of expert systems include:

- Advice on legal implications during labour-management negotiations
- Tax computations
- Selection of training methods

9   Primary stakeholders include shareholders and investors, employees, customers, suppliers, and residents of the communities where the company operates. Secondary stakeholders include the media and pressure groups, regulators and competitors.

ANSWERS TO ACTIVITIES

1   There are many possible suggestions, including those given below.

(a)   The organisation's bankers take decisions affecting the amount of money they are prepared to lend.

(b)   The public might have an interest in information relating to an organisation's products or services.

(c)   The media (press, television etc) use information generated by organisations in news stories, and such information can adversely or favourably affect an organisation's relationship with its environment.

(d)   The government (for example the Department for Business, Innovation and Skills) regularly requires organisational information.

(e)   HM Revenue and Customs require information for taxation and VAT assessments.

(f)   An organisation's suppliers and customers take decisions whether or not to trade with the organisation.

2   The first is a tactical control decision, the second is an operational control decision and the third is a strategic planning decision.

3   They are examples of operational information.

4   The data will be related to:

- Suppliers – the standing of the organisation (you do not want to be dealing with a company that is on the verge of bankruptcy), the quality of their service, the discounts they offer, their after-sales service, the delivery charges and times etc.

- Products and services – the prices, availability, quality assurance, quantities supplied

5

	Secondary information	Primary information
What it is	Data neither collected directly by the user nor specifically for the user, often under conditions unknown to the user- in other words, data collected not by you but by someone else for their own purposes or for general use.	Data that is collected specifically by or for the user, at source, in other words by you.
Quantitative, 'factual' or 'objective' example	A company's published financial statements summarise and interpret company transactions data for the benefit of shareholders, not necessarily for your precise needs.	A survey you conduct with a questionnaire you have designed, with regard to a sample. You aim to get a statistically significant result.
Qualitative example	An article in a student publication or in a book about theories of motivation.	A focus group you have conducted to talk about a specific topic.

6   (a)   Expert systems bring the power of expertise to the desk. Say a person wants a loan from a bank. An expert system can be used for credit scoring, so the request will not have to be directed back to a superior.

(b)   Executive information systems mean that senior management can focus easily on operations so the middle management function of information processing might disappear.

This points to delayering of management hierarchies, counterbalanced by the creation of new jobs in information management.

Chapter 08

Develop communication processes

Introduction

The efficient running of organisations requires that all the members of the organisation work together towards the achievement of the organisation's objectives. This working together requires the adequate understanding of what others are doing. It requires a high level of coordination and control, and fundamentally it requires communications, which are efficient and effective.

This chapter focuses on communication in the organisation, its nature and operation. The design of the formal communication system is considered as well as the types of informal communications channels that probably will exist in an organisation. If management is the art of 'achieving results through other people' then interpersonal skills are a key part of the job.

This chapter deals with the use of the Internet and the World Wide Web in business. It will consider the impact of e-commerce and the growing use of intranet by organisations in order to manage their information.

Your objectives

After completing this chapter you should be able to:

- Report on existing processes of communication in an organisation

- Design ways to improve appropriateness

- Implement improvements to ensure greater integration of systems of communication in that organisation

- Create a personal plan to improve own communication skills

1 THE PROCESS OF COMMUNICATION

1.1 FUNCTIONS AND OBJECTIVES OF COMMUNICATION

Communication in an organisation can serve a number of functions.

(a) It can be a vehicle for the exchange of information, so that people are told about an event or state of affairs, or what other people are doing.

(b) It can be a vehicle for instruction (eg a superior communicating by giving orders to a subordinate).

(c) It can be a vehicle of persuasion in which a person can be won over to a particular viewpoint or proposal.

(d) It can reinforce (by encouragement) existing behaviour.

(e) It may be directed towards the establishment of relationships.

(f) It can publicise needs and requirements.

The objective of communication by a manager or administrator is to exchange, impart or receive *information*. This does not mean that unedited data should be transmitted to all and sundry. Good information will have the following qualities.

(a) Relevance to a user's needs

(i) *Identifying the user.* Information must be suited and sent to the right person (one who needs it to do a job, make a decision etc).

(ii) *Getting the purpose right.* Information is effective only when it helps a user to act or make a decision.

If you ask someone the way to the nearest train station, you do not expect or need to be told that the weather is fine, or even that there is a very interesting train station in another town some miles away.

(iii) *Getting the volume right.* Information must be complete for its purpose, ie not omitting any necessary item: it should also be no more in volume than the user will find helpful or be able to take in.

(b) *Accuracy within the user's needs.* Information should be 'accurate' in the sense of 'correct': downright falsehood and error are fatal to effective communication of any sort. It may, however, be impossible – or at least time-consuming and expensive – to gather, process and assimilate information that is minutely detailed. An approximation or an average figure is often sufficient to our needs. If you asked: 'Is it hot in Brighton in August?' because you were planning a holiday, you would be happy to hear that it 'averaged 78 F': you would not waste time and effort poring through a sheet of daily temperature readings for the last five years.

(c) *Inspiring the user's confidence.* Information should not give the user reason to mistrust, disbelieve or ignore it, eg because it is out-of-date, badly presented or from an unreliable source. It should be *verifiable* by reference, or by application (which risks finding out the hard way, if the information is incorrect).

(d) *Timeliness.* Information must be readily available within the time period, which makes it useful: ie it must be in the right place at the right time.

(e) *Appropriately communicated.* Information will lose its value if it is not clearly communicated to the user in a suitable format and through a suitable medium.

(f) *Cost effective.* Good information should not cost more than it is worth. Gathering, storing, retrieving and communicating an item of information may require expense of time, energy and resources: if the expense is greater than the potential value of the item, re-consider whether the information is necessary to such a degree of accuracy, completeness etc – or even necessary at all.

1.2 EFFECTIVE COMMUNICATION

Effective communication is a two-way process, perhaps best expressed as a cycle. Signals or 'messages' are sent by the communicator and received by the other party, who sends back some form of confirmation that the message has been received and understood. This is enormously complicated in practice, especially in face-to-face communication: you may send a letter and receive an acknowledgement back, which would correspond to a single cycle of communication, but face-to-face, the workings of two or more minds and bodies (nodding understanding, gesturing and so on) complicate the picture.

ACTIVITY 1 (10 MINS)

One definition of business communication is 'the transmission of information so that it is received, understood and leads to action'. Evaluate the key items included in this definition

Within the communication process it is also important to note the problem of 'noise', ie anything in the environment that impedes the transmission of the message, is significant. Noise can arise from many sources, eg factors as diverse as loud machinery, status differentials between sender and receiver, distractions of pressure at work or emotional upsets. The effective communicator must ensure that noise does not interfere with successful transmission of the message.

ACTIVITY 2 (10 MINS)

Give five examples of what you would interpret as:

(a) Negative feedback (a sign that your message was not having the desired effect)
(b) Positive feedback (a sign that your message was received and understood)

1.3 CHOOSING THE COMMUNICATION CHANNEL

Choosing the right method of communication is important. How information is communicated will impact on how it is interpreted. A channel that will help the receiver correctly interpret the information should be used. The choice of medium will depend on numerous factors, including:

Factor	Considerations
Time	How long will be needed to prepare the message, and how long will it take to transmit it in the chosen form? This must be weighed against the urgency with which the message must be sent.
Complexity	How long will be needed to prepare the message, and how long will it take to transmit it in the chosen form? This must be weighed against the urgency with which the message must be sent.
Distance	How far is the message required to travel? Must it be transmitted to an office on a different floor of the building, or across town, or to the other end of the country?
Written record	A written record may be needed as proof, confirming a transaction, or for legal purposes, or as an aid to memory. It can be duplicated and sent to many recipients. It can be stored and later retrieved for reference and analysis as required.
Feedback/interaction	Sometimes instant feedback is needed for effective communication eg when you are questioning a customer to find out his precise requirements (small, medium or large) (green, red or blue).
Confidentiality	Telephone calls may be overheard; faxed messages can be read by whoever is standing by the fax machine; internal memos may be read by colleagues or by internal mail staff; highly personal letters may be read by the recipient's secretary. On the other hand a message may need to be spread widely and quickly to all staff: the notice-board, or a public announcement or the company newsletter may be appropriate.
Recipient	It may be necessary to be reserved and tactful, warm and friendly, or impersonal, depending upon the desired effect on the recipient. If you are trying to impress him, a high quality document may be needed.
Cost	Cost must be considered in relation to all of the above factors. The aim is to achieve the best possible result at the least possible expense.

As regards **confidentiality**, remember:

- Telephone calls can be overheard
- Faxed messages can be read by whoever is standing by the fax machine
- Internal memos may be read by colleagues or internal mail staff
- Personal letters may be read by the recipient's secretary
- E-mail may not be completely secure

An overview of the features and limitations of common communication tools are outlined in the following table.

Tool	Features /Advantages	Limitations
Conversation	Usually unstructured so can discuss a wide range of topics Requires little or no planning Gives a real impression of feelings	Temptation to lose focus May be easily forgotten
Meeting	Allows multiple opinions to be expressed Can discuss and resolve a wide range of issues	Can highlight differences and conflict if not managed efficiently – have been known to turn into time-wasting confrontations
Memorandum	Provides a permanent record of an internal message Adds formality to internal communications	If used too often or the message is too general people may ignore it Can come across as impersonal
Letter	Provides a permanent record of an external message Adds formality to external communications	If inaccurate or poorly pre-sented provides a permanent record of incompetence May be slow to arrive depending on distance and the postal service
Report	Provides a permanent, often comprehensive written record. Use a clear, simple structure	Complex messages may be misunderstood in the absence of immediate feedback
Presentation	Complex ideas can be communicated Visual aids such as slides can help the communication process The best presentations will leave a lasting impression	Requires planning and skill Poorly researched or presented material can lead to an audience
Telephone	Good for communications that do not require (or you would prefer not to have) a permanent written record Can provide some of the 'personal touch' to people in geographically remote locations Conference calls allow multiple participants	Receiver may not be available Can be disruptive to receiver if in the middle of another task No written record gives greater opportunity for misunderstandings
Facsimile	Enables reports and messages to reach remote locations quickly	Easily seen by others Fax machine may not be checked for messages Complex images do not transmit well
Electronic mail	Provides a written record Attachments can be included Quick – regardless of location	Requires some computer literacy to use effectively People may not check their e-mail regularly

Tool	Features /Advantages	Limitations
	Automated 'Read receipts' or a simple request to acknowledge receipt by return message mean you know if the message has been received Can be sent to multiple recipients easily, can be forwarded on to others	Lack of privacy – can be forwarded on without your knowledge Is impersonal

ACTIVITY 3   (10 MINS)

Because of the advantages and disadvantages associated with each type of communication, organisations use more than one method in conjunction. What methods would you suggest for the sales launch of a new product?

2   CURRENT DEVELOPMENTS

2.1 CHANGING ENVIRONMENT

The changing economic and business climate is likely to put increased pressures upon communication systems. The challenges require an enhanced commitment to quality, profitability and the ability to manage change.

- The changing demographic profile is introducing **new working practices**, with more job sharing, full-time women workers and multi-skilling becoming standard. These new working practices inevitably mean different values, attitudes, skills and aspirations for the future. Workers of the future will require more challenging occupations, more variety and continual development together with increased flexibility to balance family and working life.

- The **flatter management structures** currently fashionable are encouraging a more dynamic and interactive working environment, which will precipitate the need for closer and more personal communication systems that contribute to maintaining the competitive position of the organisation.

- The growth of **multi-national enterprises** will ultimately require the establishment of global information systems that can effectively integrate differing cultures, languages and operating systems throughout the organisation.

- Increased numbers of **people working from home** will mean that more effort must be directed towards fostering a feeling of belonging to the organisation, since such workers may well suffer a sense of isolation. Electronic media will undoubtedly assist in the maintenance of links (both formally and informally) between worker and employer.

- Recent years have witnessed unprecedented **downsizing**, both within the manufacturing base and also the service sector, where jobs are being sacrificed in pursuit of improved efficiency and profitability. Consequently, employees are increasingly concerned with job security and less confident in the competence of senior level management. Those responsible for stabilising a climate of distrust need to engender greater levels of confidence and openness within the organisation. Indeed, criticism of downsizing has emerged: so-called 'corporate anorexia' inhibits growth.

2.2 CHANGING COMMUNICATION

In the last few years, the infrastructure and tools of communication have radically changed. The phone is swiftly being overtaken by e-mail as the most popular method of remote interpersonal communication. The Internet has changed the way people access information. Even 'old' media like the television and telephone are being transformed by new data transmission infrastructures and integration with computer systems. Broadly, communication has changed in the following ways.

(a) **Higher speed** – the development of 'facsimile transfer' (fax) was breakthrough in its day: enabling documents, which previously had to be posted, to be transferred down a phone line. Now, messages can be transferred via a local computer network or the Internet almost instantly, to the point where real time conversations can be held using online messaging and chat rooms. Recent infrastructure innovations such as ISDN (Integrated Systems Digital Network), DSL (Digital Subscriber Lines), satellite transmission (for telephone and television signals), fibre optic cabling and increased 'band width' (allowing more data to pass through networks more swiftly) have supported this process.

(b) **Wider access to information** – once you are connected to the Internet, you have instant access to an almost indescribable wealth of information. Through electronic mail and bulletin boards (newsgroups) you can use a different kind of resource: a worldwide supply of knowledgeable people, some of whom are bound to share your interests, no matter how obscure... There are also more (and better) resources, including museums, exhibitions, art galleries and shops.

(c) **24–7 global communication** – information and communications technology (ICT) has enabled 24-hour 7-day global communication: across working or office hours, time zones and geographical distances. Telex, fax and answer machines were a start in this direction – but they required (possibly delayed) human intervention to initiate a response. The Internet allows users to access information/services and perform transactions at any time of any day. Nor is there any distinction between local and international sites, in terms of speed or cost of access. (Physical delivery of products ordered will, of course, re-erect some of the geographical barriers.)

(d) **Interactivity and multi-media** – Interactivity is mutual responsiveness. Consumers are increasingly demanding in terms of interactivity in accessing and responding to promotional messages. Consumers are also increasingly demanding in terms of the stimulation provided by promotional messages. Multi media communication implies the use of written, visual and audio elements to enhance a message's impact and interest.

The Internet and related technologies have habituated people (particularly young media and IT consumers) to multi-media presentations, high-level animated/video-based graphics and interaction with material. Although the impact of such trends may be limited by the power of the individual user's PC and the speed of the modem, printed matter may seem relatively unstimulating in comparison: some of the features of online and multi-media presentation are being added to traditional print advertising and information: simulated 'links' and buttons, multi-directional graphics and so on.

(e) **Personalisation** – database, document generation and web technologies have improved the ease and sophistication of targeting and personalisation of contact between organisations and customers. Examples include:

(i) Allowing users to customise web pages for their personal interests and tastes

(ii) Making individually-targeted product offers and recommendations based on browsing/buying behaviour

(iii) Sending personally addressed and targeted-content messages to customers

(iv) Encouraging users/customers to form 'virtual communities' (for example, using chat rooms, discussion boards and newsgroups)

ACTIVITY 4 (10 MINS)

Suggest the most effective medium for communication in the following situations.

(a) New printer cartridges are urgently required from the office goods supplier.

(b) The managing director wants to give a message to all staff.

(c) Fred Bloggs has been absent five times in the past month and his manager intends to take action.

(d) You need information quickly from another department.

(e) You have to explain a complicated operation to a group of people.

---

3   MEETINGS AND CONFERENCES

3.1   MEETINGS

Meetings play an important part in the life of any organisation. Meetings include:

(a)   **Formal meetings** required by government legislation or the Articles of a company.

(b)   **Regular or 'one-off' internal management meetings**. These may involve the gathering of, communication of, or review of, information. Alternately, the meeting may have a problem-solving or decision-making purpose.

(c)   Some **discussions** held informally may 'qualify' as a meeting – there are no hard and fast rules as to what constitutes an informal meeting.

One-to-one communication is necessary at all levels of an organisation. Communication does not happen by chance – it requires structure and discipline! While meetings can be time consuming, effective meetings use that time to drive to specific outcomes, utilise the input of all participants, and assign accountability for business results.

The face-to-face or one-to-one meeting can be formal or informal, vertical, horizontal, or diagonal, but it is always the richest communication medium. Here the full play of verbal and non-verbal cues is available to both sender and receiver. Meetings take place in offices and boardrooms, but many meetings are the more informal ones in the hallways at work (by chance or by design); breakfast, lunch or dinner meetings; and those that take place at the club or on the golf course. These more informal meetings should not be underestimated for their importance to activities at work, for it is here that many relationships are built and deals are made.

Organisational members who are excluded from such meetings by their sex or age are discriminated against because they do not have the same opportunities to communicate, as do others. This discrimination can be as simple as the men at a meeting taking a washroom break and continuing to discuss business while women present at the meeting are excluded.

3.2   FORMAL MEETINGS – STRUCTURED

Most managers seem to spend half of their life in meetings, so understanding how they work and how to make them more effective is very important.

DEFINITION

A **meeting** is a group of people coming together for the purpose of resolving problems or making decisions.

Meetings can be held for a wide range of purposes, but it is important that the purpose of the meeting is made clear to the participants in advance. If this is done, the meeting is more likely to be a success.

A well-organised, well-aimed and well-led meeting can be extremely effective in many different contexts.

- The relaying of decisions and instructions (eg briefings)
- The dissemination of information and the collection of feedback
- Participative problem-solving
- Brainstorming: free exchanges with a view to generating new approaches and ideas
- Coordinating the efforts of a large number of people from different interest groups

A meeting may be responsible for taking a final decision on an issue of great importance.

Formal meetings – are planned and structured and include Board meetings, committees, working groups, public meetings, conferences, Annual General Meetings (AGMs), team meetings, appraisals, interviews and brainstorming.

Formal meetings, such as the Board meeting of a company, the Annual General Meeting (AGM) of a society, or a local council meeting, are governed by strict conventions. These may establish procedure on such matters as:

(a)   attendance rights (for members of the public, shareholders etc)
(b)   adequate notice of forthcoming meetings
(c)   the minimum number of members required to hold the meeting (the 'quorum')
(d)   the timing of meetings
(e)   the type of business to be discussed
(f)   the binding power of decisions made upon the participants

Formal meetings generally conform to a system where there is usually a chairperson who guides the proceedings and aims to maintain order. They generate formal documentation for the announcement, planning, conduct and recording of the proceedings. These include the following:

- **Notice** – the invitation or announcement of the meeting, which is prepared and circulated in advance. The communication can be by e-mail, a personal letter, a memo, a notice on the internal notice board or an official card like an invitation.

- **Agenda** – the items of business to be discussed at the meeting. This is often attached to the notice to give participants a guide to the business that will be discussed and the preparations they will need to make. The minutes of the previous meeting might also be included so that any queries or objections relating to them may also be prepared.

- **Minutes** – the written record of the proceedings at the meeting, approved by those present. They provide a source of reference, particularly with regard to decisions and action points agreed by participants.

3.3 PROJECT MEETINGS

Project team members should meet regularly to maintain and improve team relationships and to ensure project objectives, progress and current priorities are communicated and understood.

(a)   **Project status meetings** – should be held regularly to keep project stakeholders informed of project status and plans. The attendees of such a meeting would usually include:

   (i)   Project manager
   (ii)   Team members
   (iii)   Customer/client representatives

   A typical agenda of a project status meeting may include the following items:

   (i)   Objectives achieved since the previous meeting
   (ii)   Current project status
   (iii)   Expected future project progress
   (iv)   Current expenditure/resource use compared to forecast
   (v)   Task assignment with due dates

(b)   **Project problem-solving meetings** – it may be necessary over the course of a project to call additional meetings to address specific problems. If a problem that has the potential to impact on project progress is identified, a meeting of all those affected may be the best way to establish an effective course of action.

   The project manager should ensure all are aware of the level of authority the problem-solving team has to make decisions, and it is clear who is responsible for ensuring the action decided on is carried out.

(c)   **Project evaluation meeting** – at the end of a project the project manager should meet each team member to thank him or her for their work, assess their contribution to the project and consider how this may be improved on future projects. The project manager should also call the whole project team together for a project evaluation meeting to see what lessons can be learnt from the project that may help with future projects.

   A typical agenda of a project evaluation meeting may include the following items:

   (i)   Was the overall objective achieved?
   (ii)   Resource use compared with the budget
   (iii)   Time taken compared with the schedule
   (iv)   The effectiveness of the project plan and management
   (v)   Problem identification and resolution
   (vi)   Team relationships and working arrangements
   (vii) Customer liaison, communication and satisfaction

The results of the meeting should be incorporated into the post-completion audit report.

3.4 CONFERENCE – A COORDINATED APPROACH

A conference is a specific method of communication. It can serve several purposes and involve visual, written and verbal communication techniques. Most conferences consist of one-way communication only. Conferences should be recognised as being distinctly different from normal meetings.

They tend to be several months apart and require a major planning effort to ensure smooth running.

- **Public conferences** – are held for speakers to present lectures to an audience drawn from many companies and many industries. Such conferences are usually one-way communication with limited opportunity to raise questions from the floor. The main purpose of such conferences must be to inform. So Cabinet ministers can use a conference to explain government thinking, an accountant can use the platform to explain the effects of the latest tax regulations; a scientist can explain the methods used in and the results of his research programme.

- **In-house conferences** – are more common. They can be:

  - *Horizontal*, ie a member of a certain status level. An example would be a partners' conference where all partners of an accountancy firm may convene to discuss business trends and policy. Frequently such a conference would also include information sessions where an outside expert would be invited to present a topic or one partner may explain developments in his/her area.

  - *Vertical*, ie members of different status levels from one department or one division of a company. An example could be the announcement of the company results to its workers or announcement of a major policy change, eg a progress report during a management buyout.

Sales conferences – a company's sale conference is usually held annually and includes all sales representatives above a certain status level or performance level. If we take as an example a company launching a new product such as a pharmaceutical company launching a new drug that is to be sold 'over the counter' at chemists shops, as well as being available on prescription through the health service.

We can readily trace the different communication approaches used in such a conference.

(a) First, the visual communication techniques of video, slide projection and handling of product packages would be used to arouse attention and achieve maximum impact. Explanations from the platform would be brief, relying on the visual images as the main focal thread.

(b) The next stage would involve mainly verbal communication when the selling attributes of the product would be explained. The selling message would be extolled and the approach to customers would be made clear. This session would be structured to encourage maximum involvement of delegates with questions periods and discussion groups established to achieve two-way flow. This is the persuasive stage when face-to-face, two-way communication will motivate the salesforce and prepare them for any customer queries.

(c) The final stage is the written communication when the salespeople will be issued with product information packs. This pack will summarise all major aspects discussed during the day including details of advertising programmes, product benefits, the selling approach, competitors' strengths/weaknesses and sales targets. This provides the permanent record that can be referred to in the future as the need arises.

3.5 TELECONFERENCING

Teleconferencing uses a communications network to connect participants' voices. Teleconferences are similar to telephone calls, but can expand discussion to more than two people.

Conferences calls can be held using Skype or similar internet calling systems, speaker telephones, or even two-way radio. In some remote areas, satellite enhancement of connections is desirable.

Teleconferencing is a method in use to connect a small to large number of people so that they can talk together. Fax machines can also be connected so that documents can be distributed to everyone in the conference at once. Documents can be e-mailed, put in a shared computer window, or posted to the web so everyone can see them at once. Teleconferencing can save organisations money by reducing travel costs. It can also be a strategic method used by organisations to reach their employees, customers, and clients. The travelling executive with a laptop and wireless internet connection can stay in constant communication by fax and e-mail.

The internet is used as a medium for holding conferences on specific topics. Those who are interested can visit the conference website to read posted documents, make contributions and read others' comments. This method does not require participants to be physically in the same location or to be communicating at the same time.

3.6 VIDEOCONFERENCING

Videoconferencing can transmit pictures as well as voices. It is the use of computer and communications technology to conduct meetings in which several participants, perhaps in different parts of the world, are linked up via computer and a video system.

Much productive time can be lost travelling to meetings. Face-to-face meetings usually provide the best channel for discussion, information exchange and relationship building. These benefits should be balanced against the lost productive time. In general a mixture of physical and virtual meetings provides the best compromise.

Arranging telephone conferences should be simple. Most major organisations already have facilities available. Alternatively, the telephone service provider should be able to make the arrangements. There are two main styles of videoconferencing: using specialist videoconference facilities or using desktop software from your PC.

Participants may either join through the network without leaving their desk, or gather at their nearest videoconference suite (internally or externally – eg conference centres, press agencies). Two-way links are just dialled directly. Multiple link ups can be achieved through 'bridges' – everyone connects to the bridge which combines and controls the multiple video and audio links.

4 WORKSHOPS AND TRAINING EVENTS

4.1   VERBAL COMMUNICATION

Verbal methods from a major channel in business communications. Some examples of verbal methods are purely voice-to-voice as in telephone conversations and public address announcements. Most methods are face-to-face:

(a)   Interviews
(b)   Lectures and presentations
(c)   Sales visits
(d)   Formal group meetings
(e)   Informal contact and discussions
(f)   Briefing sessions
(g)   The grapevine

Verbal methods have several important advantages when used in workshops or training sessions:

- There is the personal touch of seeing the face and/or hearing the voice.

- There is instant feedback with the opportunity to respond quickly to questions of misunderstanding and disagreement.

- Because of the strong personal aspect, it is a good persuasive medium encouraging people to take a certain course of action.

- The message can be unique to you as an individual; no one else is likely to select your mix of words or emphasise the same key phrases.

The obvious disadvantages are:

- There is no permanent record, so disagreement can arise as to what was said.

- Vocabulary shrinkage occurs, in that we use only 66% of our full vocabulary when communicating verbally. The full vocabulary is available to us only when writing.

- We do not have the facility, as with writing, to go back, cancel out and replace an earlier sentence because we wish to amend its meaning.

4.2   USER WORKSHOPS

A workshop may be conference style or skill development style. In conference- style events, the trainer stands at the front of the room and speaks, using audio-visual or other props where appropriate. Participants learn what they can from the performance and from the distributed handouts. In skill development workshops, participants have the opportunity to practice and develop specific skills throughout the course of the event. This type of workshop is a meeting with the emphasis on practical exercises.

User workshops are often used in systems analysis to help establish and record user requirements.

At this type of user workshop, user input is obtained by the analyst to analyse business functions and define the data associated with the current and future systems. An outline of the proposed new system is produced, which is used to design more detailed system procedures.

Depending on the complexity of the system, the workshop may devise a plan for implementation. More complex systems may conduct a workshop early in the design stage and hold a later workshop with the aim of producing a detailed system model. Prototyping may be used at such a workshop to prepare preliminary screen layouts.

User workshops should be facilitated by a facilitator. The facilitator coordinates the workshop activities with the aim of ensuring the objectives of the session are achieved.

The facilitator would most likely be a systems analyst with excellent communication and leadership skills. The skills of the person in this role are critical to the success of the workshop. Many user workshops also utilise a scribe. The scribe is an active participant who is responsible for producing the outputs of the workshop.

4.3 TRAINING EVENTS

There are many training methods available to choose from. Some of these methods are well established – lecture talks and discussions are the obvious examples of this sort. Others are found to be useful but need to be properly designed and administered – these include all forms of simulation, eg, business games. The method chosen should match the needs of the particular training event and be based upon sound learning principles. It should generally speaking allow for the following:

(a)   the trainee's participation;
(b)   the provision of feedback to the trainee about his or her performance;
(c)   the transfer of the training experience to the job;
(d)   reinforcement for desired behaviour;
(e)   practical application of things learned;
(f)   improved performance through motivation.

Training may be given on, or off, the job and either within the firm or outside (for example, a training scheme at a college workshop). The place of training may well, of course, have a bearing on the method(s) of training used, the structure of the training programme and its content. On-the-job training is a systematic approach for a particular job, normally used by supervisors when training those who report to them. It consists of four steps:

(a)   preparing the trainee;

(b)   giving the trainee the necessary knowledge or information and demonstrating how the job is to be done;

(c)   allowing the trainee to do the job; *and*

(d)   checking the trainees' performance.

4.4 PRESENTATIONS

A presentation is a combination of both verbal and visual form of communication that is used by managers at some meetings, training sessions, lectures and conferences. Before any presentation is made it is necessary to establish the objectives of the presentation, why it is being done and what you want it to achieve. Once these things have been identified, the best way to achieve the objectives can be established. Compiling a presentation that holds the audience's interest and drives the point home with clarity is not as easy as it looks. Some professional presenters advise that you divide your presentation into three sections.

(a)   The *introduction* summarises your overall message and should begin with a title slide, or transparency, that succinctly states the purpose of the presentation.

(b)   The *main section*, sometimes called the *rationale*, delivers your main points. In general, each point should be made in a simple, powerful text slide and then bolstered with more detail from charts and subsidiary text slides. For some reason, three items of supporting data for each main point seems to work best for most audiences and most arguments.

(c) Section three winds up with re-emphasis, starting with a summary, moving on to a *conclusion* and leaving the audience with a message that will persuade them to act – this may be to applaud your department's progress or to buy your scheme. The final line of the presentation must be a definite close.

The presentation must be summarised throughout, because you cannot rely on the audience having read any handouts prior to the presentations.

The audience should be given the opportunity to ask questions and whether this is done at regular intervals or at the end of the presentation will depend upon the topic of the presentation and the audience to which it is addressed.

Graphics, in the form of still or moving pictures, can be a particularly effective method of communication. They have *advantages* in that they are attention-catching, have a dramatic impact, they facilitate the understanding of complex material and are comprehensive to those of poor linguistic ability.

4.5 COACHING

Coaching is a specialised form of communication that is concerned with training. Its need becomes apparent to management when there is a need to extend the depth and range of an employee's knowledge very quickly for reasons which may range from the introduction of new techniques to the need to train for a particular job, perhaps on the unexpected retirement of the present job holder.

Planning of the scheme of work so that any coaching is done on a systematic basis is an important aspect of the process and the teaching undertaken should be directly related to the style preferred by the student. This is usually a one to one learning situation and care should be taken to hold the attention of the student very closely throughout the coaching process. As individuals differ in their response to alternative learning styles, coaching may take any form from the academic, where the student is geared to research and knowledge based learning, to activity based learning – such as projects.

Coaching is a considerable drain on managerial time. Support has to be given from the planning stage and will continue during the learning process, with the value of constructive criticism being particularly relevant. There is a need for goals to be set and agreed by both the management and the student with regular evaluation and feedback being incorporated in the coaching plan.

Well planned coaching is an effective way of communicating information in a concentrated form.

5   INTERNET AND E-MAIL

5.1 THE INTERNET

The **Internet** (also known as 'the net', the 'information super-highway' or 'cyberspace') is a vast computer network offering the ability for computers across the world to communicate via telecommunications links. Information can be exchanged either through e-mail or through accessing and entering data via a website: a collection of screens providing information in text and graphic form, any of which can be viewed by clicking the appropriate link (shown as a button, word or icon) on the screen.

The '**World Wide Web**' (or 'Web') is a navigation system within the Internet. It is based on a technology called 'hypertext' which allows documents stored on host computers on the Internet to be linked to one another. When you view a document that contains hypertext links, you can view any of the connected documents or pages simply by clicking on a link. The web is the most powerful and flexible information and navigation service on the Internet. In order to 'surf' or navigate the web, users need a web browser, which interprets and displays hypertext documents and locates documents pointed to by links. Browsers include Firefox, Safari and Microsoft's Internet Explorer.

Access to the Internet has become more and more widespread in recent years. New computers are pre-loaded with the necessary hardware and software, and smaller, cheaper devices designed solely for Internet browsing, such as Apple's iPad tablet, are increasing in popularity. Wireless and mobile connections allow users to surf the Web and send and receive e-mail from almost any location.

5.2 THE INTERNET AS A PROMOTIONAL COMMUNICATION

The Internet can be used across the promotion mix.

Advertising	• Dedicated corporate websites, banner/button advertising, ranking on Internet search engines such as Google (to increase site exposure)
	• The forecast global penetration of the Internet over the next few years would give it a significantly larger audience than any of the television networks, print media outlets or other advertising vehicles
	• Studies show that brand awareness increases some 5% after using banner advertising
Direct marketing	• E-mail messages sent to targeted mailing lists (rented, or developed by the marketing organisation itself)
	• 'Permission marketing' (targeting consumers who have opted to receive commercial mailings)
Direct response advertising	• Immediate contact (information/transaction facilities) to follow-up customer responses to TV/radio/print advertising
Sales promotion	• Online prize draws and competitions
	• Online discounts (offset by lower transaction costs)
	• Downloadable or e-mailed discount vouchers

Customer loyalty programmes	• Value-added benefits that enhance the Internet buying experience • User home page customisation • Virtual communities (chat rooms etc) • Free e-cards/SMS messages
Media/press relations	• Online media/press kits • E-mailed media releases • 'About us' and 'contacts' pages • Technical briefings and articles on key issues
Public relations	• 'About us' and 'FAQ' (frequently asked question) features • News bulletins (eg for crisis or issues management) • Publicity/information for sponsorships, exhibitions and events • Sponsorship of popular/ useful information sites
Relationship marketing	• Customisation of Web pages and targeting of offers/promotions • E-mail follow-up contacts • E-zines – special interest newsletters published on the Web, or distributed by e-mail direct to subscribers and mailing lists
Grass roots marketing	• Generating word of mouth promotion and recommendation among customers • Online chat or message board forums and 'introduce a friend' schemes/incentives
Direct distribution	• Products (through online shopping) and services (including access to information databases) • Products can be ordered via the Net • Some can also be delivered via the Net, by downloading direct to the purchaser's PC: examples include music, computer software, product catalogues and instruction manuals
Partnership development	• Strategic promotional collaborations with synergistic content-specific sites or 'portals' (search engines, Web directories or other high-traffic sites such as Yahoo! or Google)
Customer service and technical support	• E-mail contact • FAQs (frequently asked questions) • Access to database information • Online messaging or voice interruption for interactive support

Market/ customer research	• Gathering information on customers and visitors for the purposes of market segmentation, personalisation/customisation of future contacts
	• Site monitoring
	• Online or e-mailed feedback questionnaires and surveys
Corporate identity	• Website and e-mail messages must be designed to create a unified and coherent marketing message alongside all other marketing messages for marketing synergy

5.3 ONLINE SHOPPING

The Internet is, subject to a few remaining security concerns, a potential means of direct selling and distribution to potential customers.

DEFINITION

E-commerce is an abbreviation of 'electronic commerce': it means business transactions carried out online via the Internet.

A transaction-based website is a virtual warehouse (or supermarket, or bookstore – or whatever its creators wish). Customers can take a virtual browsing tour; download catalogues; explore products; put items in 'shopping baskets'; proceed to 'checkout' and pay by debit or credit card (in some cases with one click of the mouse, enabled by a database containing the customer details); select delivery options; print out accompanying documentation; monitor the progress of their order; receive e-mailed confirmations and notifications and so on.

Although online shopping has not lived up to initial (inflated) forecasts, surveys now suggest that it is growing at a steady rate, particularly in the business-to-business market and for products such as niche market/rare items (such as craft supplies and out of print books), books, CD/cassettes, software, transport/travel and groceries. (You will need to monitor the quality press and marketing magazines for up-to-date figures and projections.)

As an alternative to e-commerce through the organisation's own transaction-based website, the following options may be considered.

(a) **Storefronts**: getting online stores such as Amazon or Yahoo! to catalogue and sell your products or services online through their sites. (In other words, an online distribution channel, with the associated benefits – and the drawbacks of competing with other brands, losing margins and so on.)

(b) **Auction sites**: putting merchandise (surplus products, used products, limited-supply items and so on) up for auction on sites such as eBay. Most auction sites charge a transaction fee, but the marketing organisation has no processing costs: it merely has to set a 'reserve' (lowest acceptable) price, write a marketing blurb and upload pictures for the auction site, and ship out the product when sold. Products may be put up for auction for promotional purposes, using the blurb, photos and a link to the company's own website. Check out: www.ebay.com.

5.4 E-MAIL

The term 'electronic mail', or e-mail, is used to describe various systems for sending data or messages electronically via a telephone or data network and a central 'server' computer. E-mail has replaced letters, memos, faxes, documents and even telephone calls – combining many of the possibilities of each medium with advantages of speed, cost and convenience.

E-mail offers many advantages for internal/external customer communication.

- Messages can be sent and received very **fast** (allowing real time messaging dialogue)

- E-mail is **economical** (estimated 20 times cheaper than fax, previously the fastest method): often allowing worldwide transmission for less than the cost of a local telephone call.

- The recipient gets a '**hard copy**' message, and the sender has documentary evidence of message transmission and retrieval by the recipient (for legal/logistical purposes).

- Messages can be sent **worldwide** at any **time**.

- The user can prepare **complex documents** (spreadsheets, graphics, photos) for sending as 'attachments' to e-mail covering messages. These can be printed out by the recipient, as a convenient alternative to fax.

- E-mail **message management** software (such as Outlook Express) has convenient features such as: message copying (to multiple recipients); integration with an 'address book' (database of contacts); automatic alert messages sent when the target recipient is unable to access his or her e-mail immediately, with alternative contact details; stationery and template features, allowing corporate identity to be applied; facilities for mail organisation and filing.

5.5 INTRANET AND EXTRANET

'Inter' means 'between': 'intra' means 'within'; 'extra' means 'outside'. This may be a useful reminder of some of the inter-related terminology in this area.

- The **Internet** is used to disseminate and exchange information among the public at large.

- An **intranet** is used to disseminate and exchange information 'in-house' within an organisation. Only employees are able to access this information. The firewall surrounding it fends off unauthorised access.

- An **extranet** is used to communicate with selected people outside the organisation.

The idea behind an intranet is that companies set up their own mini versions of the Internet, using a combination of their own networked computers and Internet technology. Each employee has a browser and a server computer distributes corporate information as well as offering access to the global Net.

Typical intranet content

- **Performance data**: linked to sales, inventory, job progress and other database and reporting systems, enabling employees to process and analyse data to fulfil their work objectives

- **Employment information**: online policy and procedures manuals (health and safety, disciplinary and grievance), training and induction material, internal contacts for help and information

- **Employee support/information**: advice on first aid, healthy working at computer terminals, training courses, offered, resources held in the corporate library and so on.

- **Notice boards** for the posting of message to and from employees: notice of meetings, events, trade union activities

- **Departmental home pages**: information and news about each department's personnel and activities to aid identification and cross-functional understanding

- **Bulletins or newsletters**: details of product launches and marketing campaigns, staff moves, changes in company policy – or whatever might be communicated through the print equivalent, plus links to relevant databases or departmental home pages.

- **E-mail facilities** for the exchange of messages, memos and reports between employees in different locations

- **Upward communication**: suggestion schemes, feedback questionnaires

- **Individual personnel files**, to which employees can download training materials, references, certificates and appraisals

Benefits of intranet

- Cost savings from the elimination of storage, printing and distribution of documents that can instead be exchanged electronically or be made available online

- More frequent use made of online documents than printed reference resources (eg procedures manuals) and more flexible and efficient interrogation and updating of data

- Wider access to corporate information. This facilitates multi-directional communication and coordination (particularly for multi-site working). It is also a mechanism of corporate culture and *esprit de corps*. The term 'virtual team' has been coined to describe how ICT can link people in structures which emulate the dynamics of teamworking (identity, solidarity, shared goals and information) despite the geographical dispersion of team members in different locations or constantly on the move (as, for example, sales representatives).

DEFINITION

An **extranet** is an intranet that is accessible to authorised outsiders.

Whereas an intranet resides behind a firewall and is accessible only to people who are members of the same company or organisation, an extranet provides various levels of accessibility to outsiders. Only those outsiders with a valid username and password can access an extranet, with varying levels of access rights enabling control over what people can view. Since information will not be available to the public in general, it can be used as part of a relationship marketing strategy. Examples include the member-only pages of professional bodies (and their student equivalents), which make information and downloads available only to registered members.

Extranets are useful tools for **business partners**. They can share data or systems to provide smoother transaction processing and more efficient services for customers. Extranets therefore allow better use of the knowledge held by an organisation – by facilitating access to that knowledge.

An extranet may be used to:

- Provide a 'pooled' service which a number of business partners can access

- Exchange news that is of use to partner companies and clients

- Share training or development resources

- Publicise loyalty schemes, sponsorships, exhibition attendance information and other promotional tools

- Exchange potentially large volumes of transaction data efficiently

- Provide online presentations to business partners and prospects (and not competitors)

5.6 ELECTRONIC DATA INTERCHANGE (EDI)

Electronic Data Interchange (EDI) is the exchange of transactional data between organisations by electronic means as a replacement for documents.

EDI is the electronic transfer of business information, with the information being sent in a format that conforms to certain standards. It introduces the possibility of 'paperless' trading and promises the end of repetitive form filling, stock orders and other forms of 'paper shifting'. EDI is used predominantly between large business customers and their suppliers eg, General Motors in the automobile industry use EDI as a part of the 'just-in-time' (JIT) organisation of the supply of components and raw materials to their assembly plants.

EDI is also of growing significance in the retail trade, enabling a large superstore such as Tesco to organise supplies from a central warehouse (and from external suppliers) to its chain of retail stores. Using EDI and electronic point of sale (EPOS) technology, Tesco deals with over 1,000 suppliers across computer networks so that stocks can be replenished exactly when needed, forecast sales patterns can be passed on to suppliers and invoices forwarded.

In banking and financial industries, EDI and related applications of IT are revolutionising the entire system of moving funds, encouraging the emergence of global or fully-internationalised money and securities markets in which the electronic transmission of funds is fast replacing 'paper-shifting'. In another thirty years, in an almost 'cashless society', most transactions to do with borrowing, paying, receiving, depositing and moving money will probably be done on wallet-sized personal communicators.

6 WRITTEN AND TELEPHONE

6.1 WRITTEN METHODS OF COMMUNICATION

Although verbal communication is the most common form of day-to-day communication, by its nature it is transitory and is often informal. Hence a verbal agreement is commonly supplemented by written confirmation – the written communication serves as a permanent formal record of what passed in what might have been a relatively informal manner (eg in a telephone conversation).

Written methods of communication of all sorts – letters, memos, bulletins, files, circulars – are the norm in many companies. The dominant characteristic of many managers' working day is paperwork and meetings. They do have the advantage that being in permanent or hard copy form they are less open to misinterpretation. With meetings, for instance, formal minutes may be taken, circulated and agreed to as the definitive written evidence of the meeting. Written methods of communication can be very flexibly used. When trying to reach a number of workers in one place notice boards are often used, typically to announce current events, meetings and similar matters which are not of crucial significance.

The advantages of written messages include the following.

(a) They provide a *permanent record* of a transaction or agreement, for confirmation and recollection of details. Evidence may also be necessary in legal affairs.

(b) They provide *confirmation* and *clarification* of verbal messages, again in case evidence should be needed, but also as an aid to memory.

(c) They are easily *duplicated* and sent out to numerous recipients: this ensures that information, operating instructions etc will be consistent.

(d) They enable a difficult piece of communication to be re-worded and rewritten over a period of time, so that the exact shade of meaning can be conveyed.

(e) They can be *stored* and later *retrieved* for reference and analysis as required.

(f) They are the cheapest form of contacting a range of individuals.

The main disadvantage is that there is no means of knowing whether the message has been received and understood by the person notified.

Other disadvantages include:

- *Time*. A written message can take time to produce, and to send (eg by post), if expensive technology is beyond the user's reach. Instant feedback is not available, and so errors in interpretation may not be corrected immediately. Because of the time factor, swift 'interactive' exchanges of opinion, attitudes etc are impossible.

- *Inflexibility.* Once sent, the message cannot immediately be altered or amended, even though circumstances change, errors are discovered etc. Written communication also tends to come across as formal and impersonal, so in situations requiring greater sensitivity or persuasion, the personal presence or voice of the sender may be more effective.

- *Perceived irrelevance?* Written messages do not have the immediacy of the phone call and so may not be read.

- *Poor drafting.* Written messages that are poorly drafted may not be understood.

6.2 WRITTEN FORMATS – PLANNED COMMUNICATION

As well as e-mail, written communications formats commonly used in business include the following.

Letters	• Used for interpersonal communication via the external mail system (eg from the organisation to external stakeholders)
	• Flexible for use in a wide variety of situations
	• Often used to provide 'covering' or confirming details
	• May be used within the organisation for confidential or personal matters
Memos	• Equivalent of a letter in internal communications within the organisation
	• Flexible for use in a wide variety of work situations
	• Efficient, especially where pre-printed stationery or e-mail formats are used
	• Can be overused, where a phone call or note would suffice
Handbooks and journals	• Used for employee communications
	• Can be used to set out work-relevant information, policies and regulations, procedures
	• Can be used to brief and update employees on performance, results, staff news and meetings
Reports	• Enable a number of people to review complex facts and arguments, for decision-making
	• Should be objective in content and impersonal in style
	• May be formal (subject to strict structural conventions) or informal (in the form of a memo or e-mail)

Reports are meant to be *useful*. There should be no such thing as 'information for information's sake' in an efficient organisation: information is stored in files and retrieved for a purpose. The information contained in a business report might be used:

- as a permanent record and source of reference; or

- as a management tool – a source of information prepared in order to assist in management decision-making. Often more junior managers do the 'legwork' in obtaining information on a matter and then prepare a report for more senior managers to consider. This saves senior managers' time and ensures that the information on which they base their decision is more objective than if it had all been gathered and used by one person only.

Depending on its ultimate purpose, a report may consist of:

(a)   *information*, retrieved from files or other sources as a basis for management activity;

(b)   *narrative* or *description*, eg of one-off events or procedures, such as a takeover target or the installation of new equipment;

(c)   *analysis*, that is a further processing of data and information to render it more useful; or

(d)   *evaluation* and *recommendation*, directly assisting in the decision-making process.

Different types of information may be presented in a report.

- *Descriptive or factual information.* This consists of a description of facts and is objective: inferences can be drawn from the facts, but they must be logical and unbiased.

- *Instructive information.* This is information that tells the report user how to do something, or what to do. A recommendation in a report is a form of advice, and is therefore instructive information.

- *Dialectical information.* This consists of opinions and ideas, based on an objective assessment of the facts and with reasons for why these opinions and ideas have been reached.

The value of recognising these different types of information is that it can help to make clear what a report writer is trying to say.

- 'These are the facts' *(factual)*.

- 'This is what the facts seem to suggest is happening, has happened or will happen' *(dialectical)*.

- 'This is what should be done about matters to sort out the situation' *(instructive)*.

6.3   TELEPHONE – INFORMAL COMMUNICATION

The telephone has been an informal medium that implies that personal contact is important in the sending of the message. The message sender has had control in when to initiate this contact. The message receiver has often been willing to give the telephone message priority over a face-to-face meeting. Most people have had the experience of talking to someone who interrupts the conversation to answer the telephone. Advances in telecommunications technology have changed the relationship between the caller and the called. Call display, call block, call return, and other services mean that the person called can now screen calls, know who called, and block incoming calls from a certain number. The widespread use of mobile telephones and computerised communication networks has changed the nature of the telephone. It is losing its personal nature and is becoming a more formal tool used to accomplish routine work.

For example, a salesperson on the road can use a mobile phone in the car to contact buyers, suppliers, and a support person at head office who is tied into the computer systems that track orders and deliveries. The telephone is used as a tool to get the latest information to the salesperson, to schedule appointments, and to relay data on orders and information on clients back to head office. The sales agent is using the telephone not as an informal way to chat but as an indispensable tool to perform the work.

The services available to users are increasing all the time, making the mobile phone a tool of **promotion** and **e-commerce** as well as interpersonal communication.

Communication services include:

Messaging	• Voice mail
	• Short message service (SMS) which allows text messages of up to 160 characters to be transmitted over a standard digital phone
	• Paging services
	• Access to e-mail messages, downloaded from the Internet
Call management	• Call barring
	• Conference calls
	• Call divert
Corporate services	• Integrated numbering, so that people have a single contact number for their desk and mobile phones
	• Virtual private networks that incorporate mobile phones as well as conventional desktop phones

6.4 COMPUTER TELEPHONY INTEGRATION (CTI)

Computer Telephony Integration (CTI) systems gather information about callers such as their telephone number and customer account number or demographic information (age, income, interests etc). This is stored on a customer database and can be called up and sent to the screen of the person dealing with the call, perhaps before the call has even been put through.

Thus sales staff dealing with hundreds of calls every day might appear to remember individual callers personally and know in advance what they are likely to order. Order forms with key details entered already can be displayed on screen automatically, saving time for both the sales staff and the caller.

Alternatively a busy manager might note that an unwelcome call is coming in on the 'screen pop' that appears on her PC and choose to direct it to her voice mailbox rather than dealing with it at once.

As another example, a bank might use CTI to prompt sales people with changes in share prices and with the details of the investors they should call to offer dealing advice.

ACTIVITY 5 (30 MINS)

'Effective communication enhances the administrative function'. Comment on this statement and highlight guidelines for effective communication.

7 INTERPERSONAL SKILLS

7.1 PERSONAL AND INTERPERSONAL SKILLS

Interpersonal skills involve inspiring, motivating, leading and controlling people to achieve goals that are often poorly defined.

> **DEFINITION**
>
> **Interpersonal skills** are the skills used in interactions and relationships between two or more people.

They include:

(a) Building rapport or a sense of 'being in tune with' another person, which draws them into a relationship

(b) Building trust and respect to develop the relationship and encourage cooperation

(c) Managing conflict in such a way that the relationship is preserved

(d) Persuading or influencing another person to do what you want them to do or to share your beliefs

(e) Negotiating or bargaining in order to reach mutually acceptable or compromise solutions to problems

(f) Communicating assertively, so that you uphold your rights and get your needs met – without violating the rights or ignoring the needs of others

(g) Communicating informatively, so that you give relevant and timely information

(h) Communicating supportively, so that you encourage the other person and gain their commitment

People need these skills to:

- understand and manage the roles, relationships, attitudes and perceptions operating in any situation in which two or more people are involved

- communicate clearly and effectively

- achieve their aims from an interpersonal encounter (ideally allowing the other parties to emerge satisfied too)

Issues to consider in interpersonal communication and work relationships:

Issue	Comment
Goal	What does the other person want from the process? What do you want from the process? What will both parties need and be trying to do to achieve their aims? Can both parties emerge satisfied?
Perceptions	What, if any, are likely to be the factors causing 'distortion' of the way both parties see the issues and each other? (Attitudes, feelings, expectations?)
Roles	What 'roles' are the parties playing? (Superior/subordinate, customer/server, complainer/soother) What expectations does this create of the way they will behave?
Resistances	What may the other person be 'afraid of? What may he or she be trying to protect? (His or her self-image/ego, attitudes?)
Attitudes	What sources of difference, conflict or lack of understanding might there be, arising from attitudes and other factors that shape them (sex, race, specialism, hierarchy)?
Relationships	What are the relative positions of the parties and the nature of the relationship between them? (Superior/subordinate? Formal/informal? Work/non-work?)
Environment	What factors in the immediate and situational environment might affect the issues and the people? (eg competitive environment: customer care; pressures of disciplinary situation: nervousness; physical surroundings: formality/informality)

7.2 WHY ARE INTERPERSONAL SKILLS IMPORTANT?

Good working relationships and good interpersonal skills can assist in the following areas.

Area	Comment
Motivation	Work can satisfy people's social needs because it provides relationships
Communication	Poor interpersonal relationships can cause a barrier to communicating effectively -messages will be misinterpreted
Team working and team-building	Good working relationships and good interpersonal skills can develop a climate in which people can communicate openly and honestly
Customer care	Good interpersonal skills are recognised as being increasingly important when dealing with customers
Career development	Good interpersonal skills are increasingly necessary to get promotion
Managerial roles	Many of the managerial roles require interpersonal skills
Power and persuasion	Interpersonal skills can be a source of personal power in an organisation and can make a manager more effective
Team management	Interpersonal skills are required for the manager's tasks of appraisal, interviewing etc

7.3 COMMUNICATION SKILLS

In addition, a range of communication skills will be deployed. The following checklist identifies and classifies communication skills.

Oral	Written	Visual/non-verbal
Clear pronunciation	Correct spelling	Understanding of control over body language and facial expressions
Suitable vocabulary	Suitable vocabulary	Drawing ability
Correct grammar/syntax	Correct grammar/syntax	
Fluency	Good writing or typing	
Expressive delivery	Suitable style	

Skills in sending messages include the following.

- **Selecting and organising your material** – marshalling your thoughts and constructing your sentences, arguments etc

- **Judging the effect of your message** on the recipient in that particular situation

- **Choosing language and media** accordingly

- **Adapting your communication style** accordingly – putting people at their ease, smoothing over difficulties (tact) or being comforting/challenging/ informal/formal as the situation and relationship demand

- Using **non-verbal signals** to reinforce (or at least not to undermine) your spoken message

- Seeking and interpreting **feedback**

Skills in receiving messages include the following.

- **Reading attentively** and actively making sure you understand the content, looking up unfamiliar words and doubtful facts if necessary and evaluating the information given: is it logical? correct? objective?

- Extracting **relevant information** from the message and filtering out the non-essentials.

- **Listening attentively** and actively – concentrating on the message and **not** on what you are going to say next; questioning and evaluating what you are hearing.

- **Interpreting** the message's underlying meaning, if any, and evaluating your own reactions. Are you reading into the message more or less than what is really there?

- Asking **questions** in a way that will elicit the information you want **to obtain.**

- Interpreting **non-verbal signals** and how they confirm or contradict **the** spoken message.

- Giving helpful **feedback** if the medium is appropriate (eg poor telephone line) or the message is unclear, insufficient etc.

ACTIVITY 6   (15 MINS)

Which written formats do you use most often in interpersonal communication (a) with colleagues or team members, (b) with your superiors and (c) with friends at work?

(a)   What do you find most convenient about each of these formats?

(b)   What factors or guidelines do you have to bear in mind when using them?

7.4   EFFECTIVE NEGOTIATION SKILLS

Negotiating is an activity that seeks to reach agreement between two or more starting positions.

The skills of a negotiator can be summarised under three main headings.

(a)   **Interpersonal skills** – the use of good communicating techniques, the user of power and influence, and the ability to impress a personal style on the tactics of negotiation

(b)   **Analytical skills** – the ability to analyse information, diagnose problems, to plan and set objectives, and the exercise of good judgement in interpreting results

(c)   **Technical skills** – attention to detail and thorough case preparation

There are behaviours that are typical of successful negotiations and distinguish them from the less successful.

Successful negotiators	Less successful negotiators
Avoid criticising or attacking the other person and concentrate instead on 'attacking' the problem in a no nonsense but constructive way.	Are more likely to get locked into an attacking spiral where one side attacks the other, which provokes a counter attack and so on.
Ask many more questions than the less skilled. The skilled negotiator asks questions not only to gain more information and understanding but also as an alternative to disagreeing bluntly, and as a means of putting forward suggestions.	Tend to assume that they understand the other person's point of view and that the other person has the same basic information. This makes asking questions redundant.
Summarise and test understanding, knowing that being explicit aids common understanding and leads to quality agreement that is more likely to stick.	
Keep the emotional temperature down by sticking to the facts.	Are inclined to exaggeration, using expressions such as 'an offer you can't refuse' and 'mutually beneficial'
Are more likely to say things that reveal what he or she is thinking, intending and feeling than the less skilled.	Feel vulnerable to losing the argument and are more likely to 'keep their cards close to their chests'.

7.5   EFFECTIVE CONSULTATION

Consultation is the process where, on a regular basis, management genuinely seeks the views, ideas and feelings of employees before a decision is taken.

The advantages that can be associated with consultation include the following.

- Improved quality of decisions because the manager is using the collected knowledge and ingenuity of those who are most affected by the decisions.

- Better cooperation between managers and employees because people will accept even those decisions that they do not like if their views have been taken into consideration, assuming they have been told why the decision has been taken.

- It serves as a valuable preliminary to negotiation. When representatives have been involved in the discussion of 'how' they will be better informed when it becomes a matter of 'how much'?

- Increased efficiency of the entire organisation by involving employees in achieving a better product or service.

- Help industrial relations by allowing managers and their subordinates the opportunity to understand each other's views and objectives.

For a process of consultation to be genuine, it must not be used when a manager has already reached a decision. His or her mind will then be closed to alternatives, the meeting will sense that it is an insulting charade of 'guess what's in my mind'. Instead of gaining commitment to the decision, the pseudo-consultation will alienate. There will be resentment, which might result in non cooperation.

7.6   PERSONAL PLAN

The communications process is composed of three parts:

1   The sender (source) of the information,
2   The receiver of the information
3   The receiver's understanding of the information received.

Information is transmitted from the source to the receiver, who interprets what he has heard or read. The better the process of transmission, the better the chances are that the message will be interpreted as the originator intended.

Within this process there are probably many areas where communication skills could be improved. A useful tool to identify and reflect upon our personal strengths and areas for development is the personal SWOT analysis.

To construct your own SWOT analysis you need to examine your current situation. What are your strengths and weaknesses? How can you capitalise on your strengths and overcome your weaknesses? What are the external opportunities and threats in your chosen career field?

Strengths	Weaknesses
- What are your advantages? Colleagues will identify this - What do you do well? Competence analysis will identify strengths and develop needs	- What could be improved? Assessment by supervisor will identify any weaknesses - What is done badly? - What should you avoid?
Opportunities	**Threats**
- What are the interesting trends? Keep up-to-date with courses, colleagues and managers as well as publications - Does your organisation have a high turnover of managerial staff? Appraisals will outline the range of opportunities	- What obstacles do you face? - Is changing technology threatening your position? - Is your job changing?

- Strengths need to be maintained or built upon.
- Weaknesses need to be remedied, changed or stopped.
- Opportunities need to be prioritised, captured, built on and optimised.
- Threats need to be countered or minimised and managed.

Your personal plan will also reflect:

- your learning needs
- what help you will need and from whom
- the resources you will need

Certain aspects of communication are critical to its success. They include listening, questioning, understanding personality differences and non-verbal communication (NVC or body language).

- **Listening** – the ability to listen and to respond with intelligent questions is more difficult than it first appears.

- **Active questioning** – indicates you are interested in the communication process. You are participating in an exchange of information.

- **Personality differences** – the trick is to use these skills appropriately when dealing with different personality types – and knowing which personality profile fits you. Bender identifies four broad personality types: the Analytical, the Amiable, the Driver and the Expressive.

  Each personality type has different strengths and weaknesses. The following table highlights traits to watch for in yourself, and in the people you work with.

Type	Strengths	Potential Weaknesses
Analytical	Thinking Thorough Disciplined	Excludes feelings from decisions Goes too far; perfectionist Too rigid or demanding of self/others
Amiable	Supportive Patient Diplomatic	Tends to conform to wishes of others No time boundaries; things do not get done Not assertive or directive
Driver	Independent Decisive Determined	Has trouble operating with others Does not take time to consider other perspectives Domineering; too focused on doing it 'my way'
Expressive	Good communicator Enthusiastic Imaginative	Talks too much Comes on too strong Dreamer; unrealistic

Once you recognise how a person is behaving, you can deal with that person on a communication level that is appropriate to the situation. Each individual responds differently. For instance, there is no sense asking the Driver extensive questions. He or she only wants answers. But when talking to the Analytical, be prepared to answer questions about everything in detail.

The Amiable wants you to be prepared to answer the 'why' questions he or she will ask. Do not push, do not rush and be a good listener. With the Expressive, ask and answer 'who' questions and keep the details minimal.

- **Non-verbal communication** - the gestures we make, the way we sit, how fast or how loud we talk, how close we stand, how much eye contact we make all send strong messages. The way you listen, look, move, and react tell the other person whether or not you care and how well you are listening. The non-verbal signals you send either produce a sense of interest, trust, and desire for connection, or they generate disinterest, distrust, and confusion. Non-verbal communication, or body language, reveals the truth about us more accurately than words.

7.7 EMOTIONAL INTELLIGENCE

Emotions are 'the glue' that connect people to one another. They are the foundation of your ability to understand yourself and relate to others. Non-verbal communication is one of the five skills of emotional intelligence. The others are:

Quick stress relief – people who are overly stressed are not able to successfully send or receive non-verbal cues. When you are upset, agitated, or frightened, you act and react differently than when you feel 'just right'. Stress tends to make you focus on yourself and lose connection to others. Stress can also make it more difficult to absorb see, hear, and experience sensory information. This makes non-verbal communication much more difficult – even impossible if the upset is sufficiently great. Because of the way stress derails non-verbal communication, you must first learn how to manage stress before you can expect to effectively send and receive wordless signals.

Emotional awareness – in order to send accurate non-verbal cues, you need to be aware of your emotions and how they influence you. You also need to be able to recognise the emotions of others and the true feelings behind the cues they are sending.

Playful communication – using gentle humour often helps you broach sensitive subjects, resolve disagreements, and reframe problems. Laughter relieves fatigue and relaxes your body, while also recharging your batteries and helping you accomplish more.

Conflict resolution – the ability to resolve conflicts positively and with confidence is the fifth of five essential emotional intelligence skills. Together, these five skills help you build strong relationships, overcome challenges, and succeed at work and in life.

EXAMPLE   EMOTIONAL INTELLIGENCE

Before you can improve any behaviour, you first have to learn to recognise it. Watch people interacting with one another. You don't want people to be aware of your presence because that would inhibit them and alter their behaviour, so be discrete. Rather than paying attention to their words, focus on their non-verbal communication:

- **Eye contact**: Is eye contact being made? If so, is it overly intense or just right?

- **Facial expression**: Are the facial expressions mask-like and inexpressive, or emotionally present and filled with interest?

- **Tone of voice**: Do their voices project warmth, confidence, and delight, or are they strained and blocked?

- **Posture and body language**: Are their bodies relaxed or stiff and immobile? Are shoulders tense and raised, or slightly sloped?

- **Touch**: Is there physical contact? If so, do both parties seem to be comfortable with it?

- **Timing and pace**: Is there an easy flow of information back and forth? Do non-verbal responses come too quickly or too slowly?

- **Sounds that convey understanding**: Do you hear sounds that indicate caring or concern?

CHAPTER ROUNDUP

- The objective of communication by a manager or administrator is to exchange, impart or receive *information*.

- Effective communication is a two-way process, perhaps best expressed as a cycle.

- The changing economic and business climate is likely to put increased pressures upon communication systems. The challenges require an enhanced commitment to quality, profitability and the ability to manage change

- Communication has changed in recent decades with the development of technologies offering higher speed, wider access to information, 24-hour, 7-day global communication (and commerce), greater interactivity and multi-media presentation and greater personalisation/customisation of communication

- A meeting is a group of people coming together for the purpose of resolving problems or making decisions.

- The face-to-face meeting can be formal or informal, vertical, horizontal, or diagonal, but it is always the richest communication medium.

- The Internet is used to disseminate and exchange information among the public at large. An intranet can be used to perform the same function within an organisation, and an extranet within a network of selected customers, prospects, members or business partners.

- The Internet (with related tools such as e-mail and website marketing) is a complex and powerful promotional tool for a wide range of promotional activities.

- E-mail has replaced letters, memos, faxes, documents and even telephone calls – combining many of the possibilities of each medium with new advantages of speed, cost and convenience.

- Electronic Data Interchange (EDI) is the exchange of transactional data between organisations by electronic means as a replacement for documents.

- The main disadvantage of written communication is that there is no means of knowing whether the message has been received and understood by the person notified.

- Interpersonal skills involve inspiring, motivating, leading and controlling people to achieve goals that are often poorly defined.

- Negotiation implies acceptance by both parties that agreement between them is required before a decision is taken. Consultation implies a willingness to listen to the views of another while reserving the right to take the final decision, with or without agreement on both sides.

QUICK QUIZ

1   Draw a model of the communication process

2   What do you understand by the term '24-7 global communication'?

3   What is a quorum?

4   How will electronic media help people working from home?

5   E-mail is cheaper than fax for transmitting hard copy messages to remote locations

   True ☐
   False ☐

6   What do the following stand for?

   (a)   E-mail
   (b)   V-mail
   (c)   SMS
   (d)   EDI

ANSWERS TO QUICK QUIZ

1   The process of communication can be modelled as follows:

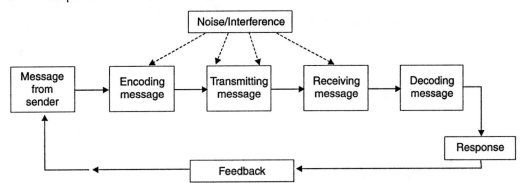

2   Information and communications technology (ICT) has enabled 24-hour 7-day global communication: across working or office hours, time zones and geographical distances. The Internet allows users to access information/ services and perform transactions at any time of any day. Nor is there any distinction between local and international sites, in terms of speed or cost of access. (Physical delivery of products ordered will, of course, re-erect some of the geographical barriers.)

3   A quorum is the minimum number of members required to hold the meeting.

4   Increased numbers of *people working from home* will mean that more effort must be directed towards fostering a feeling of belonging to the organisation. Electronic media will help in the maintenance of links (both formally and informally) between worker and employer.

5   True.

6   (a)   Electronic mail
     (b)   Voice mail
     (c)   Short Message Service
     (d)   Electronic Data Interchange (5)

ANSWERS TO ACTIVITIES

1   The main items are:

- 'transmission' ie: onus on the sender to sent the information;

- 'information' not data. Data is dead, historic or irrelevant; information tells the recipient something he does not know;

- 'received and understood' ie, in the sense intended by the sender;

- 'leads to action' ie, if it does not lead to action was communication necessary?

2

Positive feedback	Negative feedback
Action taken as requested	No action taken or wrong action taken
Letter/memo/note confirming receipt of message and replying in an appropriate way	No written response where expected
Accurate reading back of message	Incorrect reading back of message
Statement: 'Yes, I've got that.'	Request for clarification or repetition
Smile, nod, murmur of agreement	Silence, blank look, frown etc

3   Initially, visual methods could be used, eg, a film or a mock-up of the TV advertisement, to grab attention and provide impact to the main message. Then verbal methods of briefing, lectures, question and answer sessions may be used to persuade and motivate the sales team, to answer any questions and to show top management's personal backing. Finally, each salesperson could be given a fact pack, containing a written record of all the details, test results, etc for later reference.

4   (a)   Telephone, confirmed in writing later (order form, letter) – or e-mail order (if both parties have access)

(b)   Noticeboard (or employee Web page, if available) or general meeting: depending on the sensitivity of the topic and the need for staff to ask questions.

(c)   Face-to-face private conversation – but it would be a good idea to confirm the outcome in writing so that records can be maintained.

(d)   Telephone, email or face-to-face (if close by).

(e)   Face-to-face, supported by clear written notes. You can then use visual aids or gestures to help explain. This will also give you the opportunity to check the group's understanding – while the notes will save the group having to memorise what you say, and enable them to focus on understanding

5   Administration is closely concerned with the processing and conveying of information and effective communication can only help this. Communication itself is necessary for a variety of reasons including:

- to exercise day-to-day control;
- to facilitate planned change;
- to cope with unplanned changes and unforeseen circumstances.

The better and more effective the communication the more efficient will be the administrative function.

BPP
LEARNING MEDIA

The three reasons shown immediately above may be broken down into more specific purposes including:

- to convey information about what is happening internally and externally;

- to explain the nature and implications of current and anticipated problems;

- to establish guidelines, policies and procedures of dealing with a number of differing situations;

- to stimulate action;

- to enhance the quality of staff relationships.

Downward communication is concerned with planning and control and upward communication is usually concerned with feedback from all levels within the organisation, together with information from external sources such as customers.

If communication is poor then it is likely that the result will be poor, with inadequate control and faulty coordination. This could result in:

- poor understanding of working instructions and responsibilities;
- poor awareness of organisational objectives;
- lack of warning of problems;
- lack of employee participation;
- isolation of management from other staff;
- disregard of real problems.

Overall the organisation will not be working as a whole but as a group of isolated individuals and sections of individuals and obviously this cannot be good for the organisation.

6   The answer to this will depend on your own situation.

BPP
LEARNING MEDIA

Chapter

09

Improve systems relating to information and knowledge

Processing business data	Developing systems – hard and soft properties	Checkland's soft systems methodology (SSM)
Access and dissemination	**Improve systems relating to information and knowledge**	Automation, rationalisation and re-engineering
Developing websites and mailing		Information and knowledge management
Data warehousing and datamining		Databases

Introduction

This chapter describes how new information systems are developed, with special attention to organisational design issues and business re-engineering. It describes systems analysis and design and other core activities involved in the building of any information system. Different methodologies emphasise different aspects of the development process. For example, Soft Systems methodology concentrates on the problem formulation stage, while structured methodologies emphasise the design of solutions.

As information systems have developed, they have allowed organisations to gather and store vast amounts of data and knowledge. Making information available quickly and easily to those who could act on it is a challenging and important task. In this chapter we explain the concepts of information management and knowledge management before identifying and evaluating various systems available for the management of knowledge.

Your objectives

After completing this chapter you should be able to:

- Report on existing approaches to the collection, formatting, storage and disseminating of information and knowledge

- Carry out appropriate changes to the collection, formatting, storage and dissemination of information and knowledge

- Implement a strategy to improve access to systems of information and knowledge

1 PROCESSING BUSINESS DATA

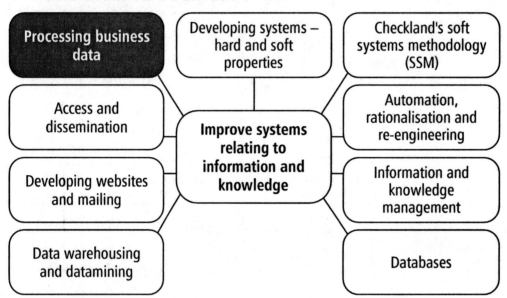

1.1 PROCESSING FEATURES

Processing business data can be said to have the following features for both manual as well as electronic data processing.

    (a)   *Collecting data in the first place.* There must be data to process and this may arise in the course of operations. There has to be a system or procedure for ensuring that all the data needed for processing is collected and made available for processing. Collecting data is an important step that must not be overlooked because the quality, accuracy and completeness of the data will affect the quality of information produced.

    (b)   *Converting the data into information,* perhaps by summarising it or classifying it and/or producing total figures etc. For example, a sales ledger system might be required to process data about goods despatched to satisfy customer orders so as to:

        (i)   produce and send out invoices;

        (i)   record the invoices sent out in the customers' personal ledgers;

        (iii)   produce a report of the total value of invoices sent out in the day/week etc;

        (iv)   record the total value of invoices sent out in the debtors' control account in the nominal ledger.

The output consists of invoices and figures for sales totals (ie management information). Updating the personal ledgers and the debtors' control account are file updating activities to keep the sales ledger records up to date.

(c) *Updating files to incorporate the processed data.* The example of sales ledger work has already been mentioned. Updating files means bringing them up to date to record current transactions.

(d) *The dissemination of information to users.* This includes a variety of reports (on-screen, or hard copy), for example:

(i) scheduled reports, routinely prepared on a regular basis (eg payroll report) and reviewed to ensure that any control information it contains is used;

(ii) exception reports which delineate deviations from plan;

(iii) reports produced on demand (ie only when requested, but not as a matter of course);

(iv) planning reports (eg forecasts).

1.2 INFORMATION IN THE ORGANISATION

Since the source of action within any organisation is decision-making, the object of communicating information within an organisation should be to serve those persons taking the relevant decisions. It is therefore natural to consider the type and level of decisions each manager has to take. Only then can the following be considered:

(a) What information is required?
(b) How should it be collected and by whom?
(c) When and from where should it be collected?

A great deal of interpreted information is disseminated within an organisation for use by its members. The organisation as an information-processing entity is shown below.

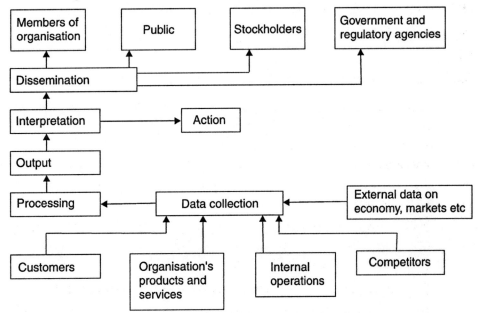

Figure 9.1: Organisation as an information-processing entity

The typical information requirements of organisations that are operating in different sectors such as manufacturing, service, the public sector and non-profit organisations such as charities will all be similar. They all have customers (sponsors, contributors and members), products or services, internal operations, competitors and the environment to obtain information from.

2 DEVELOPING SYSTEMS – HARD AND SOFT PROPERTIES

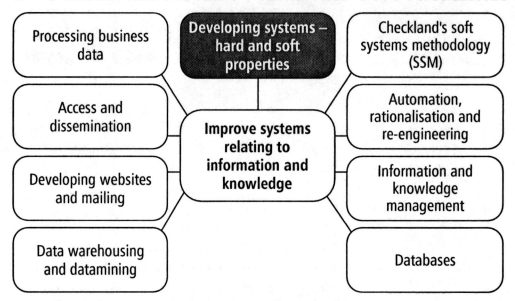

Systems thinking is central to collaboration, placing the organisation within the web of relationships that define and sustain it. A systems view of the world implies a focus on the whole – not just the constituent parts. To identify and establish productive relationships, an organisation and its employees must understand how they fit into the larger systems of which they are a part.

2.1 HARD AND SOFT PROPERTIES

Systems theory explores the nature of systems and the characteristics of systems and approaches that are suited to different situations. Organisations are social systems. All social systems are open to a wide range of influences, which means they are sensitive to a wide variety of environmental factors and are often exposed to unstructured problems.

Unstructured problems are sometimes referred to as 'soft' problems. Different people might have different views of what the problem that needs to be addressed is, and a solution might have to satisfy a variety of different objectives.

On the other hand, a 'hard' approach is based on structured, logical problems, where the objective is clear.

A **hard** approach is suitable in circumstances when:

- The problem can be clearly defined
- Objectives are clear
- The problem is self-contained
- Information needs are known
- A solution can be recognised
- Standard solution techniques are applicable

A **soft** approach is suitable in circumstances when:

- The problem is difficult to define
- Tastes, values, judgement and opinions are involved
- It is not clear what is known and what is needed
- It is not clear what the solution should achieve
- The problem is 'people' oriented
- There are no standard solution techniques available

Many problems or situations have both hard and soft properties, for example an information systems project. Properties can be classified as either hard or soft – although in practise the two will, in some circumstances, be related.

The hard properties would include the specifications of the system, for example processing speeds, the space required to accommodate the system and the budget available to develop the system. Soft properties are usually people related.

2.2 HARD SYSTEMS APPROACH

Different approaches to systems development place differing emphasis on hard or soft areas. Early systems development approaches, such as the systems lifecycle, tended to be 'harder' in their approach than more modern approaches.

In the early days of business computing, computers were used to automate processing activities. To a large extent, the systems that were developed simply matched previous manual procedures. However, the process of managing information systems development has moved on from being a matter of technical control over a few computer programmers to being a major management operation involving large parts of an organisation and elements of its environment.

2.3 SYSTEMS LIFECYCLE

The systems lifecycle (sometimes referred to as the Systems Development Lifecycle or SDLC) is a traditional method of building information systems. This disciplined approach to systems development identifies several stages of development. (Note that the number and name of the stages varies depending on the author or organisation referred to – but the principle of a structured approach is consistent.)

DEFINITION

The term '**systems lifecycle**' describes the stages a system moves through from inception until it is discarded or replaced.

Stage	Comment
Project definition	Involves an investigation and analysis of the organisation's information requirements to decide if a new or modified information system is required. If a new project is identified its objectives, scope and project plan are developed.
Feasibility study	This involves a review of the existing system and the identification of a range of possible alternative solutions. A feasible (technical, operational, economic, social) solution will be selected – or a decision not to proceed made. Findings are usually contained in a feasibility study report that describes the activities required in the remaining lifecycle phases.

Stage	Comment
Design	The logical and physical design specifications are produced in a detailed specification of the new system.
Programming or software selection	If bespoke software is to be produced, analysts work with programmers to prepare program specifications and then the programs. If off-the-shelf software is suitable, packages are evaluated (perhaps in a report) and selected.
Installation	Steps are taken to put the system into operation. Testing, file conversion and user training are carried out. A formal conversion plan is developed.
Post-implementation	The system is used and evaluated. A formal post-implementation audit determines how well the system has met its objectives and whether any modifications are required.

2.4 DRAWBACKS OF THE LIFECYCLE APPROACH

The systems lifecycle is considered a hard systems approach as it has a narrow focus. The approach efficiently automates existing procedures within easily defined processing requirements. The resulting systems are modelled on the manual systems they are replacing.

Sequential models (such as the lifecycle model) restrict user input throughout much of the process. (A sequential model is one where a stage is not started until the previous stage is complete.) This often results in substantial and costly modifications late in the development process. It becomes increasingly difficult and expensive to change system requirements the further a system is developed.

Time overruns are common. The sequential nature of the process means a hold-up on one stage would stop development completely – contributing to time overruns. Time pressures and lack of user involvement often result in a poor quality system.

Because of these drawbacks the lifecycle approach is not as widely used today as in the past. However, it is still used with success for building systems where requirements are highly structured and well-defined eg large transaction processing systems.

2.5 SOFT SYSTEMS APPROACH

The soft systems approach to systems development aims to take into account the soft properties of the implementation – this approach looks at the wider picture. Some examples of soft properties that should be considered during systems development and implementation are:

- **Job security and status** – employees might think that a new system will put them out of a job, because the computer will perform routines that are currently done manually, and so reduce the need for human intervention. In some cases, the resistance to a new system might stem from a fear that it will result in a loss of status for the department concerned. For example, the management of the department might believe that a computer system will give 'control' over information gathering and dissemination to another group.

- **Career prospects** – managers and staff might think that a new system will damage their career prospects by reducing the requirement for middle managers and therefore reducing opportunities for promotion.

- **Social change** – new systems might disrupt the established social system in the office. Individuals who are used to working together might be separated into different groups, and individuals used to working on their own might be expected to join a group.

- **Fear of depersonalisation** – staff may be afraid that the computer will 'take over' and they will be reduced to being operators chained to the machine, losing the ability to introduce the 'human touch' to the work they do. This is not wholly unrealistic.

Another fear is that the new system will expose how inefficient previous methods of information gathering and information use had been. Individuals may feel that they are being criticised by the revelation of any such deficiencies.

To overcome the human problems with systems design and implementation, management and systems analysts must recognise them, and do what they can to resolve them.

3 CHECKLAND'S SOFT SYSTEMS METHODOLOGY (SSM)

3.1 COMPLEX RELATIONSHIPS

Checkland's 'soft systems methodology' is a response to difficulty in applying the approach of hard systems (engineering) thinking to business problems. Hard systems engineering tends to emphasise:

- measurable system objectives
- top-down decomposition of systems into sub-systems.

Advanced systems engineering may show systems with unexpected and counter-intuitive behaviour and complex feedback loops between components but systems engineering when applied to 'human systems' leads to problems.

Organisation goals may be in dispute. It is wrong to assume that all organisational members accept the views and goals of top management.

Formal methods usually begin with a problem statement but fixing the problem too early tends to hide problems. The method itself can restrict what will be elicited – conclusions will reflect methods and starting positions.

With SSM the process is as important as the outcome. The experience itself of applying an SSM approach will change the organisation. This will arise from changed views about the problem and possible solutions.

SSM is based on a number of assumptions:

- People attempt to place a meaning on their observations and experiences

- This meaning is the individual's interpretation of the event/situation

- The interpretation leads to the intention to follow a particular course of action

- Once the course is decided, purposeful action is taken – altering the event or situation leading to the action and creating a cycle of activity

- SSM involves a circular process of enquiry leading to action – shown in the diagram below:

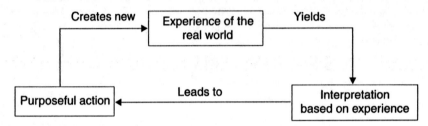

Figure 9.2: Soft systems methodology

3.2 SEVEN-STAGE PROCESS

In principle, an SSM project is done by the people of the organisation, with a consultant-facilitator. It is divided into seven distinct stages. These are:

1. **Problem situation** – finding out about the problem situation. This is basic research into the problem area. Who are the key players? How does the process work now?

2. **Analysis** – expressing the problem situation in three steps – intervention, prevalent culture and power relationships. (Rich picture)

3. **Root definition** of relevant systems – selecting how to view the situation and producing root definitions. From what different perspectives can we look at this problem situation?

4. **Conceptualisation** – based on the root definition for each area defined, build a conceptual model of the required capabilities

5. **Comparison** of the conceptual models with the real world. Use gap analysis, compare scenarios, and tables of comparisons and key-players' contrasting opinions to identify what part(s) of the conceptual models are lacking or poorly supported in the existing problem situation

6. **Changes** – identify culturally feasible and systemically desirable changes. Are there ways of improving the situation?

7. **Action** – the decision to implement the defined changes thus changing the problem situation itself and restarting the cycle.

A key feature of SSM is to keep the project vague and wide ranging for as long as possible – don't jump to conclusions, and don't ignore the current situation by concentrating on some idealised future.

There may be checklists of things to look for, models and frameworks of consideration may be used but without getting stuck with one model. Typically brainstorming techniques and force-field analysis may be used.

3.3 STREAMS OF ENQUIRY

SSM incorporates two related streams of enquiry:

(a)   The logic-driven stream of enquiry
(b)   The cultural stream of enquiry

The cultural stream of enquiry

There are three types of analysis involved in the cultural stream of enquiry:

(a)   An analysis of the relationship between the client, the would-be problem solver and the problem owner.

(b)   The second analysis considers the evolving set of relationships between roles, norms and values.

(c)   The third analysis focuses on how different interests reach accommodation and how power is expressed.

In combination all three types of analysis complement and enrich the logic-based stream of analysis.

This examination of the background of the problem can be expressed in the form of a rich picture, which is a representation of the situation showing the relevant relationships. It can be any sort of picture, a diagram or a cartoon – it can be funny, sad or political. It shows:

- Structural elements eg, departmental boundaries, product types and activities
- Process elements indicating what actually takes place in the system
- Relationships – indicated by arrows and symbols

The rich picture:

- provides an idea of the 'climate' of the situation

- includes components such as clients, people involved, tasks performed, environment

- is an important communication tools

- has a focus on perspectives and shared understanding

We can use the following example to try to draw a rich picture:

A local choral society always has difficulty in obtaining nominations for its officers and committee and attracting people to participate in choral related works. As it is a performing society a number of non-choral tasks must be managed. How can this difficulty be addressed and examined?

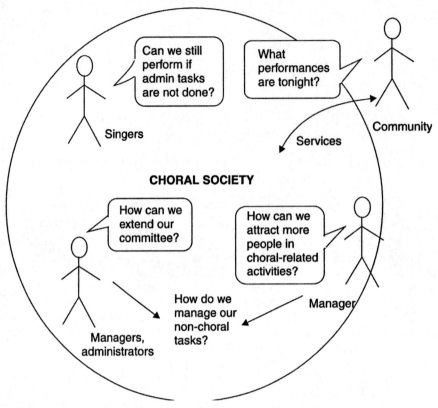

Figure 9.3: Example rich picture

Checkland describes his rich pictures as diagrams 'without rules'. Rich pictures have some distinguishing features. They show:

- the people involved

- their stated purposes

- their desires and fears (usually in think bubbles)

- more environmental detail than most diagrams (human activities, like processes, cross organisational boundaries)

- how interests agree or conflict

The logic-driven stream of enquiry

Under the logic-driven stream of enquiry the core purpose of the system is established. This is known as the root definition. A root definition is a statement defining:

- what a system is,
- who will be in it,
- persons who could be affected by it,
- persons who could affect it, and
- persons who are taking part in it.

In the choral society example, activities such as: identify needs of local community; attract membership; generate funds; attract audiences; could be used for the problem situation.

ACTIVITY 1 (10 MINS)

Root definitions can vary. As well as being a system to punish criminals, what other root definitions for a prison could there be?

In formulating the root definition, *Checkland* uses the mnemonic CATWOE to describe the human activity and its situation.

- **Clients** (customers) – those who more or less directly benefit or suffer from the system
- **Actors** – those that will carry out the transformation process
- **Transformation process** – the conversion of input to output. What transformations, movements, conversions of X take place? What is the nature of the transformations? What is the content and process of transformation from ingredients to a sandwich, from mixed, varied data to information, from an idea to a performance concept or marketable product etc?
- **Weltanschauung** – the worldview underlying the assumptions behind the root definition. What is going on in the wider world that is influencing and shaping the system and need for the system to adapt?
- **Owner** – the person who is responsible for the system and could also stop the transformation process
- **Environmental** (the political, legal, economic, social, demographic, technological, ethical, competitive and natural) constraints – fixed elements outside the system

Transformation example

Checkland offers the case of an aircraft landing system. The transformation involves getting the incoming aircraft from a height and a distance safely on the runway. The actors would be the pilots (human and auto), the clients would be the passengers and crew, the owners the owners of the airline, and the environment: the air traffic controllers, air lanes, traffic conditions and geographic features. The Weltanschauung may involve competition between international airports, the airport-housing environment, and high concern for safety and high technology operations.

3.4 CONCEPTUAL MODEL

Once the SSM team has agreed on a root definition and the CATWOE participants, a conceptual model of the relevant system is created.

The steps involved in building a conceptual model from a root definition are:

- Use the root definition and CATWOE elements to form an impression of the system carrying out a transformation process
- Decide on key verbs to describe the fundamental activities in the system
- Structure key related activities in groups
- Connect the groups with arrows to indicate logical dependencies
- Check that the root definition and conceptual model together give a clear impression of what type of system it is and what the system does.

In our example, the choral society manages fluid relationships between those involved with choral and non-choral related tasks in order to perform outstanding choral performances.

Figure 9.4: Conceptual model

The success or failure of the transformation process in the model is assessed.

Checkland's Five Es for selection criteria are:

- efficacy (will it work at all?)
- efficiency (will it work with minimum resources?)
- effectiveness (does it contribute to the enterprise?)
- ethicality (is it moral?)
- elegance (is it beautiful?)

3.5 COMPARISON

Comparing the model to the real world should stimulate debate about whether the model improves the current situation. The comparison process might include:

- Formal questioning
- Informal discussion
- Event reconstruction
- Model overlay

The aim is to:

- understand the problem and the gaps better and be able to identify potential improvements

- determine mismatches between the actual situation and the model

- raise questions about which models should exist in reality

- evaluate the models in terms of the 3Es

- determine which models are workable

- compare the models with one found in practice

At this point, the changes that would improve the problem situation are defined and agreed and measures are taken to implement these changes.

4 AUTOMATION, RATIONALISATION AND RE-ENGINEERING

4.1 FORMS OF ORGANISATIONAL CHANGE

Developing and introducing a new information system can lead to organisational change, enabling organisations to redesign their structure, scope, power relationships, work flows, products, and services.

Four types of change, encouraged by IT, have been identified.

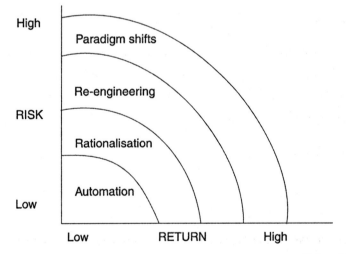

Figure 9.5: Change types

Automation

Business automation is the use of computerised working methods to speed up the performance of existing tasks. The first applications of automation using IT were introduced to help employees perform their tasks more efficiently and effectively eg, calculating pay.

Rationalisation

Rationalisation involves streamlining operating procedures and eliminating obvious bottlenecks and inefficiencies that are revealed by automation, for enhanced efficiency of operations.

As well as automating a process, rationalisation includes efficient process design. An automated banking system needs standardised account numbers and rules for calculating the daily balances.

Re-engineering

The aim of re-engineering is to reorganise business around processes rather than around functions or departments. *Davenport and Short* suggest a five-step approach to re-engineering:

(a) Develop the business vision and process objectives
(b) Identify the processes to be redesigned
(c) Understand and measure the existing processes
(d) Identify IT levers
(e) Design and build a prototype of the new process

Many businesses recognise that value is delivered through processes, but still define themselves in terms of their functional roles. To properly harness the resources within a business a clear agreement of the management and implementation of processes is needed. Without this focus on processes:

(a) It is unclear how value is achieved or can continue to be achieved.

(b) The effects of change on the operation of the business are hard to predict.

(c) There is no basis to achieve consistent business improvement.

(d) Knowledge is lost as people move around or out of the business.

(e) Cross-functional interaction is not encouraged.

(f) It is difficult to align the strategy of an organisation with the people and the systems resources through which that strategy will be accomplished.

Paradigm shifts

A paradigm shift involves rethinking the nature of the business and the nature of the organisation itself. In terms of knowledge and knowledge management, the transformation from the old world of business to the new world of e-business includes transitions that are paradigm shifts.

These changes have implications for turning the 'tried and tested' management theories and assumptions on their head. They change how managers think about:

- business strategy
- information technology
- organisational knowledge processes
- corporate assets
- organisational design
- the role of senior management

4.2 THE EFFECT OF COMPUTERS ON INFORMATION SYSTEMS

Computers have revolutionised information systems for the following reasons:

Speed – Computers are ideal for dealing with repetitive processes. The limiting factors, for example, in processing a payroll by computer are not the speed of calculation by the computer, but the speed with which data can be input and the speed of the printer at the output.

Accuracy – In general, computers do not suffer from errors, or lapses of concentration but process data perfectly. Any mistakes which computers make nowadays are not caused by electronic error, but by human error, for example at the input stage, or in designing and programming software.

Volume – Not only do computers work fast, but also they do not need to rest. They can work twenty-four hour days when required. They are therefore able to handle vast volumes of data.

Complexity – Once subsystems are computerised they can generally function more reliably than human beings. This makes it easier to integrate various subsystems. Computers are therefore able to handle complex information systems efficiently. However, one of the problems with this is that when the computer does fail, there is often a major breakdown in the system, with many personnel unable to perform their work functions.

Cost – All the above advantages mean that computers have become highly cost-effective providers of information. The process of substituting computers for human beings has revolutionised information-oriented industries such as accountancy, banking and insurance and this process is continuing.

Presentation – More recently, emphasis has been placed on displaying information in as 'user-friendly' a way as possible. Modern packages containing sophisticated word processors, spreadsheets and graphics combined with the development of the laser printer now enable boring reports to be presented in new and exciting ways!

Judgement – It is necessary, however, to remember the advantages that human beings have as providers of information. Chief amongst these is judgement of reasonableness. Human beings can usually see when an item of information looks unreasonable. Although it is possible to program limited reasonableness tests into computer systems, it is still very difficult to program judgement. The computer remains a highly trained idiot, which is particularly apparent when a programming error is made or it is subject to a computer virus.

ACTIVITY 2   (5 MINS)

Why does a computer system process information better than a manual system?

---

5   INFORMATION AND KNOWLEDGE MANAGEMENT

5.1   INFORMATION MANAGEMENT

Information must be managed just like any other organisational resource.

Information management entails the following tasks.

(a)   Identifying current and future information needs.

(b)   Identifying information sources.

(c)   Collecting the information.

(d)   Storing the information.

(e)   Facilitating existing methods of using information and identifying new ways of using it.

(f)   Ensuring that information is communicated to those who need it, and is not communicated to those who are not entitled to see it.

Developments in technology provide new sources of information, new ways of collecting it, storing it and processing it, and new methods of communicating and sharing it.

5.2 KNOWLEDGE MANAGEMENT

Knowledge management (KM) describes the process of collecting, storing and using the knowledge held within an organisation.

DEFINITION

Knowledge Management is a strategy, framework or system designed to help organisations create, capture, analyse, apply, and reuse knowledge to achieve competitive advantage

Knowledge is now commonly viewed as a sustainable source of **competitive advantage**. Producing unique products or services or producing products or services at a lower cost than competitors is based on superior knowledge.

Knowledge is valuable as it may be used to create new ideas, insights and interpretations and for decision-making. However knowledge, like information, is of no value unless it is applied. As the importance of knowledge increases, the success of an organisation becomes increasingly dependant on its ability to gather, produce, hold and disseminate knowledge.

There are dozens of different approaches to KM, including document management, information management, business intelligence, competence management, information systems management, intellectual asset management, innovation, business process design, and so on.

Many KM projects have a significant element of information management. After all, people need information about where knowledge resides, and to share knowledge they need to transform it into more or less transient forms of information.

But beyond that, KM does have two distinctive tasks:

•   To facilitate the **creation** of knowledge – designing and creating environments and activities to discover and release **tacit knowledge** (expertise held by people within the organisation that has not been formally documented).

•   To manage the way people **share** and **apply** it – designing and installing techniques and processes to create, protect and use **explicit knowledge** (knowledge that the company knows that it has eg, facts, transactions and events that can be clearly stated and stored in management information systems).

The **motivation to share** hard-won experience is sometimes low; the individual is 'giving away' their value and may be very reluctant to lose a position of influence and respect by making it available to everyone.

Organisations should encourage people to share their knowledge. This can be done through a culture of openness and rewards for sharing knowledge and information.

Companies that prosper with KM will be those that realise that it is as much about managing people as about information and technology.

EXAMPLE   HOW TO FACILITATE KNOWLEDGE SHARING

A well-designed and implemented knowledge management initiative can result in higher agent productivity as well as shorter call times, greater self-service customer satisfaction, and reduced costs thanks to call deflection. In contrast, a poorly designed and implemented knowledge management system can drive up call time, annoy customers (leading them to abandon self-service), and increase agent frustration (due to the distraction of too many tools on agents' desktops).

To succeed, knowledge management initiatives require well-thought-out strategies that align closely with the needs of contact centre agents and self-service customers. By adopting the following practices, you can deliver an outstanding customer experience and gain significant return on your knowledge management investment.

Start with a clear definition

Set realistic, precisely defined goals and objectives for the initiative. Avoid "big bang" implementation in favour of a phased approach that enables knowledge management to be fine-tuned before wider application.

Take a "less is more" approach

Rather than bludgeoning customers with results lists containing hundreds of possible answers, provide a relevant, focused, and structured response that targets the intent of your customers' inquiries.

Foster collaborative knowledge creation

By embracing social networking as a part of your knowledge management strategy, you can rapidly develop useful content at a lower cost.

Recognize the value of what you don't know

Leverage analytics to identify gaps in your implementation. By gathering intelligence on what you don't know, you can react faster to growing customer needs, continuously improve in areas you have yet to tap for efficiencies, and create a better service experience.

Think globally

Although you may start small with your initiative, do not limit your thinking about the uses and value of knowledge management in your business division or geography. It can have broad advantages across the enterprise and should be treated as a corporate initiative, not just a divisional solution.

Adapted from an Oracle White Paper

November 2011

Getting Knowledge Management Right: Five Best Practices for a Better Service Experience

---

5.3 WHERE DOES KNOWLEDGE RESIDE?

The following actions can be taken to determine the prevalence of knowledge in an organisation.

- One is the identification and development of informal networks and communities of practice within organisations. These self-organising groups share common work interests, usually cutting across a company's functions and processes. People exchange what they know freely and develop a shared language that allows knowledge to flow more efficiently.

- It is then possible to 'map' a knowledge network and make it available to others in the organisation. Knowledge maps are guides that assist employees to ascertain who knows what. This methodology involves the discovery of tacit knowledge in order to facilitate eventual sharing.

- Expert databases are similar to mapping the knowledge. They map experts by identifying knowledge of each expert and providing a guide map to help employees find those experts. Knowledge databases, similar to standard document databases facilitates the storage and sharing of explicit knowledge.

- Another means of establishing the prevalence of knowledge is to look at knowledge-related business outcomes. One example is product development and service innovation. While the knowledge embedded within these innovations is invisible, the products themselves are tangible.

Every day companies make substantial investments in improving their employees' knowledge and enabling them to use it more effectively. Analysis of these investments is a third way of making KM activities visible. For example how much technical and non-technical training are individuals consuming? How much is invested in competitive and environmental scanning, and in other forms of strategic research?

Japanese companies have a strong focus on **tacit knowledge**. They motivate knowledge creation through visions of products and strategies coupled with organisational cultures that promote sharing, transparency and proactive use of knowledge and innovation.

Human resource policies such as rotation of employees through different jobs and functions support the expansion of knowledge.

The process by which an organisation develops its store of knowledge is sometimes called organisational learning.

A learning organisation is centred on the **people** that make up the organisation and the **knowledge** they hold. The organisation and employees feed off and into the central pool of knowledge. The organisation uses the knowledge pool as a tool to teach itself and its employees.

5.4 SYSTEMS THAT AID KNOWLEDGE MANAGEMENT

Information systems play an important role in knowledge management, helping with information flows and helping formally capture the knowledge held within the organisation.

Any system that encourages people to work together and share information and knowledge will aid knowledge management.

Distributing knowledge

Office automation systems (OAS) – are the systems that create, store, modify, display and communicate the correspondence of the business. Communication can be written, verbal, facsimile or in video form.

Now that most computers are networked there is the ability to share computer files and send messages to one another via the communications network. This service is provided by electronic mail systems and electronic bulletin boards. The electronic bulletin boards are a public sector service whereby public messages can be posted.

OAS also includes voice mail systems, image processing systems, collaborative writing systems, and video conferencing facilities.

Knowledge work is dependant on the efficient production and distribution of documents and other forms of communication such as voice messaging systems.

Document imaging systems convert documents and images to digital form, reducing the amount of paper required. Electronic information should be easier to retrieve as electronic searches should be quicker than hunting through a mountain of paper.

Knowledge workers themselves perform many essential tasks within an organisation including:

- Keeping the organisation up-to-date with new knowledge as it develops outside the company, in areas such as technology, science and the humanities.

- Providing advice inside the organisation on the use of new knowledge.

- Acting as change agents by actually recommending and implementing change within an organisation.

Knowledge sharing

We have already discussed Groupware and its uses in Chapter 7. Typically, groups utilising groupware are small project-oriented teams that have important tasks and tight deadlines Perhaps the best known groupware product at present is **Lotus Notes**. However, there are many related products and technologies.

Creating knowledge

Knowledge work systems (KWS)

Knowledge Work Systems (KWS) are information systems that facilitate the creation and integration of new knowledge into an organisation. They provide knowledge workers with tools such as:

- Analytical tools
- Powerful graphics facilities
- Communication tools
- Access to external databases
- A user-friendly interface

The workstations of knowledge workers are often designed for the specific tasks they perform. For example, a design engineer would require sufficient graphics power to manipulate 3-D computer-aided design (**CAD**) images; a financial analyst would require a powerful desktop computer to access and manipulate a large amount of financial data (an investment workstation).

The components of a KWS are shown in the following diagram.

Figure 9.6: Components of a knowledge work system

Virtual reality systems are another example of KWS. These systems create computer-generated simulations that emulate real-world activities. Interactive software and hardware (eg special headgear) provide simulations so realistic that users experience sensations that would normally only occur in the real world.

EXAMPLE	VIRTUAL REALITY

Burger King has used virtual reality stores to test new store designs.

Volvo has used virtual reality test drives in vehicle development.

Capturing and codifying knowledge

Artificial intelligence (AI) is the development of computer-based systems designed to behave as humans. Artificial intelligence systems are based on human expertise, knowledge and reasoning patterns.

The field of AI includes:

- Robotics
- Natural language' programming tools
- Perceptive systems
- Expert systems (ES)

The main commercial applications of AI have involved **expert systems**.

An **expert system** is a computer program that captures human expertise in a limited domain of knowledge. An organisation can use an expert system when a number of conditions are met.

(a)   The problem is **well defined**.
(b)   The expert can define **rules** by which the problem can be solved.
(c)   The **investment** in an expert system is cost-justified.

The system enables a person with expertise in a particular situation to transfer knowledge into the computer from where someone needing that expertise can receive advice. An ES must have:

- A way of storing the information that is fed into it (the knowledge base). The **knowledge base** contains facts (for example 'Postcode AX9 9ZZ had 104 reported burglaries in 2003') and rules ('next year the burglary rate is likely to be 5% higher than last year'). These facts and rules enable the system to make a 'judgement' such as; 'In 2004 homes in postcode AX9 9ZZ have a 6% chance of being burgled'.

- A way of transferring information from the expert into the knowledge base (a knowledge acquisition program which enables the expert system to acquire new knowledge and rules).

- A way of reaching conclusions in a particular situation (the inferencing engine is the software that executes the reasoning. It needs to discern which rules apply, and allocate priorities).

- An easy to use interface so that a non-expert can interrogate the system (a user interface).

The knowledge base of an expert system must be kept up-to-date. Expert systems are not suited to high-level unstructured problems, as these require information from a wide range of sources rather than simply deciding between a few known alternatives.

ACTIVITY 3 (15 MINS)

Why do you think organisations wish to automate reasoning or decision-making tasks which humans are naturally better able to perform than computers?

Neural networks

Neural networks are another application of AI, seen by some as the 'next step' in computing. Neural computing is modelled on the biological processes of the human brain.

Neural networks can learn from experience. They can analyse vast quantities of complex data and identify patterns from which predictions can be made. They have the ability to cope with incomplete or 'fuzzy' data, and can deal with previously unspecified or new situations.

Neural techniques have been applied to similar areas as expert systems eg credit risks. They are more advanced in that they don't rely on a set of hard rules, but develop a 'hidden' layer of experience and come to a decision based on this hidden layer.

5.5 DIAGRAMS AND TEXT

Any successful company must react quickly to changing trends in the market. New products should be designed and manufactured quicker and cheaper than competitors do. A shorter design time provides a distinct competitive advantage. In many cases, communication may best be achieved if information is presented in a visual form such as a chart or a graph. CAD provides the means for capturing system requirements and for the visual modelling and design of systems on a high level of abstraction.

Graphs and charts can be complex and highly technical, so they should, like any other medium of communication, be adapted to suit the understanding and information needs of the intended recipient: they should be simplified and explained as necessary, and include only as much data as can clearly be presented and assimilated.

6 DATABASES

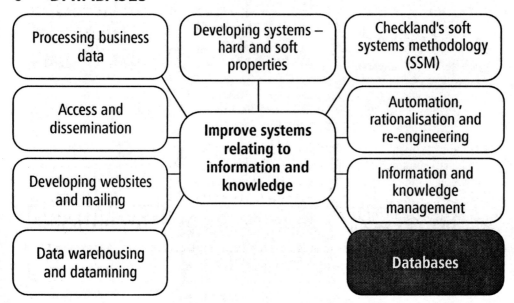

6.1 WHAT IS A DATABASE?

The way in which data is held on a system affects the ease by which the data can be accessed and manipulated. To maintain data in a database, data must be organised and stored in a consistent, reliable, and efficient manner. Many modern software packages are built around a database. A database provides a comprehensive set of data for a number of different users.

DEFINITION

A **database** is a collection of data organised to service many applications. The database provides convenient access to data for a wide variety of users and user needs.

A **database management system** (DBMS) is the software that centralises data and manages access to the database. It is a system that allows numerous applications to extract the data they need without the need for separate files.

Other key terms associated with databases include the following:

- The logical structure of a database refers to how various application programs access the data. The physical structure relates to how data is organised within the database.

- The independence of data items from the programs which access them is referred to as data independence.

- Duplication of data items is referred to as data redundancy.

- In a database environment, the ease with which applications access the central pool of data is referred to as integration.

- Integrity relates to data accuracy and consistency.

- Data independence and integration should reduce data redundancy resulting in improved data integrity.

6.2 CONSISTENCY AND RELIABILITY

In the database approach the three data requirements that are much-emphasised are: integrity of data; data integration and data independence.

(a) A database must have integrity. This means that it must be consistent, accurate and reliable. *Integrity* signifies that a single user cannot be permitted to amend the data on file and thereby ruin the usage of the database for other users. Yet users must be able to make valid amendments to the stored data by updating. Furthermore there is no inconsistency occurring due to wrongly duplicated data held in different files, because a single update proffers new data to all database users.

(b) *Data integration* – means that information retrieved from various files must be accessed and subjected to coordination and manipulation exactly as though it originated from a single file. In logical terms the data is centralised, but it is very probably stored in devices that are located in a number of organisational areas. The concept of centralisation/integration must be actively maintained to allow links between data, normally utilising direct-access approaches.

(c) *Data independence* – is the characteristic existing when amendments are made to both the organisation and content of the stored (physical) data without any effect upon the applications utilising the data. In other words, there is no need for reprogramming.

6.3 THE CHARACTERISTICS OF A DATABASE SYSTEM

A database system has the following characteristics.

- **Shared**. Different users are able to access the same data for their own processing applications. This removes the need for duplicating data on different files.

- **Controls** to preserve the **integrity** of the database. Users should not be able to alter the data on file so as to **spoil** the database records for other users. However, users must be able to make **valid** alterations to the data.

- **Flexibility**. The database system should provide for the **needs of different users**, who each have their own processing requirements and data access methods. The database should be capable of **evolving** to meet **future** needs.

The **advantages** of a database system are as follows.

(a) **Avoidance of unnecessary duplication of data** – it recognises that data can be used for many purposes but only needs to be input and stored once.

(b) **Multi-purpose data** – from (a), it follows that although data is input once, it can be used for several purposes.

(c) **Data for the organisation as a whole, not just for individual departments** – the database concept encourages management to regard data as a resource that must be properly managed just as any other resource. Database systems encourage management to analyse data, relationships between data items, and how data is used in different applications.

(d) **Consistency** – because data is only held once, it is easier to ensure that it is up-to-date and consistent across departments.

(e) **New uses for data** – data is held independently of the programs that access the data. This allows greater flexibility in the ways that data can be used. New programs can be easily introduced to make use of existing data in a different way.

(f) **New applications** – developing new application programs with a database system is easier as a central pool of data is already available to be drawn upon.

(g) **Flexibility** – relational systems are extremely flexible, allowing information from several different sources to be combined and providing answers to *ad-hoc* queries.

The **disadvantages** of a database system relate mainly to security and control.

(a) There are potential problems of **data security** and data privacy. Administrative procedures for data security should supplement software controls.

(b) Since there is only one set of data, it is essential that the data should be accurate and **free from corruption**. A back-up routine is essential.

(c) Initial development **costs** may be high.

(d) For hierarchical and network structures, the **access paths** through the data must be specified in advance.

(e) Both hierarchical and network systems require **intensive programming** and are **inflexible**.

7   DATA WAREHOUSING AND DATAMINING

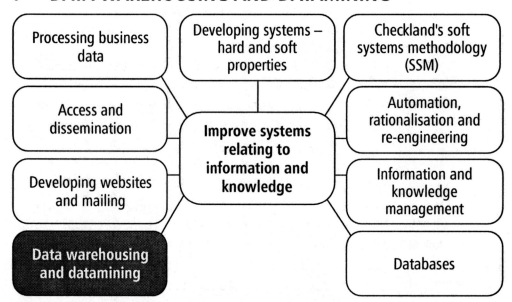

Two techniques designed to utilise the ever-increasing amounts of data held by organisations are **data warehousing** and **datamining**.

7.1 DATA WAREHOUSING

> **DEFINITION**
>
> A **data warehouse** consists of a database, containing data from various operational systems, and reporting and query tools.

A data warehouse contains data from a range of external (customer care systems, outside agencies or websites) and internal (eg sales order processing system, nominal ledger from newer channels such as customer care systems, outside agencies or websites) sources. It is loaded with a database product such as Oracle or Microsoft SQL server. This database is configured to hold the key information you want to look at and is interfaced with the 'transaction processing' systems.

For larger volumes of data a toolset has been developed called OLAP (on-line analytical processing) which allows summary information to be created and stored across the different business performance metrics. As a consequence of this, on-line and instant enquiries can potentially be made on the balances of any combination of customer/product/regional performance by date/period range.

The performance of the transaction-processing systems will not be affected by heavy use of the data warehouse for a complex set of enquiries, as you will not be working with the live information.

Once this warehouse has been set up, information can be combined from the different operations systems into a consistent format and can be accessed by a wide variety of reporting/analysis/web tools.

Data is copied to the data warehouse as often as required – usually daily, weekly or monthly. The process of making any required changes to the format of data and copying it to the warehouse is usually automated.

The result should be a coherent set of information available to be used across the organisation for management analysis and decision-making. The reporting and query tools available within the warehouse should facilitate management reporting and analysis.

7.2 FEATURES OF DATA WAREHOUSES

A data warehouse is subject-oriented, integrated, time-variant, and non-volatile.

- **Subject-oriented** – a data warehouse is focused on data groups not application boundaries. Whereas the operational world is designed around applications and functions such as sales and purchases, a data warehouse world is organised around major **subjects** such as customers, supplier, product and activity.

- **Integrated** – data within the data warehouse must be consistent in format and codes used – this is referred to as integrated in the context of data warehouses. For example, one operational application feeding the warehouse may represent gender as an 'M' and an 'F' while another represents gender as '1' and '0'. While it does not matter how gender is represented in the data warehouse (let us say that 'M' and 'F' is chosen), it must arrive in the data warehouse in a consistent integrated state. The data import routine should 'cleanse' any inconsistencies.

- **Time-variant** – data is organised by time and stored in 'time-slices'. Data warehouse data tends to deal with **trends** rather than single points in time. As a result, each data element in the data warehouse environment must carry with it the time for which it applies.

- **Non-volatile** – data cannot be changed within the warehouse. Only load and retrieval operations are made.

Organisations may build a single central data warehouse to serve the entire organisation or may create a series of smaller data marts. A data mart holds a selection of the organisation's data for a specific purpose.

A data mart can be constructed more quickly and cheaply than a data warehouse. However, if too many individual data marts are built, organisations may find it is more efficient to have a single data warehouse serving all areas.

The components of a data warehouse are shown in the following diagram.

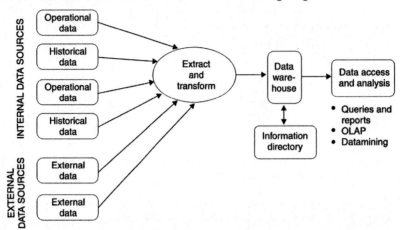

Figure 9.7: Components of a data warehouse

7.3 ADVANTAGES AND LIMITATIONS OF DATA WAREHOUSES

The advantages of setting-up a data warehouse system include the following.

(a) Decision-makers can access data without affecting the use of operational systems.

(b) Having a wide range of data available to be queried easily encourages the taking of a wide perspective on organisational activities.

(c) Data warehouses have proved successful in some businesses for:

(i) Quantifying the effect of marketing initiatives.

(ii) Improving knowledge of customers.

(iii) Identifying and understanding an enterprise's most profitable revenues streams.

Some organisations have found they have invested considerable resources implementing a data warehouse for little return. To benefit from the information a data warehouse can provide, organisations need to be flexible and prepared to act on what they find. If a warehouse system is implemented simply to follow current practice it will be of little value.

Other limitations exist, particularly if a data warehouse is intended to be used as an operational system rather than as an analytical tool. For example:

(a) The data held may be outdated.

(b) An efficient regular routine must be established to transfer data into the warehouse.

(c) A warehouse may be implemented and then, as it is not required on a day-to-day basis, be ignored.

7.4 DATAMINING – TRENDS, PATTERNS AND RELATIONSHIPS

New data management techniques have been developed to provide managers with better and quicker access to data analysis.

DEFINITION

Datamining is a set of statistical techniques that are used to identify trends, patterns and relationships in data

Datamining techniques have been available for many years, but they have only recently grown popular, as more data is being created, data processing power (in the form of computers) is becoming more accessible and datamining software tools are becoming available. Most datamining models are either:

- **Predictive**: using known observations to predict future events (for example, predicting the probability that a recipient will opt out of an e-mail list)

- **Descriptive**: interrogating the database to identify patterns and relationships (for example, profiling the audience of a particular advertising campaign).

Datamining software looks for hidden patterns and relationships in large pools of data.

True datamining software discovers previously unknown relationships. The hidden patterns and relationships the software identifies can be used to guide decision-making and to predict future behaviour.

EXAMPLE   (DATAMINING)

(1)   The American retailer Wal-Mart discovered an unexpected relationship between the sale of **nappies** and **beer!** Wal-Mart found that both tended to sell at the same time, just after working hours, and concluded that men with small children stopped off to buy nappies on their way home, and bought beer at the same time. Logically therefore, if the two items were put in the same shopping aisle, sales of both should increase. Wal-Mart tried this and it worked.

(2)   Some credit card companies have used datamining to predict which customers are likely to switch to a competitor in the next few months. Based on the datamining results, the bank can take action to retain these customers.

Datamining uses statistical analysis tools as well as neural networks, fuzzy logic and other **intelligent techniques**.

The types of relationships or patterns that datamining may uncover may be classified as follows.

Relationship\Discovery	Comment
Classification or cluster	These terms refer to the identification of patterns within the database between a range of data items. For example, datamining may find that unmarried males aged between 20 and 30, who have an income above £50,000 are more likely to purchase a high performance sports car than people from other demographic groups. This group could then be targeted when marketing material is produced/distributed.
Association	One event can be linked or correlated to another event – such as in Wal-Mart example (1) above.
Forecasting	Trends are identified within the data that can be extrapolated into the future.

8 DEVELOPING WEBSITES AND MAILING

8.1 WEBSITE DESIGN

Websites are now a key form of corporate communication. Almost every major company has some type of web presence. Increasingly, advertisers are using websites as key marketing tools – and using their conventional media advertising (especially print) to point consumers to the website. (Some print/poster ads now simply feature a prominent web address.)

Website design is a relatively new skill and the technology is constantly changing. The following, however, are some of the key issues.

Design issues	Comments
House style	The website should be consistent with corporate identity guidelines and other promotional messages.
Interest	The website should offer content that is relevant, original or regularly changing/expanding, in order to encourage repeat visits. This may be product information, links, news features, and free e-cards or chat communities.
Interactivity (and/or entertainment)	Colour, graphics, audio, video and movement add impact and entertainment value. Information can be presented as database applications, search tools, notice boards, calculators and other interactive formats.
'Stickiness'	Website 'stickiness' refers to (a) how often visitors return to a site and (b) how long they spend there. Stickiness can be improved by continually updated content, and also by promotional techniques such as chat rooms, games and reviews. Keeping visitors longer at the site gives you more time to build up awareness, and gives them more time to take in promotional messages and/or make purchases.
Credibility	Websites often contain 'about us' pages to bolster consumer confidence (and public relations) by providing information about the company.

Design issues	Comments
Transaction efficiency	As well as encouraging 'browsing' with mechanisms such as virtual 'shopping trolleys' and 'wish lists', websites can offer 1 Click or other convenient order mechanisms, automatic e-mail order confirmations and order tracing. A secure site for transactions (using various forms of encryption) is also important.

8.2 CURRENT AND VALID

Once a website is 'live' on the Internet, it can be used as a 24-hour source of information on your products, services and organisation news. The more up-to-date it is, the more likely your customers will come. One of the most important parts of having a website is to make sure that the information on the site is current. A website is a work in progress and a reflection of the business. As the business grows and changes, so should the website – it should always be up-to-date. For example, when including a press release area on the site, you should make sure that you are regularly adding press releases. Visitors who hit the site and find that the last press release is dated a year ago may think that the site has not been updated since then. It is better to have no dates than old dates. If you are selling products on your site, make sure that your prices are current. Customers may very well use your site as a point of reference before calling. Should they get one price on the phone and another on the site, they will not be very impressed with your company.

The domain registration must also be kept current and valid because the company that it is registered with may need to contact you to renew your registration. This information is also used when you try to transfer your domain from one hosting company to another.

8.3 MAILING

E-mail is one of the most popular uses of the Internet. According to Allen *et al (One-to-One Web Marketing)* 'there are more people in the world with access to e-mail than with access to the World Wide Web. This means e-mail marketing can grab attention and interest without requiring users to even start their web browsers.

E-mail lists can be obtained by buying or renting suitably targeted/segmented lists (of willing subscribers) from list brokers or permission marketing agencies.

Organisations can also build their own lists, by inviting people to subscribe to an online e-mail list (to participate in two-way discussion or receive one-way announcements) or by inputting customer and contact data from other sources (such as trade exhibitions, sales promotions and so on).

Various software-based tools exist to enable marketing organisations to maintain and manage e-mail lists and to send **mass mailings** (batched to avoid over-loading individual servers). There are even tools available online, free of charge (but supported through the placing of advertisements at the bottom of the e-mail messages).

Using e-mail as an alternative to (or support for) direct mail and direct response advertising has the following advantages.

- **Cost-effectiveness**. E-mail is one of the least expensive ways to reach people in a highly targeted, personalised manner – whether one person in the office across the hall or millions of people all over the world.

- **Speed of delivery/response**. Apart from instant transmission (unlike postal direct mail packages), most e-mail campaigns are said to elicit 5% of their responses within 24 hours and 15% of their responses within 72 hours.

- **Targeting**. E-mail messages can be written for the interests of a highly targeted audience, using integrated address books and databased information to personalise content for individual recipients.

- **Acceptability**. 'People look forward to receiving e-mail from friends, relatives and co-workers. This means that their attitude is more open and accepting than in more advertising-oriented media, such as advertising-supported websites, as well as traditional print and electronic media and direct mail.' (*Allen et al*)

Almost all commentators on e-mail marketing note the fine line that exists between legitimate use of the medium and 'spam' – unsolicited, untargeted mass e-mail broadcasts. Much of the controversy comes from companies 'harvesting' e-mail addresses from web pages, discussion lists, newsgroups and other sources and using them to target users. (It is now illegal in the UK to disclose or sell these addresses to third parties without users' permission.) Spam not only annoys recipients (and the complaint departments of their Internet Service Providers), but also frequently causes network traffic problems.

9 ACCESS AND DISSEMINATION

9.1 ACCESSING INFORMATION

We are seeing massive changes in the way that researchers/specialists in different countries communicate with one another and in how they produce and gain access to information. If they are 'connected' to various information and communication technologies (ICTs), and have access to some essential skills, they can keep in touch with their peers at the click of a few buttons, rapidly publish and disseminate their own work, and browse through whole libraries of reports and data, downloading the latest ideas needed for their work.

We have also seen changes in the information management 'business.' Fifteen years ago, information 'handling' and its management was the job of professionals and specialists (in publishing, libraries, archives, and computers). Usually located in specialist units inside organisations (sometimes specialist information organisations), these people tracked down and organised scarce information.

This situation is different today. More access to more powerful and easier to use ICTs has turned us all into information specialists, allowing us to handle our own information management needs. Around the world, researchers build websites, manage databases, publish newsletters, organise workshops, and find their own information. The old information professionals are still around, sometimes re-branded as 'knowledge' specialists, and struggling to provide services and products to people who appear to have their own access to the same technical tools.

9.2 RESEARCH INFORMATION

Researchers in general wish to make the results of their work widely and easily available to their colleagues because the whole edifice of progress is built on the gradual build-up of information and ideas from the whole community. Journal articles have been the traditional form of this dissemination and over time specific journal publishing has become a sophisticated operation offering (in print on paper) quality assurance through peer review and effective distribution. It has become highly competitive with some journals commanding important positions in their field by using subjective criteria for material that is particularly important and topical.

The system has also become very expensive as journals have proliferated and print numbers declined, so that even the biggest libraries have found it impossible to maintain subscriptions to all the available journals, while smaller institutions and in particular developing countries have been effectively priced out of the market.

Electronic publishing provides a whole new range of opportunities to improve the information chain, of which wide and apparently free dissemination via the Internet is one of the most obvious. It has encouraged more and more self-publication through individual websites, through institutional information providers, and through subject oriented preprint servers.

9.3 LEGAL AND CONFIDENTIALITY CONCERNS

Keeping some information confidential is an important **legal requirement**. It may also be part of your organisation's **policy**.

Some requirements are pure common sense. For example, most of us would expect details of our wages, salaries, health etc to be kept confidential. Others are less obvious. For example some information about your organisation may be valuable to competitors. This is known as **commercially sensitive information**.

The Data Protection Act 1998 lays down strict rules about the storage, purposes or uses, accuracy, processing and transfer of personal data.

Due to the explosion in the use of computers, concerns were expressed about:

- Access to personal information by unauthorised parties
- The likelihood that an individual could be harmed by the existence of computerised data about him or her which was inaccurate or misleading, and which could be transferred to unauthorised third parties at high speed and little cost
- The possibility that personal information could be used for purposes other than those for which it was requested and disclosed

The list of people that have the organisational and technical opportunity to collect information about users and their computers includes resource owners, e-mail recipients, Internet providers who control users' access to the net and maintain information about them, third persons with the widest range of motives, up to and including criminal intentions, and other parties.

When connected to the Internet there is the potential to collect the following information, whether comprehensively or in part:

- The IP address of a computer that is connected to the Internet, and information about the Internet provider and services rendered to the user.

- The user's e-mail address.

- Information about installed software and computer configuration.

- Information obtained through the use of cookies, indicating the users' access to websites, and their activities on those sites, including all sorts of information on logins and passwords required for access to resources and services.

- Personal data entered by the user while using various Internet sites and resources.

- User information that the provider maintains incident to rendering telecommunications services, including passwords and logins for access to the provider's information systems.

The **Data Protection Act 1998** applies to information held in any form. Therefore it does not matter whether the information is held on paper, in computer files or in another form – it is all covered by the Act. The strictest requirements of the Act apply to **'sensitive data'** such as racial origin, health, sexual orientation or political or religious beliefs. The processing of sensitive data is generally forbidden without the consent of the subject.

So who does the Act affect? You must first look at the definitions under the Act.

DEFINITION

'Data' is any information processed by automated equipment or recorded so that it forms part of a relevant filing system or accessible record.

'Personal Data' is information pertaining to a living individual who can be identified from that data. It also includes any expression of opinion about them.

A **'Data Subject'** is a living individual, so we are all to that extent data subjects. Organisations or businesses cannot be data subjects.

A **'Data Controller'** is any legal person who alone or jointly determines the manner or purposes of processing of any data.

A **'Data Processor'** is any employee other than an employee of the data controller who processes data.

A **'Recipient'** is anyone to whom information is disclosed.

'Data users' are organisations or individuals which use personal data covered by the Act.

The most obvious use is actually processing the data. However use also includes controlling the contents of personal data files. Processing covers 'obtaining, holding, recording, carrying out operations such as the organisation, adaptation and alteration of information, the retrieval, consultation or use of the same, disclosure, transmission or dissemination thereof, and the alignment, combination, blocking, erasure or destruction of information'. Consequently there are very few if any business practices which will not need to be notified under the Act.

Data subjects can **sue** data users for **damage** or **distress** caused by inaccurate data, loss of data or unauthorised disclosure. They also have a legal right to see their own personal data.

9.4 INTERNAL REQUIREMENTS

Within an organisation, the policy manual will often lay down other confidentiality rules. For example, some organisations forbid employees to talk to the press without authorisation, or to publish their research results. You can imagine that businesses planning large redundancies or the launch of a new product will not want the information to become public prematurely.

Paper files with **restricted access** should be

- Listed
- Stored securely
- Only accessible by specific people

Computer systems often use **passwords** to restrict access to information that is held on computer. You should never divulge your password to an unauthorised person or keep it in view on your desk. Think of your password as needing as much secrecy as your bank PIN number.

Use of the **Internet** can pose particular problems in maintaining confidentiality. Many companies have a policy on the purposes for which the Internet should and should not be used. The law surrounding Internet information and its protection is still developing.

If you have access to restricted information in any form, you are responsible for protecting it to comply with company policy and the law. You should lock confidential papers or computer disks away when you are not using them. You should not leave them lying around on your desk (or in the photocopier!).

You should also **not provide confidential information** to **others** outside your department without checking with a supervisor.

ACTIVITY 4 (5 MINS)

Your company's planning department asks for a copy of the monthly research cost reports for the last six months. Your computer password does not give you access to this information. What should you do?

A   Refer the query to your supervisor
B   Ask someone what the password is that will access the information
C   Ask for your password to be changed so that it will access the information
D   Try and find a hard copy of the information

CHAPTER ROUNDUP

- Organisations are social systems that are exposed to a wide range of influences and environmental factors. Organisations are often exposed to unstructured or 'soft' problems.

- The Systems Development Lifecycle (SDLC) is a disciplined, hard approach to systems development that identifies several stages of development.

- The soft systems approach to systems development aims to take into account the soft properties of the implementation – this approach looks at the wider picture.

- Checkland's Soft Systems Methodology (SSM) is a way of analysing situations in systems – such as an organisation. It provides an organised approach which can be used to tackle unstructured and poorly defined problems.

- The purpose of SSM is to enhance understanding of complex social situations which entail many divergent perspectives.

- In SSM the root definition is a concise description of a human activity system that states what the system is and what the system does. The root definition is established using the mnemonic CATWOE.

- A rich picture is a diagrammatic representation of a situation compiled through examining elements of structure, process and the situation climate.

- Knowledge management describes the process of collecting, storing and using the knowledge held within an organisation.

- Knowledge is now commonly viewed as a sustainable source of competitive advantage. Producing unique products or services or producing products or services at a lower cost than competitors is based on superior knowledge.

- Information systems play an important role in knowledge management, helping with information flows and helping formally capture the knowledge held within the organisation.

- A database is a collection of data organised to service many applications. The database provides convenient access to data for a wide variety of users and user needs.

- Advantages of a database system include the avoidance of data duplication, management is encouraged to manage data as a valuable resource, data consistency across the organisation, and the flexibility for answering *ad-hoc* queries.

- A data warehouse consists of a database, containing data from various operational systems, and reporting and query tools.

- Organisations may build a single central data warehouse to serve the entire organisation or may create a series of smaller data marts.

- Datamining software looks for hidden patterns and relationships in large pools of data. Datamining uses statistical analysis tools as well as neural networks, fuzzy logic and other intelligent techniques.

? QUICK QUIZ

1　List five characteristics of problems or situations that would make a hard approach to problem solving suitable.

2　The term 'systems lifecycle' describes the stages a system moves through from inception until it is discarded or replaced. What are the six stages of the lifecycle?

3　List five examples of soft properties that should be considered during the development and implementation of an information system.

4　Although SSM is not intended to follow a rigid sequential approach, some writers have identified 'stages of SSM'. Briefly outline these seven stages.

5　List the steps involved in building a conceptual model from a root definition.

6　Distinguish between business automation and business rationalisation.

7　Business process re-engineering involves computerising tasks previously done by people. TRUE or FALSE?

8　Under what circumstances can data subjects sue data users?

9　Why should companies have a policy on Internet use?

10　What rules should govern the control of confidential papers?

ANSWERS TO QUICK QUIZ

1   Any five of those given below. You may have thought of others.

Objectives are clear
The problem is self-contained
The problem can be clearly defined
Information needs are known
A solution can be recognised
Standard solution techniques are applicable

2   The model used in this Course Book has the stages Project definition; Feasibility study; Design; Programming or software selection; Installation and Post-implementation.

3   Any five of those given below. You may have thought of others.

Tastes, values, judgement and opinions are involved
It is not clear what is known and what is needed
The problem is difficult to define
It is not clear what the solution should achieve
The problem is 'people'-oriented
There are no standard solution techniques available

4   SSM is divided into seven distinct stages. These are: Problem situation, Analysis, Root definition, Conceptualisation, Comparison, Changes and Action.

5   Step 1   Use the root definition and CATWOE elements to form an impression of the system carrying out a transformation process.

     Step 2   Decide on a number of key verbs that describe the fundamental activities necessary in the system.

     Step 3   Structure key related activities in groups.

     Step 4   Connect the groups of activities by arrows which indicate logical dependencies.

     Step 5   Check that the root definition and conceptual model together give a clear impression of what the system is and what the system does.

6   Business automation is the use of computerised working methods to speed up the performance of existing tasks. Business rationalisation is the streamlining of operating procedures to eliminate obvious inefficiencies. Rationalisation usually involves automation.

7   FALSE. BPR uses IT to allow a business to do things that it is not doing already.

8   Data subjects can sue data users who have caused them damage or distress by loss of data, inaccurate data or unauthorised disclosure of data.

9   Companies need a policy on Internet use because it is a potential source of breaches of confidentiality.

10   Confidential papers should be locked away unless in use, used discreetly and not copied to unauthorised people without checking with a supervisor.

ANSWERS TO ACTIVITIES

1 • A system to punish criminals by locking them up (the victim's perspective).

   • A system to rehabilitate offenders by showing them the error of their ways in order to help them adjust to society (the state's perspective, perhaps).

   • A system to train criminals and increase criminal behaviour by bringing criminals' into contact with one another so that they can share their skills (the 'criminal' perspective).

   • A system to produce mailbags by using a captive workforce in order to utilise cheap labour (the Post Office's perspective).

   • A system to store people by keeping them in cells (the architect's perspective perhaps).

   • A distribution system for narcotics (the Mafia's perspective).

   • An opportunity for profit (as in the case of privatised prisons).

2 The functions of computers in information processing include:

   • processing information more quickly;
   • handling bigger volumes of processing;
   • undertaking complex operations;
   • processing information more reliably ie, with less chance of errors and mistakes;
   • processing information at less cost than a manual system;
   • improving the scope and quality of management information.

3 The primary reason has to do with the relative cost of information. A human expert builds up a specialised body of knowledge over time. This knowledge has a commercial value. With human resource 'time is money'. Expert systems aim to use this expertise without requiring the human expert to spend time making the decision. The system also protects the organisation against loss of this expertise should the human expert leave the organisation.

   Capturing knowledge in a computer system means that more people can access this wisdom. Thus, the delivery of complicated services to customers, decisions whether or not to extend credit and so forth, can be made by less experienced members of staff if the expert's knowledge is available to them.

   If a manufacturing company has a complicated mixture of plant and machinery, then the repair engineer may accumulate a lot of knowledge over a period of time about the way it behaves: if a problem occurs, the engineer will be able to make a reasoned guess as to where the likely cause is to be found. If this accumulated expert information is made available to less experienced staff, it means that some of their learning curve is avoided. An expert system is advantageous because it saves time, and therefore costs less. It is particularly useful, as it possesses both knowledge and a reasoning ability.

4 Refer the query to your supervisor.

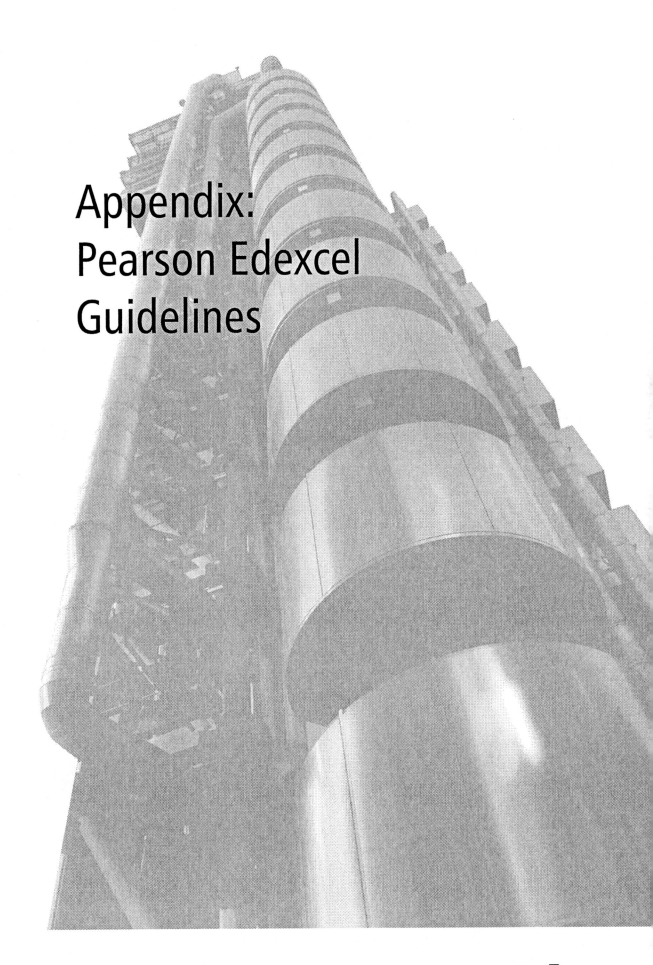

Appendix:
Pearson Edexcel
Guidelines

Pearson Edexcel Guidelines for the Pearson BTEC Higher Nationals in business

This book is designed to be of value to anyone who is studying Management, whether as a subject in its own right or as a module forming part of any business-related degree or diploma.

However, it provides complete coverage of the topics listed in the Pearson Edexcel guidelines for Units 15 (Managing Business Activities to Achieve Results) and 16 (Managing Communications, Knowledge and Information). We include the Pearson Edexcel Guidelines here for your reference, mapped to the topics covered in this book.

Units 13 (Personal and Professional Development) and 14 (Working with and Leading People) are covered in the Business Essentials course book, *Management: Leading People and Professional Development.*

BPP
LEARNING MEDIA

PEARSON EDEXCEL GUIDELINES FOR UNIT 15:
MANAGING BUSINESS ACTIVITIES TO ACHIEVE RESULTS

Aim

The aim of this unit is to provide learners with the understanding and skills to manage their activities in the business workplace to improve their effectiveness and efficiency.

Unit abstract

This unit focuses on the effective and efficient planning and management of business work activities. It gives learners with understanding and skills needed to design and implement operational systems to improve their effectiveness and efficiency and achieve the desired results for the business.

Learners are encouraged to consider the importance and interrelationship of business processes and the implementation of operational plans, together with quality systems and health and safety, in achieving satisfactory results.

Learning outcomes

On successful completion of this unit a learner will:

1. Understand the importance of business processes in delivering outcomes based upon business goals and objectives

2. Be able to develop plans for own area of responsibility to implement operational plans

3. Be able to monitor appropriate systems to improve organisational performance

4. Be able to manage health and safety in the workplace.

Unit content

		Chapter coverage
1	**Understand the importance of business processes in delivering outcomes based upon business goals and objectives** *Functions:* interrelationships of functions, mission, aims, objectives and culture; interrelationship with processes *Processes:* principles and models of effective process management; types of business process measures, output; quality gateways; how to evaluate suitability	1
2	**Be able to develop plans for own area of responsibility to implement operational plans** *Areas of responsibility:* internal and external customers; customer orientation; market research; product development, principles and methods of short- to medium-term planning; designing plans; PERT; critical path analysis; work flow, prioritising workloads; how to develop SMART objectives; time management; how to analyse and manage risk; how to align resources with objectives; legal, regulatory and ethical requirements *Operational plans:* product and service specifications and standards; meeting quality, quantity, time and cost objectives; systems eg Just-in-Time; value-added chains; statistical process control; coordinating activities; working within organisational constraints and limitations	2 3
3	**Be able to monitor appropriate systems to improve organisational performance** *Systems:* Total Quality Management (TQM), TQM philosophy, principles, methods and techniques; quality systems, quality circles, ISO9000/EN29000 or subsequent current amendments, managing and monitoring quality *Organisational performance:* principles of models which underpin organizational performance; types of performance measures and how to determine and set them; cost/benefit analysis; risk analysis; the value of a customer-focused culture; the importance of prevention rather than correction; importance of developing a continual improvement culture and how to involve others; planning, proposing, implementing and evaluating change; identifying wider implications of change within the organisation; Business Process Reengineering (BPR)	4 6
4	**Be able to manage health and safety in the workplace** *Health and safety:* legislation and regulations relating to health and safety at work; organisational policies and procedures regarding health and safety; risk assessment and monitoring; practical application of regulations; public attitudes and concerns relating to health and safety	5

Learning outcomes and assessment criteria

The learning outcomes and the criteria used to assess them are shown in the table below.

Learning outcomes On successful completion of this unit a learner will:		Assessment criteria for pass The learner can:	
LO1	Understand the importance of business processes in delivering outcomes based upon business goals and objectives	1.1	evaluate the interrelationship between the different processes and functions of the organisation
		1.2	justify the methodology to be used to map processes to the organisation's goals and objectives
		1.3	evaluate the output of the process and the quality gateways
LO2	Be able to develop plans for own area of responsibility to implement operational plans	2.1	design plans which promote goals and objectives for own area of responsibility
		2.2	write objectives, which are specific, measurable, achievable, realistic and time-based to align people and other resources in an effective and efficient way
		2.3	implement appropriate systems to achieve objectives in the most efficient way, on time, to budget and meeting organisational standards of quality
		2.4	carry out work activities meeting the operational plan through effective monitoring and control
LO3	Be able to monitor appropriate systems to improve organizational performance	3.1	design systems to manage and monitor quality standards specified by the organisation
		3.2	demonstrate a quality culture to ensure continuous monitoring, evaluation and development of the process
		3.3	recommend improvements which align with the organisation's objectives and goals and which result in improvements
		3.4	report on the wider implications of proposed changes within the organisation

Learning outcomes On successful completion of this unit a learner will:	Assessment criteria for pass The learner can:	
LO4 Be able to manage health and safety in the workplace	4.1	carry out risk assessments as required by legislation, regulation and organisational requirements ensuring appropriate action is taken
	4.2	demonstrate that health and safety regulations and legislation applicable in specific work situations are correctly and effectively applied
	4.3	carry out a systematic review of organisational health and safety policies and procedures in order to ensure they are effective and compliant
	4.4	carry out practical application of health and safety policies and procedures in the workplace.

Guidance

Links

This unit has links with all other management unit within this specification.

This unit also links to the Management and Leadership NOS as mapped in *Annexe B.*

Essential requirements

Tutors must build a bank of resource materials to ensure there is a sufficient supply of relevant information across a range of activities and processes.

Employer engagement and vocational contexts

Learner can generate evidence from a work placement or work experience. Some learners may have access to information from family owned and run businesses.

Centres should develop links with local businesses. Many businesses and chambers of commerce want to promote local business and are often willing to provide work placements, visit opportunities, information about businesses and the local business context and guest speakers.

PEARSON EDEXCEL GUIDELINES FOR UNIT 16:
MANAGING COMMUNICATIONS, KNOWLEDGE AND INFORMATION

Aim

The aim of this unit is to show how communications, knowledge and information can be improved within an organisation including making better use of IT systems.

Unit abstract

This unit recognises that communications do not automatically take place effectively in organisations and that both information and work-based knowledge is often insufficient when decisions are made. Learners will look at how managers can improve the planning of their communications processes as well as their communication skills. Learners will understand why managers need to adopt a more inclusive approach to stakeholders affected by the decisions they make and why they need to network on a more structured basis. The unit also looks at how managers can make the information and knowledge they gain accessible to other parts of the organisation.

The unit is designed to develop learner understanding of the interaction between communications, knowledge and information. It also covers how IT systems can be used as a management tool for collecting, storing, disseminating and providing access to knowledge and information.

Learning outcomes

On successful completion of this unit a learner will:

1 Understand how to assess information and knowledge needs

2 Be able to create strategies to increase personal networking to widen involvement in the decision-making process

3 Be able to develop communication processes

4 Be able to improve systems relating to information and knowledge.

Unit content

		Chapter coverage
1	**Understand how to assess information and knowledge needs** *Sources:* internal and external, primary and secondary, formal and informal, team workers, customers and other stakeholders *Types:* qualitative and quantitative, tacit and explicit, official and unofficial, policy and opinion	7
2	**Be able to create strategies to increase personal networking to widen involvement in the decision-making process** *Sources:* stakeholders and useful contacts, internal and external *Methods:* formal, informal *Strategies:* formal and informal, direct or via media, relating and interacting, trust and confidentiality, forming business relationships, decision-making and decision taking	8
3	**Be able to develop communication processes** *Types:* meetings and conferences, workshops and training events, internet and email, written, telephone, video conferencing, one-to-one meetings *Approaches:* structured and coordinated, planned, formal and informal *Strategy:* advantages, disadvantages; informal, face-to-face, formal in writing, emotional, intelligence	9
4	**Be able to improve systems relating to information and knowledge** *Type:* hard and soft, websites and mailings, access and dissemination *Style:* trends and patterns, diagrams and text, consistent and reliable, current and valid; legal and confidential	9

Learning outcomes and assessment criteria

Learning outcomes On successful completion of this unit a learner will:		Assessment criteria for pass The learner can:	
LO1	Understand how to assess information and knowledge needs	1.1	discuss the range of decisions to be taken
		1.2	examine the information and knowledge needed to ensure effective decision taking
		1.3	assess internal and external sources of information and understanding
		1.4	justify recommendations for improvement
LO2	Be able to create strategies to increase personal networking to widen involvement in the decision-making process	2.1	identify stakeholders for a decision-making process
		2.2	make contact with those identified and develop business relationships
		2.3	involve those identified in the decision making as appropriate
		2.4	design strategies for improvement
LO3	Be able to develop communication processes	3.1	report on existing processes of communication in an organisation
		3.2	design ways to improve appropriateness
		3.3	implement improvements to ensure greater integration of systems of communication in that organisation
		3.4	create a personal plan to improve own communication skills
LO4	Be able to improve systems relating to information and knowledge	4.1	report on existing approaches to the collection, formatting, storage and dissemination of information and knowledge
		4.2	carry out appropriate changes to improve the collection, formatting, storage and dissemination of information and knowledge
		4.3	implement a strategy to improve access to systems of information and knowledge.

Guidance

Links

This unit has links with all other management units within this specification.

This unit also links with the Management and Leadership NOS. See *Annexe B* for a mapping.

Essential requirements

There are no essential or unique resources required for the delivery of this unit.

Employer engagement and vocational contexts

Centres should develop links with local business and are often willing to provide work placements, visit opportunities, information about businesses and the local business context and guest speakers.

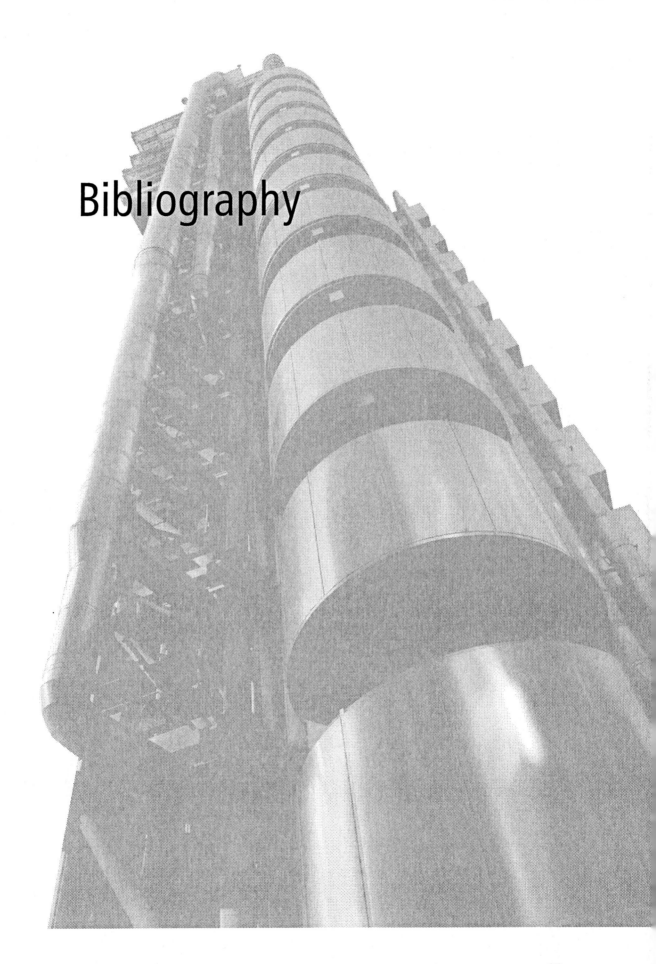

Bibliography

Adair, J. and Allen, M. (1999) *Time Management and Personal Development.* London: Hawksmere.

Beck, U. (1994) *Reflexive Modernization: Politics, Tradition, and Aesthetics in the Modern Social Order* Stanford University Press

Bryce, L. (1989) *The Influential Woman: How to Achieve Success without Losing Your Femininity.* Piatkus Books

Buchanan and Huczynski. (2004) *Organizational Behaviour: An Introductory Text.* Financial Times/ Prentice Hall; 5th edition

De Bono, E. (1990) *Six Thinking Hats.* Penguin Books Ltd

Drucker, P. (2007) *The Practice of Management.* A Butterworth-Heinemann Title; 2nd edition

Festinger, L. (1957) *A Theory of Cognitive Dissonance.* Stanford University Press

Gardner, H. (1993) *Frames of Mind: The Theory of Multiple Intelligence.* Basic Books; 10th edition

Goleman, D. (1998) *Working with Emotional Intelligence.* London: Bloomsbury.

Guirdham, M. (1995) *Interpersonal Skills at Work* (2nd ed.) Harlow, Essex: Prentice Hall.

Handy, C. (1993) *Understanding Organisations.* Penguin; Fourth Edition

Herzberg, F. (2008) *One More Time: How Do You Motivate Employees?* Harvard Business School Press

Higgs and Dulewicz (2002) *Making Sense of Emotional Intelligence.* National Foundation for Educational Research; 2nd Revised edition

Honey, P. and Mumford, A. (1992) *The Manual of Learning Styles.* Maidenhead: Peter Honey.

Kolb (1984) *Experiential Learning.* New York: Prentice Hall.

Koontz, O'Donnell, Weihrich. (1980) *Management.* McGraw-Hill Education; 7th edition

Kotter, J. (1988) *The Leadership Factor.* The Free Press; 1st Edition.

Krol, E and Ferguson, P. (1 Nov 1995) *The Whole Internet for Windows 95.* O'Reilly Media

Likert, R (1961) *New patterns of Management.* McGraw-Hill Inc., US

Luft, J. (1961) The Johari window, *Human Relations Training News,* No. 5.

Maslow, A. H.(1998) *Toward a Psychology of Being.* John Wiley & Sons; 3rd Edition

Pareto, V. (1980) *Manual of Political Economy.* Kelley, USA; Reprint edition

Pedler, M., Burgoyne, J. and Boydell, T. (2001) *A Manager's Guide to Self Development* (4th ed.) Maidenhead: McGraw Hill.

Peter, L. (1972) *The Peter Principle.* Bantam

Rodger, A. (1952) *The seven point plan.* London NIIP

Rogers, C. (1961) *On Becoming a Person.* Boston: Houghton Mifflin.

Tannenbaum, R. and Schmidt, W.H. (2009) *How to Choose a Leadership Pattern,* Harvard Business School Press; Reprint edition

Whetten, D. and Cameron, K. (2002) *Developing Management Skills* (5th ed.) New Jersey: Prentice Hall.

Yukl, G.A (2009) *Leadership in Organizations.* Pearson Education; 7th edition

Index

Notes

Review Form – Business Essentials – Management: Communications and Achieving Results (6/13)

BPP Learning Media always appreciates feedback from the students who use our books. We would be very grateful if you would take the time to complete this feedback form, and return it to the address below.

Name: _____   Address: _____

_____

_____

How have you used this Course Book?
(Tick one box only)

☐ Home study (book only)

☐ On a course: college _____

☐ Other _____

Why did you decide to purchase this Course book? *(Tick one box only)*

☐ Have used BPP Learning Media Texts in the past

☐ Recommendation by friend/colleague

☐ Recommendation by a lecturer at college

☐ Saw advertising

☐ Other _____

During the past six months do you recall seeing/receiving any of the following?
(Tick as many boxes as are relevant)

☐ Our advertisement

☐ Our brochure with a letter through the post

Your ratings, comments and suggestions would be appreciated on the following areas

	Very useful	Useful	Not useful
Introductory pages	☐	☐	☐
Topic coverage	☐	☐	☐
Summary diagrams	☐	☐	☐
Chapter roundups	☐	☐	☐
Quick quizzes	☐	☐	☐
Activities	☐	☐	☐
Discussion points	☐	☐	☐

	Excellent	Good	Adequate	Poor
Overall opinion of this Course book	☐	☐	☐	☐

Do you intend to continue using BPP Learning Media Business Essentials Course books?   ☐ Yes   ☐ No

Please note any further comments and suggestions/errors on the reverse of this page.

The BPP author of this edition can be emailed at: pippariley@bpp.com

Please return this form to: Pippa Riley, BPP Learning Media Ltd, FREEPOST, London, W12 8AA

Review Form (continued)

Please note any further comments and suggestions/errors below